Energy Security

Energy Security

Visions from Asia and Europe

Edited by Antonio Marquina
Chair in International Security and Cooperation, Complutense University of Madrid, Spain

palgrave
macmillan

First published 2008 by
PALGRAVE MACMILLAN
Houndmills, Basingstoke, Hampshire RG21 6XS and
175 Fifth Avenue, New York, N.Y. 10010
Companies and representatives throughout the world

PALGRAVE MACMILLAN is the global academic imprint of the
Palgrave Macmillan division of St. Martin's Press, LLC and of
Palgrave Macmillan Ltd. Macmillan® is a registered trademark
in the United States, United Kingdom and other countries.
Palgrave is a registered trademark in the European Union
and other countries.

ISBN-13: 978–0–230–21970–0   hardback
ISBN-10: 0–230–21970–5   hardback

This book is printed on paper suitable for recycling and made from
fully managed and sustained forest sources. Logging, pulping and
manufacturing processes are expected to conform to the
environmental regulations of the country of origin.

A catalogue record for this book is available from the British Library.

Library of Congress Cataloging-in-Publication Data
Energy security : visions from Asia and Europe / [edited by] Antonio
    Marquina.
        p. cm.
    Includes bibliographical references and index.
    ISBN 978–0–230–21970–0 (alk. paper)
    1. Energy policy — Europe. 2. Energy policy — Asia. 3. Energy
    supply — Europe. 4. Energy supply — Asia. I. Marquina Barrio,
    Antonio.
    HD9502.E852M37 2008
    333.79094—dc22   2008025125

10   9   8   7   6   5   4   3   2   1
17 16 15 14 13 12 11 10 09 08

Printed and bound in Great Britain by
CPI Antony Rowe, Chippenham and Eastbourne

Contents

List of Figures

List of Tables

Notes on the Contributors

Mely Caballero-Anthony is Associate Professor and Coordinator of the Non-Traditional Security Programme at the S. Rajaratnam School of International Studies, Nanyang Technological University, Singapore.

Weerawat Chantanakome is the Executive Director of the ASEAN Centre for Energy (ACE) in Jakarta since 2004. He has more than 30 years of experience, expertise and network in the energy sector.

Shi Dan is a Research Fellow, Director of the Energy Economics Research Center at the Institute of Industrial Economics, Chinese Academy of Social Sciences.

Eduardo González is President of Spain's Nuclear Industry Forum and former president of FORATOM (European Nuclear Forum). He was vice-president of Spain's Nuclear Safety Council.

Carolina G. Hernandez is the Founding President and Chair of the Board of Directors of the Institute for Strategic and Development Studies (ISDS), Philippines.

Kostas Ifantis is an Associate Professor of International Relations at the Department of Political Science, University of Athens.

Linda Jakobson is the Bejing-based Director of the China Programme at the Finnish Institute of International Affairs (FIIA). Her present research focuses on China's energy security and climate change policies.

Tai Hwan Lee is a Senior Research Fellow in the Regional Studies Programme, and a former director of the Foreign Policy and Security Studies Programme, at the Sejong Institute in Seoul.

Julián López is Professor of Economics at the University of Alicante, Spain. His main research area is the liberalization and regulation changes in the energy sector, especially with regard to electricity.

Antonio Marquina holds the Chair in International Security and Cooperation at the Department of International Studies, Complutense University of Madrid. He is the director of the Research Unit on International Security and Cooperation (UNISCI) and the leader of the ASEM Education Hub Thematic Network on Human Security.

José María Martínez-Val is Professor of Nuclear Technology at Madrid Polytechnic University, and current Chairman of the EURATOM Scientific and Technical Committee.

Michal Meidan is a Research Associate at Asia Centre – Centre études Asie, where she heads the activities of the Energy and Environment Programme. She also teaches at the East Asia Department at Haifa University, Israel. Her research focuses on China's energy security policy and policy-making mechanisms and their implications for China's diplomacy.

Javier Morales is a Research Fellow at the Department of International Studies, Complutense University of Madrid, and a member of its Research Unit on International Security and Cooperation (UNISCI). His main research areas are international security and Russia's foreign and security policy.

Akhmad Nidlom is the Energy Policy and Planning Specialist at the ASEAN Centre for Energy (ACE) in Jakarta. His main tasks are to monitor and evaluate the ASEAN Plan of Action for Energy Cooperation Programmes, preparing project proposals on energy activities and updating ASEAN energy data.

Gianluca Pastori is Professor of History of Political Relations between North America and Europe at the Faculty of Political Sciences of the Catholic University of the Sacred Heart, in Milan. He works on political and economic security issues of the Wider Mediterranean region and is author and editor of books and essays on historical, political and military issues related to Turkey, the Persian Gulf, the Afghan/Pakistani area and Former Soviet Central Asia.

Edy Prasetyono is a Senior Researcher at the Department of International Relations, Centre for Strategic and International Studies (CSIS), Jakarta. Currently, he is Member of the Indonesian Committee, Council for Security for Security Cooperation in Asia Pacific (CSCAP) and a Senior Fellow at the Centre for East Asian Cooperation Studies (CEACOS), University of Indonesia. Dr Prasetyono also teaches at the Department of International Studies, University of Indonesia.

Javier de Quinto is Director attached to the Presidency of the company Red Eléctrica de España, and member of the board of directors of Transportadora de Electricidad (Bolivia) and Red Eléctrica del Sur (Peru). He is also Professor of Economics at the San Pablo-CEU University, and Senior Researcher at the Research Unit on International Security and Cooperation (UNISCI), Complutense University of Madrid. He was head of the advisory board to the Spanish Minister of Industry from 1993 to 1996.

Shigeru Sudo is the Director of the Energy and Environment Programme at the International Development Centre of Japan.

Frank Umbach is the Head of the Research Programme 'Security Policies in Asia-Pacific' and also responsible for International Energy Security at the Research Institute of the German Council on Foreign Relations (DGAP). He is also Co-Chair of the European Committee of the Council for Security Cooperation in Asia-Pacific (ESC-SCAP or CSCAP-Europe). His main research interests are global energy security and energy foreign policies (in Europe, Russia and the Caspian region and Asia-Pacific), and foreign, security and defence policies.

The ASEM Education Hub: ASEM's Platform for University Cooperation

The **Asia-Europe Foundation (ASEF)** advances mutual understanding and collaboration between Asia and Europe through intellectual, cultural, and people-to-people exchanges. These exchanges include conferences, lecture tours, workshops, seminars and the use of web-based platforms. The major achievement of ASEF is the establishment of permanent bi-regional networks focused on areas and issues that help to strengthen Asia–Europe relations.

Established in February 1997, ASEF is the only permanent institution of the ASEM[1] process. ASEF works in partnership with other public institutions and civil society actors to ensure that its work is broad-based and balanced among the partner countries.

The overall aim of intensifying university and academic co-operation between Europe and Asia naturally relates to the broader issue of globalization and the consecutive need for the internationalization of higher education.

The ASEM Education Hub is ASEF's multi-dimensional platform for bi-regional co-operation in higher education which was established in 1998 at the Second ASEM Summit in London. The Hub organizes an annual Colloquium for dialogue on transversal issues (including quality assurance, joint curriculum development and university governance) among Asian and European educators. It also fosters institutional linkages with universities and centres of academic excellence through its Advisory Committee, a consultative body gathering representatives of important associations and networks in higher education. The ASEM Education Hub manages ASEM's first comprehensive online portal on education and scholarships, called the Database on Education Exchange Programmes (or DEEP), launched in April 2007 on the occasion of ASEF's tenth anniversary. DEEP lists over 4,000 universities and hundreds of official institutions, national agencies and youth and student organizations related to education. Finally, through its Thematic Networks, the ASEM Education Hub promotes cooperation in priority areas such as Lifelong Learning, e-Learning, the Environment, Peace and Conflict Resolution and Human Security.

---

[1] **ASEM** (the Asia-Europe Meeting) is an informal process of dialogue and cooperation. It brings together Austria, Belgium, Brunei, Bulgaria, Cambodia, China, Cyprus, Czech Republic, Denmark, Estonia, Finland, France, Germany, Greece, Hungary, India, Indonesia, Ireland, Italy, Japan, Korea, Laos, Latvia, Lithuania, Luxembourg, Malaysia, Malta, Mongolia, Myanmar, the Netherlands, Pakistan, the Philippines, Poland, Portugal, Romania, Singapore, Slovakia, Slovenia, Spain, Sweden, Thailand, United Kingdom, Vietnam, the ASEAN Secretariat and the European Commission. http://www.aseminfoboard.org

The Thematic Network on Human Security aims at fostering academic high level exchanges and cooperation among universities and centres of excellence from Europe and Asia, with a special emphasis on non-traditional aspects of security. ASEF is proud to be a partner of the Asia-Europe Network on Human Security since it tackles key issues of the ASEM agenda. This book is the result of the work and cooperation of the Network's first year of existence and it represents an excellent basis for the future enrichment of its activities.

Given the growth and dynamism of our two regions, Asia and Europe are and will continue to be natural partners in advancing the quality and outreach of higher education and mobility of the academic community in the ASEM partner-countries. The ASEM Education Hub will continue to respond to this challenge and ambition.

Ramon Molina
Director, People-to-People Exchange Asia-Europe Foundation, www.asef.org

Introduction

Antonio Marquina

This book is the result of the discussions held in Jakarta by the members of the ASEM Education Hub Thematic Network on Human Security from 8–10 November 2007. This Network of scholars and researchers was created in 2007, supported by the Asia-Europe Foundation (ASEF), and will be expanded in 2008. Apart from the central ASEF support, other institutions and companies sponsored the conference: Bergé, Red Eléctrica de España and Foro Nuclear. The Network is very grateful to all of them.

The first topic for discussion that we considered appropriate was energy security, before moving to other possible topics such as global warming and climate change, migration and environmental refugees, food security and health. Later we realized the salience of the national security approaches that this topic entailed. In fact the majority of the discussions revolved around geopolitical and strategic factors; this could not be avoided.

This book presents an approach to energy security both from a European perspective and from an Asian perspective. These perspectives are differentiated by various factors. In the case of European states, their perspective is complemented by that of the European Union, which has tried to confront the challenges of energy security and to include energy policy in its Common Foreign and Security Policy. The first chapters deal with the definition of what energy security is. Frank Umbach offers a traditional definition of energy security as 'adequate, affordable and reliable supplies of energy'. Michal Meidan presents some principles shared by the EU member states, summed up by the EU Commission definition as

> the ability to ensure that essential future energy needs can be met, both by means of adequate domestic resources worked under economically acceptable conditions or maintained as strategic reserves and by calling upon accessible and stable external sources supplemented where appropriate by strategic stocks.

Other definitions can be found in the White Papers or documents of the different European governments. But all these definitions show that energy security in Europe basically relies on markets and market approaches. Consequently, oil and gas shortages manifest themselves in higher prices rather than in physical shortages.

The problem is that after the Russia-Ukraine and Russia-Belarus crises, the EU recognized that there were important risks in securing reliable flows of affordable and environmentally sustainable energy supplies. The EU mentioned the following risks in 2006:

- Increasing dependence on imports from unstable regions and suppliers.
- Some major producers and consumers using energy as a political lever.
- The effects on the internal EU market of external actors not playing by the same market rules because of not being subject to the same competitive pressures domestically.

Russia's new 'energy nationalism' and China's rise as a global consumer are critical factors for understanding the new trends in the European approaches. With regard to Russia, the chapter by Javier Morales explains the relationship between Russia's self-perception as an international actor and its role as an energy exporter. Energy has become an instrument of Russian foreign policy and oil and gas have been considered as strategic reserves controlled by state companies. As such, oil and gas cannot be left to free market mechanisms. For this very reason Russia did not sign the EU Energy Charter and has obliged domestic and foreign companies to accept government orientations. This much is clear: Russia has demonstrated the profound deficiencies of the EU free market approach for dealing with energy security.

With regard to China, Michal Meidan explains the change of thinking on energy security in this country. Although the focus is on the demand side measures aimed at making energy use more efficient, the perceptions of US attempts to control – and possibly manipulate – the oil supply and protectionist trends have promoted the strategic component of China's thinking. Now the solid and influential Chinese state-owned energy companies are regarded as instruments for securing oil and gas for China, supported by Chinese diplomacy. China has put forward the unreliability of markets as the reason for increasing bilateral ties with producer countries. This approach is substantially different from the EU approach. In addition to this, poverty alleviation, not human rights and good governance, is considered its fundamental policy towards developing countries. Although there are increasing numbers of voices asking for Chinese integration into the markets, opaque Chinese practices and activities have given rise to mounting speculation on both intent and means.

Linda Jakobson, for her part, explains Chinese energy diplomacy in a slightly different way. Chinese government officials do not direct the overseas activities of the national oil and gas companies. The state companies are strong, but the bureaucracy is weak and fragmented. The government does not have a coordinated and well-planned policy. The Chinese companies, as latecomers to the international oil scene, have often gone to places considered too risky or politically problematic by Western and Japanese companies. They have to purchase oil from where it is available, putting aside the questions of good governance and human rights. In parallel, Chinese government aid does not take labour standards or corrupt practices of the recipients into consideration. All this explains the lack of chemistry with Western countries. However, Jakobson cautions the reader, explaining the divisions existing among researchers and officials on the principle of non-interference and its application. China is well aware of its lack of credibility and will probably try to move to a modified approach to its non-interference principle.

Frank Umbach explains that the emergence of China as one of the largest importers of oil and gas as well as other raw materials was largely overlooked by many EU countries until 2004. Chinese import dependencies on energy and raw materials entailed important consequences for present and future EU foreign, security and defence policies. Market approaches or strategic approaches have different consequences in the international context and expand or limit the possibilities of cooperation.

On the other hand, state-owned companies control around 85 per cent of oil and 70–80 per cent of gas reserves. These companies do not follow the laws and policies of the market. At present we have to look to the policies of the states with important energy reserves, in particular authoritarian and non-democratic countries. These countries have asserted themselves domestically and in the international arena, weakening the global democratization trend. The result is that Western and European foreign and security interests in many producer states in Central Asia, the Middle East and Africa have been undermined.

The book presents different national and regional perspectives. On the Asian side, Shigeru Sudo explains the Japanese viewpoint on energy security, its energy policies, objectives and targets on energy conservation, reduction of the oil ratio in primary energy supply from 50 per cent to 40 per cent, reduction of oil dependence in the transport sector, nuclear power generation for electricity above 30–40 per cent and overseas natural resources development. Japan, despite its efforts to diversify oil imports, in fact has increased its dependence on the Middle East. Interestingly, Japan aims to increase exploration and development of overseas oil and gas resources to around 40 per cent by 2030, from 15 per cent at present. Given Japanese dependency on the Middle East, the need to develop a relationship of closer economic cooperation with the Gulf Cooperation Council is also stressed. The experiences in Iran and Russia contribute to this choice.

Shi Dan portrays the evolution of China's energy policy since 1978 and the problems that China has to solve. China's energy policy has shifted from promoting production and increasing supply to optimizing the energy structure, the development of clean energy sources, protecting the environment and establishing a collaboration framework for energy security. On this last point the author underlines the importance of solving national and international supply problems through friendly cooperation with other countries, avoiding disputes that could undermine world peace and building a good environment for Chinese development.

The chapter by Tai Hwan Lee explores the possibility of energy competition and cooperation in Northeast Asia. China, Japan and Korea need to import most of their oil and gas. They have to diversify energy supplies given their heavy dependence on the Middle East. Energy security in Northeast Asia is closely related to the Middle East. China has become the world's second largest oil consumer after the US. Japan is the third and South Korea is the ninth. The chapter explains how the geopolitical environment of Northeast Asia is basically competitive rather than cooperative. The competition between Japan and China over access to Russian oil and over the Chunxiao (Shirakaba) gas fields in the East China Sea plus the rivalry over Middle East supplies are important factors to take into consideration in understanding one of the possible regional fault lines. In addition to this, the control of the sea lines of communication and trade routes by the US is perceived by China as very challenging. In this context the chapter explains the energy security strategies of China, Japan and South Korea. The prospects for cooperation are complicated because these countries do not share a common understanding on the ultimate goal of energy cooperation and, on the other hand, multilateral cooperation is also complex. Ideological differences and lack of trust complicate the panorama in the geopolitical context, while the economic dimensions, such as the energy market and efficiency, tend to induce more cooperation.

Moving to Southeast Asia, in Chapter 12 Akhmad Nidlom and several specialists of the ASEAN Centre for Energy introduce the subject of energy security in ASEAN, explaining what they are doing to accelerate the integration of energy strategies within ASEAN. The five-year action plan for energy cooperation covers six major programmes that include a trans-ASEAN gas pipeline and an ASEAN power grid. Pipeline delivery of natural gas from country to country is growing. Over time the present figure of 17 per cent bilateral gas transfers will increase and many new pipelines have been proposed to meet the forecasts of strong demand. The incentives for closer economic integration between Myanmar, a major producer of natural gas, and ASEAN using gas pipelines are obvious. On the other hand, the role of potential Indonesian and Malaysian gas and oil reserves are important and will become central in securing ASEAN energy supplies. Although the oil and gas reserves in Malaysia are declining, it has sufficient resources to actively pursue a strategy of regional cooperation with neighbouring countries. Edy Prasetyono deals with the huge Indonesian energy potential in his chapter.

Carolina Hernandez clarifies the case of the Philippines. Traditionally, this country has sought energy self-sufficiency to ensure energy security. In response to the recent competition for reserves and high prices of oil and gas, the President Arroyo government has updated the energy plan, looking for 60 per cent sustainable self-sufficiency and the effective implementation of reforms. Regional cooperation within ASEAN and the broader East Asia region can help in achieving the goals of energy security.

On the European side the debates are more complex and deep than in Asia. The reasons for this are discussed in the chapters dealing with the Southeast–Southwest energy corridors, the German, Italian and Greek approaches, and finally the Spanish approach.

Frank Umbach describes German energy policies until 2006, explaining the narrow debates on energy policies and ideological disputes between advocates and opponents of nuclear energy, opponents of coal and supporters of renewable energies. The concerns expressed by other countries, such as the United Kingdom and France, on growing German energy dependence on Russia had a small impact in Germany, which followed narrow national interests as was shown in the lack of consultation with Poland for the construction of the new Baltic gas pipeline coming from Russia (Nord Stream pipeline). As is explained, Germany discovered the need for a national and European energy policy and also an energy foreign policy once the Russia–Ukraine gas conflict broke out in December 2005–January 2006. After this, energy security become one of the most important foreign and security issues of the German Ministry of Foreign Affairs, debunking at the same time a series of long-standing assumptions underlying energy foreign policies. The discussion, with the creation of working groups, led to emphasis on a new national energy security concept and to diversification of German energy imports. But it created a dilemma: maintaining the special relationship with Russia or looking for energy imports from Central Asia and the Caspian Sea that bypass Russia.

During the German EU presidency in the first semester of 2007, Germany failed to establish a common position among EU members towards Russia and this created new opportunities for Russia for bilateralism of its energy policies with the different EU countries and companies, following the axiom of divide and rule. In this regard, the chapter on the Southeast–Southwest corridor by Antonio Marquina is very telling. The EU tried to establish a new relationship with the new countries of Central Asia after the Cold War. The EU signed Partnership and Cooperation Agreements with almost all the countries in the region. Energy was one of the items for cooperation. But the problem was that the EU, even taking into account its role as the principal donor in the region, was an outsider in the organization of the Southeast–Southwest energy corridor. The main reason for this was its ultraliberal approach. Energy was considered a question of markets: the strategic decision on pipeline routes and the specific routes chosen should remain essentially a commercial one for the companies concerned. The Commission's role was merely that of facilitator: helping to create the conditions for investments and business. The EU did not have a geopolitical or strategic design like the US and Russia had.

The philosophy of the EU approach was also noteworthy: to achieve political reforms, good governance and a transition to a market economy. The problem was that the norms of behaviour of the Central Asian republics could not be promoted or dictated by the EU as conditions for engagement. In a very short period of time Russia and China have demonstrated the fragility of the EU approach. The EU cannot compete and the norms of behaviour of these republics, as is obvious now, cannot be designed alone by the EU as a 'normative power'.

In this context, Russia has won all the recent battles for pipeline control and export routes from Central Asia. It is now quite uncertain whether the EU Nabucco project will be accomplished. At the same time, Russia has used different tactics and policies for disaggregating European companies and EU countries through bilateral deals. The result is clearly a chaotic EU energy strategy.

The chapters dealing with energy security in Greece, Italy and Spain provide significant information about national policies, lack of consensus on the European common energy policies to be implemented, the divisive role of European energy champions and the critical question of market liberalization. In the case of Spain, Javier de Quinto and Julián López explain Spanish singularity. Spain does not import substantial amounts of gas from Russia but it is highly dependent on North Africa, the Persian Gulf, Nigeria and Norway. Spain can make a contribution to the security of EU supply by reducing the dependence of other EU states on Russian gas.

Kostas Ifantis explains the present Greek interest in normalizing the relationship with Turkey, and the joint development projects of energy transport infrastructure constitute one important aspect. However, the inauguration of the Turkey–Greece (–Italy) interconnection in November 2007 cannot hide the participation of Greece in other initiatives that circumvent Turkey as an energy hub. Another important point to mention is the Greek initiative to establish an Energy Community of Southeast Europe, looking to secure itself a position on the oil and gas routes. This last point is crucial for understanding Greek policies: Greece, as a net energy importer, considers that its importance lies in its ability and willingness to be part of the development of major transit systems for gas and oil. The author develops several attractive arguments against the critics characterizing Greece as Moscow's Trojan horse.

Gianluca Pastori raises several interesting points to explain the apparent contradictions in Italian energy security policies in the EU context. Traditionally ENI has replaced the Italian government in the definition of energy policies and EU membership did not substantially affect Italian national policies. ENI and ENEL are still 30 per cent controlled by the government, which enjoys special rights through the 'golden share'. Italian suppliers of oil and gas are quite concentrated in a few countries, Russia being an important partner in oil and gas supplies. At present, Italy is trying to diversify, forging new links in the areas adjoining the Mediterranean basin, but strengthening the ties already existing with old partners at the same time. Italian energy companies are key actors in developing this strategy, including the development of new infrastructure and alternative routes. Curiously, ENI is a partner of Russia in the Blue Stream and the South Stream pipelines and at the same time is an important partner in the main infrastructure projects involving Turkey: CPC, BTC, TAP and the Kirkuk–Ceyhan pipeline.

The book includes a chapter by Eduardo González and José María Martínez-Val on the importance of nuclear energy for energy security, given the strong debates going on in several countries of the EU. In Asia the role of nuclear energy is not problematic: even Indonesia, Vietnam and Thailand are planning the construction of nuclear power plants and ASEAN has to adopt and implement programmes to develop nuclear energy, as is clearly presented in the chapter by several members of the ASEAN Centre for Energy. The authors defend the role of nuclear energy as a main contributor to security of supply in electricity generation. They argue that the new reactors can give better performance with higher safety standards using the same fuel cycle; that nuclear energy represents 17 per cent of worldwide electricity production at a very competitive cost; that there has been a change in public opinion concerns based on nuclear safety; and that other concerns such as the long-term waste disposal risks and proliferation of nuclear materials can be lessened. The question of low CO_2 emissions coming from nuclear energy is emphasized in particular.

Finally, the last chapter, by Antonio Marquina and Mely Caballero-Anthony, presents the current debates going on regarding human security in Europe and Asia. Unfortunately the question of energy security has become a crucial question for state security and is very high on the national security agenda, as the different chapters of this book show. This casts a shadow over the deep importance of the subject for human security. Some chapters dismiss this importance given the strong geopolitical games going on and states' designs; very few of them, such as the one in the Philippines, try to show its relevance for human security.

What is clear is that in a very short period of time the globalization process has fallen into disarray; the appearance of the EU as an international agent for good, conditioning its engagement with other developing countries with respect to human rights, good governance, democratization and the market economy has turned out to be a mirage. The EU cannot transmit its values and rules conditioning its engagement with international actors if other powerful countries do not play by the same rules and values. That is an important lesson. It shows the limits of the EU and European countries on the present world stage. Some central EU approaches have become a real disaster for the Union. It is time to learn the lessons and improve the quality of European policies and approaches.

In Asia there are strong possibilities for cooperation in ASEAN. In Northeast Asia, competition is the rule but the seeds for growing cooperation still exist. It is a question of first, create a better climate of trust, and second, develop common projects that could generate increasing interdependence. Energy is one of them.

1

German Debates on Energy Security and Impacts on Germany's 2007 EU Presidency

Frank Umbach

Introduction: global challenges and the need to redefine Germany's and the EU's energy security policies

Traditionally, energy security has been defined as adequate, affordable and reliable supplies of energy. Energy is essential for economic development and human security alike. Secure energy supply can be seen as a public good for societies, for which governments must ultimately take responsibility to minimize market supply failures. Disruptions of oil, gas and electricity can have severe consequences for societies, economies and individuals.

In contrast to energy security and its vulnerabilities, climate change is a more recent concern, but closely linked with energy policies and energy security. Thus energy supply disruptions are also the result of extreme weather conditions or accidents: in August and September 2005, hurricanes Katrina and Rita shut down 27 per cent of US oil production and 21 per cent of US refining capacity in the Gulf of Mexico[1] – with worldwide implications for global oil prices, energy policies, climate change, strategic oil stocks and perceptions of supply security. Policy-makers need to address these twin challenges of energy security and climate change to ensure the security of our global energy system and to reduce greenhouse gas emissions as part of an overall strategy of human security.

As long as fossil fuels continue to dominate the global fuel mix, energy-related greenhouse gas emissions and increased reliance on imports of oil, gas and coal from politically unstable countries will increase concerns about climate change as well as energy security. Having no adequate and secure supplies of energy at affordable prices is being perceived as a major threat as soaring energy prices and consumption cause irreversible environmental damage to human beings. If energy prices stay high, the big losers will be poor countries in particular, because they will be hit much harder economically, socially and politically in comparison with the OECD countries. It may curtail their economic development prospects and lead to social or political unrest, state failure, new terrorist havens or large-scale migration.[2]

However, with rising oil prices beyond US$100 per barrel of oil or with a future contraction of oil supplies even the less energy efficient countries of the OECD, such as the US, will suffer economically much more than efficient energy users such as Germany: 'weakening its international position relatively as well as absolutely' as US experts have warned.[3]

But even in the EU, an electricity power failure in November 2006 blacked out the homes of 10 million people in Germany. It caused further disruptions across much of Western Europe, France, Austria, Belgium, the Netherlands, Italy, Spain and even Morocco. It highlighted the vulnerability of the interconnected European grid and the need for its transnational modernization as well as for a common EU energy policy.

The new global attention to energy security is explained in particular by the new emerging giants of the world economy and their rapidly rising energy demand. They transform the global energy system just by their sheer size and growing weight in international fossil fuel trade. According to the global energy forecasts of the International Energy Agency (IEA), European Energy Agency (EEA), the World Energy Council (WEC) and international energy experts, the global primary energy demand might be over 50 per cent higher in 2030 than today, at an average annual rate of 1.8 per cent.[4] Since 2000, China alone has accounted for 40 per cent of the world's crude oil demand. In 2003, it displaced Japan as the world's second largest energy consumer and oil importer after the US, and surpassed Tokyo as the third largest exporter (after the US and Germany). As a consequence of a continuation of current world energy trends, leading to underinvestment, vulnerability and accelerated climate change, 'the need to curb the growth in fossil-energy demand, to increase geographic and fuel-supply diversity and to mitigate climate-destabilizing emissions is more urgent than ever', as the IEA concluded in its *World Energy Outlook* of 2006.[5]

However, this rising demand is not confined just to energy resources. During the last few years, China has already replaced the United States as the centre of the world's raw materials market and as a price setter for these industrial raw materials.[6] In 2008, it is expected to surpass even Germany as the largest exporter of goods in the world.

Like many other Asian countries (with the exceptions of South Korea, Japan, Singapore and Hong Kong), China has long subsidized energy consumption. The result has been an increasing inefficiency: China consumes up to five times more energy to produce each dollar of economic output, according to the Asian Development Bank.[7] While China's energy policy seems to be based on a strategic approach, thereby focusing on guaranteeing rising energy imports for its social and economic stability and, therefore, its supply security, it has neglected energy conservation, economic efficiency factors and the environmental costs of its past and present policies. At the same time, China has experienced an acute shortage of energy since 2003, which has severely disrupted its industrial output and electricity supply.

As a result of its hunger for energy and industrial raw materials, China has become ever more dependent on imports from distant, often politically unstable parts of the world. It was forced to be much more pro-active in its foreign and security policies both on the regional as well as global level – reflecting China's self-perception of its energy insecurity. In the last fifteen years, the economic rise of Asia, and above all China, has created an enormous regional and global energy demand that raises not only important economic issues, but also countless foreign and security policy issues for both regional and global stability.[8]

Although growing trade will strengthen the mutual dependence among exporting and importing countries, it will also increase political risks that wells or pipelines could be closed or tankers blocked by piracy or terrorist attacks. Rapid worldwide growth in natural gas consumption and trade will foster similar concerns, as the IEA warned in 2004.[9] At the same time, and partly as a result of a developing global gas market with liquefied natural gas (LNG), concerns about a future 'Gas OPEC', consisting of undemocratic countries and leading to price regulation and dividing up of consumer markets between its members, have increased.

Furthermore, state-owned companies now control far more oil (around 85 per cent) and gas reserves (70–80 per cent) than do the traditional private energy companies, once known as the 'seven sisters'. Many of these state-owned companies, such as in Russia and Venezuela, are not merely following the policies of market forces, but represent a new-found pricing power for political forces such as foreign policy objectives in a new global energy environment of a 'sellers' market'. The *New York Times* columnist Thomas L. Friedman and others have identified a direct correlation between the negative impact of average crude oil prices on political freedom, democratization and the direction of cooperative or confrontational foreign policies.

According to the 'First Law of Petropolitics', the higher the average oil and gas prices on the international market, the lower the internal political and economic reform willingness of governments and the more confrontational their foreign and security policies, leading to 'petro-authoritarianism' and 'petropolitics'. Presently, it explains the policies of those 'petro-ist' states such as Russia, Iran, Venezuela, Nigeria, Sudan and others, which are highly dependent on oil and gas for their GDP and have either weak institutions or authoritarian systems. They have started asserting themselves domestically as well as in their foreign policy environment by weakening the global democratization trend. This strategic trend even has the potential to distort 'the whole international system and the very character of the post-Cold War world'.[10] As a result of those dysfunctional energy politics, Western and European foreign and security interests in many producer states in the Middle East, Africa and Central Asia will be undermined.

In Germany and many other EU member states, the emergence of the People's Republic of China as the world's leading consumer (overtaking the US in 2004) and one of the largest importers of oil and gas as well as many industrial raw materials – like many other global developments and challenges – was largely overlooked until 2004. But Beijing's import dependencies on energy and raw materials have numerous consequences for, and impacts on, its present and future foreign, security and defence policies, as its policies towards the EU or the Iranian nuclear question have demonstrated during recent years. The EU, China, India and other great powers may compete for the same energy resources in the Middle East, Russia and Central Asia. In this regard, whether they follow a 'market strategy' or a 'strategic approach' may ultimately answer the question of whether they are able to cooperate for regional and global energy security or whether they will increasingly compete. As a Chinese expert admitted in 2006, 'China must now view energy security in terms of economic threats and market solutions rather than military threats and diplomatic responses.'[11]

The German Presidency of the EU in the first half of 2007 and the last G8 summit in June 2007 selected energy security and climate change as two of the most important policy issues on its agenda. On 9 March 2007, the European Council agreed on an integrated climate and energy policy and an 'Energy Action Plan' for the next few years (2007–9). It favours a liberalized internal market for gas and electricity, enhanced measures for security of supply and a common approach to an external energy policy with a global dimension. At the same time, the EU's relationship with PR China has become much more complicated. It highlights a growing economic–political interdependence as well as competition and rivalries, as the EU's new strategy towards China of October 2006 indicated.[12]

This chapter will give an overview of Germany's energy policies during recent years, explain the role of the state and national energy companies in shaping and defining Germany's energy policies and analyse their perception of national, regional and global energy challenges. This section also presents the background for understanding Germany's policies for its EU Presidency in the first half of 2007, in which the German government put energy and climate change policies on to the highest EU policy agenda and agreed with the other twenty-six EU member states on the creation of 'an integrated climate and energy policy' in March 2007.[13] The chapter will focus in particular on the significant changes of Germany energy policies as well as traditional and new understandings of the challenges Germany and the EU are facing in the years and decades ahead.

'Sleeping through the night': Germany's energy policies until 2006

During the last 15–20 years, the EU and its member states' energy policies, including Germany's, have been increasingly determined by market forces and a separation of energy questions from political factors and strategic developments. Ultimately, energy policies have been left to the industry. Their business interests, however, are primarily guided by short-term economic benefits in an increasingly competitive environment. At the same time, medium and long-term national interests of energy supply security have been neglected by both energy companies as well as national governments such as Germany.

Whereas the traditional separation of economics from politics has made sense for the internal EU market due to the existing common norms and understanding of the overall importance of market forces, energy policies determined outside of Europe are more than ever defined by those strategic and geopolitical interests of national foreign and security policies (particularly in Russia, China, OPEC countries, the US and others).[14]

Since the end of the 1990s, international energy experts have stressed the increasing strategic importance of supply security in the 'energy triad', to which economic competitiveness and environmental compatibility also belong. But only in the aftermath of the winter 2005–6 gas conflict between Russia and Ukraine has the future security of German and European energy supplies become the focus of a broader political debate.

For many years, Germany and Western Europe have largely ignored the fact that Moscow has indeed used its energy exports and pipeline monopoly as an instrument of foreign policy to intimidate and blackmail neighbouring states – albeit with little success – since the demise of the Soviet Union. Holding more than 25 per cent of the world's natural gas and hard coal reserves and 6 per cent of the world's oil reserves, Russia has also considerably increased its strategic position in many of the successor states to the USSR and in the new EU member states. It has bought up utility companies, pipelines, refineries and infrastructure through Gazprom and other giant energy corporations, thus expanding its monopoly.[15] Until 2006, however, neither Germany nor Europe had engaged in sustained analysis and discussion of how, under these circumstances, to liberalize the German and European gas markets, which are in the grip of oligopolies in any case.

Until 2004, economic experts and political observers in Germany also overlooked Asia's, especially China's, energy demand and its implications for Europe's foreign and energy security policy. Germany did not wake up to the new geopolitical and geoeconomic realities until its industry experienced mounting difficulty with imports of raw materials because China, India and other states were prepared to pay far more than customary international market prices for them.

On 8 March 2005, the Federal Association of German Industry (BDI) held a congress on protecting Germany's supply of raw materials and energy, its first such event in more than twenty years. Since then, a high-ranking BDI group with three working groups have been created to address issues of international raw materials and to formulate a national supply concept for them by 2008.

Given this state of affairs, it was not surprising that the matter of securing Germany's energy supplies still lay solely in the hands of the ministries of the economy and the environment until the end of 2005, an arrangement unlike those in many other EU member states. However, it meant that the expertise existing in the foreign ministry and the defence ministry of foreign countries and global regions had largely been overlooked in shaping a coherent state policy on energy security.

By contrast, the EU Commission's 2000 Green Paper on aspects of the European energy supply systematically examined the future of its security. Indeed, the EU's Green Paper of November 2000 has already warned that in the next 20–30 years up to 70 per cent of the Union's energy demand (presently 50 per cent) will have to be imported. With regard to oil, the EU's dependence could even reach 90 per cent for oil, 70 per cent for gas and 100 per cent for coal.[16]

Since 2003, energy security has already become an integral part of the EU's common foreign and security policy (CFSP). It was incorporated into the EU's first global 'European Security Strategy' – the most important document of its CFSP.[17] The topic of 'energy security' and its related foreign policy dimensions have also been taken up by the foreign ministries of major EU member states. In 2004, the British Foreign & Commonwealth Office published an international *Energy Strategy* with a specific foreign policy view,[18] while the foreign ministry of the Netherlands produced a similar internal policy document during the summer of 2005.

In Germany, this EU policy went almost unnoticed. Instead, the debates on energy policy were narrowed down to ideological disputes between advocates and opponents of nuclear energy and renewable energies and remained exceedingly parochial. Non-economic, particularly geopolitical, factors (such as the political stability of the crude oil and natural gas exporters or about their interests and motivations) did not figure therefore in apolitical analyses of international energy security. In forecasts of oil and gas prices, these factors have been defined as singular or temporary events and, thus, dismissed as distortions.

In this light, Germany's policies were in contradiction to those of the European Commission which had identified the EU's energy supply security and the energy triangle (supply security, economic competitiveness and environmental sustainability) as the most important energy challenge within the next decades. The European Commission for Transport and Energy and the experts of Javier Solana's office (the High Representative of the EU's CFSP), in particular, have intensified their analyses on the EU's future energy and supply security, as the publication of the two Green Papers on energy security of 2000 and 2006 have highlighted.[19]

Without an EU constitution in place, however, the national differences in their energy policies and strategies have increasingly threatened political cohesion and undermined the EU's evolving common energy policies, as well as the CFSP. Although the EU has established its own energy partnership with Russia, for instance, many new EU member states and even France and Great Britain have voiced criticisms or expressed their concerns about the ever-growing energy dependence of Germany on Russia in 2004 and 2005 because it may have unwanted implications for their own energy, foreign and security policies.

The controversial discussions of a new underwater Baltic gas pipeline from Russia to Germany (the 'Nordstream' pipeline)[20] and the failure of Germany to consult Poland and the Baltic states, for instance, have highlighted the unilateralist tendencies in German and European energy policies and the lack of a common and coherent EU energy security strategy. Those national policies, justified by narrow-minded national interests, however, are extremely short-sighted because they also undermine the EU's CFSP and ignore the lesson that any individual EU member state is too weak to establish itself as a strategic actor in the light of growing energy resource competition vis-à-vis the US, China, Russia, India, Japan and OPEC.[21]

Germany defines energy security and climate change as a comprehensive security threat: theory, practices and contradictions

Germany's Foreign Ministry discovered the need for a national and European energy and energy foreign policy only after the Russian–Ukrainian gas conflict in January 2006. Germany's Foreign Minister Frank-Walter Steinmeier, however, had already become more interested in energy security challenges at the time when he worked as the closest adviser in former Chancellor Schröder's office. At that time, he was reading more and more alarming reports from the German Federal Secret Service (BND), which followed the international energy developments more closely than any German ministry.

With Steinmeier's appointment as Foreign Minister, the Foreign Ministry began to analyse international energy security developments and to consider the manifold implications they have for Germany's energy and foreign as well as security policies. Thus energy security has become one of the most important foreign and security issues on his Foreign Ministry's agenda. Hence security of supply and energy foreign policy were put on Germany's and the EU's highest foreign policy agendas. In March 2006, the German Foreign Minister stated:

> Energy security will strongly influence the global security agenda in the 21st century ... Energy security involves the security of all stakeholders, producers, transit states and consumers. National efforts alone are inadequate. We must not allow energy to become the currency of power in international relations. That is the goal of German foreign and security policy in this field. It plays a vital role in securing our country's energy

supply by eliminating one-sided energy dependency, stabilizing unsettled world regions and promoting innovative German energy and climate protection concepts in the international arena. First and foremost, our policy is one of peace and stability.[22]

The Russian cutbacks in gas deliveries affected Ukraine as well as EU member states. Hence, the gas conflict has debunked a number of long-standing assumptions underlying Germany's energy and foreign policies, among them that:

- Oil and gas are exclusively economic goods, not strategic ones. According to this view, energy resources are not part of the foreign and security policy strategy of other countries, and the energy policies of other countries strictly adhere to the rules of market economics.
- The security of the energy supply is no longer an important factor and can be left to private utility companies.
- Disruptions in regional or global energy supply can be offset by other oil and gas imports at any time.
- Russia under President Putin has steadily strengthened its market orientation.
- Never having used energy exports as a political weapon even during the Cold War, Russia will always prove to be a reliable energy partner for Europe.
- Russia's need to export its oil and gas to the European market has led to mutual dependence that precludes the instrumentalization of Russian energy and pipeline policy as a factor of foreign policy in the age of globalization.[23]

As a result, the German government initiated a national summit in April 2006 with its ministries and the German energy companies participating. It established three working groups and a process of continuing discussions with the goal of developing a long-term national energy concept by 2008. The 'Working Group on International Aspects' has been chaired by the Foreign Ministry. It highlights its new role in the German decision-making process on energy security and energy foreign policy.

As a result of those discussions between the government and the private German energy companies in 2006, Germany's government has emphasized raising energy efficiency as a top priority in a new national energy security concept and diversifying its energy imports, including gas, by building new pipelines and a LNG terminal in Wilhelmshaven. But given the new emphasis on the need for an active German energy foreign policy and its traditional close energy partnership with Russia, particularly with regard to Germany's gas companies, the significant policy changes have also created new problems and conflicts of goals: Germany's and the EU's energy foreign policy will

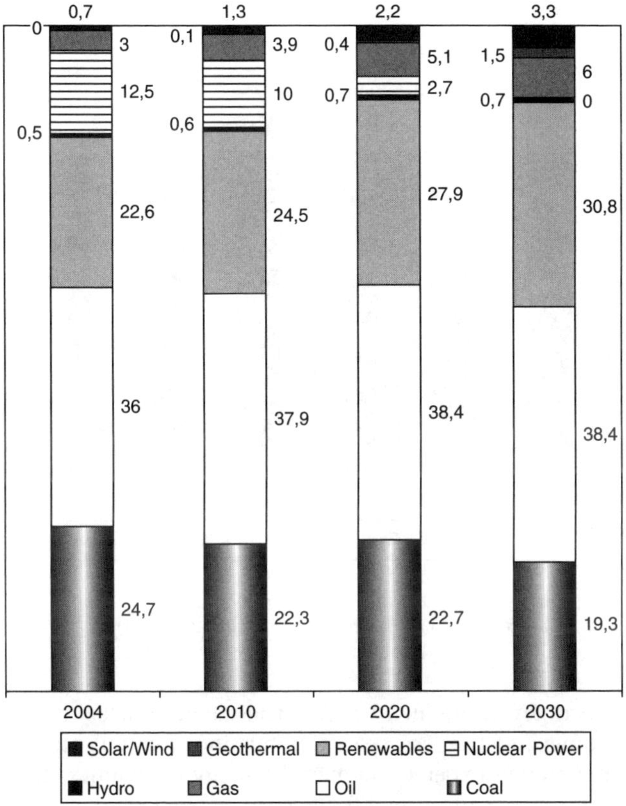

Figure 1.1   Germany's shares of energy resources (2004–30) (in %)
Source: International Energy Agency (IEA), *Energy Policies of IEA Countries. 2006 Review* (Paris: IEA, 2006), p. 267.

either further complicate their proclaimed special relations with Russia, or put into question the diversification strategy of oil and gas imports from Central Asia and the Caspian Region (CACR).[24]

Although the Merkel government has recognized the manifold challenges of energy supply security in the twenty-first century and is promoting an active foreign energy policy on a national as well as EU level, it maintains the promise made to its coalition government partner, the Social Democratic Party (SPD), to phase out nuclear power by 2021. At the same time, it has called for greater investment in renewable energy sources, steep cuts in greenhouse gas emissions and a reduction of Germany's rising dependence on Russian fossil fuels. Meanwhile, Merkel's own political party and Economy Minister Michael Glos warned that the EU will not be able to fulfil its targets

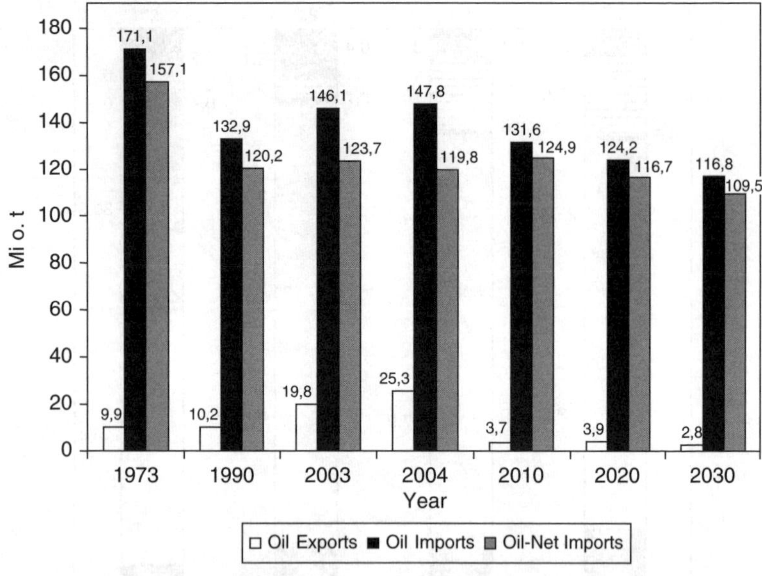

Figure 1.2   Germany's oil exports and imports (1973–2030)
Source: IEA, *Energy Policies of IEA Countries. 2006 Review* (Paris: IEA, 2006), p. 267.

on emissions unless more member countries favour nuclear energy. Following the argument of the European Commission, many German as well as international energy experts, Germany's energy companies, the Deutsche Bank and others have all warned that Germany will experience significantly higher electricity prices, become even more dependent on gas imports from Russia and fail to meet greenhouse gas emissions targets if the anti-nuclear policy is maintained. A study by the German Institute for Economic Research (DIW) in Berlin concluded in the summer of 2007 that the climate protection measures of the German government and the EU from March that year will cost Germany economically around 1.9–5.7 billion euros per year until 2020, depending on fair European burden-sharing and the implementation of a comprehensive package of climate protection measures domestically. This takes into account the emissions reductions achieved to date in the different EU-27 member states; for Germany it would mean reducing 31 per cent of its emissions on 1990 levels. But the study also warns that it would be very difficult for Germany to achieve its reduction target by phasing out nuclear power.[25]

Germany's energy policies are to a certain extent still very idealistic, ambitious, provincial and over-optimistic at the same time. It has long been a leader in the area of renewable energy in order to reduce carbon emissions and the phasing out of nuclear energy. As the world's biggest windpower

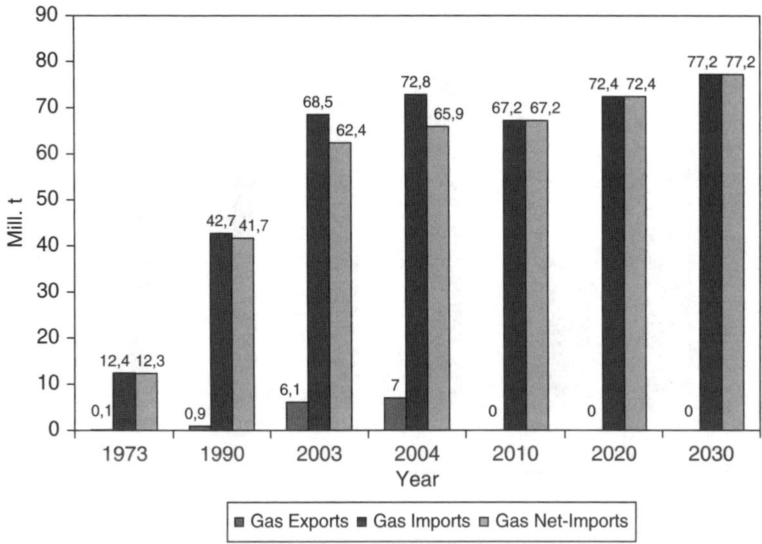

Figure 1.3   Germany's gas net imports (1973–2030)
Source: IEA, *Energy Policies of IEA Countries. 2006 Review* (Paris: IEA, 2006), p. 267.

systems manufacturer (producing 37 per cent of all systems and components worldwide), it is benefiting more than others from the current global expansion of windpower.[26] The coalition agreement between Germany's coalition government parties stipulates targets of a 4.2 per cent share of renewables in primary energy consumption (PEC) by 2010, and 10 per cent by 2020, whereas the share of renewables in electricity generation will have to rise to around 12.5 per cent by 2010 and 20 per cent by 2020. As the result of its Renewable Energy Sources Act ('Erneuerbare-Energien-Gesetz/EEG'), renewables already accounted for 5.8 per cent of PEC and 12 per cent of electricity generation in 2006. The German Ministry for Environment, Nature Conservation and Nuclear Safety (BMU) hopes to achieve 16 per cent of PEC and 27 per cent of electricity generation by 2020. However, it also creates new problems for Germany's base load supply and economic efficiency. Furthermore, it does not answer the question of where the rest of the energy supply will come from and to what extent the plans for phasing out nuclear energy will increase the dependencies on gas imports from Russia or from the unstable Middle East – and, therefore, threaten Germany's future energy supply security.

But Germany is already the world's second largest importer of gas. In 2006, it imported 88 billion cubic metres (bcm) and is, with 18 per cent of the overall European gas demand, the second largest gas market after Great Britain (with 20 per cent). According to an optimistic scenario, Germany's gas import

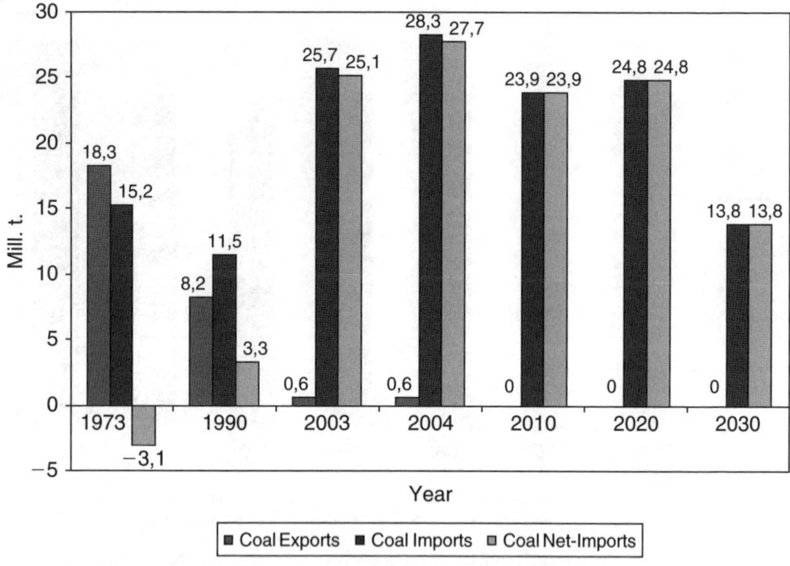

Figure 1.4   Germany's coal exports and imports (1973–2030)
Source: IEA, *Energy Policies of IEA Countries. 2006 Review* (Paris: IEA, 2006), p. 267.

demand will increase only slightly until 2030 (see Figure 1.3). However, it depends on uncertain conditions (that is, development of oil and gas prices vis-à-vis coal and climate policies etc.). According to some new scenarios, its gas imports may increase up to 100 bcm by 2020. In this case, the gas share of the PEC will increase from 23 per cent in 2004 up to 29 per cent in 2020.

As a matter of fact, Berlin has limited its energy policy options even more by announcing an end to its domestic hard coal production (Steinkohle) by 2018. Although the decision does not imply another exit strategy from overall coal production, it makes Germany even more dependent on energy imports. Furthermore, the decision is based on the assumption that the principal conditions of the worldwide coal market (cheap prices versus other fossil resources and a stable availability of coal worldwide) will not change in the next decades. However, as new studies in Europe and the US are showing this might be an over-optimistic scenario which even ignores present strategic developments in global coal markets.[27]

Meanwhile, by emphasizing the need for a national, European and global policy on climate change, the public got the impression that the declared need to preserve the balance in the triangle of objectives in energy policy and to subordinate energy policy to environmental protection and climate change policies as a single determining factor should be given up. At the same time, the anti-nuclear movement of the 1970s and 1980s has developed into

Table 1.1   EU primary energy demand (1971–2030) (mtoe)

	1971	2002	2010	2030	2003–2030*
Coal	426	303	307	274	−0.4%
Oil	633	648	687	743	0.5%
Gas	93	389	468	649	1.8%
Nuclear	13	251	251	146	−1.9%
Hydro	20	26	30	33	0.8%
Biomass and waste	25	65	84	147	3.0%
Other renewables	2	8	21	57	7.2%
Total	1211	1690	1848	2048	0.7%

*Average annual rate of growth.
Source: IEA, *World Energy Outlook 2004* (Paris: IEA, 2004), p. 251.

a new anti-coal movement that is calling for an end to coal as a national energy resource. In addition to the exit strategy of nuclear power, it would further narrow down the national energy mix, lead to higher gas imports from Russia as well as politically unstable countries and further weaken its national security of energy supply.

Future energy security challenges for the EU

Rising dependencies on energy imports

Historically, energy questions dominated the negotiations leading up to the treaties of Paris (1951) and Rome (1957). But the specific institutional provisions were made just for coal and the nuclear industries (leading to the EURATOM treaty in 1957). With regard to oil, gas and renewable energy sources, presently each EU member is free to decide its own national energy policies.

EU members possess only about 0.6 per cent of the world's proven oil reserves, 2.0 per cent of the global gas reserves and, at least, 7.3 per cent of proven coal reserves. With its eastward extension, the EU has only been able to increase its coal reserves substantially (by 41 per cent), but not its oil and gas reserves. In 2004, the EU-27's total primary energy supply was generated by oil (38 per cent), gas (24 per cent), solid fuels (18 per cent), nuclear energy (14 per cent) and renewables (6 per cent). The future new capacity will still be predominantly generated by fossil resources with a rising percentage of gas, while the number of oil and solid-fuel power stations will continue to decline.

In November 2000, the EU's Green Paper warned that in the next 20–30 years up to 70 per cent of the Union's energy demand (presently 50 per cent) will have to be imported. With regard to oil, the EU's dependence could even reach 90 per cent, 70 per cent for gas, and 100 per cent for coal.[28]

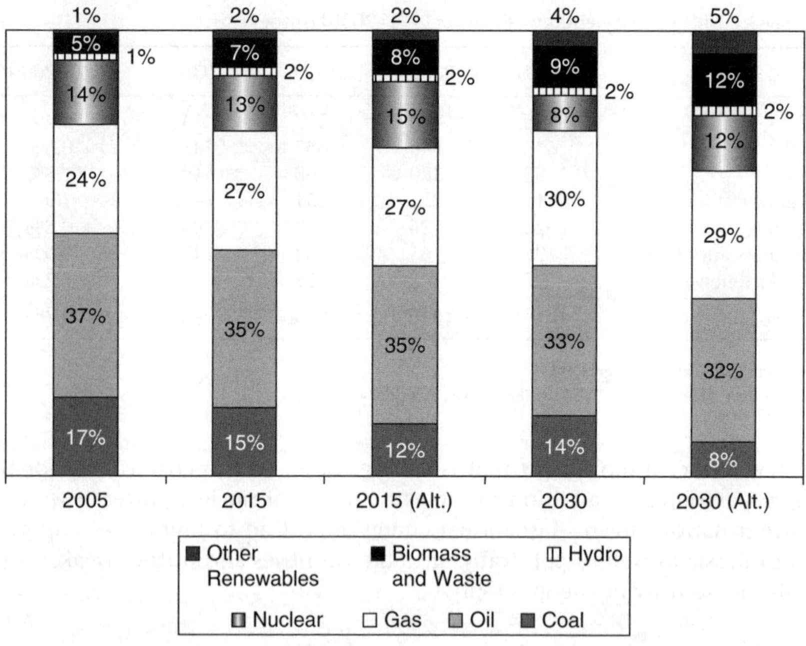

Figure 1.5 EU total primary energy demand (2005–30) (Reference and alternative policy scenarios)
Source: IEA, *World Energy Outlook 2007* (Paris: IEA, 2007), p. 616.

With the EU's enlargement policies of accepting new East European countries, Europe's energy dependence has reached even more worrying levels. Demand for natural gas imports, for instance, may rise from 60 to 90 per cent and oil from 90 to 94 per cent. In 2004, the EU-25 imported 33 per cent of its oil imports from Russia, 32 per cent from the Middle East, 19 per cent from Norway, 4 per cent from Kazakhstan, 3 per cent from Nigeria and 9 per cent from other countries (see Figure 1.6). In 2020, 45 per cent of its oil imports may come from the Middle East.

Thus the EU's long-term strategy for energy supply security has, more than ever, to cope with uninterrupted physical availability of energy products on the market, at a price which is affordable for all private and industrial consumers. At the same time, the EU needs to balance its future energy supply policies with growing environmental concerns, which has become an even more important objective in the light of the Kyoto Protocol.

Given the Green Paper's concern with regard to the projected increased external dependence over the next few decades, it has criticized the five (Germany, Sweden, Spain, Netherlands and Belgium) out of eight EU member states (the other three are France, the United Kingdom and Finland) with nuclear power who have adopted or announced a moratorium on nuclear power or decided to give up nuclear energy production. Presently, nuclear energy does play a vital role – in 2004 it produced 31 per cent of electricity in Europe compared with 14 per cent from renewables – in the sustainable production of electricity. It is also the only industrially mature energy source with negligible greenhouse gas emissions which can be expanded. The Green Paper of 2000 warned that the EU would not meet its obligations under the Kyoto Protocol without nuclear energy. Annually, it saves some 300 million tonnes of carbon dioxide emissions – equivalent to half the amount produced by all the cars in the EU.

Against this background, some of the EU member states are rethinking the nuclear option as the EU Commission, the IEA, the World Energy Council and numerous international energy experts are urging precisely that. Even Germany's unilateral withdrawal from the use of nuclear power may not last for ever. Besides Russia and Ukraine as non-EU member states, Finland, France, Great Britain and many new Central European members of the EU have already indicated that they do not want to renounce the nuclear power option. In fact, the construction of new nuclear power plants is being declared or at least seriously considered (as in Sweden, despite the recent nuclear accident). For economic, environmental, technological and political reasons, the nuclear power option is also undergoing a renaissance in the US, Russia and particularly in Asia.

If no significant changes are made to Europe's energy policy, the total energy picture in 2030 will still be dominated by fossil fuels. Although the energy demand is projected to rise much slower than GDP (by 90 per cent) between 1998 and 2030, gross energy demand is expected to be 11 per cent higher in 2030 than in 1998. Against this background, the EU has called for a mix of energy strategies that include maintaining nuclear energy, improving energy efficiency, changing consumer behaviour through taxation and other measures, as well as doubling the share of renewable energy in the overall energy supply quota from 6 per cent in 1997 to 12 per cent by 2010 and raising their part in electricity production from 14 per cent to 22 per cent by 2010. But until now, only a few members have implemented attractive strategies for renewable energy sources. Hence, even the EU may not be able to live up to its Kyoto Protocol obligations, which envisages cutting greenhouse gas emissions 8 per cent between 2008 and 2012 from 1990 levels. At the end of 2005, only Sweden and Great Britain had fulfilled their Kyoto Protocol obligations.

In a new 'Green Paper on Energy Efficiency' in September 2005, the new Energy Commissioner Andris Piebalgs called for stronger action and strengthening the EU's energy efficiency efforts.[29] The European Commission hopes that the EU could save at least 20 per cent of its present energy consumption in a cost-effective manner. It would be equivalent to 60 billion euros per year or the present combined energy consumption of Germany and Finland.

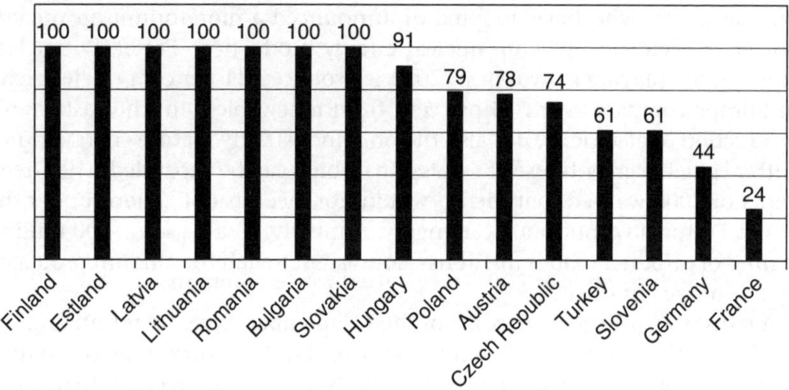

Figure 1.6 European natural gas imports from Russia in 2005 (in %)
Source: EU, IEA, Eurostat, 2005.

Its energy demand management strategy gives added emphasis to diversification in energy supply, promotion of renewable energies and a neutral look
at the nuclear option. After years of discrediting coal, the Commission also
views coal as an important energy source in the future which can contribute
to enhanced security of supply in the EU. It decided to support technical
progress in terms of the clean burning process of coal.[30]

Moreover, the expansion of natural gas as an environmentally clean
energy source will probably be the most problematic factor in the next two
decades for the EU member states. Europe is already today the largest natural gas import market and will continue to be the world champion of gas
importers until 2030. But today, almost half of the EU's gas consumption
is being imported from only three countries: Russia (23 per cent), Norway
(14 per cent) and Algeria (10 per cent) (see again Figure 1.6). The new EU
members and former allies of the Soviet Union, in particular, are still very
much dependent on their gas imports from Russia (see Figure 1.6).

Given current trends, gas imports will increase to 80 per cent over the next
twenty-five years. In 2030, Europe will have to import 488 bcm (North America, 159 bcm and China/India just 85 bcm).[31] The share of gas in total primary
demand will rise from 23 per cent at present to 32 per cent in 2030. In the
future, a growing share of EU gas imports will be shipped as liquefied natural
gas which would offer better crisis stability for gas imports. But currently,
only France, Spain, Greece, Italy, Belgium and Portugal have LNG import
regasification facilities. At present, Europe's combined LNG import facilities
can handle up to 76 bcm a year – a third of the EU's present gas imports.

Meanwhile, it has become increasingly uncertain whether Moscow will be
able to increase its gas exports beyond 180–200 bcm after 2020 due to an

emerging domestic gas crisis.[32] In other words: the EU will be forced to diversify its gas imports anyway. In this respect, the EU is in a very favourable position: unlike any other region of the world, the EU is geographically surrounded by many gas-exporting countries. Eighty per cent of the global gas reserves are within a range of 4500 km; most of those reserves can be connected to the EU by pipelines. However, most of those gas export countries are considered as politically unstable.

The EU March summit of 2007: conceptualizing a common energy policy

Prior to the spring 2007 summit, EU member states were at odds with regard to sovereign prerogatives concerning the national energy mix (i.e. nuclear energy), the agreement on a binding commitment to increase the share of renewable energy resources, the separation of production and supply activities from network operations and the agreement on a common European energy policy towards Russia.

In this light, the EU-27 states were able to agree on a set of tasks and targets at the March summit of 2007:

- energy efficiency should be increased by 20 per cent across the EU;
- the goals of the Kyoto Protocol should be exceeded and carbon emissions should be reduced by 20 per cent by 2020 compared to 1990 (if other industrialized countries such as the US, India and China commit themselves to similar policies, the EU would be willing to reduce emissions by 30 per cent);
- additionally, a 20 per cent share of the energy mix should be generated from renewable energy sources. Latvia, Sweden, Finland and Austria have already attained this target, although the Swedish and Finnish success is due to the use of nuclear energy.

Disagreements existed concerning the ambitious climate policy targets, such as the increase in the share of renewable energies in overall EU energy consumption by 2020 and whether nuclear energy can be considered as a carbon free energy source. Controversies especially erupted around the question of to what extent nuclear energy could be used to reach this target. Furthermore, hitherto only a few members have implemented attractive strategies for renewable energy sources.

In contrast to the EU's climate protection plan, its *Energy Action Plan*, which will accelerate the development and strategic orientation of the external European Energy Policy (EEP), received little public attention. In the area of security of energy supply four 'priority projects of European interest' were articulated, which includes the Nabucco pipeline, bringing gas from the Caspian to central Europe, as the only pipeline project with the support of all twenty-seven member states of the EU. It also means that the planned Nord-Stream gas pipeline in the Baltic Sea is not listed among these priority projects.

The public debate about the results of the spring summit widely concentrated on the 'historic agreement on climate change'. This rather narrow focus, however, jeopardizes the balance within the energy triangle between security of supply, competitiveness and sustainability.

Moreover, the painful decisions of the spring summit in the field of climate protection are still in the offing. With 75 per cent of CO_2 reductions, Germany takes up the lion's share of EU contributions to the goals of the Kyoto Protocol for 2012. But closing the old industrial plants in the German east – which accounted for much of the reduction – has already been done. With regard to carbon reductions by 2020 as envisaged by the EU, Germany will not be able to maintain this high percentage. It also remains questionable whether the leadership role of the EU on climate policies will be honoured and followed by the US and by China, India and other transition countries.

Concerning nuclear energy, Germany has again (as during the G8 summit in 2006) been largely isolated and failed to assert itself on the European level. The spring 2007 summit concluded that the lifetime extension of nuclear power plants can improve the CO_2 balance. Yet the European Council's agreement in March 2007 is clearly a compromise and a common European response on the future of nuclear energy is still missing. France, a country that generates 40 per cent of its energy supply from nuclear energy (and 77 per cent of its electricity supply), is thus able to comply with the required share of renewable energies without implementing any additional measures. With regard to German domestic politics, the summit's compromise backed the position of German Chancellor Merkel, her CDU/CSU parliamentary group and German energy companies. They have argued that a 'withdrawal from the withdrawal' from nuclear energy programmes is needed because it simultaneously enhances the achievement of climate protection targets and strengthens the security of supply.

Even more important is the fact that the EU heads of states and governments have failed to agree upon a common strategy towards Russia, the bloc's most important energy supplier. The lack of coherence of the bloc's external energy policy enables Russia to continue the 'bilateralization' of energy partnerships. With Russia's traditional politics of 'divide and rule', the country is in a powerful position to play off individual European states against large energy companies, as the EU has experienced since April 2007 with a bilateralization of new individual energy deals between Russia and Austria, Italy, Hungary, Greece and Bulgaria.[33] Russia's approach is most visible in its efforts to undermine a common European policy towards Central Asia. Moscow is currently trying to torpedo the Nabucco pipeline project, which is of crucial importance for European energy autonomy and the diversification of energy supply.[34]

Conclusions and perspectives: first results – the EU's successful diversification policies versus dangers of an increasing fragmentation of a unified EU gas market

Due to the environmental obligations of the Kyoto Protocol, the phasing out of nuclear energy programmes in important EU member states, and the increasing depletion of oil and gas fields in the North Sea until 2020, the EU will become much more dependent on oil and particularly gas imports from outside Europe – both from Russia as an increasingly unreliable energy partner as well as from unstable countries and regions in the Middle East, Central Asia and Africa. Despite new energy saving measures and the promotion of renewable energy sources, the fossil fuels of oil, gas and coal will remain the primary energy sources up to 2030. Moreover, the important question of how the burden of the ambitious climate protection goals will be shared between the twenty-seven EU member states has yet to be addressed.

Irrespective of many improvements in shaping a coherent and united EU energy security and foreign energy policy, the German EU Presidency failed to establish a common position of the EU members towards Russia as their single most important energy supplier. After the summit in March, the lack of coherence in foreign energy relations made it easy for Moscow to enforce the 'bilateralization' of its political cooperation in terms of energy with the single EU member states and European energy enterprises. By the means of its traditional policy of 'divide and rule', the Kremlin has successfully played off the individual European states and enterprises against each other. Hence the EU's internal disagreements vis-à-vis Europe's main energy supplier, Russia, remain the most serious problem of the envisaged common European approach.

The aftermath of the spring summit has seen European energy companies, with the backing of their respective governments, intensifying their relations with Moscow. In the light of such bilateral energy deals, the European Council conclusions run the risk of becoming political lip service. The construction of the Nabucco pipeline needs to be supported more decisively by Germany and the EU.

For the EU member states, an additional conflict of interests has occurred in their already ambivalent relationship with Moscow. The EU's foreign energy policy will either further complicate EU–Russia relations, or, given the EU's consideration of Russia's energy and security interests, put into question the Central Asia and diversification strategy of oil and gas imports from CACR. However, the EU cannot forgo diversifying its imports of natural gas from the Caspian region because: firstly, the Kremlin is exploiting energy dependencies as a means of foreign policy; and secondly, Russia alone cannot meet the forecasted EU natural gas demand up to 2030. Furthermore, in the light of the EU's wider foreign energy and security interests, it has no alternative other than to extend and to deepen its relations with CACR.

On the energy foreign policy front of strengthening energy security and supply, the EU has proceeded with a number of pipeline and LNG projects to import non-Russian natural gas sources. These new projects have a combined addition of more than 100 bcm. These alternatives will give the EU more leverage and bargaining power vis-à-vis Moscow. If the EU is successful in reducing total European energy demand by 20 per cent by 2020 and in obtaining 20 per cent from renewable energy sources, it would significantly reduce the EU's overall energy demand as well as its gas imports from Russia. Furthermore, many new EU member states are now increasing their own coal production, which has become cheaper than importing Russian gas. It also coincides with their supply strategies to reduce their dependence on Russia, to diversify their gas imports and to expand the production of gas from biomass. In the future, the EU's future gas imports might be much lower (300–350 bcm) than previously forecasted (up to 490 bcm).[35]

In regard to the EU's and Germany's growing interest in global and interregional energy cooperation and joint initiatives for containing climate change, particularly with Asia, the following recommendations of the Working Group of the Council for Asia-Europe Cooperation (CAEC) of 2004[36] are still relevant, but need to be revised with more concrete ideas:

- accommodating newly emerging Asian consumers and importers within existing cooperative schemes;
- providing assistance to countries lacking a complete energy policy;
- inferring lessons for Asia from European experience of regional cooperation (government level dialogue);
- experience sharing on national public policies (government level dialogue) on energy sector liberalization, specific market-oriented mechanisms and the most appropriate mechanisms to enhance energy efficiency;
- experience sharing, information exchange and cooperation on scientific and technical issues (expert level dialogue and public–private partnerships);
- joint initiatives in international forums dealing with energy issues and climate policies;
- promotion of public campaigns on the issue of pacific nuclear use.

In this context, the following recommendations are made for enhanced interregional dialogue and cooperation on energy security between the EU, Asia and the ASEM process:

- A long-term solution for global energy and climate change policies can only lie in the most international division of labour and multilateral policy (e.g. the creation of regional and national strategic oil and reserves) as well as enhancing worldwide energy efficiency. It would also promote the opening up to outsiders, deregulation and privatization of the Chinese and other Asian energy sectors.

- The international community, including the EU, should not only offer new technologies for renewable energy sources (like wind energy) and improving energy efficiency, but also support multilateral approaches and concrete cooperation models (such as the Treaty of the European Energy Charter, the Transit Protocol, the Extractive Industries Transparency Initiative (EITI) or the International Energy Forum (IEF). Those approaches require a fundamentally cooperative foreign and security policy in China and other Asian countries. Therefore, the EU needs to widen and deepen its energy agenda with China and other Asian countries by offering not just technology transfers and EU support of the modernization of its energy infrastructure, but also its underlying strategies and policies.

Notes

1. See D. Yergin, 'Ensuring Energy Security', *Foreign Affairs*, Vol. 85, No. 2, March–April 2006, p. 74.
2. See also M. Burrows and G. F. Treverton, 'A Strategic View of Energy Futures', *Survival*, Vol. 49, No. 3, Autumn 2007, p. 83.
3. N. Elhefnawy, 'Toward a Long-Range Energy Security Policy', *Parameters*, Spring 2006, p. 108.
4. See International Energy Agency (IEA), *World Energy Outlook 2007* (Paris: IEA, 2007, pp. 41 and 73ff.
5. IEA, *World Energy Outlook 2006* (Paris: IEA, 2006), p. 37.
6. See D. Hale, 'China's Growing Appetites', *The National Interest*, Summer 2004, pp. 137–47.
7. See K. Bradsher, 'Asian States Move to Curb Demand for Oil', *International Herald Tribune*, 7 September 2005, p. 14.
8. See also F. Umbach, *Globale Energiesicherheit. Herausforderungen für die europäische und deutsche Außenpolitik* (Munich: Oldenbourg Verlag, 2003), pp. 122ff.; and F. Umbach, 'Global Energy Supply and Geopolitical Challenges', in F. Godement, F. Nicolas and T. Yakushiji (eds), *Asia and Europe: Cooperating for Energy Security: a Council for Asia-Europe Cooperation (CAEC) Task Force Report* (Paris: IFRI, 2004), pp. 137–68.
9. See the executive summary, called 'Energy Security in a Dangerous World' in IEA, *World Energy Outlook 2004* (Paris: IEA, 2004), pp. 29–30.
10. T. L. Friedman, 'The First Law of Petropolitics', *Foreign Policy*, May–June 2006, p. 35. See also M. L. Ross, 'Does Oil Hinder Democracy?', *World Politics*, April 2001, pp. 325–61.
11. Z. Daojiong, 'China's Energy Security: Domestic and International Issues', *Survival*, Spring 2006, p. 181.
12. See F. Umbach, 'The Legs of the Triangle – The EU–China Relations', in W. Jung (ed.), *The New Strategic Triangle: China, Europe and the United States in a Changing International System*, KAS-Schriftenreihe No. 76 (Beijing: Konrad-Adenauer-Stiftung, 2007), pp. 36–45.
13. See European Council, *Presidency Conclusions*, Brussels, 8–9 March 2007.

14. See F. Umbach, *Globale Energiesicherheit*; F. Umbach, 'Europe's Energy Non-Policy', *Internationale Politik (Transatlantic Edition)*, No. 4, 2004, pp. 17–28; and F. Umbach, 'Europäische und deutsche Energieversorgungssicherheit am Scheideweg', *Energiewirtschaftliche Tagesfragen*, No. 9, 2005, pp. 629–39.

15. See Umbach, *Globale Energiesicherheit*, pp. 186ff. and R. L. Larson, *Russia's Energy Policy: Security Dimensions and Russia's Reliability as an Energy Supplier*, FOI (Stockholm: Swedish Defence Research Agency, 2006), FOI-R-1934-SE, Scientific Report.

16. See European Commission, *Green Paper: Towards a European Strategy for the Security of Energy Supply*, 2001, adopted on 29 November 2000.

17. See European Council, *A Secure Europe in a Better World*, 12 December 2003.

18. See Foreign & Commonwealth Office, *Energy Strategy*, 28 October 2004, http:/www.fco.gov.uk/Files/hfile/Energy_Report_281004.0.pdf, accessed 12 December 2004.

19. See European Commission, *Green Paper: Towards a European Strategy for the Security of Energy Supply*, 2001; European Commission, *Green Paper: a European Strategy for Sustainable, Competitive and Secure Energy*, COM (2006) 105 final, Brussels, 8 March 2006.

20. See also R. L. Larsson, *Sweden and the NEGP: a Pilot Study of the North European Gas Pipeline and Sweden's Dependence on Russian Energy*, FOI (Stockholm: Swedish Defence Research Agency, June 2006), FOI-R-1984-SE, Base data report; and A. Cohen, 'The North European Gas Pipeline Threatens Europe's Energy Security', *Backgrounder*, No. 1980, 26 October 2006 (Washington, DC: Heritage Foundation).

21. See F. Umbach, 'Europe's Next Cold War', *Internationale Politik (Global Edition)*, Summer 2006, pp. 64–71; F. Umbach, 'Deutsche Außenpolitik und Energiesicherheit', in T. Jäger, A. Höse and K. Oppermann (eds), *Deutsche Außenpolitik: Sicherheit, Wohlfahrt, Institutionen und Normen* (Wiesbaden: Verlag für Sozialwissenschaften, 2007), pp. 354–73.

22. F.-W. Steinmeier, 'Avoiding Conflict over Fuel', *International Herald Tribune*, 23 March 2006, p. 6.

23. See Umbach, 'Europe's Next Cold War', p. 64.

24. See F. Umbach, *Zielkonflikte der europäischen Energiesicherheit: Dilemmata zwischen Russland und Zentralasien. DGAPanalyse*, No. 3 (Berlin: DGAP, 2007).

25. See C. Kemfert, T. Traber and T. P. Truong, *Comprehensive Package of Climate Protection Measures Could Substantially Decrease Costs of Emission Reductions in Germany*, DIW-Weekly Report, Vol. 3, 1 June 2007 (Berlin: DIW).

26. See J. Auer, *Germany: the Global Force in Wind Energy* (Frankfurt: Deutsche Bank Research, 2007).

27. See F. Umbach, 'Kohle auch in Zukunft unverzichtbar', in J. Petermann (ed.), *Sichere Energie im 21. Jahrhundert*, 2nd edition (Hamburg: Hoffmann und Campe, forthcoming 2008).

28. See European Commission, *Green Paper*, 2001; and IEA, *World Energy Outlook 2002* (Paris: IEA, 2002), pp. 177ff.

29. See European Commission, *Green Paper on Energy Efficiency: Doing More with Less*, COM (2005) 265 final, 22 June 2005.

30. See European Commission, *Report on the Green Paper on Energy: Four Years of European Initiatives*, 2005, p. 10.

31. See IEA, *World Energy Outlook 2006*, pp. 117–18.

32. See A. Riley and F. Umbach, 'Out of Gas: Looming Russian Gas Deficits Demand Readjustment of European Energy Policy', *Internationale Politik (Global Edition)*, No. 1, Spring 2007, pp. 83–90.
33. See Umbach, *Zielkonflikte der europäischen Energiesicherheit*, pp. 18–19.
34. Ibid.; F. Umbach, *Licht und Schatten auf dem EU-Frühjahrsgipfel 2007 – Gemeinsame Energie – und Energieaußenpolitik oder nationale Sonderbeziehungen mit Russland*, Berlin, No. 3, 24 April 2007.
35. See R. Goetz, *Russlands Erdgas und Europas Energiesicherheit*, SWP-Studie S21 (Berlin: SWP, 2007), pp. 9–12.
36. See F. Nicolas, F. Godement and T. Yakushij, 'Appendix: Summary and Policy Recommendations' in Godement et al., *Asia and Europe*, pp. 229–33.

2

Russia as an Energy Great Power: Consequences for EU Energy Security

Javier Morales

Introduction

In the past few years, energy security has become one of the European Union's foremost concerns. The rise in world energy prices, the instability in the Middle East, and the challenges of reducing the environmental impact of energy production and consumption have made EU member states include the diversification of energy supply among their main priorities. The spread of a new 'energy nationalism' in producer countries like Russia – which has pursued increasingly assertive policies since the beginning of Putin's presidency – has been an additional reason for this preoccupation.[1]

Russia's evolution after the March 2008 elections is of crucial importance for Europe, considering that many EU members depend on Russian energy exports. The chances for a better mutual understanding depend not only on the actual negotiations, but also on how the Russian political leadership perceives the role that the country must play in the world arena and how energy can be used in the Kremlin's international strategy. In this regard, Dmitry Medvedev's project seems at this moment to be one of continuity, without any major shift from Putin's policies.

The purpose of this chapter, therefore, is to study the relationship between Russia's self-perception as an international actor and its role as an energy exporter. Our starting point consists of two alternative questions. First, has the current situation of high energy prices – and the consequent leverage over neighbouring countries – been the cause of Putin's more assertive policies, convincing him to take a tougher stand in international affairs? Or, on the contrary, has the use of energy exports been just an instrument for the Kremlin to restore Russia's greatness in the world, a long-term objective which they would have pursued in any case, but by other means? The available options for ensuring the energy security of the EU in the future depend on the answers.

The first part of this chapter analyses the Russian conception of energy as a foreign policy instrument. The second part contextualizes these ideas within the ideology of 'sovereign democracy' espoused by Putin and the United Russia party. The third part describes the impact of Russian energy policies on the country's relations with Europe. Finally, our conclusions include some proposals for ensuring the energy security of EU member states, considering the probable evolution of Russia in the next few years.

Energy as an instrument of Russian foreign policy

Putin's vision of Russia's role in the world could be described as a 'Great Eurasian Power', a concept which comprises two elements. First, the Russian leadership are conscious that their days of competition with the United States are over, but that does not mean that they want to relinquish their status as one of the main world powers. Secondly, the territorial base for consolidating Russia as one of the world centres of power has continued to be the post-Soviet space – or, as it has been termed in the official discourse, the 'near abroad' – which Moscow still perceives as its own sphere of influence.

Consequently, the Russian leadership have actively supported the formation of a multipolar international system where their country – together with others like China – presents an alternative to US hegemony, trying to maintain Russia's influence over the members of the Commonwealth of Independent States (CIS). This strategy had already been formulated as the 'Primakov doctrine' by Yevgeny Primakov, one of Yeltsin's foreign ministers. However, in contrast to his predecessor in the Kremlin, Putin has followed a more realistic approach to relations with Washington, more based on national interests and less influenced by personal relations.[2]

That said, neither the domestic nor the international situations were too favourable for these ambitious objectives when Putin came to power. There was a general consensus that Russia's role was declining and its status as a 'great power' could no longer be taken for granted. In addition to that, the new US administration of George W. Bush did not consider relations with Moscow as important a priority as it had been for Bill Clinton; consequently, they announced their intentions to proceed with their plans of missile defence or NATO enlargement in spite of Russian objections.

But two unforeseen series of events would provide Russia with the opportunity to reverse this trend to neglect their role in world politics. The first was the 9/11 terrorist attacks and the US-led 'war on terror', which echoed Moscow's discourse in the previous years about the threat of Islamic radicalism. However, the initial consensus on the need to collaborate with the West against terrorism was diluted by the different threat perceptions and the disagreements over the best strategies to combat it, especially when the Bush administration argued that Saddam Hussein had links to Islamist terrorism in order to justify the invasion of Iraq.

The second series of events, more relevant to our topic in this chapter, was the post-war instability in the Middle East after the Iraq War, with the consequent rise in world energy prices. Although the first signs of Russia's post-crisis economic recovery had already appeared in 1999, exports at these more favourable prices have been to a great extent the cause of its recent economic growth. According to World Bank data, in Putin's first term in office (2000–4) the oil and gas sector's share of GDP increased from 8 to 19 per cent. Hydrocarbons accounted for more than 50 per cent of total exports; more than 40 per cent in the case of oil, which increased export volumes by 80 per cent in the same period.[3]

Moscow has realized that energy exports are one of the most useful resources at its disposal in its quest for *derzhavnost*, or great power status, compared to the limitations of other symbolic attributes like its military nuclear power and its permanent seat at the United Nations (UN) Security Council. Therefore, Russia has consistently tried to use energy as one of its main foreign policy instruments: if Russia was no longer a military superpower at the same level as the United States, then it could become an energy superpower.[4] An example of this linkage between energy and foreign policy was the establishment of an International Institute of Energy Policy and Diplomacy at the Moscow State Institute of International Relations (MGIMO), the university of the Ministry of Foreign Affairs, where Russian diplomats and many in the country's elite are educated.[5]

This strategy is not completely new, nor is it merely a consequence of the Iraq War. The 2000 Foreign Policy Concept, drafted under Putin's supervision, already stated that 'Russia must be prepared to utilize all its available economic levers and resources for upholding its national interests', an obvious reference to energy resources.[6] As the number one country in natural gas reserves, second in coal reserves and eighth in oil reserves, Russia has gradually oriented itself to become an 'energy great power', becoming the world's largest gas exporter and the second largest oil exporter.[7] This is a field where it has a comparative advantage over other world powers, preserving its role as Europe's main supplier while it develops energy trade with Asian countries.

However, this reliance on oil and gas exports is also a cause of vulnerability for Russia, which depends on world energy prices and on the availability of customers, transport routes and reserves for its economic growth. A study by the International Monetary Fund concluded in 2004 that the Russian federal budget is five times more sensitive to world oil prices than before 1998–9.[8] Therefore, experts like Isbell have argued that mutual interdependence prevents Russia from carrying out prolonged supply cuts to Europe in peacetime;[9] problems could arise as a result of a conflict with a third party, such as the gas crisis with Ukraine, but not as a direct action against the EU, which would be detrimental to Moscow's own interests. This corresponds to repeated assurances by the Kremlin, most recently by Medvedev during the presidential campaign: 'We will unquestionably fulfil all of our international oil and gas supply commitments.'[10]

In addition to that, since 2003 the slowdown in oil extraction – due to lack of investment, the state campaign against Yukos and increasing taxes – has started to have a negative impact on economic growth.[11] As Åslund notes, production declined because state companies have not invested enough in the exploration of new fields or in upgrading their technology.[12] The same is also true for natural gas, which combined with high domestic demand could make it difficult to maintain exports at their current level. An indication of this was the reduction of supplies to several European countries in January 2006, when it was argued that the extremely low temperatures in Russia had increased domestic consumption. This makes investment all the more necessary.[13]

However, increasing state control and uncertainty about the rules of the game have made foreign companies more reluctant to invest in Russian projects: for example, the annulment in 2004 of a 1993 tender that gave ExxonMobil, Chevron Texaco and Rosneft the same rights to develop one of the Sakhalin oil fields.[14] This makes it more unlikely that the decline in production will be reversed.

Russia is also a very energy-intensive economy, with domestic prices regulated by the state at a much lower level than real market prices. Therefore, investment is an urgent need if oil and gas exports are to be maintained in the future, as well as to satisfy internal demand. For the EU, the mid-term security of production could be considered as a more serious risk than short-term security of supply.[15]

Energy and the ideology of 'sovereign democracy'

Russian official discourse, in spite of its ambiguity and instrumental use for electoral purposes, is the framework where the conceptions about the domestic and international situations are made explicit. Therefore, in order to better understand Putin's energy policy we have to refer to the concept of 'sovereign democracy' espoused by him and his chosen successor, Medvedev, as well as the party that supports them, United Russia (*Yedinaya Rossiya*).

According to their views, 'democracy' and 'sovereignty' are considered as the two necessary conditions for stable development of the country. But democracy is merely defined as a system of political competition to select the best leaders, with the aim of becoming integrated into the world economy, having access to technologies and investment from the most developed countries. State sovereignty, on the other hand, is considered to have retained its importance in the face of globalization; but not just in the traditional sense of responsibility over a territory, people and governing structure. It is also understood in a negative sense, as freedom and independence of the state from external influences; which includes the control of strategic sectors of the economy, such as energy resources.[16]

However, the energy policy that has been implemented by Putin cannot be considered as an attempt at re-enacting the planned economy under the Soviet regime, because it has been limited by pragmatic interests rather than ideological concerns. It has been described as 'state capitalism', that is, neither a public nor a truly private ownership of energy companies, but state control over them. Foreign investment is allowed, but always limited to a minority share;[17] as Olcott notes, 'for Putin, this investment must be made in a manner that is consistent with the Russian state's ability to exert guardianship over the country's oil and gas assets'.[18]

The roots of this conception can be traced to the years before Putin came to power, when he defended state control of energy companies in his doctoral dissertation at St Petersburg Mining Institute, invoking the country's national interests to limit the rights of private owners:

> Regardless of whose property the natural resources and in particular the mineral resources might be, the state has the right to regulate the process of their development and use, acting in the interests of society as a whole and of individual property owners, whose interests come into conflict with each other, and who need the help of state organs of power to reach compromises when their interests conflict.[19]

Oil and gas are therefore considered as strategic resources: a guarantee of the country's economic security, not to be left to the mechanisms of the free market. As a result, the role of private companies must in Putin's opinion be limited to a 'stewardship' or 'guardianship' over energy resources, while true ownership remains in the hands of the state. These concerns are behind Russia's unwillingness to ratify the Energy Charter treaty, which would give other countries access to their pipeline system. This is also linked to the defence of a 'strong state', considered the central element in the Russian political tradition by the ideologues of 'sovereign democracy'.[20]

Another consequence is that there are many obstacles to foreign investment, and private companies must accept the orientations given by the state when making strategic decisions. The clearest example was the campaign against Yukos, caused by Mikhail Khodorkovsy's rejection of state intervention. Khodorkovsky attracted the Kremlin's wrath by funding the political opposition, planning alternative pipelines to those controlled by the state – including one to China – and being willing to sell a portion of Yukos to the American companies Chevron Texaco or ExxonMobil.[21]

There have also been problems for foreign energy companies with the Russian security services. In October 2005, for example, several facilities of the Russian–British consortium TNK-BP in Western Siberia were closed down by the FSB, arguing that state secrets were in danger.[22]

In addition to that, state control has been implemented through direct personal appointments. Several high-ranking officials of the presidential administration – Putin's closest collaborators – have simultaneously chaired the boards of some of the main energy corporations: Medvedev in Gazprom, Igor Sechin in Rosneft, and Vladislav Surkov in Transnefteprodukt; additionally, Arkadi Dvorkovich had a seat on the board of Transneft.[23]

The clearest example of Putin's views is Gazprom, used as a political instrument against Ukraine after the 'Orange Revolution'. The state-controlled gas corporation has consistently tried to expand into the European market, signing deals with several of the main energy corporations: Eni, BASF, E.ON Ruhrgas or Gaz de France. Although these agreements have tried to ensure a continuing supply in the face of a slowdown in oil and gas production and increasing domestic consumption in Russia, they have also increased Europe's energy dependence.[24] But on the other hand, taking into account the uneasy relations between Russia and Ukraine, the construction of new routes bypassing the latter – such as the South Stream gas pipeline – could make supplies more stable, not affected by the periodical bilateral crisis between Moscow and Kiev.[25] This is, of course, not incompatible with diversifying energy imports to reduce this dependence as much as possible; as well as developing alternative energy sources, especially to replace oil consumption.

The paradoxes of EU–Russia interdependence

The EU is for Russia the traditional geographic space for integration into the developed world, a possible support in the creation of a multipolar world and – last but not least – a source of income, in the form of trade, investment and aid. However, it is at the same time a rival great power, an external influence from whose control it has to protect itself and a source of destabilization for the regime (criticizing violations of human rights, and so on). The EU is Russia's most important trading partner; European countries are the source of more than 60 per cent of direct foreign investment. Putin has recognized this importance by making closer economic relations with the EU a top priority, although there have been disagreements on other issues such as democracy and human rights.[26]

The situation with regard to energy is of mutual dependence. Russia is the main energy provider to the EU, especially of natural gas, the demand for which is expected to grow over oil demand as it is less contaminating and is increasingly used for producing electricity. On the other hand, Russia needs energy export revenues to maintain current levels of economic growth and to fund the state budget. Infrastructures are another cause of vulnerability for Russia: the existing pipelines determine the countries to which they can export, as gas is still not transported in its liquefied form (LNG).[27]

The only alternative markets for Russia are the energy-hungry Asian economies; China and Japan are the main candidates for receiving oil and gas from East Siberia, the Russian Far East and Sakhalin.[28] In 2006, Putin complained to the German chancellor Angela Merkel about the obstacles to the expansion of Russian energy companies, such as Gazprom's attempts to control the British gas distributor Centrica: 'What are we supposed to do in these circumstances, when every day we hear the same thing? We start to look for other markets.' But it would take many years to develop a transport network to Asia which could effectively replace the exports that Russia receives from Europe, which makes Russian threats appear rather empty in the short term.[29]

This is also true for the EU: if Russia decides to stop supplies to Central and Eastern Europe, there would be no ready alternative, especially for natural gas. This has happened several times since Putin came to power: in January 2003 Russia switched off supplies through an oil pipeline to Latvia; in July 2006, the same happened to Lithuania; and once again to Ukraine in January 2006. In February 2008, the situation was repeated when Gazprom threatened to cut supplies to Ukraine again if a debt was not paid off, ahead of a summit between Putin and Yuschenko; this time the EU received assurances that its members would not be affected.[30]

However difficult the everyday political relations between Russia and the EU may be, especially after the latter's latest enlargement to Central and Eastern Europe, more drastic unilateral moves are prevented by mutual interdependence. Europe needs a stable and secure energy supply, and Russia needs to export energy to support its current economic growth, as well as to upgrade its oil and gas complex. It must also be remembered that energy trade with Russia was initially considered by Europe as the main alternative to supplies from the Middle East, that is, as a means to increase energy security by diversifying imports.[31] The current instability after the Iraq War is, therefore, an additional reason for further cooperation between both sides: attacks against pipelines by insurgency and the risks for oil tankers in the Persian Gulf – especially in the case of a hypothetical conflict involving Iran – make continuing the energy relationship with Russia even more necessary.[32]

But to achieve this, the EU needs a common energy policy to ensure its energy security. Up to now, energy policies have been left to member states and to the 'free market'. Russia has used this lack of unity to maximize its advantages as an energy supplier, preferring to sign bilateral agreements with certain countries: for example, the North European gas pipeline through the Baltic Sea, the result of a Russian–German agreement – paradoxically signed just before the 'gas crisis' with Ukraine – which benefited Russia by bypassing Poland and Ukraine. Added to this are the effects of the agreement between Italy and Russia to build the 'South Stream' gas pipeline, also supported by Hungary; this route will link Russia to Bulgaria through the Black Sea, directly competing with the European 'Nabucco' project.[33]

Conclusions

First of all, with regard to the institutional framework of EU–Russia energy relations, both sides should recognize the clear differences in values and perceptions on a wide range of issues, from the concept of sovereignty or the role of the state in a market economy to the relationship between economic and human security. The Kremlin seems to be focused on increasing the economic potential of the state as an instrument to restore the country's 'greatness', disregarding the impact of economic policies on the welfare of individual citizens. This is apparent, for instance, in the case of environmental issues: the energy sector is the most contaminating in the Russian economy, being responsible for 70 per cent of greenhouse gas emissions.[34]

The current assertiveness in foreign policy is likely to continue with Putin's successor: the objective of consolidating itself as one of the world's great powers will continue, even in a less favourable economic situation for Russia. Within this context, in order to engage Russia in a fruitful dialogue, the EU has to make Moscow feel that its views are respected as those of a great power and an equal partner; without being unrealistically expected to behave as a candidate to accession. Therefore, the EU should aim at integrating Russia as much as possible into its activities, to influence the political elites through their socialization in European values. Emphasis should be placed on common interests, rather than on defending itself against Moscow's influence; an attitude that mirrors the Kremlin's continuing reassertion of 'sovereignty' in its relations with Europe.

That said, EU members should not forget common European interests and principles in their relations with Moscow, not only for their economic decisions – like bilateral energy contracts – but also for promoting a more open and democratic regime in Russia, within the limits of respect for the other side's views and not as a precondition. Although – in Lord Palmerston's famous words – states have permanent interests but not permanent allies, Europe has no alternative to cooperating with its neighbour; without any dialogue, Russian mistrust of Europe and European values will continue, thus preventing any significant advancement.

The practical consequences are twofold. First, EU member states need to continue developing a common energy strategy, making the most of mutual interdependence with Russia and using Moscow's reliance on export revenues to their own advantage. Secondly, this cooperation can be increased by offering incentives such as investment and technology to explore new fields, improving energy efficiency and reducing the environmental impact; which would contribute to stable, long-term production and security of supply. The energy security of Russia and the EU can either be considered as a zero-sum game or an opportunity for better understanding; the choice is ours to make.[35]

Notes

1. R. Mabro, 'Oil Nationalism, the Oil Industry and Energy Security Concerns', ARI 114/2007, http://www.realinstitutoelcano.org

2. The personalization of US–Russia relations between Clinton and Yeltsin is evident in B. Yeltsin, *Midnight Diaries* (London: Phoenix, 2001); S. Talbott, *The Russia Hand: a Memoir of Presidential Diplomacy* (New York: Random House, 2003).
3. R. Ahrend, 'Towards a Post-Putin Russia: Economic Prospects', in H. Blakkisrud (ed.), *Towards a Post-Putin Russia* (Oslo: Norwegian Institute of International Affairs, 2006), pp. 41–2, 46.
4. F. Hill, *Energy Empire: Oil, Gas and Russia's Revival* (London: Foreign Policy Centre, 2004), p. 1.
5. http://www.miep-mgimo.ru. See also M. Smith, 'Russia's Energy Diplomacy', Conflict Studies Research Centre Russian Series, F75, 2002, http://www.da. mod.uk, p. 1.
6. Federation of American Scientists, *The Foreign Policy Concept of the Russian Federation*, 2000, http://www.fas.org
7. US Department of Energy, Energy Information Administration, 'Russia', Country Analysis Briefs, 2007, http://www.eia.doe.gov, p. 1.
8. Quoted in Hill, *Energy Empire*, p. 34.
9. P. Isbell, 'Revisiting Energy Security', ARI 123/2007, http://www.realinstitutoelcano.org, p. 2.
10. D. Medvedev, 'Speech at the V Krasnoyarsk Economic Forum', 2008, http://www.medvedev2008.ru
11. Ahrend, 'Towards a Post-Putin Russia'.
12. A. Åslund, 'Russia's Energy Policy: a Framing Comment', *Eurasian Geography and Economics*, Vol. 47, No. 3, 2006, p. 325.
13. R. Götz, 'Russian Economic Security in a Medium-Term Perspective', in J. Hegenskog, V. Konnander, B. Nygren, I. Oldberg and C. Pursiainen (eds), *Russia as a Great Power: Dimensions of Security under Putin* (London and New York: Routledge, 2005), pp. 249–50; M. Fredholm, 'Gazprom in Crisis', Conflict Studies Research Centre Russian Series, 06/48, 2006, http://www.da.mod.uk, pp. 5–7; Hill, *Energy Empire*, p. 56.
14. Hill, *Energy Empire*, p. 31; Smith, 'Russia's Energy Diplomacy', p. 4; M. B. Olcott, 'The Energy Dimension in Russian Global Strategy: Vladimir Putin and the Geopolitics of Oil', James A. Baker III Institute for Public Policy, Rice University, 2004, http://bakerinstitute.org, p. 2.
15. Isbell, 'Revisiting Energy Security', ARI 123/2007, p. 4; V. Milov, L. L. Coburn and I. Danchenko, 'Russia's Energy Policy, 1992–2005', *Eurasian Geography and Economics*, Vol. 47, No. 3, 2006, p. 290; Åslund, 'Russia's Energy Policy', pp. 325–7; Fredholm, 'Gazprom in Crisis', pp. 7–8; J. Hardt, 'Putin's Window of Economic Opportunity', *Problems of Post-Communism*, Vol. 52, No. 4, 2005, p. 17; A. M. Jaffe and R. A. Manning, 'Russia, Energy and the West', *Survival*, Vol. 43, No. 2, 2001, p. 138.
16. M. Smith, 'Sovereign Democracy: the Ideology of Yedinaya Rossiya', Conflict Studies Research Centre Russian Series, 06/37, 2006, http://www.da.mod.uk
17. Åslund, 'Russia's Energy Policy', p. 324; Fredholm, 'Gazprom in Crisis', p. 2.
18. Olcott, 'The Energy Dimension in Russian Global Strategy', p. 3.
19. Fredholm, 'Gazprom in Crisis', p. 2.
20. M. Fredholm, 'The Russian Energy Strategy and Energy Policy: Pipeline Diplomacy or Mutual Dependence', Conflict Studies Research Centre Russian Series, 05/41, 2005, http://www.da.mod.uk, p. 7; Smith, 'Sovereign Democracy', p. 4; *The Economist*, 'A Bear at the Throat', *The Economist*, 12 April 2007,

http://www.economist.com; Olcott, 'The Energy Dimension in Russian Global Strategy', pp. 16, 19; Isbell, 'Revisiting Energy Security', p. 3.

21. Olcott, 'The Energy Dimension in Russian Global Strategy', pp. 1, 13–14; Hill, *Energy Empire*, pp. 35–6.

22. BBC, 'BP admits Kremlin security talks', *BBC News*, 24 October 2005, http://news.bbc.co.uk

23. J. Cooper, 'The Economy', in E. Bacon and B. Renz, with J. Cooper, *Securitising Russia: the Domestic Politics of Putin* (Manchester: Manchester University Press, 2006), pp. 167–8; Fredholm, 'The Russian Energy Strategy and Energy Policy', p. 10.

24. See Marquina's chapter in this book.

25. N. Abdullaev and S. Saradzhyan, 'Russia's Gas Showdown', *ISN Security Watch*, 30 December 2005, http://www.isn.ethz.ch; Smith, 'Russia's Energy Diplomacy', p. 5; Z. Baran, 'EU Energy Security: Time to End Russian Leverage', *Washington Quarterly*, Vol. 30, No. 4, 2007, p. 132; *The Economist*, 'A Bear at the Throat'; see also Ifantis's chapter in this book.

26. T. Casier, 'Putin's Policy Towards the West: Reflections on the Nature of Russian Foreign Policy', *International Politics*, Vol. 43, 2006, pp. 389, 393.

27. Fredholm, 'The Russian Energy Strategy and Energy Policy', pp. 6–7; Baran, 'EU Energy Security', p. 132; M. Light, 'Russian Political Engagement with the European Union', in R. Allison, M. Light and S. White, *Putin's Russia and the Enlarged Europe*, Chatham House Papers (Oxford: Blackwell, 2006), p. 65.

28. Hill, *Energy Empire*, pp. 28–9, 32–3.

29. BBC, 'Putin criticises West over energy', *BBC News*, 27 April 2006, http://news.bbc.co.uk; *The Economist*, 'A Bear at the Throat'.

30. BBC, 'Gazprom threatens Ukraine gas cut', *BBC News*, 7 February 2008, http://news.bbc.co.uk; BBC, 'Urgent talks on Ukraine gas row', *BBC News*, 12 February 2008, http://news.bbc.co.uk; BBC, 'Gazprom restarts row with Ukraine', *BBC News*, 26 February 2008, http://news.bbc.co.uk; Baran, 'EU Energy Security', pp. 132–3.

31. Hill, *Energy Empire*, pp. 29–30.

32. Smith, 'Russia's Energy Diplomacy', pp. 3–4.

33. Baran, 'EU Energy Security', pp. 131, 135; Light, 'Russian Political Engagement with the European Union', p. 66; *The Economist*, 'A Bear at the Throat'; O. Shchedrov, 'Russia wins Hungary for South Stream gas project', 2008, http://uk.reuters.com.

34. Götz, 'Russian Economic Security in a Medium-Term Perspective', p. 230.

35. Jaffe and Manning, 'Russia, Energy and the West', p. 148.

3
Perceptions and Misperceptions of Energy Supply Security in Europe and the 'China Factor'

Michal Meidan

Introduction

Energy security has been the subject of increasing debate in the last few years. Spurred by widespread political instability in the major producing countries, the emergence of new consumers with strong demand for energy as well as inefficient consumption patterns, and the inevitable hike in prices that ensues, energy policies and politics are becoming the focus of increased attention.

'Energy security' is most traditionally defined as the 'availability of energy at all times, in various forms, in sufficient quantities, and at afford-able prices',[1] meaning essentially the adequate match between supply and demand at a cost deemed affordable to a country's economy. The European Union has championed the fight against another source of insecurity, namely the growing concern with natural and environmental costs incurred by the use of fossil fuels.[2] The main threats to energy security are therefore supply disruptions, price hikes making the purchase of a certain energy resource unsustainable for the economy and, the more recent addition to the list of conventional threats, the risks to the environment. Nevertheless, different countries focus on certain aspects of this definition according to their natural resource endowment, their economic structure and their ideological views and perceptions.

In the late 1990s, China's view of supply security was categorized as a 'strategic approach'[3] which favours strong intervention on the domestic markets and political ties with producer countries in order to link the producer more directly to the consumer and to foster a political atmosphere conducive to the national energy companies' activities within that country. This is reinforced by financial aid and investments, which could, theoretically, also be accompanied by political and strategic concessions. The European attitude has been, on the other hand, classified as a 'market approach', which advocates greater transparency, a freer flow of information and collaboration with other consumers in order to ensure that markets function properly and as efficiently as possible.

By taking a closer look at the 'market component' and the 'political components' of energy security problems and the solutions offered by China and the EU, we will address the following questions: Can markets solve all our energy problems as some analysts have been claiming (and as has been the common approach in the EU for the last decade or so)? Is geopolitics necessarily a destabilizing factor? How is China's emergence in this context perceived by the EU and how is it affecting energy security trends?

This chapter is organized as follows: it will first look at some of the different definitions of 'energy security' in the European Union and in China. Then, it will assess how the changes in global energy politics, and especially the emergence of new producer and consumer countries, have shaped these definitions before analysing how the perceived Chinese strategy is influencing European approaches, both on the national level and on the corporate level. Finally, it will turn to look at the common threats to energy security that both Europe and China face and see where approaches to solutions diverge and how they could converge.

Defining energy security

European definitions of energy security

European definitions of energy security are closely related to the economic structure and consumption patterns in these countries. In 2004, total EU-27 energy supply reached 1800 million tons oil equivalent (mtoe), and was a little higher than in China (over 1400 mtoe) but lower than in the US, where supply totalled 2340 mtoe.[4] Supply was largely dominated by oil and gas with nearly 60 per cent (36 per cent and 24 per cent respectively), with nuclear and renewable energy representing an additional 21 per cent. Solid fuels (coal, lignite and peat) made up the rest. This supply structure is not expected to change drastically in the near future, and total consumption is expected to remain stable (as shown in Figure 3.1) due to the relatively efficient use of energy in most EU-27 states.

However, only a small share of this supply comes from indigenous European sources (37 per cent of natural gas and 18 per cent of oil in 2004 were from European production)[5] and in the future Europe will remain dependent on external sources of energy, especially oil and gas (Figure 3.2). While the introduction of nuclear and renewable energy could offset these trends slightly, they are not likely to have a major impact on external dependencies.

These attributes mean shared concerns with regard to market functioning (and managing the risks related to deregulation[6]), import dependency and environmental degradation due to the growing use of solid fuels. Some common trends are shared by the EU-27 and even though it is still premature to speak of a coherent and unified energy policy for the European Union,

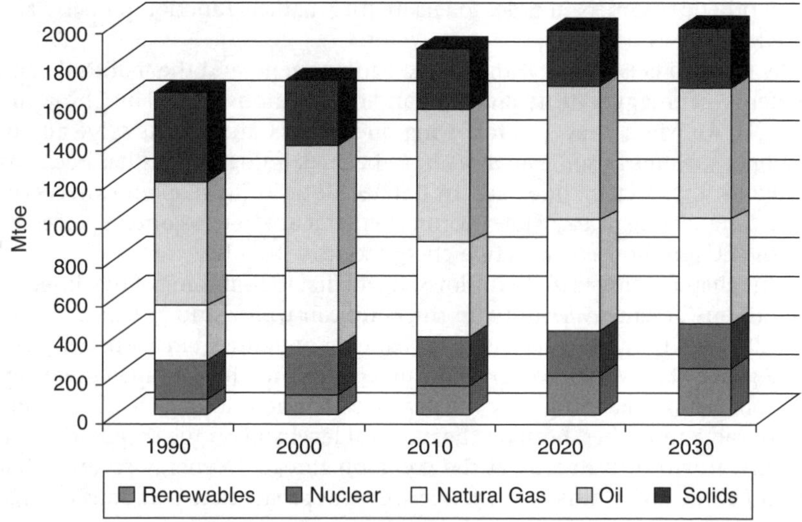

Figure 3.1   EU-27 total primary energy supply[7]

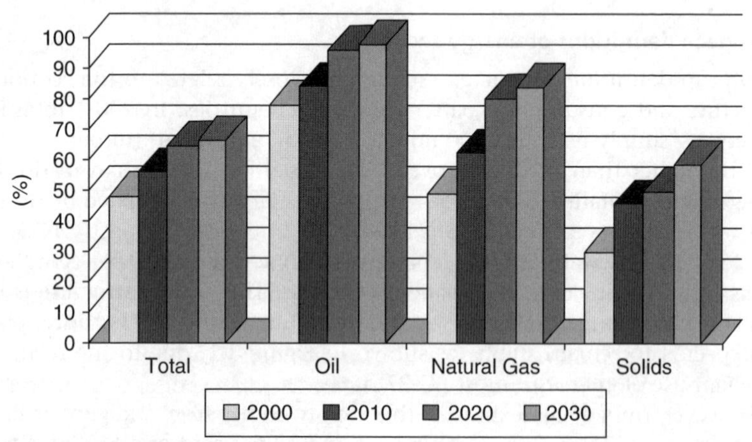

Figure 3.2   EU-27 import dependence up to 2030[8]

one can, nevertheless, speak of common approaches and of a shared belief in multilateral energy markets. This is best seen in the attempts to interconnect electricity grids, in drafting laws and regulations at EU level and in the European emissions trading scheme.[9]

While the dichotomy between the different member states and EU institutions cannot be disregarded,[10] some principles are, however, shared within the EU member states and have provided a basis for policies and priorities thus far. More fundamentally, current international energy markets are the outcome of policies that were adopted in and encouraged by developed countries after the shared experiences of the 1970s oil shocks (increased energy efficiency and shifting to service-oriented economies) and reflect the predominant thinking on energy security in Europe and more widely in OECD countries. These can therefore be summed up by the EU Commission's definition of energy security:

> the ability to ensure that future essential energy needs can be met, both by means of adequate domestic resources worked under economically acceptable conditions or maintained as strategic reserves and by calling upon accessible and stable external sources supplemented where appropriate by strategic stocks.[11]

In the United Kingdom, the recent White Paper on Energy[12] states that its strategy '[t]o deliver energy security and accelerate the transition to a low carbon economy', 'requires urgent and ambitious action at home and abroad'. For this,

> [w]e need to: save energy; develop cleaner energy supplies; secure reliable energy supplies at prices set in competitive markets. *Our strategy continues to be based on the principle that independently regulated, competitive energy markets are the most cost-effective and efficient way of delivering our objectives.* (emphasis added)[13]

In line with this emphasis on economic viability, the Polish government has also defined energy security as 'a condition of the economy which makes it possible to cover the current and prospective demand of consumers for fuels and energy, in a technically and economically justified way'.[14]

Finally, the Legal Act of 13 July 2005 lays down the four fundamentals of France's energy policy: the first objective is 'energy independence and the security of supply', which aims to moderate the effects of energy price fluctuations on the French economy and to ensure sufficient access to reserves in case of energy shortages.[15] The second objective is the 'Protection of the environment', followed by 'Energy at low cost for households and industries', meaning the availability of energy resources at a price and quality that allow the French economy to remain competitive. Finally, the Legal Act speaks of 'Social and territorial cohesion', meaning access to energy at affordable prices for all parts of society.[16] While France still holds the banner of energy independence high and aims to maintain a dominant role for its energy companies in its domestic market,[17] it strives to achieve its energy independence through 'demand side management, diversification of energy sources, developing energy-related research and ensuring means of energy transport and stockpiling adapted to needs'.[18] Out of these three examples, France can be considered as the most 'strategic' in the orientation of its rhetoric on energy security, but the fact remains that the main policy tools for achieving these goals are still market mechanisms. Even though the above definitions are those of three out of 27 EU member states, they are taken from countries with very different levels of external dependence, consumption structures and history of integration within the EU.[19] These definitions reflect the fundamental consensus within Europe that energy security relies essentially on markets. Since the 1970s oil crises and the creation of the International Energy Agency (IEA), followed by two decades of relatively stable oil prices, OECD countries have basically maintained a 'market approach' to energy security.

While on the diplomatic front the EU has great difficulties in 'speaking with one voice', in terms of energy, up until recently the need for a common approach on external energy issues was not felt. Some foreign policy tools do exist, such as the Energy Charter Treaty and the various dialogues with other producer countries, and are examples of existing strategies and attempts to reinforce coordination between consumers and producers.[20] These efforts to improve and enhance dialogues are sometimes weakened by the individual activities of member states but the basis for these activities is the assumption, as stated by EU documents, that the major source of uncertainty surrounds 'the ability and willingness of major oil and gas producers to step up investment in order to meet rising global demand',[21] meaning that policies envisage a supply crunch due to underinvestment, not due to political manoeuvring or the producer or a third state denying physical access to resources. 'Locking up' oil is therefore not an option and the 'concept of physical shortage is misleading and unhelpful. In a reasonably competitive market for a reasonably fungible commodity like oil, "shortage" is manifested by higher prices rather than physical shortages'.[22]

Hence, EU energy policy priorities on the supply side focus on improving investment climates in producer countries in order to encourage investments in energy diversification. A new trend has, however, emerged with the rise of new consumers and producers who seem to be playing by different rules, and the need for a diplomatic and strategic component to energy security is being clearly felt in the EU. China's rise as a global consumer and its perceived energy security strategy have been among the factors contributing to this change.

The evolving Chinese definitions of energy security

The situation in China is radically different in terms of resource endowment, economic structure, consumption patterns and the view of energy as a strategic commodity.

The Chinese energy mix is dominated by coal. While it accounts for almost 70 per cent of the country's primary energy demand, it also gives rise to a wide array of problems such as environmental degradation (of air, land and

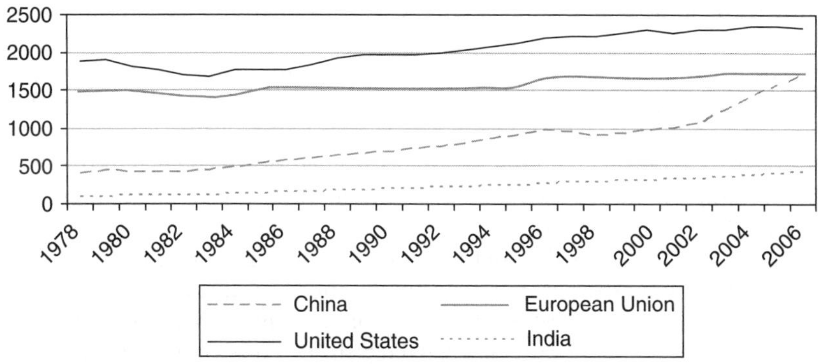

Figure 3.3   Chinese primary energy demand, in mtoe

water); transport bottlenecks from producer to consumer areas; the need to increase economically viable mining; and the very poor safety record of coal mining. With an additional 21 per cent supplied by oil, 3 per cent by gas and 6 per cent by renewable energy, China's dependence on external sources is almost insignificant in relative terms.

Currently, the country is self-sufficient for almost 90 per cent of its primary energy but in the future, with increased urbanization and growing car ownership, this situation is bound to change and Beijing will have to rely increasingly on international sources of oil, gas, and even coal.[23] Furthermore, the country's energy use is highly inefficient and in recent years energy demand has soared at a worrisome pace not only in comparison with developed countries, but also when compared to trends in India (Figure 3.3).

Thus, as a relatively self-sufficient country, the issue of energy security was non-existent until 1993 when China became a net oil importer for the first time. Maoist ideals of self-sufficiency had to be abandoned in favour of reliance on international markets that were deemed unreliable.

China's inexperience with international trading mechanisms was often cited as a source of vulnerability,[24] as was its dependence on foreign countries for strategic commodities such as oil. Along the oil supply chain, which comes mainly from the Middle East and Africa, other sources of concern emerged, in particular the Chinese navy's relative weakness in securing the Sea Lanes of Communication (SLOC) and the dependence on the US Navy this entailed.

In the mid and late 1990s, energy security policies in China were described as a 'shortage-equals-security-threat', reminiscent of 1970s scenarios in developed countries.[25] In the late 1990s, definitions of energy security focused on supply security and the strategic vulnerabilities linked to oil supplies;[26] however, this bias on supply-side measures has evolved with the growing realization that China's energy woes came from mismanagement of the sector and that insecurity is influenced just as much by domestic factors as it is by international factors.[27] Nevertheless, the 'strategic' rhetoric and reasoning still prevail in China,[28] albeit with a certain moderation in the last few years and especially since the arrival of President Hu Jintao and Premier Wen Jiabao to power. Not only did they assume office at the height of strategic thinking on energy security in the aftermath of the 11 September 2001 attacks, but more significantly, their arrival coincided with major energy shortages *within* China that highlighted that the threat to energy security was also of a domestic nature.[29] The energy shortages inside China, coupled with Western observers ostracizing Chinese activities in the Middle East for trying to 'lock up' oil resources, triggered a shift in thinking[30] on the nature of 'energy security' and on the tools to achieve it.

The shift in thinking is also manifest in the guidelines for energy policy within the framework of the 11th Five-Year Plan: the focus is less on supply security and increasingly on demand-side measures aimed at making energy use in China more efficient, less polluting and more sustainable. The government has put forward new ambitious guidelines, promulgated new laws (the Renewable Energy Law in 2005, and extensive work is being done towards the Energy Law) and announced regulations to rationalize and rein in energy use in the country, but the efficiency of these measures has been limited. This stems from a number of factors, including the weak authority of the legal system, the largely administrative incentive measures rather than fiscal and economic incentives, and also the overall weakness of China's energy policy-making, which is segmented and ill-coordinated.

A 'strategic' component of thinking on energy security does, however, still exist and is fuelled by perceptions of American attempts to 'dominate' oil (as was the case, according to some Chinese analysts, in the Iraq War[31]), or protectionist trends that deny China the right to take action on the international market, as seemed to be the lesson from the failed Unocal bid.[32] Moreover, Chinese energy companies are strong and influential stakeholders in the energy decision-making system and have the power to initiate activities overseas, thereby introducing a diplomatic and strategic dimension to the country's energy activities. Being state-owned enterprises they are regarded as tools of the government aiming to secure oil for China. While this is not the case,[33] on some occasions Beijing's diplomats have sought to facilitate market entry for its companies.[34]

In the light of China's new-found dependence on international markets (and its inexperience with crises like the 1970s oil crises that triggered major changes in energy policies in OECD countries) and its oil companies' increased overseas activities, the 'strategic' component of energy security remains a source of concern for Chinese leaders and analysts, which in turn, reflects on European decision-makers and energy observers.

Geopolitics on the rise?

In the last two decades, through the Cold War and intense periods of ideological rivalry, oil and gas still flowed from the Soviet Union to Europe. The global markets seemed to be keeping the allocation of resources and the balance between supply and demand at bay, albeit with the help of the OPEC cartel. When markets kept prices relatively low, and resources seemed sufficient (even though the debate on the 'peak of oil' re-emerges periodically), oil geopolitics were kept on the back burner.

A series of events and actions brought politics back to the forefront of energy security, first and foremost due to the significant hike in world market prices for crude oil that has ensued since 2004 (Figure 3.4). The surge in oil prices can be explained by growing demand from developing countries, and especially China and India, the political situation in the Middle East and uncertainties over the future of Venezuela's energy sector.

Furthermore, non-OPEC countries are squeezing OPEC's market share and reducing its ability (or desire) to balance prices, and psychological factors are entering the physical realm of energy supply and demand: the American-led invasion of Iraq and the assessment by some that its purpose was domination of Iraqi natural resources, the emergence of Russia as a strong producer country that fully uses its energy resources as a political tool, recentralized into the hands of the President, and more frequent terrorist attacks are all pushing prices up even further.

In reaction, as early as 2002 the British House of Lords noted that, 'markets on their own cannot cope with the geopolitical problems that are the main source of security concerns',[36] and after the oil skirmish between Russia and Ukraine in January 2006, a response to 'adverse influence on market

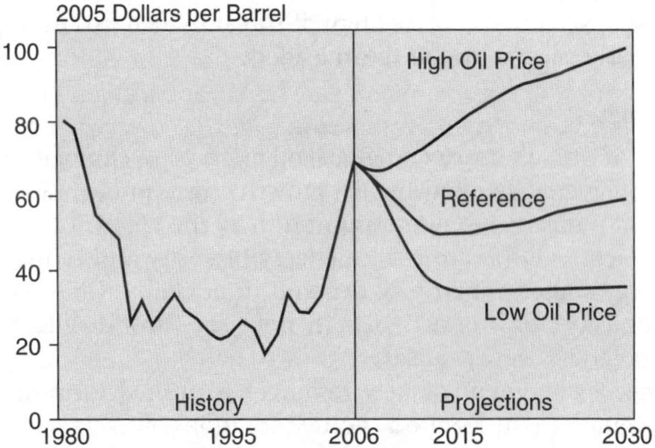

Figure 3.4   World oil prices in three cases, 1980–2030[35]

fundamentals'[37] became urgent. Indeed, the EU paper defined 'Increasing dependence on imports from unstable regions and suppliers' as 'a serious risk'. Coupled with the fact that 'Some major producers and consumers have been using energy as a political lever' and with the emergence 'of external actors not playing by the same market rules nor being subject to the same competitive pressures domestically, the development of a coherent and focused external EU energy policy, drawing on the full range of EU internal and external policies, would enhance the collective external energy security of the Union'.

Nevertheless, the paper goes on to emphasize that 'Well-functioning world markets are the best way of ensuring safe and affordable energy supplies.'[38] Nevertheless, the European Union has introduced a series of initiatives including dialogues with key producers and consumers, the focus being essentially on Russia, Central Asia and key regional bilateral partners in order to improve legal and regulatory frameworks in their energy sectors and to help integrate regional electricity markets. Dialogues with other consumers, (such as China, the US and Brazil) emphasize cooperation on low carbon energy technologies, increasing energy efficiency and promoting the use of renewable energy.[39]

Two main contradictory trends have therefore emerged, highlighting a new readjustment phase between the perceived importance of markets and geopolitics. On the one hand, market signals have set in motion a new round of investments. More oil companies are now seeking to develop new resources in fields that were once deemed unprofitable, in the Central Asian republics or in China's Western provinces. The Canadian tar sands are now no longer considered a pipe dream and the hunt for new sources of energy is back on. But on the other hand, access to oil and gas is often intrinsically linked to political stability in the producer country and to diplomatic manoeuvres for market access. All the major global actors seem to be beefing up their diplomatic activities to address this new situation, be it an opportunity, as is the case for new investments, or a potential threat, which, for example, Russia may potentially become to European leaders.

The 'China factor'

While some of China's impact on global oil prices is psychologically induced, the fast rise in energy demand and the growth targets put forward by the Chinese leadership mean that oil consumption in the country is not expected to subside. Despite efforts to reduce energy intensity and to introduce new cleaner energy sources, the rising demand from China will strain resources and refining capacities, and be felt in price rises worldwide. But China's impact is rooted in deeper causes.

While the development of new resources is pushed forward by market prices and signals, the attribution of oil exploration contracts is rarely a purely economic affair. Oil diplomacy was not invented by China even though Beijing is attracting all the attention in this regard.[40] But most multinationals still retain strong national colours, and often have a close relationship with diplomats if they are overseas. Furthermore, most producer countries have nationalized their energy companies and sectors, and investments in exploration and production are rarely a matter between two oil companies. So while Chinese activities in this regard are not all that different from Western practices (or at least from their practices from the 1950s to the 1970s), the Chinese National Oil Companies (NOCs) stand out due to the fact that they are not accountable to investors, other than the state which is the majority stakeholder, and do not operate according to bottom-line imperatives as their tendency to overbid for their overseas projects seems to indicate.

Many reasons can be put forward for this: first, their relative inexperience in overseas acquisitions leads them to badly estimate their costs; second, the lack of hard budget constraints encourages them to develop their expertise and technology despite its uneconomic nature; third, the belief that oil fields are relatively scarce and those that open up, be they in politically problematic countries or in difficult geological areas, should be grabbed in order to enhance the NOCs' asset base. Finally, the fact that overseas acquisitions were put forward as a priority by the government in its 'going out' policy, and the financial and administrative incentives to do so were given, has naturally led the NOCs to seize this opportunity to develop themselves as multinationals.[41]

The issue of supply security has been the focus of policies in the last decade or so because it is the newest challenge to the Chinese energy sector and therefore deemed to be the most problematic. Chinese rhetoric has put forward 'unreliable markets' as the reason for increased bilateral ties with producer countries, entailing an image of Beijing's diplomats and leaders securing market access for their companies through diplomatic ties and of a foreign policy that will support the country's energy needs even if it means turning its back on the wider international community.[42]

Nevertheless, there are increasing voices in China calling for greater oil interdependence, and for deeper Chinese integration in the markets.[43] It would seem therefore that a shift in Chinese thinking on energy security will bring it closer to European thinking on the need to reinforce market mechanisms and encourage more transparency and a better flow of information.

But with opaque practices, Chinese activities are giving rise to mounting speculation on both intent and means. On the one hand, China is being accused of paying for its Iranian oil with consumer goods (and even arms),[44] but on the other hand, there is an 'Asian premium' on Middle Eastern oil shipped to China, making it unlikely that a producer would be willing to secure the Chinese markets with important price concessions.

The view from below: competition in business practices

From an economic point of view, China's activities in exploration and production are bringing new resources to the markets and thereby alleviating the pressure on them, so while they may be in competition with European (and American) companies, they have done nothing more than beat them to it. Which brings us to the question of: how do we decide which means are 'fair' or 'justified' in order to win a bid?

When looking at China's overseas acquisitions and exploration, the details are often blurred. How much of China's production overseas is physically shipped to China and how much of it is traded internationally? Chinese analysts and industry experts claim that most of the resources developed abroad are sold on the international markets and only a small share of around 10 per cent is shipped back to China's shores.[45] This is also due to the fact that assets sold internationally make higher profits than resources sold in China at state-controlled prices. But in their overseas ventures, Chinese companies seem to be providing producer countries with an alternative to business practices pursued until now. Questions on financing methods, risk assessment and managerial choices remain opaque, posing a problem on the business level. European firms now have to deal with different investment rules and a new business configuration. Chinese companies are offering 'package deals' including not only resource development but also infrastructure work and affiliated services at relatively low cost.[46] Western industrial actors who operate according to established business practices find it difficult to compete, not because of technical or technological capacities or even because of new quality standards, but because the rules of the investment game seem to be changing. While many Chinese analysts argue that Chinese business practices are coming closer in line with Western practices, including risk assessment and insurance policies for activities in politically unstable countries, Western industrial actors are perplexed about financing, legal and managerial practices in Chinese NOCs.[47]

The view from above: shifting policies

China's activities in Africa are, on a different level, challenging the 'comprehensive Africa-Europe Energy Partnership' as defined by the EU Commission in its Green Paper:

> The importance of Africa as an energy supplier has increased greatly in recent years, but its potential is still greater. The dialogue should include security of supply, technology transfer in renewable energy, sustainable exploitation of resources, transparency of energy markets and respect for good governance.[48]

But China is competing for projects and providing aid with no strings attached, thereby weakening the EU's stance. Valid arguments are made saying that despite this incompatibility of views, China is helping to develop African resources and thus helping to pull African states out of poverty, but the fact remains that China is also gradually contributing to a change in the rules of the game as the EU has perceived them so far.[49]

So while China becomes gradually more familiar with international trading mechanisms and the current predominant business practices, European businesses are increasingly wary that they might be losing out to an actor who manages to shore up state support, both financial and diplomatic, while governments fear that the new global geopolitical context requires more than just markets. The EU has therefore integrated the need for a 'coherent external energy policy' that includes 'energy partnerships with producer, transit countries and other international actors'[50] in its energy policy. However, China's newly released 'White Paper on Energy Conditions and Policies'[51] vows that its worldwide search for oil and gas will be carried out in a spirit of fair play and international cooperation so as not to disrupt sensitive international markets and reiterates that 'China did not, does not and will not pose any threat to the world's energy security.'[52]

It would therefore seem that intense international scrutiny and domestic pressures have incited China to change its thinking and rhetoric on supply security. The Chinese report places relatively little emphasis on international cooperation and the supply security dimension is the last of seven chapters in this new White Paper that deals essentially with energy conservation, efficiency and greenhouse gas emissions reduction. It seems therefore that while European businesses and governments are gearing up for a new strategic rival, Chinese companies and leaders are trying to integrate global markets through enhancing global practices and greater transparency, albeit at their own pace.

Nevertheless, greater efforts to moderate fears with regard to perceived energy security policies are still needed. Even though many concerns are common to China and the EU, the choice of responses is different and these divergences will have to be addressed.

Common threats, different approaches

In Europe and Asia, as shown above, consumption habits, development levels and past experiences have led to different policy choices and perceptions of energy supply. European markets are more mature and better regulated and reliance on these mechanisms is a result of several decades of functioning and perfecting. The emphasis in terms of supply security is therefore on market efficiency and affordable supply prices on the consumer side and, whenever and however possible, on encouraging stability in producer countries. The case in China is radically different as is the time span in which the country has had to deal with the various aspects of its economic transition. Furthermore, China did not experience the oil shocks or any other strong external crises like Europe did.[53] It is, arguably, the domestic shortages that have triggered a comparable response in the sense that the urgency of new consumption patterns and demand-side measures in China are clearly felt, but this is work in progress that began with the new leadership and requires more time in order to have visible effects. But along with demand-side measures, activities meant to secure the 'supply side' are also common. Both China and the EU have raised the need to diversify foreign energy sources and are fully aware of the effects of political turmoil in producer countries.

Common threats to supply security

The threats to supply security are, as mentioned above, first and foremost those of physical disruptions and these are, essentially, the following. First, there is the possibility of an embargo by a producer country that decides willingly to stop exports to a targeted country or countries. But ever since the use of the oil weapon by Arab countries in 1973, the global oil market and risk-minimizing mechanisms have been developed in such a way as to moderate the effects of such an event if it reoccurred: this is due to the growth in new producers that have increased the available resources, and to the fact that producers are also reliant on their consumer markets in order to keep their economies running. It is estimated that if Saudi Arabia voluntarily stops exporting oil its foreign exchange reserves would allow for around three months of imports.[54] Moreover, diversification of energy resources means that there is always somewhere to buy oil and gas; and finally, the emergence of oil trading markets and hedging mechanisms means that in case of physical disruptions the prices go up for everyone, and that physical disruptions are hard to sustain for a long time due to the very active spot markets and the emergency preparedness mechanisms designed for such events. Voluntary disruptions are therefore a double-edged sword. But physical disruption of supply can be an option if the physical movement of oil and gas can be cut off. The most salient example of this is the Russian cut-off of Georgian resources in the winter of 2005 and the beginning of the winter in 2006. In that sense, gas imports have become more vulnerable to physical disruptions than oil transit and China's desire to import directly from producer countries puts it in a position of potential vulnerability.

When comparing China's vulnerability to that of the EU, in terms of voluntary physical cut-offs, European states have more to lose: 287 mt out of Europe's 655 mt of oil in 2005 came from the former Soviet Union[55] and perhaps more worrying is the fact that 36.5 bcm of gas was exported in 2005 from Russia to Germany by pipeline (out of 85.9 bcm consumed in Germany in 2005). In the light of the strong recentralization trend of control over the energy sector in Russia[56] it would seem that maintaining stable political relations with Russia should become a political priority. While the Russian question is beyond the scope of this chapter, Moscow's use of energy as a political tool has alarmed decision-makers in the West, even if Moscow remains highly dependent on Europe as an outlet for its gas and cannot replace this consumer market quickly with an Asian alternative. It is generally assumed, though, that the possibility of a voluntary embargo initiated by producer countries (other than Russia targeting its close neighbours in its 'near abroad'), has declined greatly since the 1970s.[57] Most producers have as much to lose as consumers do because oil and gas, for them too, is often not only a resource, but also a source of revenue and political legitimacy. Moreover, the political and diplomatic price for initiating a voluntary disruption is high. Nevertheless, it may not be such a far-fetched scenario, as Moscow has shown.

Secondly, disruptions to oil supply can be of an involuntary nature due to terrorist attacks or natural disasters affecting infrastructures. These events also affect all consumers alike as the immediate result is price hikes for all parties concerned. The damage to the affected infrastructure could, arguably, have greater effects on the country in which it is based, be it oil wells in producer countries, pipelines in transit states or on the seas, or ports in consumer countries.

Third on the list of causes of disruption is the possibility of manipulation by a third party: the United States could for example try to influence oil-producing states to stop supplies to a third country, such as China. While some Chinese strategists have raised the American monopoly over markets as a main cause of concern for China's energy security, it seems highly unlikely that one nation could coerce another into cutting off supplies. Even if it did succeed, as mentioned above, an alternative source of supply can quite readily be found. Furthermore, a country often buys its oil indiscriminately: the US, for example, imports directly or indirectly from Iran and Libya, despite their 'pariah state' status and most of the oil exports from Venezuela, despite Chavez's combative rhetoric, still end up in the US.[58]

Is China more in danger of being targeted by the US rather than the EU as vulnerable to attempts such as the Russian one? While these nightmare scenarios are taken into account as worst-case scenarios, recent history has shown that they are no more than scenarios and, as argued above, their effect is mitigated and felt on prices, not on actual supplies.

In these first cases, the link between markets and geopolitics is unidirectional: political actions influence the markets. In both instances, however, global market mechanisms have found a way to moderate the effects of these occurrences, albeit not to fully prevent them. Despite the argument that markets can allocate resources and that politics need not play a part in oil and gas distribution, it can still become a highly political question. In an ideal world the markets could run the show, as they did to a certain extent in the last two decades, but the above-mentioned hypotheses can occur and cannot be disregarded, especially in view of recent trends in the global energy system.

Physical disruption could also emanate from events on supply routes. Be they voluntary or accidental, US-initiated blockades of Chinese resources or piracy on the Malacca Straits are not unimaginable events. While the likelihood of the former is highly debatable, the fact remains that these are non-market events that could have repercussions on market prices. Securing

Sea Lines of Communication (SLOCs) or the political stability of transit states such as the Central Asian independent republics is therefore an increasingly important task. These, however, affect both China and the EU equally. While the Malacca Straits are a question for Asia and the Pacific, securing transit states in Central Asia is a common concern. The current amounts of oil and gas shipped from Central Asia to both China and the EU are relatively limited but their importance is as much for their present supplies as their future potential, both as new sources of production and as transit states providing solutions to the dependency on one (or few) transport route(s). Securing the transit states should therefore be an issue of common concern; however, the question that comes to mind is whether China and the EU can find common solutions. The means required to achieve political (and military) stability in Central Asia may be a major bone of contention between China and the EU, but it does not mean that the question should not be addressed jointly.

Diverging solutions to common threats

As shown above, many of the threats of physical disruption will eventually affect all consumers equally and are, therefore, common causes for concern. But after having identified the causes of insecurity, it is still important to look at the solutions.

When dealing with unstable producer countries, the responses are not always the same. What constitutes the main cause of 'instability': political regime or economic development? The African example comes to mind again. When looking at the conditions to 'stabilize' African countries, Chinese scholars will often argue that democracy can only come after poverty alleviation, whereas the European attitude focuses on good governance as the basis for aid to African countries. Acknowledging this difference is the first step; addressing it and finding a level playing field is the next step that requires enhanced dialogue between China, the EU and African leaders.

China's stance on 'pariah states' is another case in point. Whilst Beijing has substantially moderated its position on Iran,[59] it still maintains that sanctions, not to mention military action, will not help solve the Iranian nuclear issue. More bemusing to international observers is the fact that state-owned oil giant Sinopec signed a deal to develop Iran's Yadavaran oil and gas field valued by Iran's oil minister at US$2 billion on 9 December 2007.[60] Even though investments in Iran's energy sector are not banned under the terms of UN sanctions, they are seen as a potentially useful point of leverage in negotiations with the country. The timing of the announcement of the deal, just a week after US intelligence published a report concluding that Iran stopped nuclear weapons development in 2003, possibly reduces risks for Sinopec in moving ahead on Yadavaran. The astute choice of timing does not, however, change the fact that practices in both diplomacy and business are different in China and the EU and must be addressed jointly in order to reduce perception gaps.

Conclusions

Chinese and European outlooks on energy supply security stem from very different economic systems, ideological perceptions, history and experiences. While they are gradually converging, the arrival of new actors on the global energy scene has warranted readjustments on all sides that indicate a bumpy road ahead.

But a few fundamental realizations should guide both Europe and China in their thinking: to different extents, both have limited potential for energy self-sufficiency and both will continue to depend on foreign supplies in order to sustain (and improve in China's case) standards of living within their borders. Second, despite liberalization efforts in the energy sectors, governments are never truly absent, be it in securing investment climates overseas or in hands-on regulation to varying degrees. European governments and various EU institutions have initiated dialogues with producing regions and, while these political initiatives may have enhanced Europe's sense of security, part of the challenge is also reaching an agreement on the rules of the investment game as Chinese companies are clearly bringing new practices and challenges that need to be addressed. Third, diversification of sources has certainly enhanced energy security but given the pivotal role of the Middle East as an energy supplier, the region's stability is of common interest, and must be achieved jointly. Fourth, oil and, to a lesser extent, natural gas markets are global and well integrated. The source of a barrel matters less than its actual availability on the market and no country can secure itself alone from physical disruptions or 'lock up' oil. More predictability on transparent oil markets should be a common goal for producers and consumers in order to enhance global economic growth and political stability.

China and the EU clearly have different perceptions of the threats to energy security and the way to deal with the related insecurities. China is making greater efforts to become more transparent in its actions and to calm fears about its means and intentions, of which the publication of its Energy White Paper is a case in point. However, the renewed attention to energy geopolitics has led the EU to rethink its energy security policy and to give energy diplomacy a more important role.[61]

On some issues, the EU and China's interests are clearly convergent: the need to maintain stable transit states is one example (even though the idea as to what constitutes a stable country, that is, which kind of political regime for example, may not be the same); the need for a stable Middle East; common concerns over environmental threats; improving market efficiency through greater transparency and freer flow of information as well as on technical aspects related to energy efficiency. Dialogue between the two partners could also be extremely useful for reducing the perception gaps that feed into the need for greater political assurances when the markets seem to falter. More joint projects between Western and Chinese multinationals in China and abroad could bring Chinese companies the know-how and technologies China requires and familiarize it with Western practices. This would also allow greater transparency that could moderate Western apprehensions and open the door for more joint investments within China, thereby advancing towards a more level playing field. The level playing field should, however, go both ways: China's failed attempts to acquire Unocal and Slavneft did not reassure Beijing that the West will greet its investments warmly. Conversely, a study of Western experience has shown that industrialized countries maintained strong control over their energy sectors when they were in transitional phases; China should therefore not be expected to open its markets immediately but it has undertaken obligations with its accession to the WTO that may be useful to proceed with jointly. The lack of experience in the Chinese regulatory authorities could be complemented by foreign assistance and expertise and, while this is already the case with some foreign experts advising the Chinese government on economic and regulatory incentives, it is lacking on an institutional level. Efforts by the IEA to work with the Chinese authorities should be enhanced and widened.

While on the more military and strategic aspects many of China's concerns emanate from the perceived American threat, there is still room for coordination with the EU as well. This may also be easier because there is relatively little room for competition between the two to turn into outright conflict.

Be it in the economics or the politics of energy, the need for real and effective dialogue is flagrant, especially at this crucial time when global energy systems seem to be in flux.

Notes

1. P. Andrews-Speed, J. X. Liao and R. Dannreuther, *The Strategic Implications of China's Energy Needs*, Adelphi Paper No. 346 (Oxford: Oxford University Press, 2002).
2. European Commission, Communication from the European Commission, *An Energy Policy for Europe*, COM (2007) 1 final, 2007, http://eur-lex.europa.eu/ LexUriServ/site/en/com/2007/com2007_0001en01.pdf, accessed 14 December 2007.
3. For a more detailed explanation and comparison of the different approaches and measures to energy security, see Andrews-Speed et al., *The Strategic Implications of China's Energy Needs*; Clingendael, *Study on Energy Supply and Geopolitics*, report prepared by the Clingendael International Energy Program, 2004, http://www.clingendael.nl/ciep/publications/studies, accessed 20 December 2007.
4. Figures for China and the US are cited from BP, *BP Statistical Review 2007*. European figures are from European Commission, *Green Paper: a European Strategy for Sustainable, Competitive and Secure Energy*, COM (2006) 105 final, 2006, http:// ec.europa.eu/energy/green-paper-energy/doc/2006_03_08_gp_document_en.pdf, accessed 17 January 2008. There is little discrepancy, however, between the figures for Europe cited in the BP *Statistical Review* and in the EU Commission paper.

5. European Commission, Commission Staff Working Document, *EU Energy Policy Data* SEC (2007) 12, http://ec.europa.eu/energy/energy_policy/doc/02_eu_energy_policy_data_en.pdf, accessed 15 January 2007.

6. D. Buchan, 'The Threat Within: Deregulation and Energy Security', *Survival*, Vol. 44, No. 3, 2002, pp. 105–16.

7. According to a baseline scenario, from European Commission, *Green Paper*, 2006.

8. European Commission, *EU Energy Policy Data* SEC (2007).

9. P. Andrews-Speed, 'A European Approach to Energy Security', in F. Godement, F. Nicolas and T. Yakushiji (eds), *Asia and Europe: Cooperating for Energy Security*, Council for Asia-Europe Cooperation-Task Force Report (Paris, 2004), pp. 85–110.

10. As pipeline projects in Europe have shown, with the Nabucco pipeline failing to emerge and the Blue-Stream pipeline creating increasing controversy.

11. European Commission, *Green Paper*, 2006.

12. Department of Trade and Industry, *Meeting the Energy Challenge: a White Paper on Energy*, CM 7124, 2007.

13. Ibid.

14. Ministry of Economy and Labour, *Energy Policy of Poland Until 2025*, 2005, http://www.mg.gov.pl/NR/rdonlyres/20205452-144A-4325-8935-B4C95FB29DBD/0/energetyka_do_2025_ang.doc, accessed 18 January 2007.

15. See also S. Meritet, 'French Perspectives in the Emerging European Union Energy Policy', *Energy Policy*, No. 35, 2007, pp. 4767–71.

16. The French Energy Bill: *LOI n° 2005-781 du 13 juillet 2005 de programme fixant les orientations de la politique énergétique*, JORF, No. 163, 14 July 2005, p. 11570, text no. 2, http://www.legifrance.gouv.fr/affichTexte.do?cidTexte=JORFTEXT000000-813253&dateTexte=, accessed 18 January 2007.

17. Ibid.

18. Ibid.

19. For a German approach, see Umbach's chapter in this volume.

20. Andrews-Speed, 'A European Approach to Energy Security'.

21. IEA, *World Energy Outlook 2006* (Paris: OECD/IEA, 2006).

22. J. Dunkerely, 'Lessons From the Past Thirty Years', *Energy Policy*, No. 24, 2006, pp. 503–7.

23. Despite its huge reserves of coal, China became a net importer in 2007, a trend that is likely to continue over the coming years. See B. Ricketts, 'Coal in China from a Global Perspective', in M. Meidan (ed.), *Shaping China's Energy Security: the Inside Perspective* (Paris: Asia Centre, 2008).

24. Interview with CASS analyst, Beijing, December 2006.

25. C. Constantin, *China's Conception of Energy Security: Sources and International Impacts*, Working Paper No. 43, Centre of International Relations (Vancouver: University of British Columbia, 2005).

26. See Andrews-Speed et al.,*The Strategic Implications of China's Energy Needs*.

27. B. Kong, *An Anatomy of China's Energy Insecurity and Its Strategies*, Pacific Northwest Center for Global Security, PNNL-15529, 2005; Meidan, *Shaping China's Energy Security*.

28. W. Zhang, 'Sea Power and China's Strategic Choices', *China Security*, No. 3, 2006.

29. On 'cyclical insecurity' see Kong, *An Anatomy of China's Energy Insecurity and Its Strategies*.

30. See M. Meidan, P. Andrews-Speed and X. Ma, 'Shaping China's Energy Security: Actors and Policies', in Meidan (ed.), *Shaping China's Energy Security*.

31. Further discussion on this matter can be found in L. Wu and X. Liu, 'China or the United States: Which Threatens Energy Security?', *OPEC Review*, Vol. 31, No. 3, 2007.
32. See Jakobson's chapter in this book.
33. The relationship between the Chinese oil companies and the government is a complex and somewhat opaque issue. An interesting form of interdependence exists between them which limits their autonomy but does still give them considerable power in the system. For more on this, see X. Ma and P. Andrews-Speed, 'The Overseas Activities of China's National Oil Companies: Rationale and Outlook', *Minerals and Energy*, Vol. 21, No. 1, 2006, pp. 17–30; M. Meidan, 'China's African Policy: Business Now, Politics Later', *Asian Perspectives*, Vol. 30, No. 4, 2006, pp. 69–93.
34. This is of course not unique to China but the way this is perceived and its repercussions are discussed below.
35. Energy Information Administration (EIA), *International Energy Outlook 2007*, http://www.eia.doe.gov/oiaf/ieo/oil.html, accessed 10 December 2007.
36. Cited in O. Geden, C. Marcelis and A. Maurer, *Perspectives for the European Union's External Energy Policy: Discourse, Ideas and Interests in Germany, the UK, Poland and France*, Working Paper FG1 2006/17 (Berlin: SWP, 2006).
37. European Commission, *An External Policy to Serve Europe's Energy Interests*, Paper from Commission/SG/HR for the European Council S160/06, 2006.
38. Ibid.
39. Europa, *Developing External Energy Policy for the EU*, MEMO/07/533, 2007, http://www.europa.eu/rapid/pressReleasesAction.do?reference=MEMO/07/533&format=HTML&aged=0&language=EN&guiLanguage=en, accessed 17 January 2008.
40. For a salient example of this, see President Sarkozy's recent visit to Beijing (November 2007) in which he signed deals for some of France's biggest energy companies.
41. See Ma and Andrews-Speed, 'The Overseas Activities of China's National Oil Companies'.
42. For a more refined analysis on China's energy diplomacy see E. Downs, *The Energy Security Series: China*, Brookings Foreign Policy Studies (Washington: Brookings Institution, 2006); M. Meidan, 'La Chine à la conquête des marchés énergétiques monidaux', *Hérodote*, No. 125, 2007.
43. H. Zhao, 'Cooperation and Dialogue on Energy Security: Strategic Choices for an Era of Energy Interdependence', *Xiandai Guoji Guanxi*, 5, 2006, pp. 38–44; F. Chen, 'New Trends in International Energy Security', *Xiandai Guoji Guanxi*, 6, 2006, pp. 41–6; D. Zha, 'Energy Interdependence', *China Security*, No. 3, 2006.
44. See M. Meidan, *Chine – Iran: des relations pragmatiques*, Asia Centre Working Paper, 2006, http://www.centreasia.org.
45. Interviews in Beijing with industry analysts, January 2007.
46. A. Goldstein, N. Pinaud, H. Reisen and X. Chen, *The Rise of China and India: What's in it for Africa?* (Paris: OECD, 2006).
47. Interviews in Beijing, December 2007.
48. European Commission, *Green Paper*, 2006.
49. It must not be overlooked that this is also made possible by 'political' producers such as Russia, the arrival of India and the perceived activities of the US and some European countries with regard to energy geopolitics.
50. European Commission, *Green Paper*, 2006.

51. Xinhua, 'Full Text: China's Energy Conditions and Policies', released on 26 December 2007, http://news.xinhuanet.com/english/2007-12/26/content_7315441_7.htm, accessed 18 January 2008.
52. Ibid.
53. For the issue of external crisis as a catalyst for domestic policy change, see T. Sano, 'Japan's Energy Policy: From Anti-Pollution to Energy Saving and Efficiency for Environmental Conservation', in Meidan (ed.), *Shaping China's Energy Security*.
54. Y. Mao, 'Markets vs. Politics', *China Security*, No. 3, 2006.
55. BP, *BP Statistical Review 2006*.
56. L. Buszynski, 'Oil and Territory in Putin's Relations with China and Japan', *Pacific Review*, Vol. 19, No. 3, 2006, pp. 287–303.
57. For China's case, see Zha, 'Energy Interdependence'.
58. E. Haght and Y. Chen, 'The Oil Weapon: Myth of China's Vulnerability', *China Security*, No. 3, 2006.
59. For an analysis on China's attitude towards 'pariah states', see S. Kleine-Ahlbrandt and A. Small, 'China's New Dictatorship Diplomacy', *Foreign Affairs*, Vol. 87, No. 1, 2008, pp. 38–56.
60. 'Sinopec to develop oil field in Iran', *International Herald Tribune*, 10 December 2007.
61. The Green Papers are available at the European Commission's website: http://ec.europa.eu/energy/green-paper-energy/index_en.htm.

4
The Southeast–Southwest European Energy Corridor

Antonio Marquina

Introduction

The European Union and NATO have paid special attention to energy security since 2005. When, from December 2005 to January 2006, Russia greatly increased gas prices to Ukraine, the European governments realized the great importance of oil and gas producers in influencing the policies of consumer states. After this incident, a similar event took place between Russia and Belarus. Later on, the creation of a gas cartel was proposed, including as possible participants Russia, Algeria, Iran and Qatar.

In this situation there were several urgent questions for Europe, related to establishing a single energy market, security of supplies, agreements between companies and member states, energy issues related to national security policy, obligations and constraints of policies respectful towards the environment and the implication for the use of nuclear energy.

The European Commission published the Green Paper, *A European Strategy for Sustainable, Competitive and Secure Energy* on 8 March 2006. The Green Paper identified six key areas where action was considered necessary in order to address the challenges. Among them, diversification of the energy mix on the supply side and a coherent external energy policy were mentioned. The goals and instruments of the external energy policy were the following:

- A clear policy on securing and diversifying energy supplies.
- Energy partnerships with producers, transit countries and other international actors.
- Reacting effectively to external crisis situations.
- Integrating energy into other policies with an external dimension.
- Energy to promote development.

The conclusion of the paper was that the EU lacked a common policy on energy and could not meet key objectives and, in particular, secure supplies.

Several months later a paper from the EU Commission's Secretary General and the High Representative for External Relations entitled 'An External Policy to Serve Europe's Energy Interests' presented the external energy risks to the European Union and how the EU's external relations, including the Common Foreign and Security Policy (CFSP), could be used to pursue the common objective of securing reliable flows of affordable and environmentally sustainable energy. The paper questioned the traditional EU market approaches on energy security and one of its guiding principles that 'well-functioning world markets are the best way of ensuring safe and affordable energy supplies'. The risks mentioned were the following:

- Increasing dependence on imports from unstable regions and suppliers.
- Some major producers and consumers using energy as a political lever.
- The effects on the EU internal market of external actors not playing by the same market rules because of not being subject to the same competitive pressures domestically.

At the same time, the right of the EU's member states to pursue their own external relations for ensuring security of energy supplies and to choose their internal energy mix was maintained.

Diversification of energy resources and geographical origin was also considered a building block of energy security. A number of infrastructure projects already decided or in an advanced stage of planning could create new energy corridors and a new import capacity for the EU. The last part of the document explained the possible initiatives that could be developed at bilateral level, regional level and multilateral level.

On 10 January 2007, the Commission published a new report, *An Energy Policy for Europe*. In this document the European Union maintained the traditional approach on energy markets and governance, and proposed the strategic objective of acting on greenhouse gas emissions, transforming the European Union into a high energy efficient and low CO_2 energy economy. This should be the guiding point for all energy policy decisions.

Finally, a European Council Action Plan (2007–9) was adopted that comprised priority actions on internal markets for gas and electricity, security of supply, international energy policy, energy efficiency and renewable energies and energy technologies. In the international energy policy one of the essential elements to be developed was the intensification of the EU's relations with Central Asia, and the Caspian and the Black Sea regions, with a view to further diversifying sources and routes.

Trans-European energy networks and energy corridors (TEN-E)

At the end of the 1980s the idea emerged of linking national energy networks and regions with a modern infrastructure. It made sense in the context of a single market. The first list of priority projects was adopted in December 1994 in the Essen European Council. It comprised ten projects, five in the electricity sector and five in the gas sector. In accordance with Article 129c of the Maastricht Treaty, the European Union established in 1996 a series of guidelines on Trans-European energy networks covering objectives, priorities and lines of action including the identification of projects of common interest. The guidelines focus on the main transportation networks for electricity and natural gas and the objectives were the effective operation of the internal market, the strengthening of economic and social cohesion and reinforcing the security of energy supply. At that time, one of the missing links was to connect Europe with Central Asia by a southern route.[1] The list of projects was revised in 1997 and 1999.

A new revision of the guidelines took place in July 2003, taking into account the enlargement of the European Union and its implications for the priorities established. The priority axes decided in 2003 were twelve in number, seven for electricity networks and five for natural gas networks. Again, one of the priority projects already agreed for natural gas networks was NG 3, Caspian Sea countries-Middle East-European Union.[2] The Commission considered that the three main suppliers of gas to Europe – Russia, Norway and Algeria – would continue to be the main suppliers by 2020. The assessment of future needs was very conservative regarding the need for diversification of suppliers. It mentioned new gas supply sources to be developed in the Middle East and in the Caspian Sea area, stimulated by the large potential market in Turkey. However, the importance of Turkey as a transit route was emphasized.[3] The security of supply was also underlined but in the context of 'a strong need for better organisation and co-ordinated use of oil and gas stocks and further, the need for a debate on the future of nuclear energy'.[4]

On 24 July 2006, several months after Moscow applied pressure on Ukraine, new TEN-E revised guidelines were again adopted by the Council. Concerning natural gas the aim was securing and diversifying additional gas import capacity from sources in Russia, the Caspian basin region, Northern Africa and the Middle East. The increase in import capacity by 2013 was established at 50 billion cubic metres per year, in addition to an import capacity of liquefied natural gas of 50 billion cubic metres per year. The projects included ten gas pipelines, two of them linking Turkey with other European countries: Turkey-Greece-Italy and Turkey-Austria.[5]

In this context, energy corridors between the European Union and its neighbouring countries were fundamental. The EU is expected to increase its dependency on gas supplies from neighbouring countries from 40 per cent to more than 70 per cent.[6] Thus Nordic, eastern and southern corridors will play an increasing role in the energy supply of Europe.

Three elements are needed for the integration of the European Union energy markets and neighbouring countries:

- Compatible interconnections.
- Compatible market framework.
- Compatible environmental policies.[7]

The corridors contemplated in the ENCOURAGED project launched by the Directorate-General for Energy and Transport were:

- Gas corridors.
- Electricity corridors.
- Hydrogen corridors (expected from 2015).

The main gas projects to the EU identified as optimal economic gas corridors were:

- North Stream (Russia to Germany – foreseen start up 2010).
- Medgaz (Algeria to Spain – foreseen start up 2008).
- Galsi (Algeria to Italy – foreseen start up 2009).
- Nabucco (Caspian and Middle East-Turkey to Austria – foreseen start up 2010).
- ITG-IGI (Caspian/Greece-Italy – foreseen start up 2011).
- Langeled (Norway-UK – foreseen start up 2006).

The realization of these gas pipeline projects could provide an additional supply capacity to the EU of 98.5–139 billion cubic metres of natural gas. These energy resources are fundamental to the EU for several reasons that are interlinked: scarcity, lack of confidence in Russia and the necessity for diversification.

In the East–West corridor Turkey is a key player. The Nabucco project, with a capacity of 25–30 billion cubic metres per year, was considered a sustainable project but difficult to complete because of the complexity of transit issues and difficulties in coordinating investments, not only in production but also in transit infrastructure.[8] According to the official information, as an outcome of the feasibility study it was decided to construct the pipeline in two major stages – first to construct the complete new route from the Turkish border to Baumgarten, and second to construct further compressor stations to increase capacity. At the same time, it was decided that construction step one would be technically split into two separate back-to-back construction phases.

The first construction phase, starting in 2009, would cover the planned route between Ankara and Baumgarten, approximately 2000 km of pipeline. After this phase, the existing pipeline facilities between Turkey and Georgia and Turkey and Iran would be used for an interim period of two years, thus linking the new pipeline to the Turkish border. By 2012, the initial capacity would be 8 billion cubic metres per year. The second construction phase would run from 2012 until the end of 2013 and would consist of the construction of the remaining section from the Turkish border to Georgia and later to Iran.

A subsequent construction step would consist of installation of further compression stations at key points of the pipeline in order to increase the capacity to 31 billion cubic metres per year.[9] To do that a fluid relationship with the suppliers in the Caspian area and Central Asia was needed. The problem is that EU policies regarding the Caspian Sea and Central Asia have been inconsistent.

EU policies regarding Central Asia

EU policies towards Central Asia after the Cold War have been quite weak, even taking into account that the EU was the main donor in the region. The problems that the EU had to manage were centred on achieving political reforms and the transition to market economies. The Commission knew very little about this region and expected that the institutional development of the new republics of Central Asia could be accomplished in a very short period. First they tried to support the transition using the Tacis programme and later with the negotiation of partnership and cooperation agreements with every republic.

But, as happened in the Caucasus, the Russian decision to unilaterally cut the traditional economic relationships with its former rouble zone and the cut in subsidies for basic products, including energy, produced profound economic unrest. To this, conflicts such as the war in Tajikistan have to be added. The final result was poverty and misery. In an economic context like this the political and economic reforms devised and needed, initially considered very easy to put into practice, were not implemented.

In fact the problems to manage and confront were quite complicated: autocratic regimes that prevented good governance and economic development; the growth of mafias and organized crime; very slow economic reforms; the problem of distribution of water among the states; radical Islam; the question of energy and monopolization of distribution channels by Russia; and the rivalry among the new republics.

Thus the first phase in the new political approach was the establishment of contractual relations and the negotiation of Partnership and Cooperation Agreements (PCAs). Economic aid was modest, with the exception of the humanitarian aid to Tajikistan and Kyrgyzstan.

In 1999 the Partnership and Cooperation Agreements (PCA) with Kazakhstan, Kyrgyzstan and Uzbekistan, signed in 1995, came into force, setting out the political, economic and trade relationship between the EU and these partner countries. Each PCA was a ten-year bilateral treaty signed and ratified by the EU and the individual state. But the PCA with Turkmenistan was not ratified. And the PCA between the EU and Tajikistan was signed late, on 11 October 2004. Energy was one of the items for cooperation. The Commission considered that the development of the energy sector in Central Asia was of special importance. However, the position of the Commission was very simple. It should act as a facilitator helping to create the conditions for investment and business. Brussels launched the INOGATE (Interstate Oil and Gas Transport to Europe) Programme in 1995, and a Tacis line of finance aimed at integrating the gas and oil networks in Caucasus and Central Asian countries. It was a technical assistance programme for the rehabilitation, modernization and expansion of the systems which transmit oil and natural gas from the Caspian basin and Russia to European and international markets. The programme addressed some supply security issues such as infrastructural deficiencies, regulatory standard requirements and possibly the improvement of the investment framework, especially for downstream projects.

By signing Partnership and Cooperation Agreements with basically all countries in the area, the EU showed some willingness to upgrade its political and economic presence in the region, along with its active participation in the so-called 'Western engagement' that characterized multilateral initiatives under several international organizations operating in the area.

The problem was that the EU was an outsider in the organization of the East–West energy corridor. In November 1999 President Clinton participated in the signing ceremonies in Istanbul that laid down the legal framework for gas and oil from the Caspian Sea to Turkey. The Trans-Caspian Gas Pipeline Framework Declaration was signed by Turkmenistan, Azerbaijan, Georgia, Turkey and the United States. Regarding oil, the intergovernmental agreement for an oil pipeline Baku-Tbilisi-Ceyhan was signed by Turkey, Georgia and Azerbaijan. Later on, Madeleine Albright and high-level officials from Azerbaijan, Georgia and Turkey signed the legal framework agreement for the Baku-Tbilisi-Ceyhan oil pipeline on 28 April 2000.[10]

The passive position adopted by the EU with respect to the development of the East–West Caspian corridor was clearly inconsistent. The main reason for these incredible policies was an ultraliberal approach. At the Luxembourg meeting of the EU Ministers of Foreign Affairs on 27 April 1998 it was declared that the construction of multiple pipeline routes was logical and desirable. The Council believed that the timing of strategic decisions on pipeline routes and the specific routes chosen should remain essentially a commercial matter for the companies concerned. This declaration probably facilitated the political approach of the United States[11] and will substantially contribute to the present chaos in the European approaches regarding Russian's central geopolitical designs using gas and oil.

Apparently a new phase in the relationship between the EU and Central Asian countries started in 1999, but it was a mirage, and the economic assistance to Central Asia was reduced. At the end of 2000, during the preparation of the Swedish EU Presidency, the government of Sweden considered that expanding the policies of the Union towards Central Asia was important. The head of the unit on Caucasus and Central Asia, Cornelis Wittebrood,[12] was in favour, but the Commissioner for External Relations, Chris Patten, refused to expand the policies to Central Asia. At that time, with very small resources used in this region, the EU presence, and its interests as well, would have substantially increased.

In parallel, the EU Commissioner for Transport and Energy, Loyola de Palacio (November 1999–November 2004), tried to encourage the energy dialogue with Russia, which was considered a more reliable partner for the security of the EU supply than the countries from the Middle East.

The consequence was evident: a lack of EU presence in the region and a lack of EU strategy towards Central Asia.[13]

In 2002, after the 11 September 2001 impact and the military intervention in Afghanistan, Central Asia became a priority on the international agenda. Thus a so-called 'Regional Strategy Paper' was adopted by the Commission on 30 October 2002. The Strategy Paper set out the cooperation objectives and assessed the Central Asian policy agenda. It was officially stated that the core objective of the new assistance was the promotion of stability and security in the countries of Central Asia and to assist in their pursuit of sustainable economic development and poverty reduction. The Tacis assistance had to be delivered via three tracks: a regional cooperation programme to promote concerted work among two or more Central Asian partner countries that could include work on transport and energy networks; regional support for programmes implemented at national level; and a pilot poverty reduction scheme in two or three selected target areas.[14]

However, this approach did not mean a departure from the traditional agenda of preventing adverse developments in the region and failed to view the region as 'a land of opportunity'.[15] The Baku Initiative of 2004, however, proposed EU investments to the Caspian countries in infrastructure and reforms in return for energy supplies.

The philosophy of the agenda changed after the Russia–Ukraine confrontation regarding the price of gas from December 2005 to January 2006. The Commission tried to improve the EU presence in the region and a new energy cell was created in order to deal with energy issues in the different regions. New proposals were made for the Caucasus, the Caspian and Central Asia in the new Black Sea Initiative. It was very late.[16] Following a reactive policy, the German Presidency in the first semester of 2007 prepared a Central Asia Strategy Paper. The EU has missed important opportunities in Central Asia: the policies of limited engagement and the primacy given to market liberalization and to the companies on decisions on pipeline routes and the specific routes chosen were a clear fiasco and could produce a disaster. The EU's normative approach to governance, energy market liberalization, human rights and the lack of political development and market economies has also meant that Russia and China have increased their influence with the countries of the region, putting aside the question of democracy, market liberalization and human rights, and thus creating more difficulties for the promotion of EU rules and values.

In the strategy approved in June 2007 by the Council it was stated from the beginning that the EU had to establish a regional political dialogue, start a European Education Initiative and an EU Rule of Law Initiative, and establish regular human rights and energy dialogues with Central Asian states.[17]

But in May 2007 Russia had won the first and most important round of the game: pipeline control and export routes from Central Asia. The companies of the EU, including companies substantially controlled by European states, could not properly react to this challenge. Or rather, they reacted following their own instincts, looking for possible profits. European states maintained different priorities and policies in a situation where common European policies were a priority. Energy was again at the top of the security agenda. The challenge was not a market challenge. It was something different, a state challenge, the possible manipulation of the European energy market by Russia.[18]

Russian policies and projects: South Stream and Novorossisk-Burgas-Alexandropolis pipelines

The South Stream gas pipeline

After Putin's announcement in December 2005 that Russia intended to be a big energy player, Russia took a tough stance in its negotiations with the EU. Regarding gas supplies, Russia maintained a de facto monopoly on the gas from Turkmenistan, Kazakhstan and Uzbekistan through the Gazprom transport infrastructures. Since the end of the Cold War, Russia had been dictating the prices it was willing to pay for the gas of the new Central Asian republics. But in April 2006, President Hu Jintao and President Saparmurat Niyazov signed a framework agreement on oil and gas cooperation. The deal involved the construction of a gas pipeline to export 30 billion cubic metres of Turkmen gas annually for 30 years to China, starting in 2009. The Russian export monopoly was thus broken. It implied a setback for Russia. Gazprom, which had resisted an increase in gas prices from $65/tcm to $100/tcm, had to agree to the new prices in September 2006. The deal covered the purchase of 50 billion cubic metres a year until 2009. Russia needed the Turkmen gas imports to meet its gas exports to the EU. The new prices were also needed to maintain Russian control of Turkmen gas supplies. In fact, Niyazov simultaneously agreed to give a preferential access to the Yolotan gas fields to Russia and to quadruple the capacity of the existing gas pipeline to transport the gas to Russia.

In December 2006 Saparmurat Niyazov died. On 11 February 2007 a new President, Gurbanguly Berdymukhammedov, was elected. The new President maintained the commitment of his predecessors to Russia. However, Turkmenistan was still not happy with the prices. Gazprom was selling Turkmen gas to Ukraine for $100/tcm while selling gas to the EU for $250/tcm at the same time. But Western countries considered that a window of opportunity existed for brokering energy deals with the new President. Speculation and official statements – not independent audits – on new gas findings and the need for new export gas pipelines fostered this dream.

In this new situation Russia acted very rapidly. On 12 May 2007, Vladimir Putin attended a summit meeting in the Turkmen Caspian port of Turkmenbashi. The presidents of Kazakhstan and Turkmenistan were there. They agreed to build a gas pipeline bordering the Caspian running from Turkmenistan through Kazakhstan connecting with the Russian pipelines to Europe. The formal agreement had to be signed in September 2008. In the first stage, the pipeline will deliver 10 billion cubic metres of gas a year by 2009–10. With a new gas infrastructure to be finalized in 2012 and the modernization of the old one, total deliveries of 90 billion cubic metres a year to Russia are expected. The three countries manifested their interest in working also with Uzbekistan to update the existing pipelines in order to get the synergies of this, the second largest gas producer in Central Asia.

The agreement was a major diplomatic victory for Russia. The President of Turkmenistan still maintained that his country could diversify the export routes and had enough gas for new pipelines with Iran, China, Afghanistan, India and the trans-Caspian for Nabucco. But few analysts considered new alternative gas pipelines of significant capacity viable in the near future. Connecting gas suppliers from the Caspian to Europe through Turkey was now difficult indeed. In the future Turkey would have to receive substantial quantities of gas from Azerbaijan, Iran and Iraq in order to be a real player. The supply of 30 billion cubic metres of gas per year to the EU, using the projected gas link Baku-Tblisi-Erzurum-Nabucco was not viable.[19]

Then Turkey tried to reactivate the dormant agreement with Turkmenistan signed on 29 October 1998 for the supply of 30 billion cubic metres a year. Of this 14,000 had to be transferred to Europe. Turkey resented the systematic policies of Russia to block its initiatives to make Turkey an energy hub corridor. Previously, Russia had tried to block the trans-Caspian gas pipeline by constructing the Blue Stream, a joint venture of Gazprom and the Italian ENI. In fact, only the first section of the pipeline, from Baku to Erzurum, was constructed.

Russia again had a clear strategy. On 23 June, the newspapers announced that Gazprom and ENI had signed a memorandum on the construction of a new gas pipeline from Russia to Europe across the Black Sea. The capacity of the pipeline, to be determined by the feasibility study, could reach 30 billion cubic metres a year. The estimated cost of building a 900 km link under the Black Sea was 10 billion euros.

The name of the new pipeline was South Stream. It would link Bulgaria-Hungary-Austria (Nabucco bis) and Bulgaria-Greece-Otranto (Italy). Bulgaria, Hungary and Greece had announced their participation in the project. Thus, Ukraine and Turkey were bypassed. It was abundantly clear that Russia was trying to monopolize gas exports,[20] and that the EU countries were deeply divided, even taking into account the common EU approaches on energy security and diversification.

With this, the Nabucco project was losing momentum. The participants in the project had not yet reached an agreement over financing and Turkey had vetoed the participation of Gaz de France. Environmental problems and concerns plus the dispute on the division of the sea among the riparian states were also critical issues that delayed the project.

But Turkey responded quickly. A failure in the Nabucco project meant a failure in the Turkey-Greece-Italy and Turkey-Greece-Balkan states projected gas corridors. On 13 July, in Ankara, the Iranian and Turkish ministers of energy signed a memorandum of understanding on gas deliveries from Turkmenistan and Iran via Turkey to Europe. The tentative amount was also 30 billion cubic metres of gas a year, 20 billion coming from Iran and 10 from Turkmenistan. But this memorandum was problematic. Iran has serious technical and production problems on the supply side. Iranian production is around 79 billion cubic metres of gas but it is consumed in the country. It urgently needs heavy investment in infrastructure to extract its important gas reserves. Several times Iran could not fulfil its commitments with Turkey, for instance in the winter of 2004–5, in the winter of 2006–7 and later in January 2008. Apparently the new gas for the pipeline would come from the development of Iran's giant South Pars gas field.

Turkmenistan, which exports 5–8 billion cubic metres a year to Iran, also cut the supplies to Iran in January 2008. To this the terrorist activities by PKK/PJAK in the pipeline corridor and the strong opposition of the United States to a deal with Iran have to be added.

Turkey also went ahead with the project to open a gas pipeline with Greece connecting the gas fields of the Caspian with Europe, bypassing Russia. On 18 November 2007, Tayyip Erdogan and Costas Karamanlis inaugurated the 300 km gas pipeline. The pipeline would initially carry 250 million cubic metres of Azerbaijan gas a year from Karacabey in Turkey to Komotini in northeast Greece. By 2012, the capacity is expected to triple once the projected Poseidon undersea pipeline, linking Greece and Italy, is in operation.

But four days later, it was announced that Gazprom and ENI would sign a deal confirming their plan to build a new pipeline to supply Russian gas to Europe. The agreement was signed in the Kremlin by the Italian Prime Minister Romano Prodi and President Vladimir Putin.

In December Russia, Kazakhstan and Turkmenistan finally signed the agreement to build the gas pipeline along the Caspian Sea. The agreement ended months of conversations and tensions over the gas prices between Gazprom and the government of Turkmenistan, which had not respected the contract signed in 2006 for the supplies in the period 2006–9 at $100 per 1000 cubic metres. The price agreed in November was $130 per 1000 cubic metres of gas in the first semester of 2008 and $150 in the second semester of 2008. The government of Turkmenistan increasingly played with Western companies showing interest in the trans-Caspian route and the eastern connection with China. Thus Russian economic leverage and influence over its former satellite zone had drastically diminished. Ukraine was also a clear loser. On 4 December Gazprom announced that Ukraine had agreed to a price of $1795 per 1000 cubic metres of gas.

In the following months Russia tried to consolidate the South Stream. Vladimir Putin visited Bulgaria in January 2008 and reached a compromise with President Georgi Parvanov. Russia and Bulgaria would each have a 50 per cent stake in the Bulgarian part of the gas pipeline. Bulgaria wanted a majority stake in the pipeline. The problem was that Bulgaria was a member of the Nabucco project and Russia obtained a de facto monopoly over Bulgaria's energy market.

Four days later, Russia signed a deal with Serbia giving control of the Serbian oil and gas monopoly, the state company NIS, to Gazprom. Serbia was promised investments for modernizing the energy infrastructure and that it could become an energy hub for Russian energy. It was another critical Russian achievement. Romania could now be bypassed. It became a weak link in Russian strategy. And Hungary, which receives 80 per cent of its supplies from Gazprom, seems a possible target more than a partner for Russia.[21] Both countries have received Russian proposals for the South Stream and, as members of the EU, have the political obligation to support the Nabucco project. Both countries, through MOL and Transgaz, are also partners of the Nabucco project. However, Hungary, in March 2007, preferred to cooperate with Gazprom in the extension of the Blue Stream and later, Prime Minister Ferenc Gyurcsany agreed to participate in the South Stream in a meeting with Russian Prime Minister Viktor Zubkov.[22]

Novorossisk-Burgas-Alexandropolis pipeline

In parallel, in the oil sector several important changes have taken place. The Baku-Tbilisi-Ceyhan (BTC) pipeline, strongly supported by the United States, was inaugurated at the Ceyhan terminal on 13 July 2006. It is the second largest pipeline, 1760 km, and the cost was quite high, $4 billion. It is expected to transport 1 million barrels of oil per day by 2008.

The pipeline was designed to provide an alternative to the Russian control of oil transport in the Caspian. Thus Azerbaijan could resist the Russian pressure on energy transport prices. But it did not last long. Russia mounted a counterattack.

In a meeting in Athens in March 2007 between President Vladimir Putin, the Greek Prime Minister Costas Karamanlis and the Bulgarian Prime Minister Sergei Stanishev an initial agreement was signed to build an oil pipeline from Burgas, a port in the Bulgarian Black Sea, and Alexandropolis, a port in the Greek Adriatic Sea. The potential of the pipeline was 50 million barrels a year. Russian tankers will alleviate the traffic in the Bosporus. In this respect, it was good news for Turkey but it was a setback for the Turkish pretension to be an energy hub corridor.

Two months later, on 10 May 2007, Vladimir Putin signed an agreement with President Nazarbayev for expanding the oil pipeline that transports oil from Tengiz fields to the Novorossisk port and from there to Burgas and Alexandropolis. Another agreement opened the Kazakhstan participation in the Burgas-Alexandropolis oil pipeline. Kazakhstan's interest in sending oil via BTC drastically diminished.[23]

A new initiative also tried to bypass Turkey. The Bulgarian Parliament on 31 May ratified an agreement with Albania and Macedonia for the construction of a trans-Balkan pipeline, the AMBO project, linking Burgas to Vlore in Albania.

In these circumstances, Western plans are in clear disarray, counting only on Azerbaijan energy reserves. In order to be an energy hub corridor Turkey now has to rely on Iran, Iraq and possibly Turkmenistan reserves. But the United States is against a rapprochement with Iran, Turkmenistan reserves need an audit, the oil pipelines from Iraq Kirkuk-Yumurtalik-Ceyhan and the exploitation of gas fields negotiated for a joint venture among TPAO-BOTAS-TEKFEN depend on the stabilization of the country and the solution of the Kurdish question. That is a complex question indeed.

Conclusion

The European Union's approach to energy security is clearly in disarray. EU policy has been late and reactive in the face of the thrust of Russia's policy. It has suffered from a lack of vision, in the first place, for believing that the norms of behaviour of the new Central Asian republics could be exclusively designed by the EU. The promotion of democracy, human rights and the market economy as conditions for European engagement have been seen to be fragile when confronted with Russia and China, whose agenda does not include these matters and, in the case of Russia, looks to maintain a dominant position at any price. Russia under President Vladimir Putin has used different tactics for discouraging foreign investors and has tried to co-opt countries, companies and regulators using upstream power, partnerships with energy companies and banks, strong and extensive lobbying and tough diplomacy, including the personal involvement of Vladimir Putin, disaggregating the European companies and the EU countries through bilateral deals.[24]

In the second place, there is the preponderant role awarded by the EU to companies in the design of routes and corridors for energy transportation. This naive position has already clashed in the past with the policies of the United States and Russia that had a strategic design in the context of deep rivalry. Subsequently this position has prevented the adoption of sufficiently strong common postures. The EU prioritized companies and markets over state policies. The result has been catastrophic.

European companies have been motivated by the search for profits. This point has been intelligently exploited by Russia in its policy of divide and conquer. It has even attracted state companies, or companies with an important European state participation, among the countries of the European Union. The attempts to carry out a common energy policy on the part of Europe have not been successful. One could even say that the European Commission's proposals and energy plans are to a large extent in disarray. It is not a mere commercial dispute between Russia and other countries. The approach to energy security as solely a matter of markets or human security is not sustainable.

Another important consequence has been that Turkey has diminished in importance as an energy corridor for the EU. Russia is to bypass Turkish and EU interest in this corridor. But Turkey still maintains its potential as a transit country for energy coming from Iraq, Iran and possibly Turkmenistan and Uzbekistan.

Notes

1. On natural gas, the interconnections in existence in 1996 were Finland with Russia; Western Europe with Russia (mainly through Ukraine and Slovakia); Greece with Russia (through Ukraine, Romania and Bulgaria); Italy and Spain/Portugal with Algeria; LNG terminals receiving mainly Algerian gas. As missing links the following were mentioned: Baltic States with Nordic and Central Europe; Balkan countries with Central Europe and Mediterranean basin; and Europe with Central Asia, by the southern route.
2. The natural gas priority projects agreed were the following: NG 1, United Kingdom-northern continental Europe, including Netherlands, Denmark and Germany (with connections to Baltic Sea region countries)-Russia; NG 2, Algeria-Spain-Italy-France-northern continental Europe; NG 3, Caspian Sea countries-Middle East-European Union; NG 4, LNG terminals in Belgium, France, Spain, Portugal, Italy; NG 5, underground storage in Spain, Portugal, Italy, Greece and the Baltic Sea region. As an additional natural gas priority the NG 6 Mediterranean member states-East Mediterranean gas ring project was proposed.
3. See 'Priority Axes and TEN-E Projects', Brussels, 25 July 2003.
4. European Commission, Commission Staff Working Paper, 'Decision of the European Parliament and of the Council laying down guidelines for

trans-European energy networks and repealing Decisions No. 3936/3391/EC and No. 1229/2003/EC', COM(2003) 742 final, 2003.

5. 'TEN-E Guidelines specify a European-wide energy transmission network', Memo/06/304, Brussels, 24 July 2006.

6. European Commission, Directorate-General for Research into Sustainable Energy Systems, 'Energy Corridors', Project Report EUR 22581 (Luxembourg: European Commission, 2007), p. 15.

7. Ibid., p. 4.

8. Ibid., p. 25.

9. 'Nabucco Project Timeline', http://www.nabucco-pipeline.com/project/project-timeline/index.html.

10. Azerbaijan, Georgia, Turkey and Turkmenistan are beneficiary countries in the INOGATE programme. It is also worth mentioning that the EU financed a viability study for the trans-Caspian pipelines. See A. Marquina, 'The EU Policies Towards the Caucasus', *Turkish Yearbook of International Relations*, 2001, pp. 157–71.

11. For a summary of the strategic US approach to the Caspian during these years see F. Hill, 'Une stratégie incertaine: la politique des États-Unis dans le Caucase et en Asie centrale depuis 1991', *Politique Étrangère*, No. 1, 2001.

12. At that time, the Directorate E: Eastern Europe (non-candidate countries), Caucasus and Central Asia was chaired by Timo Summa, and the head of unit E3: Caucasus and Central Asia (including Mongolia) was Cornelis Wittebrood.

13. During the Swedish Presidency in the first semester of 2001 an EU strategy for the Caucasus was not finally approved. Instead the EU adopted a confidential document. On Central Asia, the role of the rotating EU Presidency has been fundamental. The Netherlands Presidency in 2004 and the Austrian Presidency in 2006 tried to engage the EU in the region. The most significant initiative was the appointment in July 2005 of Jan Kubis as EU Special Representative for Central Asia.

14. European Commission, *Strategy Paper 2002–2006 & Indicative Programme 2002–2004 for Central Asia*, 2002, http://ec.europa.eu/external_relations/ceeca/rsp2.

15. A. Matveera, *EU Stake in Central Asia*, Chaillot Paper No. 91 (Paris: EU Institute for Security Studies, 2006), p. 83.

16. The EU never had a lobby on Central Asia and the political engagement depended in good part on the will of the rotating EU presidencies. This was the case of the Dutch Presidency in 2004 and the Austrian Presidency in 2006. Ibid., p. 91.

17. Council of the European Union, 'The EU and Central Asia: Strategy for a New Partnership', 2007, http://register.consilium.europa.eu/pdf/en/07/st10/st10113.en07.pdf.

18. See also in this regard the approach of Z. Baran, 'EU Energy Security: Time to End Russian Leverage', *The Washington Quarterly*, Vol. 30, No. 4, 2007, pp. 131–44.

19. The summit meeting took place in parallel with a summit meeting in Krakow attended by the presidents of Poland, Ukraine, Lithuania, Georgia Azerbaijan and a representative from the government of Kazakhstan. In a joint declaration they manifested their interest in the construction of a pipeline from Odessa to Gdansk. The project did not materialize.

20. Some of the gas for the pipeline will come from a Russian gas field previously operated by Yukos, sold to Gazprom and operated by ENI. At the same time, Gazprom planned to build the Nord Stream under the Baltic Sea from Russia to Germany, bypassing Poland. The partners were the German companies EON and BASF, Gasunie from Netherlands and ENI unit Saipem. The South Stream and the Nord Stream had a projected capacity of 85 billion cubic metres of gas per year.

21. B. Bösze, 'Security of Energy Supply in Hungary', *Regio: Minorities, Politics, Society*, No. 1, 2006, http://www.ceeol.com/aspx/getdocument.aspx?logid=5&id=62b11187-4748-4448-af40-0943af652404.

22. J. Dempsey, 'Hungary Chooses Gazprom over EU', *International Herald Tribune*, 12 March 2007; 'Hungary to Join South Stream Gas Pipeline Project', *RIA Novosti*, 7 December 2007.

23. A. Vershinin, 'Russia, Central Asia in Crucial Gas Deal', *Los Angeles Times*, 12 May 2007; 'Can Caspian Oil Flow to the West?', *People's Daily Online*, 18 May 2007.

24. To this has to be added the preventive acquisitions; this was the case of the energy sector acquisition in Armenia, avoiding Iranian competition and expansion, the market flooding in Turkey or punitive actions in Lithuania and Ukraine. See R. R. Amsterdam, 'The Gazpromization of European Energy Security', *Today's Zaman*, 21 February 2008, http://www.todayszaman.com.

5

Greece's Energy Security Policy: Between Energy Needs and Geopolitical Imperatives

Kostas Ifantis

Introduction

There is no doubt that, over the last few years, energy has been at the centre of global attention. Achieving energy security and diversification, combined with fighting climate change, have become the number one issue in almost every country in the world. On Wednesday, 2 January 2008, oil prices rose above the symbolic level of 100 dollars a barrel, a long-awaited milestone in an era of rapidly escalating energy demand. Oil prices, which had fallen to a low of 50 dollars a barrel at the beginning of 2007, have quadrupled since 2003. The rise has been driven by an unprecedented surge in demand from the United States, China and other Asian and Middle Eastern countries.[1] Booming economies have led to more consumption of oil-derived products like gasoline, jet fuel and diesel. Meanwhile, new oil supplies have struggled to catch up. Oil markets have grown increasingly unpredictable over the past few years, with large swings that have been attributed partly to financial speculation, not just market fundamentals. Political tensions in the Middle East, where more than two-thirds of the world's proven oil reserves are located, have also fuelled the rise in prices.[2]

Oil is now within reach of its historic inflation-adjusted high, reached in April 1980 in the aftermath of the Iranian revolution, when prices jumped to the equivalent of 102 dollars per barrel in 2008 money. Unlike the oil shocks of the 1970s and 1980s, which were caused by sudden interruptions in oil supplies from the Middle East, the current surge is fundamentally different. Prices have risen steadily over several years because of a rise in demand for oil and gasoline in both developed and developing countries.[3] Higher prices have been cast as vindication of a theory that the world has reached the maximum rate of oil production. Explorers have failed to discover major new fields to replace ageing deposits being tapped in countries like Saudi Arabia, Kuwait and Iran. One thing looks certain: the uncertainties are enormous. The big questions are how fast the likes of China and India can and will reduce the high energy intensity of their own rapid growth and how rapidly new energy resources can come on line. Energy security is a multi-faceted issue and is about much more than where the oil comes from and at which price. According to Burrows and Treverton:

> The big strategic issues are not high prices at home but political effects abroad: which countries will be the big winners and which the big losers, what challenges both winners and losers will pose for international security and global welfare, and the implications of changes in the global oil and gas markets, especially the control of resources by national oil companies ... International oil companies, with their technological and management skills, are no longer in charge; producer countries and their national oil companies have control over nearly three-quarters of the world's proven oil reserves.[4]

There is as yet no generally recognized definition of energy security. For consuming countries, energy security equates to security of supply, while for producing countries it equates to security of demand. It could be said that global energy security means a set of measures intent on ensuring an optimized balance of supply and demand on the world market with due account to the interests of both consumers and producers. In its most fundamental sense, however, energy security is assured when a country can deliver energy economically, reliably, environmentally soundly and safely, and in quantities sufficient to support its economic growth and defence needs. To do so requires policies that support expansion of all elements of the energy supply and delivery infrastructure, with sufficient storage and generating reserves, diversity and redundancy to meet the demands of economic growth.

Today, the challenges of global energy security include high and volatile oil prices, increasingly poor geographical correlations between energy sources and users, vulnerability of the critical energy infrastructure and political instability, natural disasters and other threats. At the same time, the growth in demand and in the increasing import requirement of each of the main consuming regions (the United States, Japan, China and Europe) potentially can make access to those resources an issue of strategic competition. The investment requirements along the entire energy chain are enormous, while the need to protect the environment and to tackle climate change has become grave.

The challenge, therefore, is to effectively manage the increasing complexity of an energy-interdependent world while striving to meet economic, security and environmental imperatives. This requires a much more sophisticated approach to energy policy-making, one that more fully appreciates the interdependencies of global markets, the complex nature of energy security and the need to manage the trade-offs inherent in energy policy decision-making.[5]

As a matter of principle, the global nature of these challenges and the growing interdependence between producing, consuming and transiting countries require strengthened partnership between all stakeholders to enhance global energy security. A look at the Eurasian map confirms that partnership is the best recipe for projects such as the Blue Stream, the Greece-Turkey Gas Interconnector, the Caspian Pipeline Consortium (CPC), the Baku-Tbilisi-Ceyhan (BTC), the Bourgas-Alexandroupolis, the Constanta-Trieste, the Greece-Italy Gas Interconnector, the Nabucco, the Blue Stream-2 and so on.

For Greece, the focus on enhancing energy security has been coupled with acquiring a new role in the 'geoenergy' matrix and in the context of a changing regional and transregional environment. Greece's role as part of a gateway through which gas and oil can enter the EU is becoming increasingly important as the EU grapples with the interrelated problems of ensuring energy security and the provision of energy supplies from multiple sources at competitive prices. The fact of the matter is that Greece suddenly claimed a position on the global energy map. And this is due to a number of reasons: the expansion of its geopolitical environment; the gravity of domestic energy needs and a subsequent as well as gradual paradigm shift in the domestic energy market; the transregional pipeline developments; and the Russian energy 'onslaught'. Equally sudden was the need to develop the kind of policies which could respond effectively to a strategic equation that seemed to be promising some favourable pay-offs in terms of relatively upgrading the country's regional power position. All these issues, however, should be seen through the more general changes affecting Greece's geopolitical environment.

Greece's changing geopolitics

According to Lesser, 'a key, defining feature of the geopolitical environment as seen from Greece is the progressive enlargement of the country's strategic space'.[6] The stabilization of relations with neighbouring countries and the fact that Greece has emerged as a champion of a clear European perspective for the whole region has reinforced the expansion of both Greek interest and the way this should be pursued. The general stabilization of Greece's northern neighbours, and a reduction in the potential for economic dislocations and security spillovers from developments in southeast Europe – with the exception of Kosovo, the risk of conflict, regional collapse and organized spillovers of political violence is quite remote – has allowed Athens to develop a rather positive geostrategic mix of regional and transregional elements. Of course, many functional issues – the most important being terrorism – cut across regional boundaries.[7] Although Greece is a small country in terms of size and population, its geographical position can confer upon it a relatively greater role in political, economic and security developments across a wide region, from Balkan reconstruction and political reform to the Middle East peace process, and from energy transport to maritime security in the Mediterranean and elsewhere.

Such a role has been easier to pursue since bilateral relations with Turkey have followed a positive trend. For Athens, relations with Turkey have traditionally been the core strategic issue. Since 1999, Greek–Turkish détente has changed the geopolitical landscape in fundamental ways – regionally, and also in terms of European and American interests and policies.[8] The prospect of continued normalization in relations with Turkey already puts a premium on bilateral initiatives aimed at managing shared challenges in Southeast Europe, around the Black Sea and the Eastern Mediterranean. One area where tangible progress has been registered is in joint development projects of energy transport infrastructure. The energy security issue and the extent to which Greece has a 'score-card' in the 'energy game' should be placed and discussed within a wider geopolitical context along with the country's energy profile and domestic energy policy developments.

Greece's energy sector[9]

According to 2006 estimates, Greece has oil reserves of just 7 million barrels. With domestic production of 6,400 barrels per day (bbl/d) in 2005, Greece relies heavily on imports – primarily from Iran, Saudi Arabia, Libya and Egypt – to meet its 439,000 bbl/d of oil consumption. Oil's market share of total energy consumption is gradually declining as the country increases its reliance on natural gas. Although the Middle East is expected to remain Greece's major oil supplier, oil from Russia and the Caspian Sea region will become more important as Greece constructs new pipelines. Today, oil accounts for 62 per cent of total energy consumption.

In the field of natural gas, in 2006, total final consumption reached 3.1 billion cubic metres (bcm) and future projections show an increase at the levels of 6 bcm for the year 2010 and 7.5 bcm for 2015. Despite the recent strong demand growth, the share of natural gas in total energy consumption is still small, reaching 7 per cent in 2005. Greece receives two-thirds of its natural gas imports from Russia, with the remainder coming as LNG from Algeria.

Lignite is Greece's only significant fossil fuel resource, with reserves totalling 4,300 million short tons (Mmst). With lignite output of 80 Mmst in 2005, Greece is second only to Germany in European lignite production. Coal accounts for 26 per cent of total energy consumption, but it is responsible for more than 70 per cent of Greece's total electricity generation.

On the renewable energy front, a total of 750 MW in renewable energy source (RES) systems is operational in Greece. It is also noteworthy that approximately half of existing capacity was installed and connected to the system in the period from March 2004 to September 2006, showing a significant increase of 55 per cent of operational RES systems. Moreover, the government's planning involves reaching a total installed capacity of 3,000 MW by 2010, thus meeting Greece's EU obligation amounting to 20.1 per cent of total gross electricity consumption originating from RES.

On average, it is estimated that 7 per cent of the country's electricity needs could be sustained over the next decade by this form of energy, though looking further into the future this percentage might exceed 30 per cent eventually, due to Greece's ample sunshine throughout the year. Wind energy can fulfil another 15 per cent. If one adds biofuel, geothermic and wave energy to the equation, it becomes clear that Greece has the ability to become a fully independent energy producer by the mid-twenty-first century, and relieve itself from the strain of energy imports.

Estimates show that 15 per cent of the country's electricity needs can be produced by wind farms, with installed windpower capacity possibly expanding to 2000 MW by 2010 from 475 MW in 2006.[10] The use of solar technology in Greece has almost tripled since 2000, and several EU reports indicate that Greece could use solar power to meet one-third of its energy requirements. Solar power projects are expected to draw investments worth 5 billion euros by 2020. Foreign companies specialized in this field – mostly from Germany – have already set up offices in order to take advantage of the new market to be created.

Finally, as far as biofuels are concerned, a proportion of 5.75 per cent of biofuels of the total diesel and petrol quantities for transport purposes will be placed on the market by 31 December 2010. In 2006, total supply of biodiesel in the Greek market reached 90,000 metric tons (MT), while for 2007 total supply was expected to rise to 115,000 MT.

Domestic energy policy developments

Since March 2004, Greece's new energy policy has been based on a twofold strategy. The first part involves the liberalization of Greece's internal energy market, aimed at the developing sector and attracting large-scale investment. The second part refers to enhancing the country's position on the international energy map, transforming Greece into an energy hub.

In this context, special focus has been given to the liberalization of the internal electricity and national gas markets, the further use of renewable energy sources, the introduction of biofuels in the Greek energy mix and the implementation of energy saving and energy efficiency measures. At the same time, priority has been given to the development of a strong external energy policy, basically through the creation of new and the upgrading of existing energy interconnections with neighbouring countries in the electricity, natural gas and oil sectors. Since 2004, Greece's energy market has undergone radical reform, aiming to open up the internal electricity and natural gas markets to new players.

Market liberalization

Greece's oil industry is dominated by Hellenic Petroleum (HP), formed in 1998 from the state-owned Public Petroleum Corporation (PPC). HP conducts oil exploration, imports crude and petroleum products and distributes and markets petroleum products throughout the country. In Greece, the Group owns and operates three refineries, in Aspropyrgos, Elefsina and Thessaloniki, with nominal annual refining capacity of 7.5 million tons, 5 million tons and 3.4 million tons of crude oil per year, respectively. The three refineries combined, cover 73 per cent of the country's total refining capacity. Since 1999, the Group, via its associated company ELPET BALKANIKI, holds the majority shares in OKTA AD SKOPJE, which operates the only refinery in FYROM. The capacity of the OKTA refinery is 2.5 million tons, which exceeds the demand of the local market, allowing for the export of extra capacity.[11] The Greek state is partially privatizing HP in stages, and the company is currently 41.5 per cent privately owned.

The electricity market became fully liberalized in July 2007 and the natural gas market in November 2009. Today, the Public Gas Corporation (DEPA S.A.) is the sole supplier of natural gas in the Greek market. However, the new regulatory legislative framework combined with the operation of the new natural gas interconnection pipeline with Turkey, means that the Greek market will be supplied with an additional 3.5 bcm per year, the construction of, at least, three new power plants by 2010, and the establishment of the three new distribution companies, laying the groundwork for the entrance of new suppliers in the Greek natural gas market.

Greece on the 'geoenergy map': what kind of player?

Greece's unique geoeconomic location between the energy producers of the Middle East, North Africa and the Caspian, as well as the vital transport routes of the Aegean Sea and Eastern Mediterranean, define it as an expanding energy hub between East and West. Several ongoing or new projects in the energy sphere attest to Athens' commitment to developing the energy sector as something vital to both economic growth and national security. On the fronts of oil and gas, Greek initiatives and projects will determine Greece's position in international energy networks.

Energy diplomacy has come to dominate the foreign policy agenda for countries on Europe's periphery and the Balkans is no exception. In the field of regional energy cooperation, Greece has taken the initiative to establish an Energy Community of Southeast Europe. The Treaty was signed in Athens on 25 October 2005 and official operation began in July 2006. It involves the creation of a unified energy market in the greater Balkan region, through the establishment of common market rules and regulation, later to be integrated with the EU's energy market. And this is rather important for Greece, since it has the potential to constitute a point of reference in the wider area. Greece and, particularly, the area of Northern Greece can become the basis for large international companies, seeking investment opportunities in Southeast Europe.

According to the World Bank, with the establishment of the Energy Community of Southeast Europe, approximately 30 billion euros will be invested, by 2020, in the electricity and natural gas sectors alone.[12] In this framework, the enhancement of regional energy integration is pursued through the upgrading of existing and the development of new electricity interconnections with neighbouring countries. At the same time, aiming to further enhance electricity cross-border exchange in Greece's northern interconnections and taking into account the electricity market integration in the wider Balkan region, a number of new electricity interconnection projects have been scheduled: such as the reinforcement of the electricity interconnection with FYROM, by upgrading the existing to 400 kV; the new interconnection line with Turkey, through the construction of a 400 kV line of total transmission capacity of 400 MW, which was commissioned in 2007; and the reinforcement of the existing interconnection line with Bulgaria, through the construction of a new line with a total capacity of 300 MW.

As the West seeks to strengthen and diversify its energy supplies, the region has become awash with proposals for new transit routes to ease the flow of resources from the Caspian. Since the mid-1990s, successive Greek governments have sought to carve out a role for the country as an 'energy hub' in this most lucrative of sectors, investing millions in new infrastructure. But how do countries like Greece expect to benefit from the array of pipelines under consideration? And how can they exploit the opportunities provided by the energy needs of the West in order to further their own strategic interests?

Of course, location alone cannot transform a small Balkan country into a major European power. Greece is a long way downstream from Russia and the Caspian, and the country's influence in Brussels – where it remains on the periphery – will benefit little from the prospect of energy diversification. Nevertheless, the geopolitical benefits of securing a position on the oil and gas routes are real enough, and it is this that seems to provide the rationale for the country's new energy policy.[13] A net energy importer itself, Greece's importance lies in its ability and willingness to be part of the development of major transit systems for gas as well as oil, thus enabling hydrocarbon resources to access European markets by pipeline from such regions as the Caspian, Central Asia and Russia.

With its current oil production and consumption levels, Greece is unable, regardless of any level of investment, to form a strategy that is going to be related to domestic production. Thus, it has reached the point at which it needs to rely on ventures with foreign corporations and states so as to use its territory as a transit route for the emerging energy networks. In setting itself up as a gateway for the flow of energy and investment into emerging Balkan markets, Greece has been able to exploit its regional expertise to advance its relative power position in the region.

The Burgas-Alexandroupolis pipeline

The clearest illustration of Greek thinking is the recent agreement regarding the 285 km Burgas-Alexandroupolis (B-A) pipeline. B-A would bypass the overcrowded Bosporus Straits by transporting Russian crude oil from the Bulgarian port of Burgas to Alexandroupoli on Greece's Aegean coast. Designed to serve West European markets, the project has been on the cards since as early as 1993, but it was only in 2004 – some eleven years after the project's conception – that it rose to the top of the Greek foreign policy agenda. So why the decade-long lag?

Greece's push to see B-A in operation was the result of a series of developments in the region spanning the course of the last decade. In the mid-1990s – the height of the infamous dispute between Athens and Skopje over FYROM's name – a similar pipeline (AMBO) came under discussion. Running from Burgas to Albania's Adriatic port of Vlore, AMBO would supply crude oil to Bulgaria, FYROM and Albania. Like B-A, its chief objective was to provide a Bosporus bypass for Caspian crude oil en route to Western markets. Despite American support for the US-registered AMBO Corporation, the project – and with it the diversification of Skopje's oil supplies – soon floundered. Instead of looking to the Balkans for new oil routes, the West had diverted its attention to the BCT pipeline, a route which could bypass Russia altogether on the way from the energy-rich Caspian.

With AMBO and B-A both grounded, Greece's state-controlled HP took the opportunity to construct its own pipeline to Skopje, one which continues to serve as FYROM's only large-scale supplier of crude oil. The subsequent acquisition of Skopje's sole refinery (OKTA) meant that, by the turn of the century, Hellenic Petroleum had established almost complete control over FYROM's oil consumption. Seen in the context of mass Greek investment – the bulk coming from Greece's large public sector – Athens' influence over Skopje had grown immeasurably.

The major problem for early B-A planners was that in the mid-1990s there was no economic *raison d'être*. B-A and any of the available counter-proposals were simply too immature to be seriously discussed in the absence of increased exports on the Russian and Kazakh side. Kazakh exports actually only started in October 1998, almost simultaneously with the steady rise in Russian oil exports.[14] These two factors, along with Turkey's decision to minimize oil exports via the heavily populated Bosporus Straits, especially after the infamous oil tanker accident of 1994, contributed to the Bosporus' eventual 'choking'.[15]

With BCT operational, production levels in the Caspian were widely considered insufficient to justify two Balkan oil routes to the West. The construction of AMBO would offer Skopje the chance to diversify its oil supplies away from Greece, while Athens hoped that progress on B-A could forestall this eventuality and consolidate a status quo favourable to Athens. Inevitably then, heightened interest in AMBO saw Greek lobbyists redouble their efforts to promote the rival B-A pipeline.[16] Since 2004, a flurry of summits were organized between leaders and foreign ministers of B-A countries Greece, Bulgaria and Russia, and high-profile visits were exchanged by Russian President Vladimir Putin, Greek Premier Costas Karamanlis, and Gazprom chief Alexei Miller.

While both projects could offer the Kremlin reduced export costs and a consolidated market share, Moscow expected an endorsement of B-A over AMBO to benefit Russia's other chief export commodity, natural gas. Discussions on B-A were paralleled by Russian approaches for access to the new Turkey-Greece gas link – billed for completion by the end of 2007 – and the possibility of concessions here was looking attractive to Russian energy companies deciding which Balkan oil route to back.

The main criterion in Russia's decision was made, in principle, on geopolitical grounds. The operationalization of the principle, following the construction of BTC, demanded that Russia, as well as Kazakhstan, diversify their oil export routes away from Turkey, namely the Bosporus Straits and its choking-off as a de facto oil conduit.

Conversely, US energy companies active in the region were looking to court B-A in order to achieve the opposite effect. Europe's demand for gas is growing faster than that for oil, and US concerns over the continent's dependency on Russia means that keeping companies like Gazprom out of new gas links is a top priority. While Miller's overtures on the subject provoked a stern warning to Athens and Ankara in 2006, the State Department appeared to have warmed to B-A, billing the pipeline as a 'positive' development for the region.

In Greece, the final agreement on 15 March 2007 was heralded as a crucial step towards establishing the country's position on the geoenergy map. With a transport capacity of 30 million tons per annum (initially), reaching 50 million, this particular pipeline greatly elevates Greece's natural geoeconomic role in the wider Southeast Europe region. Firstly, it effectively bypasses the Turkish Bosporus Straits and eases the exports of Eurasian oil to Western Europe. Therefore, through it, Greece becomes an important country for European energy security, a factor that would seem to translate into some degree of political clout.[17] The Russian side, which owns 51 per cent of pipeline shares through Lukoil, is interested in investing in refinery capabilities in Greece. Already it operates a similar facility in the Bulgarian port city of Burgas and, according to reports in the Greek press, has an interest in similar construction in the Greek northeastern Aegean port of Alexandroupolis, or buying a share in the Motor Oil Hellas Corporation which runs the second-largest refinery in Greece. In any case, the pipeline seems to ignite wider commercial interest in the Greek energy market, and consequently transforms the role of Greece from that of a sole importer to a regional energy point.

However, these developments and the B-A reception around European capitals show both progress and tension. The final agreement of the shareholders, signed by the trilateral committee of Russia-Bulgaria and Greece during Vladimir Putin's visit to Sofia on 18 January 2008, stipulates the creation of a company to be based in the Netherlands that will seek funds from the international banking system. It is estimated that all technical and feasibility studies will be completed by the end of 2008, and the pipeline will begin its operations by late 2011.

The Turkey-Greece (-Italy) interconnector

Natural gas is another vital resource by which Greece is seeking to enhance its energy 'reputation'. The Turkey-Greece natural gas interconnector, which began in July 2005 and was inaugurated in November 2007, stretching from Karacabey in Turkey to Komotini in Greece with a total length of 295 kilometres, will for the first time allow the delivery of Caspian gas to Europe without crossing Russian territory. In its current form, the interconnector will transport only limited amounts.[18] The new pipeline will provide Greece with a third supplier of natural gas and an additional quantity of 3.5 bcm coming from Turkey, thus diversifying its existing supply of natural gas from Russia, via Bulgaria, and liquefied natural gas (LNG) from Algeria. The gas flowing through the pipeline will be bought by the Turkish BOTAS company.

There are, however, ambitious plans to link it to a mooted Greek-Italian sub-sea line and boost its capacity. The construction of the Greece-Italy underwater pipeline will, essentially, constitute the extension of the Greece-Turkey pipeline (the Poseidon Project). The pipeline is designed to carry 8 billion cubic metres per year and its total budget is 300 million euros. It will extend from western Greece to the city of Otrando in Italy and will have a total length of 212 km.

The project has long enjoyed EU backing – one of the five priority axes of the Trans-European Networks – with the then (2003) EU External Relations Commissioner Chris Patten providing early vocal support and the Commission itself financing initial studies. The very concept of an interconnector is strategic, in that the line as envisaged would be able to carry gas from Turkey to Greece and Italy. In other words, it would serve as a link between two main supply systems, increasing flexibility of supply.[19]

Once the two projects are completed, the Greek-Turkish and the Greek-Italian interconnectors, Greece will be transformed into an energy hub, through which significant quantities of natural gas will be transported from the Caspian region to the high consumption markets of Western Europe. It will be the first time that Europe is supplied with Caspian gas bypassing Russia and the Middle East.[20] However, fears are expressed that Azerbaijan might have difficulty meeting the demand. To be able to put 11.6 bcm into this pipeline alone, Azerbaijan – which has other commitments and must retain quantities for domestic use – must more than double production in the next four or five years. Its 2006 production was 6.8 bcm. At this point this seems particularly unlikely. In that case, the project might have to fall back on Russian gas. The assumption is that ultimately it will be a mixture of Azeri, Iranian and Russian gas.

For Greek–Turkish relations, this is the first major joint project to link the two countries. Reason dictates that there will no longer be so many causes of tension as both countries will be bound by mutually advantageous economic interests. Neither Greece nor Turkey would want to be held responsible for disrupting the flow of gas to EU markets.[21]

The South Stream gas pipeline

On 25 June 2007, Greece's participation in the construction of the new South Stream natural gas pipeline, linking Russia with Europe, through Greece, was announced after a meeting of the Greek Prime Minister Costas Karamanlis with Russian President Vladimir Putin in Istanbul and following the agreement between Gazprom and ENI. Although, from a financial point of view, this investment seems very ambitious, in terms of providing satisfactory returns to the investors, from Greece's point of view, a pipeline transferring gas that will meet Italian and European needs is another beneficial development since it will secure for decades to come a steady flow of gas to Greece, and it will add to its relatively expanding energy position.

The South Stream agreement signals the culmination of a major political and economic process. The Russian Gazprom and the Italian ENI agreed to invest 15 billion dollars to construct a 900 km pipeline stretching from the Russian Black Sea coast via Bulgaria, Greece and ending in Otranto, Italy. The pipeline should be constructed by 2011. However, as it will bypass countries such as Ukraine, it may exacerbate the rift between American and Russian geopolitical interests. American uneasiness stems from the fear of an ever-expanding increase of Russian energy exports to Europe.

Russia's 2006 transit crises with Ukraine – and to a much smaller extent Belarus in January 2007 – evoked the 'spectre' of a Russian 'gas weapon' in many circles in Europe and the US and catapulted energy security to the forefront of the EU agenda. Nevertheless, a closer analysis of what actually happened in January 2006 indicates that the real problem with EU import security does not lie in the unlikely event of a Russian 'gas embargo', but with the deteriorating condition of Russian–Ukrainian relations. Ever since the emergence of the 'Orange Revolution' in late 2004, the state of affairs between Moscow and Kiev has teetered on the brink of a disastrous break-down. The immense gas pipeline network that feeds more than 70 per cent of all Russian gas exports, and more than 90 per cent of Russian exports to Europe, lies in the middle of this increasingly volatile fault line. Russia is only a little less dependent on Ukraine than vice versa, and is likely to remain so for as long as Moscow does not have alternative hard currency markets outside Europe and/or export routes that bypass Ukraine.[22] The fact is that Russia's willingness to diversify away from its transit dependence on Ukraine and other East European countries is much more justifiable and pragmatic than the risk of an embargo. The South Stream is the southern equivalent of the nearly equal capacity-strong Nord Stream pipeline linking Russia directly to its greatest European client, Germany. It should be noted that in the case of Nord Stream, the opposition by the new EU members is not due to the prospect of increased Russian leverage. Rather, Ukraine, Belarus, the Baltic countries and Poland stand to lose transit money and counter-leverage on Russia.[23]

This transit diversification constitutes a cardinal interest for Europe's security of supply and does not necessarily increase the share of Russia's control over European gas markets. It merely makes that critical supply more geopolitically secure. The idea that Moscow is somehow trying to pre-empt the construction of 'antagonistic' projects such as Nabucco does not survive closer scrutiny.[24] The European Commission, and the countries involved in very capital-intensive infrastructure projects like Nabucco, can exclude Russian gas from utilizing the EC-funded pipeline networks.

Yet, this does not mean that Moscow cannot come to terms with those same countries so as to construct an exclusively Russian network spanning the Baltic Sea as well as Southeast Europe. More to the point, Russian gas cannot be excluded from flowing via privately owned networks such as the Trans-Adriatic Gas Pipeline (TAP) promoted by Swiss-based EGL. EGL is following an open-access strategy that focuses on the volumes of exported gas, not its nationality.

Another important point is that the goal of Europe's import diversification away from Gazprom is not served by the construction of alternative pipeline routes but by the monetization of available export volumes from non-Russian producers. The critical problem for Europe is that there is no major alternative gas producer that could challenge Gazprom's dominant position, other than Iran, at least not in the medium term.[25] What needs to be underlined is that the South Stream and the other alternative pipelines (IGI, TAP and Nabucco) are in the long term complementary in that they can both diversify Russian export options away from increasingly volatile transit routes and maintain the option open for an increased diversification of EU gas imports from potentially crucial medium-term sources such as Iran and Iraq.

Conclusions

The optimism for Greece's energy-related future endeavours is surely being justified by the latest developments. Nevertheless, as has been noted, quite a few of these projects are inexorably related to wider geopolitical moves, and in particular are concentrated between the tripartite relations, and conflicts, between Russia, the US and the Islamic world.

Questions regarding the security and sustainability of energy supply have been left to individual EU members and to powerful market forces. The majority of European governments, even when they agree on the need for the EU to acquire a common energy policy, prefer not to discuss the geopolitics of energy, searching for a unified stance. The truth is that there is little unity among member states' energy policies, especially vis-à-vis Russia, while European corporate energy champions, such as ENI, Gasunie, BASF, EON Ruhrgas and Gaz de France, seem to ignore political preferences and they instead push hard to secure access to Russian energy and the profits it brings.[26] In addition, many in the EU are hesitant to engage in energy deals with countries such as Kazakhstan because of their rather poor record on human rights and the rule of law.

In this framework, Greece is doing nothing more than securing its energy interests the same way Germany, Italy, Hungary or France are doing. Analyses identifying Athens as Moscow's 'Trojan Horse' are rather superficial and definitely ahistorical.[27] While the future seems very encouraging, ensuring success through political initiatives that will secure the deals signed are seen as the utmost priority for Greek policy-makers. Their successes or failures will determine the country's future role as a player in the Southeast European energy game.

Notes

1. Global energy demand is projected to increase approximately 50 per cent in the next 25 years, with nearly 70 per cent of that growth coming from developing economies, 20 per cent from China alone. International Energy Agency (IEA), *World Energy Outlook 2007* (Paris: IEA, 2007), p. 65.
2. '$100 oil a reality over worries in "dangerous world"', *International Herald Tribune*, 3 January 2008.
3. China has more than doubled its use of oil since New York crude dropped to this century's low of $16.70 on 19 November 2001. That has soaked up most of the world's spare production capacity amid supply cuts in Nigeria, Iraq and Venezuela. The 11 per cent slide of the dollar in 2007 against the euro also fed into higher oil prices because it made commodities cheaper for buyers outside the United States and attracted investors as a hedge against inflation. See Z. Daojiong, 'China's Energy Security: Domestic and International Issues', *Survival*, Vol. 48, No. 1, Spring 2006, pp. 179–90.
4. M. Burrows and G. Treverton, 'A Strategic View of Energy Futures', *Survival*, Vol. 49, No. 3, Autumn 2007, pp. 79–80.
5. F. Verrastro and S. Ladislaw, 'Providing Energy Security in an Interdependent World', *The Washington Quarterly*, Vol. 30, No. 4, Autumn 2007, p. 95.
6. I. O. Lesser, 'Greece's New Geopolitical Environment', *Southeast European and Black Sea Studies*, Vol. 5, No. 3, September 2005, p. 347.
7. Ibid.

8. K. Ifantis, 'Greece's Turkish Dilemmas: There and Back Again…', *Southeast European and Black Sea Studies*, Vol. 5, No. 3, September 2005, pp. 379–94.

9. US Department of Energy, Energy Information Administration, 'Greece', Country Analysis Briefs, 2006, http://www.eia.doe.gov, accessed 26 September 2007.

10. Wind farms are already located on the Greek islands of Crete, Evia, Andros and Samos. In May 2006, Greek wind farm operator Rokas announced that it would invest more than two billion euros in a wind farm and power transmission system. The company plans to install 44 wind parks with a combined generated capacity of 1363 MW and to link them to the Chios, Lesvos and Limnos islands in the northern Aegean. The project is one of the biggest investments in wind energy in the world.

11. Hellenic Petroleum, *2006 Annual Report* (Athens: Hellenic Petroleum, 2006).

12. http://go.worldbank.org/JOVI8N7BP0.

13. J. Demopoulos, 'Greek Energy Diplomacy and Future Balkan Pipelines', 11 February 2006, http://www.balkananalysis.com.

14. N. Yotov and D. Kiriakov, 'Balkan Pipeline Dreams', *The Region*, March 2006, pp. 31–4.

15. T. G. Tsakiris, 'The Odyssey in the Caspian Sea', *Worldpipelines*, 1–6 December 2006, p. 1.

16. The project's backers have put forward an ingenious proposal whereby there would be an equalization of tariff, on a genuine average cost basis, for tankers using the Bosporus and for shippers using the B-A line. Since Bosporus costs are, at present, indirect (indeed direct tariffs are illegal under the 1936 Montreaux Convention which governs traffic through the straits), such averaging would indeed lower the overall cost for pipeline throughput, at the expense of increasing it for the Bosporus. But were all the Black Sea littoral nations and the shipping companies using the Bosporus to agree, this would indeed help resolve one of the key Bosporus bypass issues: how to overcome the gap that still exists – despite demurrage and other charges caused by routine tanker delays in the Bosporus – between passage through the Bosporus and a commercial rate for using a bypass pipeline. The project's main strength is its relative cost and length.

17. I. Michaletos, 'The Greek Energy Sector: Developments and Opportunities', 25 January 2008, http://www.balkananalysis.com.

18. K. Barysch, 'Turkey's Role in European Energy Security', *Centre for European Reform Essays*, December 2007, pp. 1–8.

19. J. Roberts, 'The Turkish Gate: Energy Transit and Security Issues', *Turkish Policy Quarterly*, Vol. 3, No. 4, 2004, p. 30.

20. A. Karaiskou and R. Psylla, 'Turkish Energy Policy and the Middle East: Determining the Nexus', *Middle East Bulletin*, 8, December 2007, http://www.idis.gr, pp. 16–18.

21. 'Greek, Turkish premiers open taps on Europe's first supply of Caspian gas', *International Herald Tribune*, 17 November 2007.

22. T. G. Tsakiris, 'The Southern "Gate": the Geostrategic Ramifications of Ukraine's Natural Gas By-passes on SE Europe', *Global Pipeline Monthly*, Vol. 2, No. 4, April 2006, p. 3.

23. R. Larson, 'Nord Stream, Sweden and Baltic Sea Security', *Swedish Defence Research Agency (FOI)*, March 2007, p. 9.

24. Z. Baran, 'EU Energy Security: Time to End Russian Leverage', *The Washington Quarterly*, Vol. 30, No. 4, 2007, p. 138.

25. Turkmenistan, the only major Caspian producer, as well as Kazakhstan, have committed in May 2007 the near entirety of their exportable volumes to the construction of an inter-Caspian pipeline connecting both countries to Russia.
26. Baran, 'EU Energy Security', p. 133.
27. M. Leonard and N. Popescu, *A Power Audit of EU–Russia Relations*, European Council on Foreign Relations ECFR/2 Policy Paper, November 2007, http://www.ecfr.eu, pp. 27–9.

6
Between Continuity and Change: the Italian Approach to Energy Security

Gianluca Pastori

Introduction

In the last few years, academics and practitioners have provided different definitions of the multifaceted concept of energy security. For the purposes of this chapter, it will be seen – from a consumer's perspective – as the guarantee of a reliable flow of energy, at affordable prices, plentiful in comparison to national needs, and sustainable in the mid-to-long term, also from an environmental point of view.[1] In this perspective, the concept is intimately linked on the one hand with national security in its 'diplomatic' and 'geopolitical' meaning, on the other with its individual and social dimension, pertaining to the sphere of welfare, development and economic growth.

Often linked – in the past – with the related but different concept of energy independence, energy security has emerged recently as a key element in many states' political agendas. Growing competition, the emergence of new high consumer markets (especially in Asia), increasing international prices and doubts about the real amount of hydrocarbon reserves, in a context of growing pressure on resources, together with the constraints imposed by international environment preservation agreements, have all created more political interest in the issue. Moreover, energy security in its individual and social dimension is intuitively linked with human security, at least since, according to what had been labelled an 'extraordinarily expansive and vague'[2] concept, a threat to human security could be construed as any menace to 'the quality of life of individuals', or as any attack on individuals' and communities' 'human, environmental and social rights'.[3]

The Italian situation in some ways mirrors the international one, although with more emphatic undertones.[4] Italian dependence on foreign imports makes the country highly vulnerable to the political and economic turbulence affecting international markets. Weak planning, uncertainties in the legal and administrative fields and the fragmentation of responsibilities between different actors, both at central and local level, all increase the country's vulnerability. Since the mid-1970s, Italy has been engaged in producing constantly revised energy plans. Their effective enforcement has been, nonetheless, only marginally pursued, mostly due to the favourable international situation of the 1980s and 1990s, which has allowed the country access for a long time to (relatively) cheap oil and gas, and to the resistance from different quarters to undertake some steps, perceived as painful, especially in the infrastructure sector, such as building the re-gasification plants seen as essential to increasing Italy's natural gas supply.

From this perspective, the Italian approach to energy security is prone to be seen through the lens of continuity. Lacking coherent political drive, in the past it has been largely delegated to 'technical' actors, especially to the state-owned companies operating in the energy sector. As has been noted, this is especially true with reference to ENI, whose action 'until the early 1970s, replaced the government's action in terms of the country's energy matters'.[5] In the following years, despite efforts made to reverse the situation and to define a national energy policy more or less comparable with that of the other European countries, results have been somewhat disappointing: domestic energy production has never really increased, while dependence has constantly grown with (imported) natural gas largely replacing (imported) oil. At the same time, growing needs have largely offset the benefits arising from the reduction of energy intensity, negatively affecting also overall national environmental performance. Neither has the 'European anchorage' provided by EU membership proved – up to now – any more successful, partly due to limitations of the European policy-making process, partly to inability to translate European guidelines into an effective national policy. However, in recent years, signs of change are emerging, both at grassroots and institutional levels. A growing consciousness of the environmental dimension – although often with strong emotional connotations – can play its part in promoting new patterns of consumption. Something similar can be said of the liberalization of the energy market that, breaking up the old energy monopolies, has led to a certain degree of differentiation on the supply side. Thirdly, increasing European commitment – despite the limits of a still often unrealistic approach – can act as a positive driving force, fostering better national governance and promoting 'virtuous' behaviour.

A brief historical sketch

Italy's dependence on fossil fuels dates back to the very beginning of its national industrial history and shaped it in many different, and sometimes conflicting, ways. It also explains the peculiar path of the country's economic development.[6] Since national unity, in the 1860s, and especially after the 1880s (the decade of the first, tentative, economic take-off), in only a few periods have energy imports accounted for less than 50 per cent of total domestic consumption. Between 1890 and 1914, coal accounted for the lion's share, gradually replacing wood and water as the main energy source (in 1913, it accounted for about 81,000 billion kcal of 144,000 billion kcal of total energy consumption). As a percentage, in 1910, coal's share was about 54 per cent, wood's share about 33 per cent and hydroelectric power's share about 11 per cent. Oil's contribution was negligible, with a share lower than 1 per cent. This state of affairs slowly evolved after World War One. Changes occurring in the energy mix were partly due to the need to overcome dependence on coal, whose price on the Italian market was significantly higher than in other countries. In the interwar period, hydroelectric power – which had been a key factor in the modernization of the industrial sector between the late 1880s and early 1910s, the so-called 'big spurt' – emerged as a cornerstone in this search for energy independence. In 1914, about 74 per cent of the installed electric power was hydroelectric. After the war, between 1921 and 1940, with the impulse of Mussolini's regime, this share rose further, growing from 1,292,000 to 5,198,000 kW. In the same period electricity production rose from 4.5 to 20 billion kWh, 90 per cent of which was hydroelectric.[7]

The other pillar of the new autarchic policy was oil. In the interwar period, oil's contribution to the national energy mix gradually grew, passing from a 4.6 per cent share in 1920 to 7.9 and 8.8 per cent in 1930 and 1940 respectively. A strong political drive lay behind this change. In 1926, Mussolini's government, upon the initiative of Giovanni Belluzzo (Minister of National Economy) and Count Giuseppe Volpi di Misurata (Minister of Finance), himself deeply involved in the energy sector as founder and president until 1943 of SADE (Società Adriatica di Elettricità), created AGIP (Azienda Generale Italiana Petroli). AGIP's task was to promote oil and gas research and production, both at home and abroad, and to refine and sell oil products on a domestic market then dominated by the duopoly of SIAP and NAFTA, the Italian branches of the two powerful multinational companies Standard Oil of New Jersey and Royal Dutch-Shell. In Mussolini's opinion, AGIP – de facto, a state-owned joint-stock company, whose shares were divided between the Ministry of the Treasury (60 per cent), the Instituto Nazionale delle Assicurazioni and the Assicurazioni Sociali (20 per cent each) – could also have been a political tool to promote Italian penetration in some key geopolitical areas, such as the Balkans and, to a lesser extent, the Middle East. This is another reason why an ad hoc legislation fostered its development until the outbreak of World War Two, although in the field of research and production results were 'absolutely negligible' and initiatives were 'de facto paralyzed by competing political and economic interests, both of a public and private nature'.[8] AGIP acquired, nonetheless, a relevant share in national refining capacity, especially through the incorporation of rival ROMSA and DICSA (the latter formerly owned by Count Volpi) and the creation of the ANIC joint venture between AIPA (Azienda Italiana Petroli Albanesi) and the privately owned Montecatini.

In the forty years between 1920 and 1960 (which are often seen as a single period in the history of Italian energy, despite the cleavage of World War

Two, of the civil war and of the shifting of political regimes), energy imports reached their lowest level, fluctuating between a minimum of 50 per cent (1920) and a maximum of 62 per cent (1930). In the same period total energy consumption steadily increased (with the exception of the war years) from 9.1 Mtoe to 48.2 Mtoe. In the same way, energy intensity increased too, although more unevenly (and it too with the exception of the war years) from 83.9 to 158.9 Toe per billion lira in 1985. Despite not breaking the overall continuity of the national energy policy and its emphasis on hydroelectric power as the main way to reduce foreign dependence, World War Two deeply affected the Italian energy sector. Allied bombing and – from September 1943 on – German requisitions and sabotage almost neutralized the efforts made in the late 1930s and early 1940s to increase domestic production, especially in the electricity sector and in the southern and central regions. Recovery was quite slow. In 1950, despite a growing population (46.9 million people against 44.9 million in 1940), a higher GDP (173.3 billion lira against 156.5 billion in 1940) and with the US-sponsored European Recovery Programme (ERP) almost fully operating, total energy supply (21.5 MToe) was still lower than in 1940 (21.7 MToe).

Between 1950 and 1960, energy imports fluctuated – in round figures – from 54 per cent to 58 per cent, being the second and the third best results since 1890. Until the second half of the 1950s, reduction of foreign dependence was still seen as a main political aim. To this end, ENI (Ente Nazionale Idrocarburi), the state-owned oil company, was formed in February 1953 with the task 'of promoting and enforcing initiatives, in the national interest, in the field of oil and natural gas' and 'of promoting and enforcing initiatives, in the national interest, in the chemical sector and in the research, production, regeneration and selling of nuclear fuels, and in the mining sector pertaining to these activities'. ENI inherited, thus, the former AGIP's role both at national and international level, and during the years it absorbed, as different branches, some of the most important actors operating in the domestic energy sector, in the petrochemical and in related industries, such as AGIP itself, ANIC, SNAM, ROMSA, SAIPEM, Snamprogetti, Liquigas and Officine del Pignone (afterwards Nuovo Pignone). From its creation, ENI also exerted exclusive rights in the exploitation of the (few) resources discovered in the Po Valley (Podenzano, Caviaga, Ripalta, Cortemaggiore, etc.) and became, in the mid-1950s, an important element in Italian foreign policy, especially towards the newly independent states of North Africa, the Middle East and the Soviet Union.[9] In this period, electricity generation increased too, with the opening – in the mid-1960s – of the first nuclear plants (Latina, Garigliano and Trino Vercellese) providing 3.9 billion kWh (about 4 per cent of total domestic production in 1966), and with the mix shifting from hydro- to thermoelectric. In 1965, the traditional dominance of the hydroelectric sector had been, de facto, reversed. Its contribution to total generation declined from 82 per cent in 1960 to 52 per cent in 1965, while the contribution of oil grew in the same five years from 7 per cent to 33 per cent, to reach 49 per cent in 1970 and 62 per cent in 1973.

Despite the expectations generated by the discovery of oil and gas reserves in the Po Valley, an ageing but still viable hydroelectric sector (according to some estimates, hydroelectric potential accounted for between 50 and 60 billion kWh, with about 45 billion actually exploited in the mid-1960s) and a greater presence on the international markets, the ambitions in terms of self-sufficiency (or, at least, of lower international dependence) nurtured in pre- and immediate post-war years were generally frustrated, and after the mid-1960s overtly abandoned except in small circles. The target to mini-mize an unavoidable external dependency was also only randomly pursued, especially after the crisis of 'neo-Atlantism' and the softening of ENI's aggres-sive commercial penetration following Enrico Mattei's death in 1962.[10] Easy access to cheap oil granted by a favourable international situation (in real terms, between 1961 and 1970, the oil price was about 1.8 dollars/bbl, with a retail price ranging from 10 to 7.3 dollars/bbl) was the main factor accounting for this change. Cheap oil also favoured a general increase in energy inten-sity (with some negative effects on overall efficiency), with the figure rising to 206.7 Toe per billion lira in 1965, to 229.8 Toe per billion lira in 1970 and to 238.9 Toe per billion lira in 1973, and a parallel increase of energy con-sumption. In 1973, at the time of the first oil shock, Italian per capita energy consumption – which in the 1950s was significantly lower than that of the other developed countries – had became roughly equal to the French one and had reached a level more than half of the American one. Quite obviously, oil's share in the national energy mix had grown dramatically too (passing from 22.1 per cent in 1950, to 44 per cent in 1960, 72.6 per cent in 1970 and about 75.3 per cent in 1973), and natural gas had entered the mix, with its share fluctuating between 11 per cent (1960) and 8 (1965) per cent.

The two oil shocks in 1973 and 1979 only partially affected this state of affairs, leading to a decrease in energy intensity per GDP unit (from 238.9 Toe per billion lira in 1973 to 194.4 Toe per billion lira in 1980) but not to a per-manent decline in energy imports (from 82 per cent to 83 per cent in the same period). Energy efficiency significantly increased, especially after 1979, when world oil prices, in real terms, jumped almost overnight from 27.9 \$/bbl to 58.9 \$/bbl (12.91 \$/bbl to 29.82 \$/bbl at current prices). Another important change affected the energy mix, with natural gas gaining an increasingly relevant weight, both in final consumption and in the field of electricity generation (from 10.2 per cent to 18.7 per cent and from 3 per cent to 13 per cent respectively between 1973 and 1985). However, these changes had been somehow reverted from the mid-1980s, and especially from 1985–6, when a change in Saudi Arabia's policy led to a general fall (sometime labelled as the 'third oil shock'[11]) in world oil prices, which plummeted, in real terms, from 35.7 \$/bbl to 17.5 \$/bbl (from 27.52 \$/bbl to 13.84 \$/bbl at current prices). It is worth noting that the oil shocks (both in the 1970s and 1980s) and the changes they triggered in domestic patterns of consumption did not significantly affect – in the long run – Italy's energy dependency, which had reached about 80 per cent of domestic consumption in 1970. In the following years, the figure fluctuated between 81 per cent and 83 per cent, reaching its peak in 1990. The increasing role of hydrocarbon in electricity generation (despite the ongoing shift from oil to natural gas) largely offset reductions in private and industrial consumption. Alternative energy sources too continued to play an almost negligible role, with geothermal (the better rooted alternative source) accounting for only 1 per cent of electricity generation between 1975 and 1985.

Present-day situation

Despite changes affecting the normative framework, in the 1990s and in the first years of the following decade few real changes took place in Italy's patterns of consumption, excluding a fast-paced substitution of oil for natural gas (both in the intermediate and final markets), mostly due to environmental concerns. Forecasts by the Ministry for Economic Development see this trend continuing in the next few years, pushing gas to a 40 per cent share of domestic energy needs by 2020 and surpassing oil, whose share – in the same year – is forecast at 37.5 per cent.[12] According to the Economist Intelligence Unit, in 2006 Italian energy imports amounted for roughly 98 per cent of total energy supply, with oil (45 per cent of primary energy supply) and natural gas (35 per cent of primary energy supply) accounting for just over 85 per cent of imported energy sources.[13] According to the figures provided by Eurostat, the statistical office of the European Communities, in 2005 Italy's net energy imports accounted – in absolute terms – for 160.74 Mtoe, i.e. 86.1 per cent of gross inland consumption (186.77 Mtoe), with a slight and uneven rising trend in comparison to mid-1990s figures. Oil imports accounted for 79.42 Mtoe and gas imports 59.84 Mtoe, i.e. 95.5 per cent and 84.7 per cent of gross inland consumption respectively. As for forecasts, according to the 2005 update of the *European Energy and Transport: Trends to 2030*[14] (which, compared to Eurostat, slightly underestimates 2005 figures, assessing 156.4 Mtoe as net energy imports and 180.98 Mtoe as gross inland consumption), in 2015 net imports will be 168.84 Mtoe (86.6 per cent of the gross inland consumption), somewhat confirming Italy's structural imbalance in the hydrocarbon sector. Figures from other sources are roughly comparable. According to the US Energy Information Administration (EIA), for example, in 2006 Italy imported about 1.7 billions bbl/d of crude oil (91 per cent of the country's domestic consumption), and about 2.3 Tcf of natural gas (82 per cent of the country's domestic consumption). It is worth noting that, unlike many other OECD countries, Italy still relies on oil for quite a large portion of its electricity generation: preliminary International Energy Agency (IEA) data for 2005 quoted by EIA show that Italy relied upon oil for 16 per cent of its electricity generation, versus 5 per cent for the OECD as a whole.[15]

This state of things is partly due to Italy's long-lasting decision to do without nuclear energy. Italy closed and deactivated its four nuclear plants – opened in the mid-1960s and located in Latina (near Rome), Caorso (in the Po Valley), Trino Vercellese (near Turin), and on the Garigliano river (between Rome and Naples) – between 1987 and 1988, following a referendum held on 8 November 1987, and deeply influenced by the emotional impact of the Chernobyl incident (26 April 1986). Following the referendum, the country also stopped the building of new plants, and reconverted some structures (such as Montalto di Castro, in the Po Valley) to thermo-electric. In the mid-to-long term, the closing of Trino and Caorso,[16] the obsolescence of the hydroelectric grid, and its reaching of almost full capacity (under the then prevailing economic constraints), together with a steadily increasing domestic demand (352,826 GWh in 2005, +1.1 per cent compared to 2004), have led to growing dependence also in the field of electricity (49.1 TWh in 2005). According to Terna – Rete Elettrica Nazionale (the operator of the electricity transmission grid), between 1986 and 1987, generation from nuclear sources dropped from 8,758 to 174 Gw, while in 1988 Italy's imports grew to 31,256 Gw from 23,146 Gw in the previous year. According to the same source, in 2006 electricity imports accounted for 44,985 Gw on 337,495 Gw of total demand (13.3 per cent).[17] Italy's main providers are France (whose nuclear plants provide some 76 per cent of total energy consumption), Greece, Switzerland and Slovenia, with an increasing role for the latter two after the opening of new connections in mid-2000. Summing up direct electric imports and fossil fuel imports related to electric generation (the sector's reliance on oil and gas is around 80 per cent, with an increasing role of gas, presently contributing a 44 per cent share), Italy's dependence in this sector is around 84 per cent.[18]

From a normative point of view, the liberalization of the domestic market, the privatization of ENI (the privatization law was passed in 1992, but the first stocks had been sold in 1995 only) and ENEL (1999), and the end of the de jure or de facto monopoly that they had held in their respective sectors with the split of the production stream among different companies, have led to a relevant increase in the number of subjects operating in the energy industry. In turn, this has favoured the flourishing of projects to increase supply, and to a certain degree of differentiation among suppliers. Presently, both ENI and ENEL are still 30 per cent state-controlled (partly through the 70 per cent state-controlled Cassa Depositi e Prestiti, holding a 10 per cent share of the two companies). National government also enjoys special rights through the so-called 'golden share', which grants it – independently from effective stock ownership – wide and somewhat contested powers of veto and governance, allows it to limit stock ownership by certain actors, and poses tight barriers to the right to vote. Although the situation is still quite fluid, in this sense the two former state-owned companies can still be seen as the main actors in the Italian energy industry, and state involvement in the sector is still deep and largely permanent. The public role is relevant in the field of the alternative and renewable energies too, whose exploitation had been actively (although not always efficiently) promoted in recent years. It is worth noting that, despite alternative and renewable energies having always played quite a relevant role in the Italian energy mix (Italy was the first country to exploit geothermal energy, with Larderello plants in 1904, and was, until the 1970s, one of the main European producers of geothermal energy) and despite the often-contended commitment to promoting their use, efforts seem not to have led to significant benefits (for example, according to Sorgenia, in 2005, renewable energies provided 16.4 per cent only – 49,920 GWh – of total electricity generation, significantly less than the 22 per cent target fixed by the EU for 2010), while shortcomings in the legislative and administrative framework cast a dim light on the sector's future development.

In both the oil and natural gas sectors, Italian suppliers are quite concentrated. Libya provides 27 per cent of total national oil imports (458,000 bbl/d), followed by Russia (268,000), Saudi Arabia (195,000), Iran (183,000), Iraq (130,000) and Azerbaijan (108,000), the balance being made by smaller suppliers accounting for 316,000 bbl/d. The situation on the gas market is similar, with Algeria providing 38 per cent of total gas imports, followed by Russia (32 per cent), the Netherlands (14 per cent), and minor partners form Africa and Northern Europe (16 per cent).[19] The Persian Gulf as a whole (especially Saudi Arabia, Iran and Iraq) is the main geographic region from which Italy draws its energy, while Russia is a key supplier in both the oil and gas sector. In the past, reliance on Russian gas has led to recurrent supply crises, the most severe one being in the winter of 2006, following quarrels between Moscow and Ukraine on the issue of transit rights. The lack of domestic production (110.000 bbl/d of crude oil in 2006 and 0.5 Tcf of natural gas in 2004, with proven reserves accounting for 0.6 trillion bbl and 5.8 Tcf respectively[20]) increases Italian vulnerability, and despite minor changes, dependence from the international markets will remain, in the foreseeable future, a structural trait of the national energy structure.

Negative implications of Italian exposure have been emphasized, both at European and national level. As has previously been said, since the mid-1970s, Italy has been engaged in producing constantly revised energy plans. However, still lacking a fully-fledged national energy strategy such as the one envisaged in the 1998 *US Comprehensive National Energy Security*, in the *Energy Policy Act* of 2005, in *US National Security Strategy* and in the US National Economic Council's *Advanced Energy Initiative* of February 2006,[21] the country has largely endorsed (at least at a formal level) European indications, whose last version was expressed in the EU *Energy Action Plan 2007–2009* (EAP).[22] Supplementing the Green Paper, *Towards a European Strategy for the Security of*

Energy Supply (2002),[23] EAP aims, among the other things, at '[addressing] the crucial issue of security of energy supply and the response to potential crises... [improving] the EU's bilateral cooperation with all suppliers... [ensuring] reliable energy flows into the Union... [and developing] clear orientations for an effective European international energy policy speaking with a common voice'. It also provides binding indications with the task of saving 20 per cent of the EU's energy consumption compared to projections for 2020 estimated by the EU Commission in its Green Paper on energy efficiency,[24] and to make good use of member countries' National Energy Efficiency Action Plans for this purpose; of reaching the binding target of a 20 per cent share of renewable energies in overall EU energy consumption by 2020, with a 10 per cent minimum target to be achieved by all member states for the share of biofuels in overall EU transport petrol and diesel consumption by 2020; and of achieving at least a 20 per cent reduction of greenhouse gas emissions by 2020 compared to 1990. Related to this, the European Council has also endorsed an EU objective of a 30 per cent reduction in greenhouse gas emissions by 2020 compared to 1990 as its contribution to a global and comprehensive agreement for the period beyond 2012 (the expiry date of the Kyoto Protocol), 'provided that other developed countries commit themselves to comparable emission reductions and economically more advanced developing countries to contributing adequately according to their responsibilities and respective capabilities'.[25]

Infrastructures and geopolitics

With regard to this, Italy's efforts to override its present condition focus on a 'whole azimuth' strategy, aimed at differentiating the supply markets, strengthening the commercial ties already existing with old partners, forging new links in the areas adjoining the Mediterranean basin and putting on stream still unexploited national reserves (both old and new), especially in central and southern regions (Val d'Agri, L'Aquila, Tempa Rossa) and in Sicily (Vega, Gela, Ragusa). Private companies are the key actors both in developing and carrying out this strategy. Special attention is also paid to the LNG sector with the aim of making Italy a LNG regional hub, and interventions on the national energy mix are envisaged as fostering the role of renewable sources, such as Eolian and geothermal. It is worth noting that, in 2006, Italy ranked fourth among the EU countries after Germany, Spain and Denmark in terms of installed wind energy (2123 MW; +23.6 per cent on 2005 1718 MW installed), and in 2005 was first in geothermal electricity production (5033 gWh on an EU total of about 5190 gWh). Finally, pressures exist to revise the traditional anti-nuclear politics. In spring 2008, the national government has endorsed the 'nuclear option', too. This is a relevant turning point in European energy alignments, since a group of member countries including Austria, Denmark, Portugal and Spain are opposed to using nuclear power as an energy source while, conversely, countries like

Italy, Germany, Sweden, the UK and the Netherlands, that were formerly opposed, and/or had bans against using nuclear power, are now supporting nuclear development.[26]

In the international field, in terms of fossil fuels, the Middle East and North Africa remain the key points of reference. In 2002, Algerian Sonatrach signed a $2 billion deal with a consortium comprising the Italian EnelEnergia, Edison Gas, EOS Energia, Progemisa e SFIRS and the German Wintershall, to link the Hassi R'Mel gas field (which fuels the huge Transmed/TTPC pipeline) to Sardinia and to mainland Italy (Castiglione della Pescaia) by 2009/2010. The Galsi (Gazoduc ligne directe Algérie-Italie) pipeline is approximately 900 kilometres long, more than 300 km of which are in waters over 2000 metres deep, and have an initial capacity of 9/10 Bcm/y. In 2005, Sonatrach also signed letters of intent with twelve potential natural gas purchasers, covering the entire planned capacity of the system.[27] Libya also improved its position with Greenstream, approaching full capacity at 8 Bcf/year (out of 10 Bcf/year from the fields of Wafa and Bahr Essalam).[28] ENI, which built the Greenstream and operates the Western Libyan Gas Project, is also widely involved in the Gulf, especially in Iran (where it operates South Pars gas field, the Darquain, Dorood and Balal oilfields and a series of technical infrastructures comprising the South Pars onshore gas treatment plant), Saudi Arabia (where it entered in 2004 with an exploration licence for a 51,687 km^2 area in the Rub al-Khali basin, at the border with Qatar and the United Arab Emirates) and Oman.[29] But Italy is also involved in the Eastern Mediterranean, in the development of alternative routes to the congested Bosporus Straits. The Italian presence in Central Asia and the Caucasus dates back to the early 1990s and includes – among others – a 32.5 per cent share in the Karachaganak gas and oil field and an 18.52 per cent share in the North Caspian Sea Production Sharing Agreement (NCPSA) on the Kashagan field.[30] ENI is also a member of the CPC (Caspian Pipeline Consortium), the owner of a 5 per cent share in the Baku-Tbilisi-Cehyan (BTC) pipeline, and 50 per cent owner (together with Russian Gazprom, with which, in November 2006, it had signed a strategic partnership agreement envisaging common activities in the up, mid and downstream sectors) of the Netherlands-based joint venture Blue Stream Pipeline B.V., a key partner in the Blue Stream, the 1213 km-long trans-Black Sea underwater gas pipeline, which is expected to reach its full capacity of 16 Bcf/year by 2010.[31]

From this point of view, infrastructures play an essential role in the framework of the Italian energy security strategy. By 2015, the Italian government has the financing of four new natural gas import plants planned (final locations to be defined among a wide range of potential competitors), accounting for 8 Bcm/year each, stipulating that, by 2010, LNG should account for at least 30 per cent of total natural gas supply. Among private companies, in 2006 Edison planned to line up eleven projects by 2010, including the Galsi, the ITGI project (a gas corridor linking Turkey to Italy via Greece) and nine LNG plants at Brindisi, Livorno, Rosignano, Gioia Tauro, Priolo, Taranto, Zaule, Trieste and Porto Empedocle, with an overall capacity of 27 Bcm/year.[32] The opening of new links between the Black Sea, Eastern Europe and the Mediterranean would increase Italian reliance on Central Asian and Caucasus oil and gas, and reduce national dependency on its traditional supply markets. It is worth noting that EAP (2007–9) suggests 'intensifying the EU relationship with Central Asia, the Caspian and the Black Sea regions, with a view to further diversifying sources and routes'.[33] EAP states also that 'regarding coordinators [of the documents] and without prejudice to further appointments, the Council notes that in its Communication, the Commission envisages the following projects: the Power-Link between Germany, Poland and Lithuania; connections to offshore wind power in Northern Europe; electricity interconnections between France and Spain; and the Nabucco pipeline, bringing gas from the Caspian to central Europe'.[34] From an Italian perspective, the opening of these links, coupled with a general improvement of the LNG sector, would enhance the country's role as one of the main energy hubs in the central Mediterranean, and strengthen its overall position in the European oil and gas industry. Italian involvement in the Turkish energy market (through ENI, Saipem and Snamprogetti, but also through newcomers such as Edison and EnelEnergia) is one of the pillars of this strategy.[35] It is worth noting that ENI is an important partner in the main infrastructural projects involving Turkey, i.e. CPC, BTC, the most recent TAP (Trans-Anatolian Project, or Samsun-Ceyhan pipeline), and the Kirkuk-Ceyhan pipeline. The other pillar is the development of stronger ties with Russia, epitomized by the strategic agreement signed with Gazprom, by the acquisition of Yukos through the Enineftegas consortium (60 per cent ENI; 40 per cent Enel) in April 2007, and by the recent (June 2007) signing of a MOU between ENI and Gazprom for the building of the new 'South Stream' pipeline, planned to carry 30 billion cubic metres of gas annually.

However, this strategy is likely to face strong international competition. Both the EU and the US have shown their concerns about the long-term political implications of the South Stream project, which would make Russia – according to its critics – the dominant actor in the European gas market. Vladimir Socor, on Jamestown Foundation's *Eurasia Daily Monitor*, for example, has pointed out that 'the project at this stage seems politically motivated to intensify competition among European countries for limited amounts of Russian gas', and that 'South Stream significantly increases Russia's options to play consumer countries and various national energy champions in Europe against each other'.[36] The *Wall Street Journal* and the *International Herald Tribune* have voiced similar concerns too, while analysts and investors have pointed out how the South Stream and Nabucco projects dangerously target the same markets of delivery. Finally, new and aggressive Russian pipeline politics has raised concerns in Turkey, whose long-coveted ambitions to become the main Mediterranean hub for Caspian and Central

Asian energy resources would be ultimately thwarted by the opening of a more direct link between Russia and Italy. From Ankara's point of view, one of the South Stream side effects is that

> Gazprom is looking to consign Turkey to a lesser transit role. Rather than serve as the main bridge for Central Asian gas to Europe, Turkey may be left in a position to accept Russia's lesser offer to serve as a north–south bridge for Russian gas to Israel. [Alexander] Medvedev [Deputy Chairman of Gazprom's Management Committee and Director General of Gazprom Export] noted that the South Stream proposal does not mean that Gazprom and ENI have abandoned a plan for 'Blue Stream-2' from Russia to Turkey via the Black Sea. However, he said that the focus of the second pipeline via Turkey would be aimed at supplying the Middle East, namely Israel but also possibly Lebanon, rather than Southern Europe.[37]

Turkey's problematic relations with the EU are another important element to deal with. In this sense, and despite the uncertainties still surrounding the EU INOGATE and TRACECA programmes, an all-European route reaching Vienna and/or the Adriatic coast through the Eastern and Western Balkans (such as Nabucco, benefiting from large EU support, or the trans-Balkan pipeline) seems to enjoy greater favour than a largely Anatolian one, gravitating towards the southeastern Mediterranean, and enhancing Ankara's bargaining power. Political and economic considerations, both at domestic and international level, will, thus, intermingle in defining the Italian strategy's effective viability. Nor should we forget the role that Asia's increasing energy demand will play in the future, and the effects it will have on the commercial decisions of the former Soviet Republics and of the Gulf countries.

Notes

1. On alternative definitions of energy security, see D. Yergin, 'Ensuring Energy Security', *Foreign Affairs*, Vol. 85, No. 2, 2006, pp. 69–82; see also A. F. Alhaji, 'What is Energy Security?', *Middle East Economic Survey*, 2007, http://www.mees.com/postedarticles/oped, accessed 28 February 2008.
2. R. Paris, 'Human Security: Paradigm Shift or Hot Air?', *International Security*, Vol. 25, No. 2, 2001, pp. 87–102; on an effort to reach a conceptual understanding of human security, see M. Weissberg, 'Conceptualizing Human Security', *Swords & Ploughshares*, Vol. 13, No. 1, 2003, pp. 3–11.
3. See M. McDonald, 'Human Security and the Construction of Security', *Global Society*, Vol. 16, No. 3, 2002, pp. 277–95; see also S. Loregan et al., *Global Environmental Change and Human Security: Science Plan*, IHDP Report Series, No. 11 (Bonn: IHDP, 1999), http://www.ihdp.uni-bonn.de, accessed 28 February 2008.
4. An overview of the debate is in *Limes. Rivista Italiana di Geopolitica*, No. 6, 2006; a supplement is at http:// limes.espresso.repubblica.it/2007/11/23/il-clima-dellenergia-20/?p=359, accessed 28 February 2008.

5. G. Sapelli and F. Carnevali, *Uno sviluppo tra politica e strategia: ENI (1953–1985)* (Milan: Franco Angeli, 1992); see also G. Sapelli, L. Orsenigo, P. A. Toninelli and C. Corduas, *Nascita e trasformazione d'impresa: Storia dell'Agip Petroli* (Bologna: Il Mulino, 1993).

6. P. A. Toninelli, 'La questione energetica', in F. Amatori et al. (eds), *Storia d'Italia: Annali 15, L'industria* (Turin: Einaudi, 1999), pp. 352–84; more in depth, see P. A. Toninelli, 'Il processo di industrializzazione: tipologie e modelli', in P. A. Toninelli (ed.), *Lo sviluppo economico moderno: Dalla rivoluzione industriale alla crisi energetica (1750–1973)* (Venice: Marsilio, 1997).

7. See R. Giannetti, *La conquista della forza: Risorse, tecnologia e economia nell'industria elettrica italiana* (Milano: Franco Angeli, 1985).

8. Toninelli, 'La questione energetica', pp. 372–3, quoting Sapelli et al., *Nascita e trasformazione d'impresa*. On AGIP's 'geopolitical' role see the trilogy by M. Pizzigallo, *Alle origini della politica petrolifera italiana 1920–1925* (Milan: Giuffrè, 1981), *L'Agip degli anni ruggenti (1926–1932)* (Milan: Giuffrè, 1984) and *La 'politica estera' dell'Agip (1937–1940): Diplomazia economica e petrolio* (Milan: Giuffrè, 1992).

9. On the political aspects of ENI's dealings with the USSR, see B. Bagnato, 'Diplomazia petrolifera e diplomazia italiana: il caso del contratto ENI-SNE dell'ottobre 1960', in M. Guderzo and M. L. Napolitano (eds), *Diplomazia delle risorse: Le materie prime e il sistema internazionale nel Novecento* (Florence: Polistampa, 2004), pp. 177–203; on ENI's North African and Middle Eastern policy see B. Bagnato, *Petrolio e politica. Mattei in Marocco* (Florence: Polistampa, 2004), and A. Tonini, 'L'ENI alla ricerca di un partner arabo: Egitto e Iraq, 1688–62', in Guderzo and Napolitano (eds), *Diplomazia delle risorse*, pp. 205–23; on ENI's Persian policy and on the 1957 deal inaugurating the so-called 'formula Mattei' on the joint management of oil reserves see E. H. Wall, 'The Iranian-Italian Oil Agreement of 1957', *International and Comparative Law Quarterly*, Vol. 7, No. 4, 1958, pp. 736–52; J. P. C. Carey, 'Iran and Control of its Oil Resources', *Political Science Quarterly*, Vol. 89, No. 1, 1977, pp. 147–74.

10. On Mattei's political strategy and its links with Neo-Atlantism, see L. Maugeri, *L'arma del petrolio: questione petrolifera globale, guerra fredda e politica italiana nella vicenda di Enrico Mattei* (Florence: Ponte alle Grazie, 1994); A. Tonini, *Il sogno proibito: Mattei, il petrolio arabo e le 'sette sorelle'* (Florence: Polistampa, 2003); and, more recently, G. Buccianti, *Enrico Mattei: assalto al potere petrolifero mondiale* (Milan: Giuffrè, 2005).

11. G. Philip, *The Political Economy of International Oil* (Edinburgh: Edinburgh University Press, 1991). Both the 1973 and the 1979 oil shocks hit the Italian economy severely; in those years, Italian energy needs were between 15 and 20 per cent higher than in the other industrial countries, its external dependency was 20 per cent higher than the EEC countries, and 45 per cent higher than in the OECD countries; it is worth noting that in Italy, energy intensity per GDP unit reached its peak in 1972, on the eve of the first oil shock.

12. Ministero dello Sviluppo Economico, *Scenario tendenziale al 2020* (Rome: Ministero dello Sviluppo Economico, 2005).

13. Economist Intelligence Unit, *Italy: Country Profile 2007* (New York: Economist Intelligence Unit, 2007), p. 28.

14. http://www.ec.europa.eu/dgs/energy_transport/figures/trends_2030_update_2005/energy_transport_ trends_2030_update_2005_en.pdf, accessed 28 February 2008.

15. US Department of Energy, Energy Information Administration, 'Italy', Country Analysis Briefs, 2007, http://www.eia.doe.gov/emeu/cabs/Italy/pdf.pdf, accessed 28 February 2008.
16. At the time of their deactivation, both Garigliano and Latina had already been stopped, the former in 1978, the latter in 1986; in 1985, nuclear plants had contributed about 1 per cent of total domestic energy supply, their best results since 1965. See Toninelli, 'La questione energetica', Table 2.
17. http://www.terna. it/default/Home/sistema_elettrico/statistiche/dati_storici/tabid/ 421/Default.aspx, accessed 28 February 2008. According to Ambrosetti (The European House, *Linee guida per la politica delle fonti energetiche primarie come chiave per la competitività e la sicurezza dell'Italia e dell'Europea in futuro* (Milan: Ambrosetti – The European House, 2007)), in 2005 the same figure was 14.9 per cent (49.1 TWh) on a gross domestic consumption of 352.8 TWh.
18. According to GSE – Gestore dei Servizi Elettrici S.p.A. – presently operating in the field of renewable energy sources, between 1 January and 31 May 2003, total import from these countries was about 22.8 billion kWh.
19. Energy Information Administration, 'Italy', Country Analysis Brief, p. 4; the Italian government provides slightly different figures:

Table 6.1   Natural gas import by country – standard Mcm at 38,1 MJ/m^3

	2002	*Share*	2003	*Share*	2004	*Share*	2005	*Share*
Algeria	24,158	40.7	24,561	39.1	25,632	37.7	27,464	37.4
Russia	20,713	34.9	21,688	34.5	23,624	34.8	23,326	31.8
Netherlands	7,825	13.2	7,630	12.2	8,074	11.9	8,040	10.9
Norway	4,884	8.2	5,030	8.0	5,190	7.6	5,723	7.8
Libya	–	–	–	–	521	0.8	4,493	6.1
Others EU	924	1.6	1,941	3.1	2,809	4.1	2,763	3.8
UK	770	1.3	1,253	2.0	1,120	1.6	543	0.7
Others non-EU	18	0.0	692	1.1	937	1.4	1,108	1.5
Total	59,291	100.0	62,794	100.0	67,908	100.0	73,460	100.0

Source: Ministero dello Sviluppo Economico – Direzione Generale dell'Energia e delle Risorse Minerarie – Osservatorio Statistico Energetico, http://dgerm.attivitaproduttive.gov.it/dgerm/ importazionigas.asp, accessed 28 February 2008.

20. Energy Information Administration figures; EU figures at http://ec.europa. eu/energy/energy_policy/doc/factsheets/mix/mix_it_en.pdf, accessed 28 February 2008, are slightly different, attesting 2004 oil production at 100,000 bbl/d and 2004 oil reserves at 0.5 trillion bbl; according to the same source, oil share in Italy's energy mix would be 45 per cent, versus a gas share of 36 per cent, the balance being made by solid fuels (9 per cent), renewable sources (7 per cent) and others (3 per cent).
21. US Department of Energy, *Comprehensive National Energy Strategy* (Washington D.C: US Department of Energy, 1998); *Energy Policy Act of 2005*, at http//www.doi.gov/iepa/EnergyPolicyActof2005.pdf; The President of the United States, *National Security Strategy of the United States of America* (Washington D.C.: White House, 2006), esp. VI, 'Ignite a New Era of Global

Economic Growth through Free Markets and Free Trade', pp. 25–30; the National Economic Council's Advanced Energy Initiative is at http://www.white house.gov/stateoftheunion/2006/energy/energy_booklet.pdf, accessed 28 February 2008.

22. See EU *Energy Action Plan 2007–2009* as Annex I at http://www.consilium.europa. eu/ueDocs/cms_Data/docs/pressData/en/ec/93135.pdf, accessed 28 February 2008; on Italian energy politics and the EU framework see Autorità per l'energia elettrica e il gas, *Relazione annuale sullo stato dei servizi e sulla attività svolta* (Rome: Autorità per l'energia elettrica e il gas, 2007).

23. http://ec.europa.eu/comm/energy_transport/doc-principal/pubfinal_en.pdf, accessed 28 February 2008.

24. http://ec.europa.eu/energy/efficiency/doc/2005_06_green_paper_book_en.pdf, accessed 28 February 2008.

25. EU, *Energy Action Plan 2007–2009*, p. 10.

26. Energy Information Administration, 'Country Analysis Brief: European Union', 2006, http://www.eia.doe.gov/emeu/cabs/European_Union/pdf.pdf, accessed 28 February 2008; according to EIA figures, in 2003, nuclear energy accounted for 14 per cent of total EU energy consumption, compared with 43 per cent for oil, 24 per cent for natural gas, and 13 per cent for coal.

27. On Sonatrach and Galsi activities in 2005 see Sonatrach's 'Rapport Annuel 2005' at http://www.sonatrach-dz.com/rap-2005fr.pdf, accessed 28 February 2008; in 2006 Sonatrach signed five sale/purchase agreements through the Galsi project with Edison, Enel, Hera, Ascopiave and Worldenergy; as stated in the 'Rapport Annuel 2006', the agreements concern a volume of 2 Gcm/year with Edison, 2 Gcm/year with Enel, 1 Gcm/year with Hera, 0.5 Gcm/year with Ascopiave and 0.5 Gcm/year with Worldenergy, and will help Sonatrach to achieve its export goal of 85 Gcm/year during 2010, 'in line with the Group's strategy to strengthen its position on the European natural gas market' (see http://www.sonatrach-dz.com/rapanu-2006fr.pdf, accessed 28 February 2008).

28. With its 520 kilometres, Greenstream (technically, the Libyan Gas Transmission System, or LGTS) is the longest underwater pipeline laid in the Mediterranean Sea; it is part of the Western Libyan Gas Project and includes the Mellitah compressor station, on the Libyan coast, the underwater gas pipeline and the reception terminal at Gela, in Sicily. Construction of the pipeline began in August 2003 and ended in February 2004; Bahr Essalam is an offshore field located 110 kilometres off the Libyan coast, while Wafa is an onshore field close to the border with Algeria. ENI is the operator, with a 50 per cent stake, for the joint development of the fields. The other partner, with an identical stake, is National Oil Corporation (NOC), the Libyan state-owned oil company.

29. Beyond Libya and the Middle East, ENI activities focus on a wide range of countries, comprising Algeria, Angola, Argentina, Australia, Austria, Brazil, China, Congo, Croatia, Egypt, France, Germany, Greece, Hungary, India, Indonesia, Ireland, Italy, Kazakhstan, Mozambique, Nigeria, Norway, Pakistan, Portugal, Russia, Slovenia, Spain, the Netherlands, Tunisia, Turkey, the United Kingdom, the United States and Venezuela.

30. Karachaganak is located in northwest Kazakhstan and is one of the world's largest oil and gas condensate fields; covering an area of over 280 km^2, it holds more than 1200 million tonnes of oil and condensate and over 1.35 Tcm of gas; the expansion of the field has involved an investment of over \$4.3 billion and it is currently the biggest internationally funded project in Kazakhstan; the field

development has being overseen by the Karachaganak Petroleum Operating B.V. (KPO), comprising British BG Group and ENI, each with a 32.5 per cent interest, US Chevron with 20 per cent, and Lukoil with 15 per cent. The NCPSA contract area extends over a territory of 5600 km² and includes the giant Kashagan oil field, the Kashagan South West (SW), Aktote, Kairan and Kalamkas discoveries; Agip KCO (a company fully owned by ENI S.p.A. via AGIP Caspian Sea B.V.) is the single operator of the appraisal, development and future production operations in the Kazakhstan sector of the Caspian Sea on behalf of seven international companies and under the North Caspian Sea Production Sharing Agreement (NCPSA); members of the NCPSA are ENI S.p.A. (Agip Caspian Sea B.V.) with an 18.52 per cent share, JSC NC KazMunayGas (KMG Kashagan B.V.) with 8.33 per cent, ExxonMobil Kazakhstan Inc. with 18.52 per cent, Shell Kazakhstan Development B.V. with 18.52 per cent, Total E&P Kazakhstan with 18.52 per cent, ConocoPhillips (Phillips Petroleum Kazakhstan Ltd.) with 9.26 per cent, and INPEX North Caspian Sea Ltd. with 8.33 per cent. The Kashagan field was discovered in July 2000; it is currently estimated that it holds up to 38 billion barrels of oil-in-place of which 13 billion is potentially recoverable with the use of gas re-injection.

31. On the CPC see http://www.cpc.ru; on the BTC pipeline see http://www.btc.com. tr/eng/project.html; on the Blue Stream see the ENI presentation page at http://www.eni.it, all accessed 28 February 2008.

32. R. Potì (2006) 'Più energia. Più progresso', presentation at the Italian Energy Summit 2006, Milan, 27–29 September.

33. EU, *Energy Action Plan 2007–2009*, p. 19.

34. Ibid., p. 18; priority projects of European interest are listed in Decision 1364/2006/EC of the European Parliament and European Council, http://eurlex.europa. eu/LexUriServ/site/en/oj/2006/l_262/l_26220060922en00010023.pdf, accessed 28 February 2008; on the Nabucco pipeline (which is, among the projects quoted in the EAP, the most relevant to Italy's energy strategy) see the presentation at http://www.nabucco-pipeline.com. Shareholders in the Nabucco consortium are the German OMV Gas International GmbH, MOL Plc, Romanian Transgaz S.A., Bulgargaz Holding EAD, and the Turkish Botas AS, each of them holding a 20 per cent share of the total capital.

35. Among Edison's main projects, a special place is devoted to the ITGI Corridor. By 2012, the plan is for ITGI to allow Italy to import (Elio Ruggeri, ITGI Project Leader, Edison, in its official presentation dated 26 July 2007, adds the specification: 'for the first time') natural gas from the Caspian via Turkey and Greece, with an overall capacity of 8 Bcm/year. It envisages the strengthening of the Turkish network and the building of two connections between Turkey and Greece (ITG Project) and between Greece and Italy (IGI Project); the Turkey-Greece connection will be operative in August 2007 with an initial capacity of about 3.5 Bcm/year; by 2012, capacity is to increase to 11.5 Bcm/year; ITG will be operative on the Greek side by DESFA and on the Turkish side by BOTAS; the Greece-Italy connection will be operative by 2012 with an initial capacity of about 8 Bcm/year; the IGI Project envisages two legs, an onshore leg between Komotinialla and the Thesprotia coast to be built by DESFA, and an offshore leg (Poseidon pipeline) between the Thesprotia coast and Otranto, to be built by Edison and DEPA through a fifty-fifty joint venture.

36. V. Socor, 'South Stream: Gazprom's New Mega Project', *Eurasia Daily Monitor*, Vol. 4, No. 123, 25 June 2007. Quite a different opinion was expressed on 28 September 2007 by EU Energy Commissioner, Latvian Andris Piebalgs,

although he cast doubts on the actual feasibility of the project;   see K. Geropoulos, 'Piebalgs says Russia's South Stream future uncertain', *New Europe*, No. 749, 29 September 2007. On the role of pipelines in promoting Russia's geopolitical ambitions, see A. Cohen, 'Europe's Strategic Dependence on Russian Energy', *Backgrounders*, No. 2083, 5 November 2007; D. Helm, 'The Russian Dimension and Europe's External Energy Policy', 2007, http://www.dieterhelm.co.uk/publications/Russian_dimension.pdf, accessed 28 February 2008; and from an Italian perspective, A. Rosato, *La 'sicurezza energetica' nelle relazioni tra Unione Europea (Italia) e Federazione Russa* (Rome: Centro Militare di Studi Strategici, 2006), http://www.difesa.it/backoffice/upload/allegati/2007/%7B3A6111B0-76E4-4617-8D56-F62D3EA798E3%7D.pdf, accessed 28 February 2008.

37. A. Neff, 'South Stream pipeline threatens Turkey's role in gas transit to Europe', *Global Insight*, 26 June 2007, at http://acturca.wordpress.com/2007/07/03/south-stream-pipeline-threatens-turkeys-role-in-gas-transit-to-europe, accessed 28 February 2008.

7
Security of Supply: Spanish Policies in the EU Context

Javier de Quinto and Julián López

Energy security in the EU

The recent Green Paper on energy policy from the European Commission to the European Council and the European Parliament states that:

> Europe needs to act now, together, to deliver sustainable, secure and competitive energy ... The point of departure for a European energy policy is threefold: combating climate change, limiting the EU's external vulnerability to imported hydrocarbons, and promoting growth and jobs, thereby providing secure and affordable energy to consumers.[1]

The increasing import dependency of the EU, the concentration of oil and gas supplies in a limited number of net-exporting countries/regions in the world and the growing competition among consuming countries for scarce supplies have put security of energy supply high on the political agenda.

Energy import dependencies for the EU as a whole are increasing. Figure 7.1 gives an indication of these developments, with overall energy import dependency rising as much as up to 65 per cent in the next twenty-five years.

The EU as a whole currently receives slightly less than half of its natural gas from the United Kingdom, the Netherlands and other EU member states. Around 50 per cent of the gas consumed by the member states of the EU is imported, and three countries, Russia, Norway and Algeria, provide Europe with the bulk of its gas imports. Russia currently provides 25 per cent of that imported gas and that is expected to rise to over 30 per cent by 2015. Several EU member states are totally dependent on Russian natural gas for their domestic energy consumption. Gas imports are expected to reach 80 per cent by 2030. Table 7.1 illustrates the levels of dependency on imported natural gas in selected nations of the EU.

EU efforts to diversify European energy supplies and decrease dependence on Russia have heightened calls within Europe for stronger political and

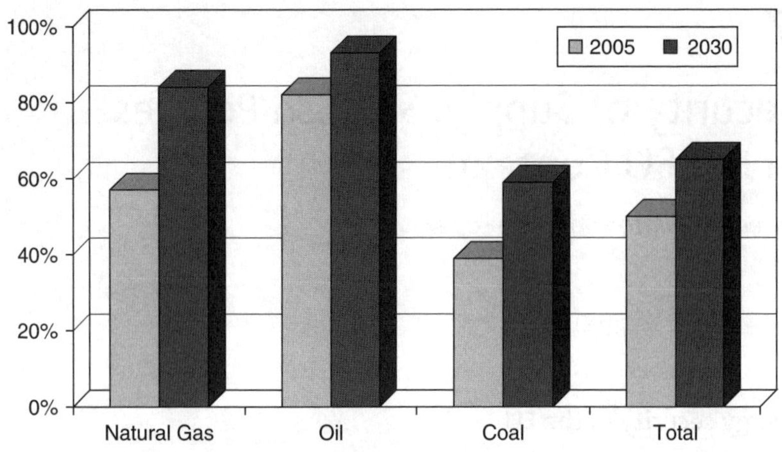

Figure 7.1   EU energy import dependencies
Source: European Commission Green Paper, *A European Strategy for Sustainable, Competitive and Secure Energy*, COM (2006) 105 final (Brussels: European Commission, 2006).

Table 7.1   Imported gas and gas from Russia (2005)

Country	Dependence on imported gas (%)	Total gas consumed, imported from Russia (%)
Austria	88	74
Czech Republic	98	70
Estonia	100	100
France	98	26
Finland	100	100
Germany	81	39
Italy	85	30
Poland	70	50

Source: V. L. Morelli, *The European Union's Energy Security Challenges*, CRS Report for Congress, Order Code RL33636 (Washington D.C.: Congressional Research Service, 2006).

economic engagement in the Middle East and North Africa. EU relations with North Africa were formalized in 1995 with the creation of the Euro-Mediterranean Energy Partnership. The EU has also created the EU-Gulf Cooperation Council (GCC) with the states of the Persian Gulf and has initiated a formal dialogue with the nations of OPEC. European energy companies have also become more involved in the Middle East.

Europe already depends on the Middle East/North Africa region for close to 30 per cent of its oil imports and approximately 15 per cent of its piped gas. The largest portion of that oil comes from Saudi Arabia, followed by

Libya and Iran. Europe's primary supplier of natural gas is Algeria, via two pipelines that enter Europe through Italy and Spain. A smaller amount comes from Libya via pipelines to Italy. Two additional gas pipelines from Algeria to Spain and Italy are under construction.

Perhaps the most important development for Europe in this region has been the growing availability of liquefied natural gas (LNG). Today, Europe accounts for approximately 8 per cent of the world's total consumption of LNG, and in 2005 LNG represented 15 per cent of European gas imports – a 21 per cent increase from 2004. The principal suppliers of LNG to Europe include Egypt, Oman, Qatar and Algeria, which is the world's third largest exporter of LNG, with almost all of its gas going to Europe.

The potential for growth in Europe's energy diversification strategy with respect to the Middle East and North Africa is significant. However, political instability in the region and strong competition for its energy resources from countries in Asia and North America will likely temper the degree to which Europe seeks to increase its reliance on the region.[2] Nevertheless, as in the Caspian region, Russia appears to be bolstering its efforts to influence Europe's energy plans: President Putin and several Gazprom officials have travelled to Algeria to discuss Russian participation in Algeria's future oil and gas projects, including its LNG export markets.

A major challenge facing the EU is the need to complete the internal gas and electricity markets. Many national markets are still harassed by protectionism and dominated by a few companies. Opening up these markets will create fair competition between companies at European level and improve the security of the energy supply.

Since July 2007 consumers have had the legal right to purchase gas and electricity from any supplier in the EU, but in order to make an internal energy market a reality, the following core areas need particular attention:

- A European grid with common rules and standards for cross-border trade is needed to give suppliers harmonized access to national grids.
- A priority interconnection plan to stimulate investment in infrastructure linking the various national grids, most of which are still not adequately interconnected.
- Investment in generation capacity to meet peaks in demand can be encouraged by opening up markets that are truly competitive.
- A more clear-cut unbundling of activities to distinguish clearly between those which generate and those which transmit and distribute gas and electricity. The confusion which is being created in certain countries is a form of protectionism.
- Energy regulators must be given not only the task of promoting the effective development of their national market, but also of promoting the development of the Internal Energy Market.

Opening up the markets is one way of guaranteeing a secure energy supply because it creates the stable, competitive environment in which companies invest. Given Europe's dependence on imported energy and fluctuations in demand, action is needed to ensure that there is an uninterrupted energy supply.

The EU is trying to establish effective mechanisms to create emergency stocks and foster solidarity to avoid energy supply crises. The Commission is proposing to create a European Energy Supply Observatory to monitor the energy market and identify potential shortfalls. It includes a mechanism for rapid solidarity that could be put in place for cases where a country's supply is in crisis following damage to its infrastructure.

The EU also needs adequate energy reserves to cope with potential supply disruptions. For this reason, the Commission also proposes re-examining existing legislation from the perspective of security of supply, particularly with regard to the EU's oil and gas stocks.

Encouraging the development and use of alternative energy supplies, including safe nuclear power, clean coal and renewable energy, will help to meet Europe's energy security goals. In the EU, each member state is free to choose its own energy mix from the sources available. These choices are important to the EU's energy security and could be coordinated at European level by means of a Strategic EU Energy Review.[3] The Commission is designing a Renewable Energy Road Map to create a stable environment in which to develop renewable energies. This Road Map must set the EU's specific objectives for 2020, subordinated to a binding target of a 20 per cent share of renewable energies in overall EU energy; and draw up a list of measures to promote the development of clean and renewable energy sources. Carbon capture and clean fossil fuel technologies must be encouraged too so that countries who choose to can keep carbon-based sources in their mix.

The competency of the EU in energy policy-making does not cover all three main goals, i.e. the market, the environment and security of supply. Both the internal energy market and the environment policies are based on an EU policy framework. Such a policy framework is nearly absent for security of supply, where the member states have largely maintained their national competence.[4]

Gas security of supply in Spain

Latest developments in the EU

The Community gas market is currently being liberalized, which is why there is a growing need to guarantee the security of gas supplies. The Gas Directive (2003/55/EC) recognizes the right of member states to regard security of supply as a public service obligation. This Directive established the common rules for the internal market in natural gas that enable member states to take the requisite measures to safeguard supply in the event of a sudden crisis in the energy market.

Directive 2004/67/EC, concerning measures to safeguard security of natural gas supply, establishes a common framework within which member states can define general security-of-supply policies that are transparent, solidarity-based, non-discriminatory and consistent with the requirements of a single market in gas. Member states must ensure that supplies for household customers inside their territory are protected at least in the event of the following circumstances.

- A partial disruption of national gas supplies during a period to be determined by member states, taking into account national circumstances.
- Extremely cold temperatures during a nationally determined peak period.
- Periods of exceptionally high gas demand during the coldest weather periods statistically occurring every 20 years.

At the same time, member states may extend the scope to small and medium-sized enterprises and other customers that cannot switch their gas consumption to other energy sources; set or require the industry to set indicative minimum targets for a possible future contribution of storage, either located within or outside the member state, for security of supply; take the appropriate measures in cooperation with another member state, including bilateral agreements, to achieve the security of supply standards using gas storage facilities located within that other member state; and adopt and publish national emergency provisions.

The Commission monitors, on the basis of reports from member states, the extent to which gas supply is covered, the level of gas in storage and the capacity of gas storage, the degree of interconnection of the national gas systems of member states and the foreseeable gas supply situation at Community level concerning specific geographic areas in the Community.

By 19 May 2008, the Commission will, in the light of the manner in which member states have implemented this Directive, report on the effectiveness of the instruments used and their effect on the internal gas market.

A Gas Coordination Group has been established to facilitate coordination of security of supply measures by the Community in the event of a major supply disruption. This group could also assist member states in coordinating measures taken at national level.

Gas consumption

The consumption of primary energy in Spain remains different to the European average value (Figure 7.2). Oil and natural gas dominate Spain's primary energy supply, with an aggregate 67 per cent of total. The consumption of both sources, but mainly of gas, has increased dramatically in recent years. The opening of the Spanish gas market has been completed for all

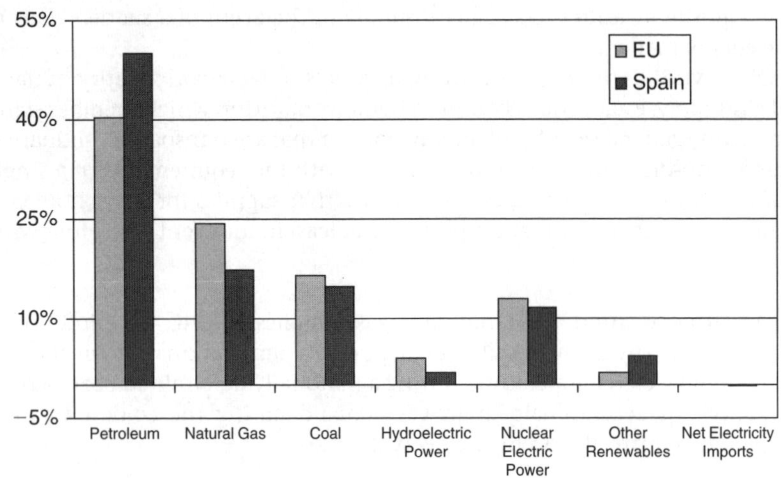

Figure 7.2   Consumption of primary energy in the EU and Spain (2004)
Source: Eurostat, http://epp.eurostat.ec.europa.eu.

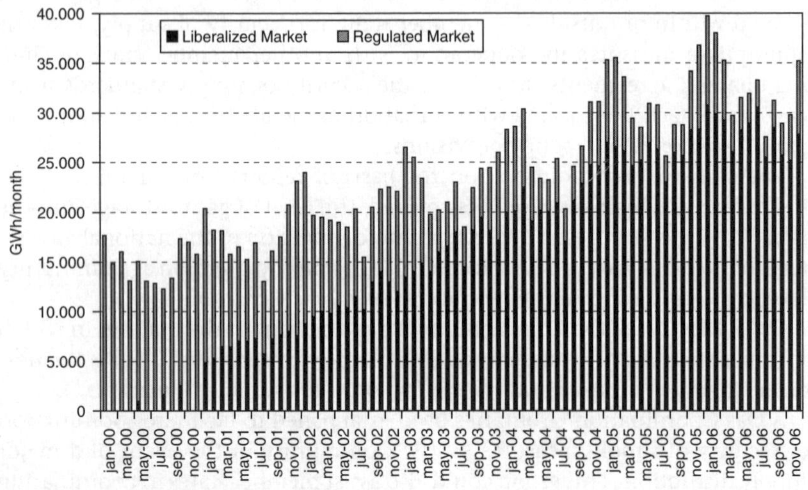

Figure 7.3   Consumption of gas in Spain
Source: Comisión Nacional de la Energía (CNE) (different years), *Boletín mensual de estadísticas de gas natural, febrero* (Madrid: CNE).

consumers since 2003, and a large share of demand has moved from the regulated to the liberalized market (Figure 7.3). The consumption of renewable sources has also increased significantly and in 2004 was at the EU average (6 per cent).

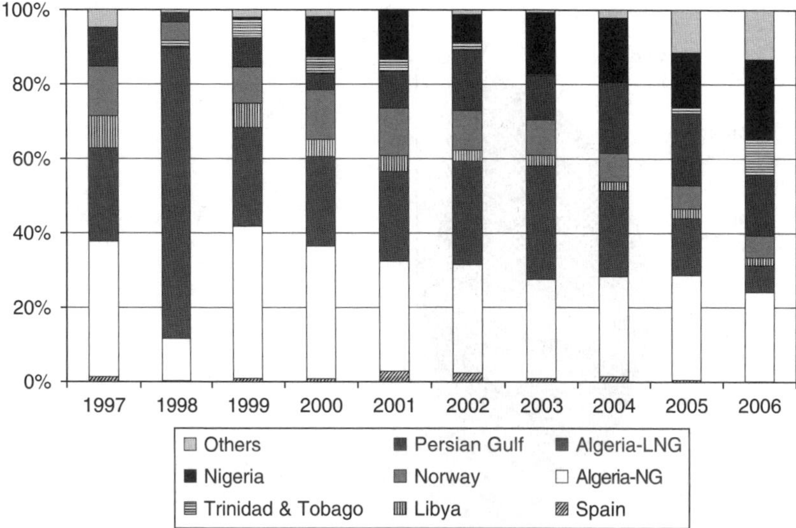

Figure 7.4   Geographical sources of supplies
Source: Comisión Nacional de la Energía (CNE) (different years), *Boletín informativo sobre la evolución del mercado de gas natural en la zona peninsular* (Madrid: CNE).

Diversification and security of supply

Spain is heavily import-dependent for its supply of natural gas with 99 per cent of gas coming from imports, both in the form of LNG and natural gas coming from pipelines with international connections (Figure 7.4 shows the geographical sources of supplies). Because of the high growth of gas consumption and the vulnerability of the Spanish import system to either technical problems, such as faults on the pipeline to North Africa, bad weather preventing unloading of LNG tankers, or competition for LNG from North America, the overall position with regard to security of gas supply has become weaker in recent years.

Spanish legislation establishes supply diversification on natural gas sources and limits the market share of gas providers: agents that deliver gas to the system must diversify their supplies in order to have less than 60 per cent of them coming from the main provider country (Algeria). There is also a market share restriction: the share of the gas supplied by each company is limited to a maximum of 70 per cent of national consumption. The entry of new retail traders has contributed to diversification (Figure 7.5): these companies have tried to get their own sources of supply, through agreements with firms that exploit the wells or build liquefaction plants in origin. The liberalization has also encouraged the entry of international groups (Figure 7.6), although their market shares are still low.

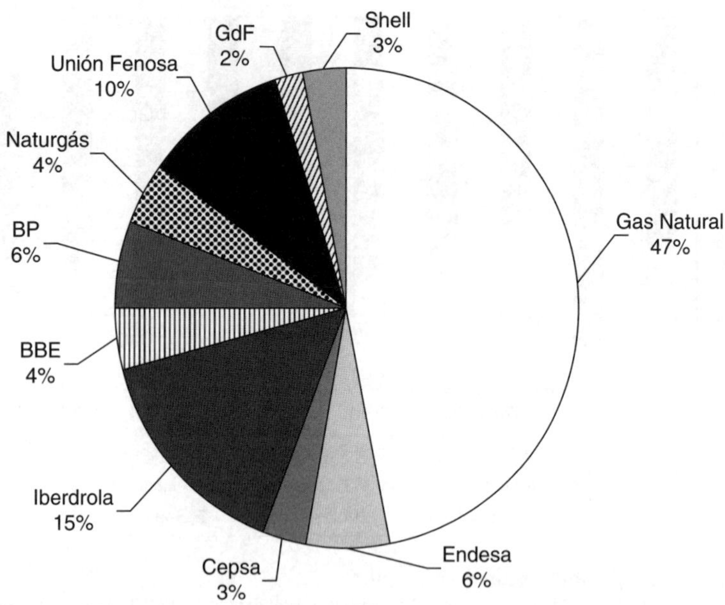

Figure 7.5   Supplies for the Spanish liberalized market
Source: Comisión Nacional de la Energía (CNE) (different years), *Boletín informativo sobre la evolución del mercado de gas natural en la zona peninsular* (Madrid: CNE).

The share of LNG is growing (Figure 7.7), and it increases the operation flexibility as well as the number of possible sources of supplies. With rising gas consumption in Spain, the volume of LNG is likely to increase in the future, despite the planned increase in Algerian deliveries through the MedGaz pipeline, due on line in 2008.

Other security of supply measures in the Spanish gas market

There are also other measures applied in the Spanish gas market in order to ensure security of supply.[5]

- A compulsory network planning (ten years ahead).
- Agents that deliver gas to the system (and consumers who take up their access entitlement and do not get their supply from an authorized trader) must maintain minimum security stocks corresponding to thirty-five days of their firm sales (or consumption).
- Emergency and exceptional situations have been defined and imbalance penalties have been established.

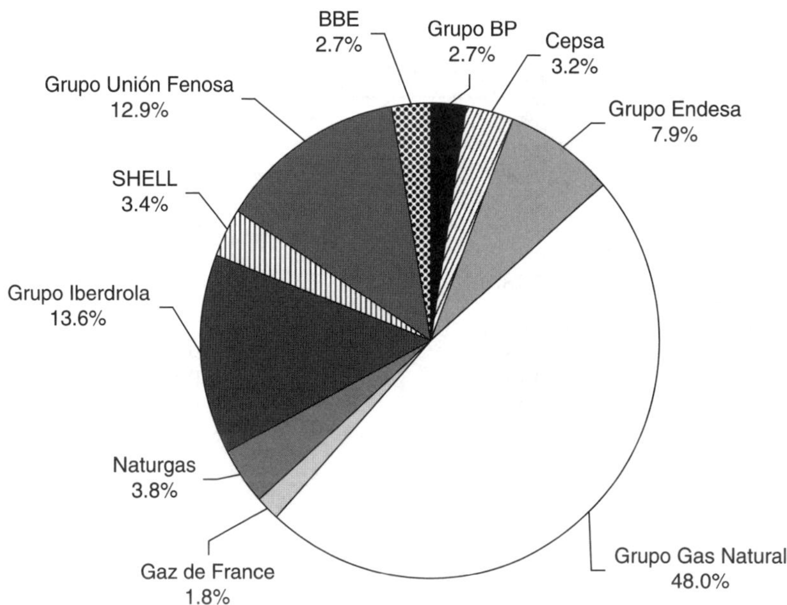

Figure 7.6 Market shares in retail supply
Source: Comisión Nacional de la Energía (CNE) (different years), *Boletín informativo sobre la evolución del mercado de gas natural en la zona peninsular* (Madrid: CNE).

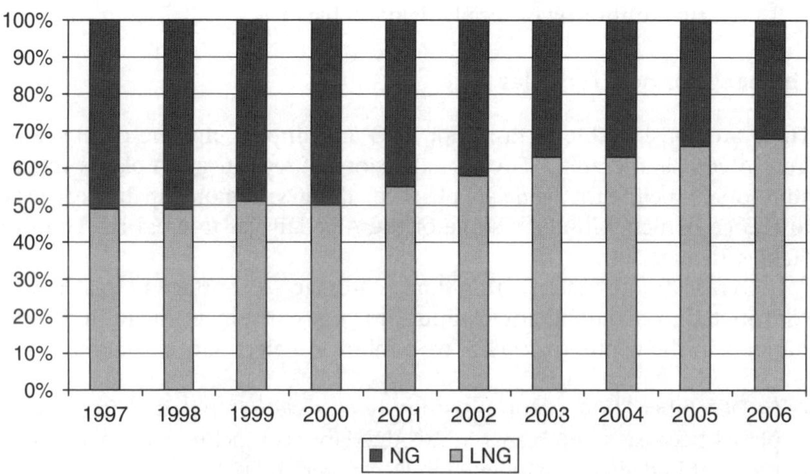

Figure 7.7 Natural gas and LNG shares
Source: Comisión Nacional de la Energía (CNE) (different years), *Boletín informativo sobre la evolución del mercado de gas natural en la zona peninsular* (Madrid: CNE).

Table 7.2   Capacity of regasification plants

LNG plant	Storage capacity (Mm³)	Regasification capacity Mm³(n)/h
Barcelona	0.54	1.65
Huelva	0.46	1.2
Cartagena	0.287	1.2
Bilbao	0.3	0.8
Sagunto	0.3	0.8
Mugardos	0.3	0.41
TOTAL (2007)	2.187	6.06
Additions to existing plants		
Barcelona	0.18	0.3
Huelva	0.15	0.15
Cartagena	0.3	0.15
Bilbao	0.3	0.4
Sagunto	0.3	0.4
New plants		
El Musel	0.3	0.8
TOTAL (2011)	3.717 (+70%)	8.26 (+36%)

Source: Comisión Nacional de la Energía (CNE) (different years), *Informe semestral de seguimiento de las infraestructuras referidas en el 'Informe marco sobre la demanda de energía eléctrica y gas natural, y su cobertura'* (Madrid: CNE).

- Supervision of supply–demand balance:
  - (a) Forecasts for five years.
  - (b) Yearly monitoring of supply-demand balance.

The need for new facilities

There are considerable facilities for LNG and import pipeline connections from Algeria and France.[6] Further extensions of regasification plants and an additional pipeline to Algeria are planned, along with more pipeline capacity to France, which will allow some of the Algerian gas to cross the country (Tables 7.2 and 7.3).

The critical bottleneck at this time is storage. A shortage of gas storage contributed to gas supply interruptions to large consumers, including power stations, in the winter of 2004/5, with follow-on electricity shortages:

- In December 2004, natural gas supply cuts were imposed at four power plants because of problems in an Algerian gas pipeline (another supply incident had already happened in December 2003).
- Another round of supply cuts were imposed in February 2005 because of bad weather preventing unloading of LNG tankers at the same time as a compressor failure on a supply pipeline.

Table 7.3 Capacity of import pipeline connections (Mm^3(n)/h)

	2007	*2011*
Larrau	0.28	0.58
GME	1.15	1.15
Tuy	0.04	0.04
Badajoz	0.15	0.15
Francia-Irun	0.057	0.285
Medgaz		0.913
TOTAL	1.677	3.119 (+86%)

Source: Comisión Nacional de la Energía (CNE) (different years), *Informe semestral de seguimiento de las infraestructuras referidas en el 'Informe marco sobre la demanda de energía eléctrica y gas natural, y su cobertura'* (Madrid: CNE).

Table 7.4 Extraction capacity of underground storage facilities (Mm^3(n)/h)

	2003	*2007*	*2011*
Serrablo	0.2875	0.2875	0.2875
Marismas		0.067	0.183
Gaviota	0.2375	0.2375	0.592
Poseidón			0.0625
Yela			0.625
Castor			1.042
TOTAL	0.525	0.592 (+13%)	2.792 (+472%)

Source: Comisión Nacional de la Energía (CNE) (different years), *Informe semestral de seguimiento de las infraestructuras referidas en el 'Informe marco sobre la demanda de energía eléctrica y gas natural, y su cobertura'* (Madrid: CNE).

The impact of the natural gas supply cuts in December 2004 and February 2005 could have been minimized if there had not been a shortage of storage facilities. The need for flexibility tools for the management of the system will increase as the grid expands and residential consumption grows. Therefore, the development of underground storage facilities is a critical concern for Spain's security of supply, both in gas and electricity (Table 7.4).

Moreover, underground storage facilities serve several functions including:

- Strategic reserves for security of supply in case of disruption.
- Seasonal load balancing to match peak demand.
- Achieving daily balance.
- Transmission support, such as mitigating localized capacity constraints or critical pressure thresholds.

Insufficient storage capacity could also prevent entry of newcomers and discourage further competition because one of the key issues facing a small supplier is balancing in the event of interruptions (if balancing is unavailable, new entrants do not have a portfolio which can react and therefore will see their profit margin eroded by system penalties).

Finally, gas storage is used for seasonal balancing (the gas is stored from May to October, when demand is lower, and is extracted from November to April, when consumption is higher and there is not enough capacity in pipelines and regasification plants), and a part of LNG storage is necessary to operate regasification plants. As a result, the requirement for minimum reserves of 35 days' worth of consumption of stocks has frequently been unfulfilled.

Electricity security of supply in Spain

Latest developments in the EU

Directive 2005/89/EC establishes a framework within which member states are to define transparent, stable and non-discriminatory policies on security of electricity supply, which is compatible with the requirements of a competitive internal market for electricity, and to ensure:

- An adequate level of generation capacity.
- An adequate balance between supply and demand.
- An appropriate level of interconnection between member states for the development of the internal market.

In implementing that framework, they shall take into account:

- The importance of a transparent and stable regulatory framework.
- The importance of ensuring continuity of electricity supplies.
- The degree of diversity in electricity generation at national or relevant regional level.
- The importance of reducing the long-term effects of the growth of electricity demand.
- The importance of encouraging energy efficiency and the adoption of new technologies, in particular demand management technologies and renewal energy technologies.
- The importance of removing administrative barriers to investment in infrastructure and generation capacity.

Member states are to ensure that transmission system operators set the minimum operational rules and obligations on network security and have to require transmission system operators to maintain an appropriate level of operational network security. To that effect, transmission system operators shall maintain an appropriate level of technical transmission reserve capacity for operational network security and cooperate with the transmission system operators concerned to which they are interconnected. Member states or the competent authorities shall ensure that transmission and, where appropriate, distribution system operators set and meet quality of supply and network security performance objectives. Member states shall also guarantee that curtailment of supply in emergency situations shall be based on predefined criteria relating to the management of imbalances by transmission system operators.

Member states have to encourage the establishment of a wholesale market framework that provides suitable price signals for generation and consumption. To this end, they must require transmission system operators to ensure that an appropriate level of generation reserve capacity is available for balancing purposes and/or to adopt equivalent market-based measures. They may also take additional measures, such as:

- Provisions facilitating new generation capacity and the entry of new generation companies to the market.
- Removal of barriers that prevent the use of interruptible contracts.
- Removal of barriers that prevent the conclusion of contracts of varying lengths for both producers and customers.
- Encouragement of the adoption of real-time demand management technologies such as advanced metering systems.
- Encouragement of energy conservation measures.

Moreover, member states shall establish a regulatory framework that provides investment signals for both the transmission and distribution system network operators to develop their networks in order to meet foreseeable demand from the market, and that facilitates maintenance and, where necessary, renewal of their networks. They shall also ensure that decisions on investments in interconnection are taken in close cooperation between relevant transmission operator systems.

Electricity demand and production

Electricity consumption in Spain has increased by an average yearly growth rate of 6.3 per cent during the last decade. This is one of the highest growth rates among developed countries, and it is mainly driven by the strong growth of the Spanish economy and the large decreases in tariffs that occurred in the first years after liberalization (Figure 7.8).

Electricity consumption traditionally peaks during the winter. The maximum demand load on the mainland was recorded on 27 January 2005 with 43,708 MW. Peak load consumption increased by an average of 6.6 per cent per year from 1996 to 2006. Historically, peak load during summer periods has traditionally been below 90 per cent of the winter peak. During the last four or five years, however, the summer peak has increased and in 2006 reached 95.6 per cent of the winter peak. This is a development mainly

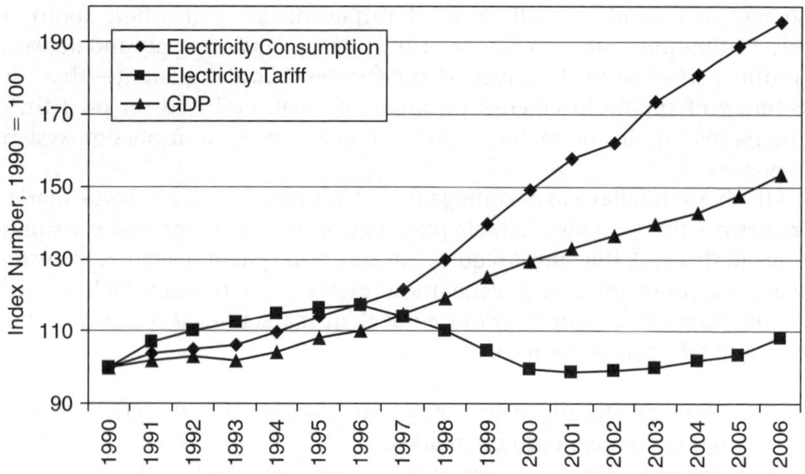

Figure 7.8   GDP, electricity consumption and electricity prices
Source: Instituto Nacional de Estadística (INE), http://www.ine.es; Asociación Española de la Industria Eléctrica (UNESA), *Memoria Estadística Eléctrica,* 2006 (Madrid: UNESA, 2007).

driven by the increased use of air-conditioning, and new rises are possible (heat pumps in air-conditioning machines).

The Spanish electricity system is not so much constrained by generating capacity, but by the fluctuation of power generation due to the significant share of hydro and wind (around one-third of installed capacity on the peninsula). Wind and hydro are dependent on weather conditions, which will limit their ability to respond. The share of hydro generation can fluctuate significantly from year to year. 2006 was a relatively dry year so the share of hydro was only 9.5 per cent. During the last five years, the installed hydro capacity has operated at an effective load factor of less than 20 per cent of its theoretical capacity. The average capacity factor of windpower during the last five years has been 26 per cent. Taking this into account, it is not surprising that the system was becoming constrained in 2000 and 2001, before the new CCGTs started to be commissioned (Figure 7.9).

Spain has insufficient energy resources of its own and depends on imports of all forms of energy resources from a variety of countries. The coal resources of Spain are not of very high quality and large hydro resources are already considerably exploited. There is also no longer a moratorium on nuclear power, but the government is committed to phasing out nuclear power over the long term. The country has transmission interconnections with France, Portugal, Morocco and Andorra, but the share of cross-border trade compared to total supply and demand is very low. Weak cross-border gas and electricity interconnections and low electricity trade compared to total demand lead to a situation not dissimilar to that of an island.

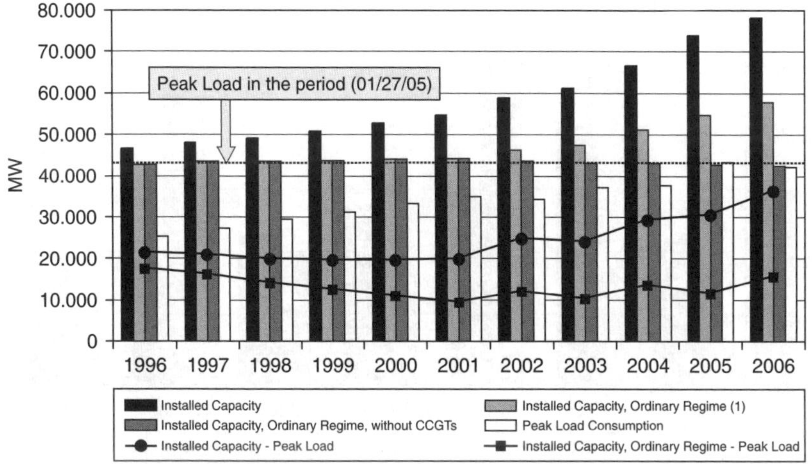

Figure 7.9   Peak load consumption and installed capacity (MW)
(1): Excludes special regimes (wind, co-generation and other renewables)
Source: Red Eléctrica de España, *Informe del Sistema Eléctrico Español en 2006* (Madrid: Red Eléctrica de España, 2007).

Spain is already attempting to increase the exploitation of new renewable sources in order to reduce import dependence and to reduce energy demand by increased energy efficiency, but coal and gas are the main fuels and the contribution of nuclear fuel is high (Figure 7.10). Gas has exhibited the most significant increase in the share in electricity generation.

The share of natural gas is increasing rapidly and new increases are expected at an even higher rate for the next ten years. Much of this capacity is being built by the incumbents and also by several newcomers (Figure 7.11).

There is an increasing dependence on gas in power generation (Figure 7.12). At the same time, the key driver in gas demand is power generation.

During the winter of 2004/5, a new system constraint emerged in the Spanish electricity system: when technical problems occurred in the gas system, strengthened by scarcity of storage capacities, they led to supply problems to CCGT plants during periods with high electric and gas loads. As we said previously, the development of underground storage facilities is a critical concern for Spain's security of supply, both in gas and electricity.

Energy security or energy nationalism?

A few days after the announcement by E.ON of a public bid for Endesa (21 February 2006), the Spanish government adopted a new urgent legislative measure increasing the supervisory powers of the CNE. Pursuant to it,

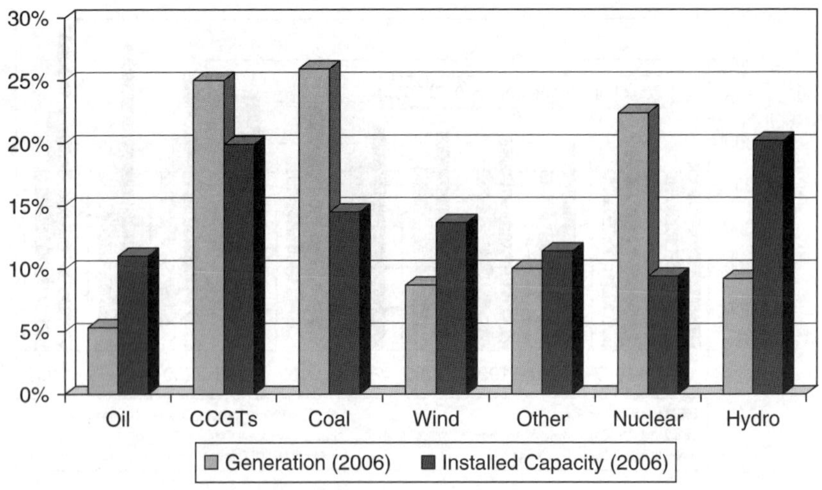

Figure 7.10   Electricity generation in Spain
Source: Red Eléctrica de España, *Informe del Sistema Eléctrico Español en 2006* (Madrid: Red Eléctrica de España, 2007).

the acquisition by any company of more than 10 per cent of the share capital, or any other participation conferring significant influence, in a company (directly or indirectly) active in a regulated activity (transmission or distribution of gas or electricity) or in certain other activities, has to be previously approved by the CNE, which has to apply a test based on the following general criteria (the same proceedings are required for the acquisition of assets):

- The existence of significant risks or negative (direct or indirect) effects on regulated activities or certain activities subject to administrative intervention.
- The protection of the public interest in the energy sector and in particular the guarantee of proper maintenance of sector policy objectives, with special consideration given to assets deemed to be strategic, such as:
  - Natural gas basic network.
  - International gas pipelines (Spain being destination/transit country).
  - Electricity transport infrastructure, non-mainland (i.e. islands and extra peninsular territories).
  - Infrastructure for generation transport and distribution of electricity.
  - Nuclear power plants and thermal plants using domestic coal.
- The possibility that an entity undertaking regulated activities or certain activities subject to administrative intervention cannot guarantee the exercise of these activities as a result of any other activities of the acquirer or the target entity.
- Public security.

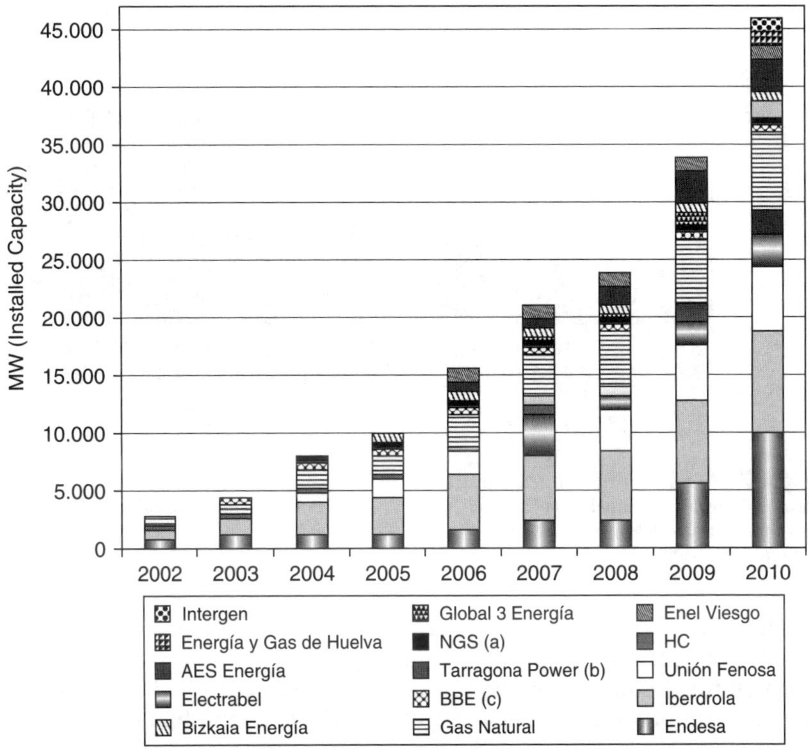

Figure 7.11   CCGTs: evolution and estimations (2002–2010)
(a) 'NGS' is shared by Cepsa and Unión Fenosa (50% & 50%).
(b) Shared by Iberdrola and RWE (50% & 50%).
(c) Iberdrola has 25% of BBE. The shares of Iberdrola and Unión Fenosa in these companies are included in their installed capacity.
Source: Comisión Nacional de la Energía (CNE) (different years), *Informe semestral de seguimiento de las infraestructuras referidas en el 'Informe marco sobre la demanda de energía eléctrica y gas natural, y su cobertura'* (Madrid: CNE).

Gas Natural, the competing bidder, had to obtain CNE authorization for its bid, but under the pre-existing rules, because it is itself an undertaking active in the regulated energy sector in Spain. The authorization was granted before the Decree Law entered in force.

The only pending operation covered by the new provision was E.ON's bid, which at the moment of its launch did not require the CNE's approval: the CNE was only required to grant prior authorization for the acquisition of stakes in any undertaking by companies directly involved in regulated activities in Spain, and not being involved in regulated activities in Spain; E.ON did not therefore have to obtain the CNE's prior authorization for its bid.

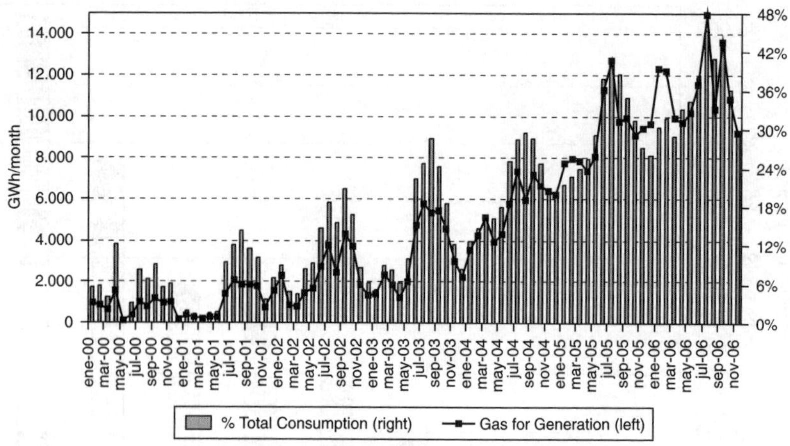

Figure 7.12 Gas for power generation
Source: Comisión Nacional de la Energía (CNE) (different years), *Informe semestral de seguimiento de las infraestructuras referidas en el 'Informe marco sobre la demanda de energía eléctrica y gas natural, y su cobertura'* (Madrid: CNE).

The European Commission opened an infringement procedure against Spain with regard to the provisions granting special powers to the CNE, stating that they could be contrary to fundamental principles of EC law, such as the freedom of capital movement and the right of establishment.

Conclusions

The increasing interaction between the natural gas and electricity systems provides new challenges as regards energy security to Spanish energy policy-makers, because failures in gas supply have the potential to lead to electricity blackouts when a significant share of electricity is produced from gas. Gas and electricity tend to have similar winter peaks and there has already been an occasion when CCGT plants had to be interrupted owing to a compressor failure on the Maghreb pipeline. Increased liberalization of the electricity market, which has led to a 'dash for gas' among Spanish electricity generators, is contributing to this effect.

It is necessary to encourage the development of interconnections, LNG terminals and new underground storage facilities, and it is critical to improve trade across the Spanish–French border and to promote an extension of the available transmission capacity.

On the other hand, given a potential increase in the connection capacity of Spain to European gas and electricity networks, Spain could contribute to EU security of supply by reducing the dependence of other EU states on Russian gas. Spain has significant entry capacity through LNG regasification terminals that could be utilized to import gas from new suppliers into the EU, either as gas or electricity.

Because of the need for investment, to meet increasing demand and to increase competitive pressure, it is important that the approval processes are continuously improved to become as transparent and fast as possible. Spain embarked on the liberalization of its electricity sector in the mid-1990s, and is now among the EU member states with the longest experience in electricity market reform. But it is still in a transitional phase where one aim has been to protect consumers from the effects of the uncertainties liberalization may bring. The electricity market has, however, evolved with a continuously high level of regulation and political involvement. This regulation has served a purpose but has also created many distortions in the market.

The Spanish electricity market is now at a stage where the regulation that was meant to ease the transition has become a hindrance for its further development. Political and regulatory involvement should then be focused on establishing a regulatory framework for the areas where transparent regulation is crucial to maintain market efficiency, such as system reliability, market design, competition, regulation of networks and public service obligations.

Spanish renewables policy is driven by environmental policy and a desire to diversify Spain's energy sources and to reduce import dependence. Spain has ambitious targets for renewable energy, of increasing the share of renewable energy sources in total primary energy supply and electricity generation to 12.1 per cent and 30.3 per cent respectively by 2010.

The Energy Efficiency Strategy (E4) covers demand-side measures to reduce energy consumption and CO_2 emissions in all sectors of the economy. The government has approved two Action Plans to implement the E4 Strategy. A reduction in energy intensity in the Spanish economy will lead to the achievement of three essential goals of EU and Spanish energy policy:

- Guaranteeing the supply of energy in Spain despite a high degree of external energy dependence.
- Improving competitiveness through more efficient use of energy resources.
- Promoting environmental protection by reducing emissions from energy use.

The attempted acquisition of Endesa, one of the two largest Spanish electricity producers, by E.ON, the largest energy company in Germany, has raised the issue of whether the creation of national champions in the energy sector promotes the security of supply. The Spanish government alleged, among other reasons, the need to ensure security of supply when it decided to increase the supervisory powers of the CNE. The CNE also referred to the security of supply when it adopted a decision to submit the operation to several conditions: energy security or energy nationalism?[7]

Notes

1. European Commission, Green Paper, *A European Strategy for Sustainable, Competitive and Secure Energy*, COM (2006) 105 final (Brussels: European Commission, 2006).
2. P. Belkin, *The European Union's Energy Security Challenges*, CRS Report for Congress, 2007, http://www.fas.org/sgp/crs/row/RL33636.pdf.
3. European Commission, Green Paper, 2006.
4. J. Gault, *The European Union: Energy Security and the Periphery*, Occasional Paper Series, No. 40 (Geneva: Geneva Centre for Security Policy, 2002).
5. J. Dolader, *Gas Security of Supply in Spain: a Liberalised Market*. Workshop with Gas Regulators on Security of Supply in Liberalized Markets, 27 June 2003, Paris, http://195.200.115.136/textbase/work/2003/gasreg/spain.pdf.
6. J. de Quinto and J. López, 'El aprovisionamiento de gas y la seguridad de suministro en el sector eléctrico', *Noticias de la UE*, No. 271–2, August–September 2007, pp. 27–40.
7. See also International Energy Agency (IEA), *Security of Gas Supply in Open Markets: LNG and Power at a Turning Point* (Paris: IEA, 2004); IEA, *Energy Policies of IEA Countries: Spain, 2005 Review* (Paris: IEA, 2005); M. Scheepers, A. Seebregts, J. de Jong and H. Maters, *EU Standards for Energy Security of Supply* (Petten and The Hague: ECN and CIEP, 2006), http://www.ecn.nl/docs/library/report/2006/c06039.pdf; M. Scheepers, A. Seebregts, J. de Jong and H. Maters, *EU Standards for Energy Security of Supply, Updates on the Crisis Capability Index and the Supply/Demand Index Quantification for EU-27* (Petten and The Hague: ECN and CIEP, 2007), http://www.ecn.nl/docs/library/report/2006/c06039.pdf.

8

Does China Have an 'Energy Diplomacy'? Reflections on China's Energy Security and its International Dimensions[1]

Linda Jakobson

Introduction: China's energy security as viewed from the outside

China's energy security is of interest to outsiders for three principal reasons. First, China's growing demand for oil has an immediate as well as long-term economic impact on the rest of the world. China is already becoming a major force in world energy markets. As is well known, China's oil imports have grown markedly in the past decade or so. This raises the question of how much oil China (and India) will need to import twenty years from now and of how quickly the world's oil reserves will be depleted if China's economic growth and its need for imported oil continue. A mere fourteen years ago China was self-sufficient in oil; today, with imports of nearly 3 million barrels per day (mbd), it is the world's third largest importer of crude oil after the United States (nearly 14 mbd) and Japan (over 5 mbd).[2] If China's rapid economic growth continues, China will need to import 60–80 per cent of its total domestic oil consumption by 2020, anywhere from 6 to 11 million barrels per day.[3] China's increasing need for foreign oil has also been blamed for rises in oil prices and volatility in the global oil spot market.[4]

Second, China's energy needs have come under scrutiny because China is now the largest emitter of greenhouse gases. How China deals with the challenges of energy conservation, energy efficiency and energy supply diversification are questions that the rest of the world also has a stake in. China will not choke to death alone. Despite the Chinese government's efforts to put incentives in place to enhance energy efficiency and increase the production of renewable energy, the amount of fossil fuel derived from energy consumption in China, in absolute terms, is going to quintuple in the next few decades. Air pollution from China already affects its neighbours, and even countries further away. Furthermore, attempts to curb global warming will be fruitless if China does not succeed in reducing its carbon dioxide emissions.

Third, the heightened level of activities by Chinese political leaders, diplomats and businessmen in oil-rich countries has provoked questions in the West concerning the type of behaviour that can be expected from China as it expands its global reach. Western policy-makers are trying to assess whether the impact of China's rising economic, political and in some cases military influence in other parts of Asia, Africa, Latin America and the Middle East will undermine Western interests in these areas. How will Beijing's energy-related commercial interests abroad affect its foreign policy thinking and actions in the international arena?

In sum, China's energy security matters to the outside world because of its effect on the global oil market, on the global environment and on international relations. This chapter focuses on the third facet described above, namely the presence and activities by an increasing number of Chinese actors in energy-rich countries, described by some analysts as China's 'energy diplomacy'. The chapter argues that this term is not entirely accurate and it gives rise to misleading perceptions. The chapter assesses energy security as one variable in the evolution of China's strategic foreign policy thinking, taking the relationship between China and Sudan as a case in point to illustrate the complexities of China's global reach.

'Energy diplomacy': misleading perceptions

As China's energy demand has grown, Chinese national oil companies (NOCs) have sought to secure the country's growing need for imported oil and gas by diversifying their overseas energy supplies. During the past ten years China's three major NOCs (CNPC, Sinopec and CNOOC)[5] have signed long-term crude supply contracts and liquefied natural gas (LNG) supply contracts in numerous countries across Africa, Asia, Latin America and the Middle East, invested in large-scale pipeline projects, and bought equity investments in overseas oil sites (so-called physical control over oil supplies). In addition, Chinese companies providing oil services, ranging from exploration to rig management and drilling equipment, have expanded their overseas operations and today constitute a growing presence on the international market.

Chinese government officials have supported the overseas activities of the NOCs by cultivating strong bilateral ties with the governments of countries that have oil and gas, promising trade advantages, investments as well as aid and other development assistance. This flurry of activity by Chinese government officials in energy-rich countries has been described by many analysts as China's 'energy diplomacy'.[6] However, the term is not entirely accurate for two reasons. First, it conveys the impression of a planned and coordinated policy enacted by government officials who direct the overseas activities of NOCs. This is not the case. Second, the term 'energy diplomacy' portrays diplomacy as solely geared to China's energy needs. This is also too black-and-white. In both cases, further examination reveals a much more nuanced and multi-faceted picture.

Weak bureaucracy, strong companies

Turning first to the notion that Chinese NOCs operate according to a comprehensive policy plan, first devised and then enacted by Chinese government officials, there is conflicting evidence with regard to which party is in the driving seat. On the one hand, there is admittedly ample evidence of a symbiotic relationship between the Chinese government and NOCs. For example, the top executives in the major Chinese NOCs are appointed by the Chinese Communist Party's Organization Department. Moreover, Chinese NOCs must at least in theory receive government approval for large overseas investments. On the other hand, the government is dependent on the NOCs. The major Chinese NOCs are powerful and wealthy entities that employ hundreds of thousands of people and provide the government with substantial tax revenue. In 2006 the net profits of major Chinese NOCs accounted for about one-third of the total net profits of state companies.[7] To succeed in the international market Chinese NOCs have had to increasingly operate as market-driven companies, seeking profits and maximizing efficiency, just as international oil companies do. Their executives maintain good ties to high-ranking government officials in order to operate effectively, just as oil company executives do the world over.[8] Delegations comprising businessmen who accompany political leaders abroad and wish to maximize the good will of an official visit are a worldwide phenomenon.[9]

Rather than following explicit government directives, Chinese NOC executives are more likely to use government policies to justify decisions they would like to make for commercial reasons. The wording of most government edicts in China is so lacking in specificity that it is usually possible to find a clause validating any sort of action.[10] The much publicized 'Go Out' policy of the Chinese government, for instance, encourages Chinese companies to invest abroad and develop their international competitiveness.[11] It provides a useful umbrella under which any and all overseas activities can be deemed appropriate. As is the case when examining the implementation of a wide array of policies during the reform period over the past three decades in China, vaguely worded policy formulation leaves room for multiple interpretations and makes it possible for initiative-taking individuals and enterprises to pursue numerous different routes. The objective of an NOC top executive is to expand his own empire by increasing revenues. When government assistance is deemed beneficial, it is sought; when government help is not needed, the NOC operates alone. For example, Chinese oil companies have not always secured approval for large overseas investments before committing to them; rather, the investment decision has only later been reported to the State Council.[12]

China's energy bureaucracy is weak and fragmented. There are several government agencies overseeing energy policies that are not subordinate to each other in terms of political power but have overlapping areas of authority, which has led to intense rivalry and ineffective management. There is no single government entity that would command the authority over all the stakeholders. Consequently, effective policy formulation is not forthcoming nor is there a comprehensive national plan for acquiring energy assets abroad.[13] The situation in 2008 has not changed markedly since Andrews-Speed wrote in 2004 about the 'chronically fragmented nature of China's energy policy for at least two decades', which was the result of the 'continuing power of the individual state energy companies combined with the lack of a strong and well-staffed agency charged with formulating energy policy'.[14]

Moreover, if China did have an 'energy diplomacy' it would not only require submission by the NOCs to government policy. It would also require close cooperation between the Chinese NOCs in the name of national interest. The three major NOCs regard each other as rivals. On occasion Chinese NOCs have bid against each other despite the admonitions by Chinese officials to avoid competition.[15]

Multi-faceted global reach

In addition to conveying the (mis)perception of a well-planned and coordinated government policy, the term 'energy diplomacy' is inaccurate because it portrays China's diplomacy as energy-centric. China's foreign policy is in a state of flux. Chinese policy-makers are not only continuously adapting and adjusting policies to changing international conditions, but also to the country's developing needs. This is a natural consequence of China's growing economic, political and military weight on a global scale. The dramatic increase in activity by Chinese government officials in energy-rich or more generally resource-rich countries is just one dimension of China's new global activism. Hence there is a need to reassess diplomatic efforts in energy-rich countries as simply one part of China's evolving foreign policy.[16]

Those responsible for Chinese foreign policy are scrambling to come to terms with the increasingly dynamic roles of a diverse group of Chinese actors in the international arena. In a mere two decades, the face of the People's Republic of China (PRC) abroad has changed. Ensuring that China's diplomacy supports China's national interests is a daunting challenge. In the Chinese bureaucracy, the Ministry of Foreign Affairs is but one actor in the realm of diplomacy; in addition the National Development and Reform Commission, People's Bank of China, China Import-Export Bank, State-owned Assets Supervision and Administration Commission, Ministry of Finance, Ministry of Commerce and several other ministries are all involved in activities abroad in the name of the PRC and are part of decision-making pertaining to China's diplomatic efforts. Most of these government entities lack personnel with sufficient international expertise. On the commercial front, there are several types of state enterprises including ones supervised by the Commission of Science, Technology and Industry for National Defence (COSTIND), private enterprises, and a growing number of individual entrepreneurs who all have their own interests and agenda when doing business overseas. For example, there are no reliable data on the number of companies doing business in Africa or the number of Chinese presently living in Africa. Estimates vary from 674[17] to more than 800 companies,[18] and 100,000 to 300,000 people,[19] respectively. It is evident that the Chinese authorities are not able to oversee or control all the activities of these diverse actors though they are increasingly aware that these actors can disrupt China's broad diplomatic efforts and taint China's image abroad.

The goal of any country's foreign policy is to enhance national interests. China's national interests include ensuring support for the 'One China Policy' in relation to Taiwan, deterring the United States from constraining China's rise while at the same time avoiding conflict with Washington (or any major power) to enable China to remain stable and concentrate on its modernization drive, as well as supporting China's continued economic growth. Furthermore, as the economic, political and military power of China grows, an increasingly significant national interest is to ensure that China's rise to international pre-eminence evokes respect rather than creates enemies.

Taiwan's unresolved political status is still of overriding importance in formulation of Chinese foreign policy. The PRC maintained close ties with several oil-rich countries long before China started to import oil because these countries recognized Beijing (and not Taipei) as the sole representative of China. The African nations, which make up more than one-quarter of the votes in the United Nations General Assembly, have for decades been viewed as crucial allies to the PRC to counter Taiwan's efforts to regain representation in the UN.

Another paramount national objective of the Beijing leadership is managing its complex relationship with Washington. This has ramifications for China's energy security too. China wants to avoid confrontation with the United States but simultaneously wants to deter Washington from containing China or impeding its modernization efforts. Chinese leaders view dependency on the global oil market as undesirable because of their perception that the United States in particular can manipulate markets.[20] Furthermore, the unsuccessful attempts by Chinese NOCs to buy the Russian oil producer Slavneft in 2002 and the American oil company Unocal in 2005 have made Chinese specialists doubt that a level playing field exists in the global oil business. China would also like to decrease its reliance on US-controlled sea lanes because of the perceived risk that Washington would disrupt energy supplies in the event of a Sino-US conflict over Taiwan.[21] Though this is highly unlikely because all consumer nations would suffer and though there is no evidence of any intentional disruption of Chinese oil supplies over the past three decades, psychologically the sheer possibility of intervention has a 'deep impact' on Chinese policy-makers.[22]

Securing oil from where it is available

As mentioned earlier, Chinese NOCs have diversified their energy supplies by negotiating bilateral deals, investing in pipelines, and acquiring oil assets overseas. This is part of a broader strategy of the companies to expand their international scope, which is also in line with the Chinese government's pursuit of energy security. The countries in which Chinese NOCs have been active include ones that are shunned by Western oil companies because of serious human rights abuses in the country in question. Chinese academics and policy-makers alike point out that China is a latecomer to the international oil scene. International oil companies had already taken the best available sites. As a result, Chinese NOCs have often gone to places that are deemed commercially too risky by Western and Japanese oil companies or decreed off-bounds by Western governments for political reasons. A recurring theme in analysis by Chinese observers of their own oil companies is that Chinese NOCs have had no other alternative than to drill and purchase oil from where it is available, regardless of political or human rights concerns.[23]

India, like China a latecomer on the international oil scene and a country needing a growing amount of imported oil, has also invested in oil-rich countries with despotic governments. For example, Indian oil companies control about 25 per cent of the Sudanese oil market while the Chinese control about 40 per cent.[24] But India has not been subjected to the kind of criticism that China has for its oil investments nor have India's equity oil investments been in the spotlight of the international media. While China, as a veto-wielding member of the United Nations Security Council, can certainly be expected to shoulder a greater degree of responsibility in solving international crises, the different treatment accorded by Western politicians to China's and India's efforts to secure oil plays into the hands of those in China who see Western nations as determined to contain China's rise.[25]

The Beijing government has been criticized by Western governments and international aid organizations for providing aid 'with no political strings attached' in conjunction with deals for, among others, petroleum projects. In giving aid the Chinese government does not hold the receiving parties accountable to ensure that aid is used for the purpose it is intended. Unlike Western aid organizations, the Chinese do not demand that labour standards or anti-corruption practices be enforced to even a minimum standard. By changing the rules for providing development aid, China has placed itself on a collision course with international aid organizations and Western governments. When confronted on this issue Chinese officials refer to China's long-standing policy of non-interference in other countries' affairs, a pillar of Chinese foreign policy since the 1950s. Nowhere has Beijing's staunch defence of its non-interference policy caused so much international outcry than in Sudan. The relationship between China and Sudan is an illuminating example of how challenging the implementation of a coherent foreign policy is in this new era of Chinese global activism.

China's controversial relationship with Sudan

Chinese–Sudanese ties are a nexus of the conflicting interests of commercial enterprises, the People's Liberation Army (PLA) and the Chinese government.

Commercially, Sudan and China are strong partners. China is Sudan's largest foreign investor. The oil sector is the main focus of Chinese investments but in addition Chinese companies are involved in building roads, railways and dams. China is northern Sudan's most important trading partner.[26]

About a third of all of the foreign equity oil pumped by China's national oil companies is from Sudanese sites. Of the dozens of Chinese oil investments overseas, the Sudan operation of the Chinese national company China National Petroleum Corporation (CNPC) represents the single greatest commercial success.[27] The Chinese company is simply not going to abandon this very lucrative operation. Or it will not as long as the Chinese government does not have the political will to force it to do so. (China has thus far been unwilling to take actions such as Western governments have done in forcing their companies to abandon drilling operations in Myanmar, for example.) Ironically, while the CNPC earns handsome profits in Sudan the Chinese government is the target of international criticism even though CNPC's oil operations in Sudan hardly enhance China's energy security, which the government so ardently pursues – the oil pumped from Chinese oil sites in Sudan is not suited for Chinese refineries and is sold elsewhere. Japan purchased most of China's 'Sudan oil' in 2006.[28]

Also on the military and defence industry front, Sudan is a valued customer of China. According to a May 2007 Amnesty International report, China sold Sudan arms and ammunition worth US$24 million in 2005.[29] China has overtaken Iran as Sudan's largest arms supplier.[30] Though this constitutes only a fraction of the revenue Chinese companies earn from arms sales worldwide, for an individual enterprise or company the revenue can be noteworthy in terms of its overall sales and in the light of the Chinese government's decision to demand profitability from defence-related enterprises. Moreover, China has also promised to strengthen exchanges and cooperation between the two armed forces.[31]

Internationally, China has lost considerable credibility because of its commercial and military dealings with Sudan. Beijing makes no secret of its close relationship with the Sudanese government and rejects being blamed for not doing enough to stop the genocide in Darfur. Beijing has repeatedly hidden behind its policy of non-interference to justify its opposition to United National Security Council sanctions against Sudan. It is as if Beijing does not acknowledge that an economy of its size inevitably interferes in the affairs of another country merely on the basis of its economic activities. First, the Al-Bahir government is strengthened by the oil revenue it accumulates from Chinese oil companies and second, China's arms sales permit the Al-Bahir government to carry out its genocidal policies more effectively. Furthermore, China first endorsed a UN Security Council arms embargo on the Darfur region in 2005, but according to the 2007 Amnesty report, China has since (together with Russia) violated the resolution by selling weapons to the Al-Bahir government for use in Darfur, in clear contravention of its earlier commitments.[32]

To China's credit, Chinese diplomats became more active with regard to Darfur during the course of 2007, presumably as a result of international outrage over the genocide, coupled with more and more attention being paid to China's passivity.[33] As Sudan's largest investor China is the one country that could possibly have some clout vis-à-vis the Sudanese government. During 2007, several senior Western officials praised Chinese diplomats for their behind-the-scenes efforts on behalf of the Darfur crisis. However, in off-the-record conversations, several Chinese foreign ministry officials have acknowledged that the attempts by Chinese diplomats to redeem China's reputation are impossible so long as Sino-Sudan military cooperation and arms sales continue.[34]

China's energy security and strategic foreign policy thinking

The Chinese leadership's sense of insecurity when it comes to guaranteeing sufficient energy supplies will not diminish. Energy security and overall domestic stability are vital for continued economic growth, which in turn is a prerequisite for the Chinese Communist Party to stay in power. Energy security, in Beijing's view, has become 'too important to be left to the markets'.[35] Therefore energy security will continue to be a driving force of China's foreign policy. As a result, Beijing will engage more broadly and deeply with producer countries. To ensure China's strategic interests it is inevitable that Chinese officials will find it necessary to attempt to influence the domestic policies of the countries it has economic interests in. Consequently, it will be increasingly difficult for China to adhere to its long-standing principle of mutual non-interference.

During the course of 2007 Chinese think-tank researchers and mid-level foreign policy officials conceded in private conversations that the principle of non-interference is untenable and impractical.[36] For example, the slaying and kidnapping of oil workers in Ethiopia and Nigeria, respectively, in 2007 were reminders that China will have to deal with a growing number of non-traditional threats in countries in which it has commercial interests. It was evident that those who formulate strategic policy were mulling over ways to free China from what can be viewed as a 'non-interference trap'.

Chinese officials are conscious of the contradiction that arises when a rising power that advocates achieving a 'harmonious world'[37] as its foreign policy objective is viewed as turning a blind eye to international crises such as genocide.

Energy security will at some point in the future prompt China to replace the long-standing principle of non-interference with a more active yet not too aggressive core principle. Commenting on the principle of non-interference at the 2007 China EU Roundtable in Beijing, a Chinese participant commented that 'in Chinese foreign policy practice, when there is a conflict between national interest and principle, national interest will prevail'.[38] A senior foreign policy specialist who consults with the country's leading policy-makers went a step further in January 2008 by stating that China is moving gradually towards a policy of 'constructive interference'.[39] Ever since 2006 there have been careful formulations in academic journals by Chinese researchers laying the groundwork for the acceptance of a modified approach to the non-interference principle due to Chinese companies' international business pursuits.[40] Some researchers have even directly alluded to humanitarian crises when contemplating China's policies of non-intervention. For example in an article about the Darfur crisis in *Encyclopaedic Knowledge*, a Chinese language journal, Shi Xianze wrote in 2007:

> China has always emphasized non-intervention in other countries' domestic affairs, and has been opposed to any form of intervention in another country's domestic affairs, based on the concept that 'sovereign rights are superior to human rights'. However, as China's views are gradually converging with the international community's mainstream values, China recognizes the existence of 'humanitarian crises', and believes that intervention is necessary when the country in question agrees to intervention or it is authorized by the international community.[41]

Officials at the Chinese Ministry of Foreign Affairs are aware of their credibility problem and the damage done to China's international standing by Chinese oil companies' operations in Sudan. In 2007 China's credibility was a recurring theme in internal discussions involving officials, foreign policy advisers, and scholars.[42] There have also been Chinese scholars who have written about this phenomenon in Chinese journals, calling on China to 'improve its credibility in the international community through enhancing the transparency of its governmental and commercial activities'.[43]

Chinese officials' perception that China is vulnerable in the realm of energy security needs to be taken into account when evaluating China's policies and actions. As mentioned earlier, Chinese officials are inclined to view the United States in particular as a country capable of manipulating global energy markets in its favour against China's interests. Africa has been described as the 'frontier of competition' between China and the United States in the oil sector.[44] Unsuccessful attempts by Chinese national oil companies to join a British Gas-led international consortium to buy a stake in the Kashgan oil fields as well as to acquire shares in Unocal have strengthened the standing of those Chinese policy-makers who see Westerners as wanting to impede China's growth.[45] Rhetoric about the need to contain China and the 'China threat' in statements by US Congressmen and other Western officials is a recurring theme in Chinese discussions about energy security.[46]

While China will continue to embrace global and regional security policies that improve its international image and are consistent with international norms, it is unclear how often in future years there will be instances – like in the case of Sudan – when Beijing will not give up pursuing self-interested national objectives. As its economic, political and military clout grows, it is possible that Beijing's inclination to be selfish could strengthen.

Conclusion

The term 'China's energy diplomacy' does not accurately reflect reality and in fact may inaccurately evoke a perception of Chinese national oil companies pursuing overseas deals according to coordinated government policy. Energy security is certainly one driving force behind China's evolving foreign policy and diplomacy, but is not in itself the basis of coherent diplomacy. Even if one examines China's diplomatic efforts from a purely commercial perspective, China needs many raw materials besides oil to ensure continued economic growth. It must also expand its export markets, both in terms of commodities and labour.

Formulating foreign policy to reflect all of China's national interests is often not possible. In some cases, conflicting interests of Chinese government and commercial actors make the implementation of a coherent foreign policy problematic. China's quest for energy abroad has had unintended consequences which undermine China's diplomatic efforts to build an image of a benign and responsible rising power. China–Sudan ties are a case in point.

Protecting the commercial interests of Chinese companies abroad – energy-related interests included – as well as fulfilling China's desire to be viewed as a responsible major power in international affairs, will inevitably propel China at some point in the future to modify its stance on its long-held principle of non-interference in other countries' affairs. Officials and scholars involved in foreign policy deliberations already privately acknowledge that the principle of non-interference is untenable in the long term, taking into account China's growing economic, political and military power. In the short term, however, China's leaders will continue to emphasize the country's adherence to non-interference, at least in rhetoric, which in turn will cause tension in its relations with Western countries.

China's leaders will not feel any more confident about energy security in the coming years. It is unrealistic to expect China to drop its stance that it has the same right as other nations to develop and prosper. The challenge for outsiders will be to find ways to deal with the vulnerable areas of China's energy security. One constructive way is to encourage China to engage in international dialogue with a focus on improving the stability of the global oil market, stability of supplies, and access to long-term crude supply contracts as the key to China's energy security, rather than outright ownership and control.[47] Global market stability needs genuine international cooperation. Furthermore, it is in the interests of major energy consumers like China, Europe and the United States to collaborate and find ways to put pressure on and entice the oil-producing nations to open up their oil and gas fields to outside investment.[48] In addition, though China is already adopting measures to reduce its reliance on oil, there are multiple unexplored avenues involving concrete collaboration between China and industrialized countries to accelerate China's own efforts. Finally, China has to be constantly reminded that to credibly pursue a 'harmonious world' one cannot hide behind outmoded principles such as its non-interference formulation. Passivity is not a plausible approach by a responsible stakeholder in a globalized world.

Notes

1. This chapter draws on parts of the author's paper 'Understanding China's Approach to Energy Security', presented at the IISS Global Strategic Review in Geneva, 8 September 2007.
2. BP, *Statistical Review of World Energy 2007*, http://www.bp.com/productlanding.do?categoryId=6848&contentId=7033471.
3. E. Downs, *China*, Energy Security Series (Washington, D.C.: Brookings Institution, 2006), pp. 9–10.
4. See, for example, Zhao Hongtu, 'New Features of the International Energy Security Situation', *Contemporary International Relations*, No. 7, 2005, p. 26; C. Hoyos, 'China's oil demand set to keep fuel prices high', *Financial Times*, 10 April 2004.
5. China National Petroleum Corporation (CNPC), China Petroleum & Chemical Corporation (Sinopec), China National Offshore Oil Corporation (CNOOC).
6. D. Zweig and Bi Jianhai, 'China's Global Hunt for Energy', *Foreign Affairs*, September/October 2005; J. Tang, *With the Grain or Against the Grain? Energy Security and Chinese Foreign Policy in the Hu Jintao Era* (Washington, D.C.: Brookings Institution, 2006); Cai Juan and Yang Zhongqiang, 'China's Energy Diplomacy and Geopolitics' (in Chinese), *Academic Exploration* (in Chinese), Vol. 3, 2006; Zhang Zhe, Tao Ye and Liu Chunjiang, 'Strategy and Construction of China's Energy Diplomacy Under the International Background' (in Chinese), *China Construction (Solar & Renewable Energy Sources)* (in Chinese), Vol. 4, 2007.
7. Qi Zhongxi, 'Oil Companies Should Use their Huge Profits Sensibly in the High Oil Price Era' (in Chinese), *Xinhua.net*, 6 February 2007, http://news.xinhuanet.com/fortune/2007-02/06/content_5704626.htm, accessed 16 January 2008.
8. Portions of this chapter are based on the author's off-the-record research interviews with Chinese and American oil industry specialists as well as Chinese diplomats in Beijing, Boston, New York, Shanghai and Washington, D.C. during 2006–7. See

also Downs, *China*, pp. 21–4. Downs provides an insightful description of the relationship between the senior executives of major Chinese NOCs and government officials.

9. Michal Meidan also refers to this phenomenon in her chapter elsewhere in this volume, alluding to the energy deals agreed upon during the 2007 visit to Beijing of French President Nicolas Sarkozy.

10. L. Jakobson, 'The Burden of "Non-interference"', *China Economic Quarterly*, Q2, 2007, p. 15.

11. Wang Yang, 'Assistant Minister of Commerce Chen Jian: Chinese Enterprises "Go Out" for New Space' (in Chinese), 10 August 2007, http://www.gov.cn/jrzg/2007-08/10/content_711929.htm, accessed 14 January 2008.

12. Downs, *China*, p. 24.

13. See, for example, ibid., pp. 24, 35.

14. P. Andrews-Speed, *Energy Policy and Regulation in the People's Republic of China* (The Hague: Kluwer Law International, 2004), p. 56.

15. Zhang Ying, 'The Two Oil Giants Fight Loudly Overseas, Competition Forces Prices Down and Both Sides Suffer' (in Chinese), *Economic Reference News* (in Chinese), 28 June 2004, http://www.southcn.com/news/china/china04/petroleum/latest/200406280680. htm, accessed 18 January 2008. For the Chinese government's attempts to rein in competition between the NOCs, see for example, Zeng Qinghong, 'The Current Economic Situation and Party Construction Work' (in Chinese), *Study Times* (in Chinese), No. 301, September 2005. At the time of writing Zeng Qinghong was a member of the Standing Committee of the CPC's Central Committee Political Bureau and Vice-President of PRC. The journal *Xuexi shibao* is published by the Chinese Communist Party School.

16. For an overview of China's global activism, see P. C. Saunders, *China's Global Activism: Strategy, Drivers and Tools* (Washington, D.C.: National Defense University Press, 2006).

17. Salimata Kone, 'Study on Chinese Enterprises' Direct Investment in Africa' (in Chinese), *Contemporary Manager* (in Chinese), Vol. 3, 2006.

18. Huang Di and Li Changyu, 'Analysis of Investment Trends of Chinese Enterprises in Africa' (in Chinese), *Perspectives of Scientific and Technological Achievement* (in Chinese), Vol. 5, 2007.

19. B. Sautman, 'Friends and Interests: China's Distinctive Links with Africa', 2006, http://www.cctr.ust.hk/articles/pdf/WorkingPaper12.pdf, accessed 16 January 2008.

20. See, for example, Wenran Jiang, 'Beijing's "New Thinking" on Energy Security', *China Brief*, The Jamestown Foundation, Vol. 6, No. 5, 12 April 2006.

21. See, for example, I. Storey, 'China's "Malacca Dilemma"', *China Brief*, The Jamestown Foundation, Vol. 6, No. 8, 12 April 2006.

22. Zha Daojiong, 'Energy Interdependence', *China Security*, Summer 2006, p. 7. See also Zha Daojiong, 'China's Energy Security: Domestic and International Issues', *Survival*, Vol. 48, No. 1, Spring 2006, p. 181.

23. Remarks by Chu Shulong at the Sino-Nordic Roundtable at the China Institute of Strategic Studies in Beijing, 30 October 2005; see also Wang Meng, 'Darfur Crisis: a Turning Point in the Challenge to Reform China's Diplomacy' (in Chinese), *World Economics and Politics* (in Chinese), June 2006, p. 37.

24. Jyoti Malhotra, 'India, China: Comrades in Oil', *Asia Times*, 19 August 2005, http://www.atimes.com/atimes/South_Asia/GH19Df04.html, accessed 16 January 2008.

25. Author's discussions and off-the-record research interviews with several Chinese foreign policy analysts in Beijing during 2006. In the same vein many Chinese interpreted the US decision in March 2006 to sign a nuclear cooperation agreement with India as a move directed against China.

26. O. Mcdoom, 'Pressure changed Beijing's Darfur stance, report says', *Reuters*, 18 August 2007, http://www.alertnet.org/thenews/newsdesk/MCD845351.htm, accessed 15 January 2008.

27. For details on China's oil explorations in Sudan, see L. Jakobson and Daojiong Zha, 'China and the Worldwide Search for Oil Security', *Asia Pacific Review*, Vol. 13, No. 2, 2006, pp. 64–71; Jakobson, 'The Burden of "Non-interference"'.

28. 'Sudan oil industry in American figures', *Sudan Tribune*, 12 May 2007.

29. Amnesty International, 'Sudan: arms continuing to fuel serious human rights violations in Darfur', 8 May 2007, http://web.amnesty.org/library/Index/ENGAFR 540192007?open&of=ENG-SDN. According to the Stockholm International Peace Research Institute (SIPRI) arms transfer database, China's arms sales to Sudan appear not to constitute a significant percentage of China's arms sales worldwide.

30. Ibid.

31. 'China, Sudan vow to boost military exchanges', *People's Daily Online*, 3 April 2007, http://english.people.com.cn/200704/03/eng20070403_363374. html, accessed 22 January 2008.

32. Amnesty International, 'Sudan'.

33. See, for example, M. Farrow and R. Farrow, 'The Genocide Olympics', *Wall Street Journal*, 28 March 2007; M. Farrow, 'Beijing Can Do More on Darfur', *Wall Street Journal*, 5 October 2007; Mcdoom, 'Pressure changed Beijing's Darfur stance, report says'.

34. Author's off-the-record discussions in Beijing in September and October 2007.

35. K. Lieberthal and M. Herberg, 'China's Search for Energy Security: Implications for US Policy', *NBR Analysis*, Vol. 17, No. 1, April 2006, p. 13.

36. Author's off-the-record discussions in Beijing, Hangzhou, Shanghai and Washington, D.C. in 2007.

37. Hu Jintao, 'Build towards a Harmonious World of Lasting Peace and Common Prosperity', speech at the United Nations Summit, New York, 15 September 2005, http://www.fmprc.gov.cn/ce/ceun/eng/zt/shnh60/t212915.htm, accessed 22 January 2008.

38. China–EU Roundtable held at the China Institute of Strategic Studies in Beijing, 28 June 2007.

39. Author's off-the-record interview in Shanghai, 17 January 2008.

40. See, for example, Wang Meng, 'Darfur Crisis', p. 38.

41. Shi Xianze, 'Darfur Crisis' (in Chinese), *Encyclopaedic Knowledge* (in Chinese), Vol. 14, 2007.

42. Author's off-the-record conversations with officials at the Ministry of Foreign Affairs of the PRC and Chinese researchers at universities and research institutes in Beijing in October and November 2007.

43. Zha Daojiong, 'China's Energy Security: a Perspective of International Relations' (in Chinese), *International Economic Review* (in Chinese), Vol. 11–12, 2005.

44. Kang Sheng, 'US Factor in China's Energy Security and Diplomacy in Africa' (in Chinese), *Journal of Socialist Theory Guide* (in Chinese), Vol. 4, 2006, p. 80.

45. Jakobson and Daojiong, 'China and the Worldwide Search for Oil Security', pp. 67–8.

46. See, for example, Zhang Shirong, 'Probe into the Complicity of China's Energy Security System' (in Chinese), *Journal of Inner Mongolia Normal University (Philosophy & Social Science)* (in Chinese), Vol. 5, 2007; Zhang Yuyan and Guan Qingyou, 'World's Energy Structure and China's Energy Security' (in Chinese), *Journal of World Economy* (in Chinese), Vol. 9, 2007; Zha Daojiong, 'China's Energy Development Strategy and International Relations' (in Chinese), *Study Monthly* (in Chinese), Vol. 19, 2006.
47. M. Herberg, 'China's Energy Consumption and Opportunities for US–China Cooperation to Address the Effects of China's Energy Use', testimony before the US–China Economic and Security Review Commission, Washington, D.C., 14 June 2007.
48. Jakobson and Zha, 'China and the Worldwide Search for Oil Security', p. 70.

9
China's Energy Policy and its Development

Shi Dan

China's energy policy in retrospect[1]

Despite the fact that China has yet to publish an energy policy White Paper, a study of the series of policies and steps the nation has taken since the adoption of policy reform and opening up to the outside world allows us to trace the origin and course of development in Chinese energy policy and to clarify the reasons and goals behind China's energy policy readjustment.

The focal points of China's energy policy, 1978–1993

The reform and opening-up policy went through its initial stage of development in the 1978–93 period, as the nation began the transition from central planning to a market economy. Economic restructuring conducted during this period unleashed the nation's productivity and boosted economic growth. However, as a legacy of central planning, supply shortages continued to trouble the national economy. Energy shortages were one of the nagging headaches at the time, and the reform and incentive measures the government adopted to tackle this problem boiled down to three aspects.

Giving priority to investment in energy construction and expanding energy production

The energy industry was given centre stage in virtually every major economic document the central government issued during the 1978–94 period. To secure funding for energy project construction, the annual economic documents issued by the State Council during the 1981–9 period never failed to give top priority to energy development investment. Even after the nation started to curtail its investment scale and rectify economic development in 1990, energy development has enjoyed the limelight in the nation's investment policy. In other words, the energy industry has always stayed at the top of the government's economic agenda.

To resolve shortages in energy supply and construction funds, the energy industry was one of the earliest fields where production boundaries and ownership limitations were eased. In coal mining, the policy was to pool the efforts of the state, collectives and individuals; in oil development, foreign companies were invited for joint prospecting; in the power industry, investment was absorbed from outside the energy industry, and bank loans were increased for it.

Using economic incentives to stimulate producer enthusiasm

From 1979 to 1994, economic restructuring in China served the goal of establishing a 'planned market economy'. That is to say, while market forces were introduced into socioeconomic activities, they were only allowed to play a supplementary role, with central planning still holding sway. Capital goods production and sales remained under state planning control. For instance, in the coal mining industry the policy was to put production on a contracted basis, with the earnings from above-norm output shared among partners; in the power industry, electricity prices were set so that the 'principal can be repaid with interest' and 'investors and users can benefit from the electricity generated'. Moreover, energy construction projects were accorded a preferential 15 per cent corporate income tax reduction.

Setting energy-conservation goals and energy-saving focal points

Great importance was attached to energy conservation as early as the initial reform years. In the Sixth Five-Year Plan (1980–5) for National Economic and Social Development, the chapter on energy began by stressing energy conservation and went on to outline energy-saving goals, along with a list of key areas and industries to watch over. That chapter demanded that the energy needed to maintain a 4 per cent annual industrial growth be obtained by conservation efforts, meaning that during the five-year period, the nation's total energy consumption should be cut by 70–90 million tons of standard coal. To attain that goal, the government published a programme on energy-saving technology policy. In the Seventh Five-Year Plan (1986–90), the government called for giving full scope to economic leverages and adopted a series of policy steps, including establishing a sound energy supply system under which companies that excelled in energy conservation were ensured of energy supplies, companies that used more energy than allowed had to pay more for the extra supply, energy-saving pace-setters were awarded, and energy-saving projects were accorded preferential credit and loans. The Eighth Five-Year Plan (1991–5) continued to set energy-conservation goals. The Ninth and Tenth Five-Year Plans (1996–2000, 2001–5) did not raise new energy-saving goals, but still listed energy conservation as a major field of endeavour. It is therefore obvious that energy conservation has been emphasized in Chinese energy policy all along.

Energy policy emphases 1995–2005

By the mid-1990s China's shortage-plagued economy came to an end. Robust energy output growth by and large rectified long years of energy shortage. In the meantime, however, indiscriminate energy development, illegal energy production, wanton tapping of energy resources and environmental pollution became serious problems. For a time, more than 20,000 private coal mines were engaged in unauthorized production and sales. The 1997–8 Asian financial crisis resulted in a glut in China's coal-production and power-generating capacities, but at the same time, low oil supply self-sufficiency turned the nation from a net oil exporter to a net oil importer. To cope with the situation, the Chinese energy policy shifted from encouraging output expansion to restructuring the nation's energy sources, rectifying production order, and speeding up market-oriented reform.

Paying due attention to developing quality energy sources and ameliorating the energy production structure

The discrepancy in energy supply and demand eased up with the fulfilment of the Eighth Five-Year Plan. Nevertheless, structural contradictions between supply and demand, between energy development and the environment, and between resources, continued to cause problems. Structural readjustment thus became a task of overriding importance during this period. A government energy development plan set the goal for national restructuring of energy sources: increasing the percentage of natural gas, hydropower and other clean, efficient and quality energy sources, while cutting down on ultimate coal consumption. One step to be taken to serve the goal was for the power industry to curtail the number of small thermal power plants. Beginning from the Ninth Five-Year Plan period, new thermal power plants were required to use high-efficiency generating units of no less than 300,000 kilowatts in generating capacity. Efforts were to be stepped up to develop hydropower plants, discover new energy sources, and strengthen power grids, especially in rural areas. The coal mining industry was asked to transform large coal mines, to build high-yielding, high-efficiency coal pits, tap coalbed gas, step up research in clean-coal technology, close down coal mines that were small, ill-located, wasteful or hazardous, and give full play to the productive capacity of large mines. With the adoption of the policy to develop western China on a big scale, the nation started projects to transmit natural gas from west to east and electricity from east to west, the idea being to improve eastern China's energy consumption pattern and accelerate development in western China.

During this period the government also issued an outline programme on the development of new, renewable energy sources, and raised the goals and tasks and formulated policy measures for this endeavour from the Ninth Five-Year Plan period to the year 2010.

*Adopting a new policy to synchronize utilization of international
oil resources, energy development and environmental treatment*

The energy policy featured in the Ninth and Tenth Five-Year Plans called for
the establishment of a national oil reserve system that consisted of reserves
at two levels – national and corporate. The policy also urged the nation to
go all out to open up new international markets, speed up natural gas development, and carry out a 'go international' strategy so as to make the most
of both internal and external resources and markets. Other new elements in
Chinese energy policy included diversifying import sources and developing
oil substitute products.

For the first time in China, the Ninth Five-Year Plan listed ecosystem conservation as a strategic goal for the development of the energy industry,
and called for simultaneous energy development and environmental treatment. The plan called for developing clean energy sources and clean-coal
technology, restricting and phasing out dusty and high-sulphur coal production, avoiding and reducing environmental pollution caused by energy
development and utilization, and promoting coordinated energy, economic
and environmental development. In the Tenth Five-Year Plan, the government suggested rectifying and raising the standards of waste-discharge fees on
energy production and consumption, guiding companies to adopt advanced
equipment and production processes and phasing out small thermal power
plants and other energy-producing and utilizing facilities handicapped by
outdated technology and low efficiency.

*Promoting reform of the energy industry's administrative system and
tightening up relevant legislation*

To vigorously promote reform and let reform steer development was an
important aspect of China's energy policy for the Ninth and Tenth Five-Year
Plan periods. As a result, institutional reform of the energy industry came a
long way during both periods. Firstly, major breakthroughs were scored in
energy price reform, in which coal prices (fuel coal for thermal power generating not included) were decontrolled and left at the mercy of the market.
Electricity prices, which used to be set according to individual project costs
to recoup the principal and pay the interest, were decided according to the
public's average optimal costs. Urban and rural electricity prices were unified, as well as their categories. Preferential in-grid prices were adopted for
electricity generated from new energy sources. Double-track oil prices were
abolished and replaced with unified prices, which were then quickly pegged
with international prices. Secondly, major progress was made in revamping
the energy industry's administrative system. Government functions were initially separated from corporate management; the reform goal of 'separating
the functions of power plants and power grids, and rewarding in-grid business
rights to the highest bidder under government supervision', and electricity

price reform began in some provinces and municipalities on a trial basis. The petrochemical and natural gas industry was regrouped, resulting in two major enterprise groups that formed the upper and lower reaches of the industry and integrated domestic and foreign trade; both groups were later successfully listed in overseas stock markets. Thirdly, state-owned energy enterprises conducted corporate reform with the goal of establishing a modern corporate system.

While pushing administrative restructuring in the energy industry, China promulgated the Electric Power Law in 1995, the Coal Law in 1996 and the Energy Conservation Law in 1997. In the meantime, a number of administrative rules and regulations were issued, thereby filling in the legal blanks in the development of the energy industry and adding legal backing for supervision in this industry.

Three problems to be solved in China's energy policy

Tackling the environmental impact of energy production and consumption

Energy production and consumption have grown dramatically since reform and the opening-up efforts began in 1978. Although this has strongly fuelled sustained high-speed economic growth, it has also brought a tremendous pressure to bear on the environment. Colossal energy production and consumption heavily dependent on coal was a major cause of China's atmospheric deterioration. It is estimated that 85 per cent of carbon dioxide emissions, 74 per cent of sulphur dioxide emissions, 60 per cent of nitrogen oxide emissions, and 70 per cent of soot in the atmosphere of China were caused by coal burning. As things stand today, coal-fuelled thermal power generating consumes approximately half of the nation's total coal output and 40 per cent of the water for industrial use. It causes more than half of the total sulphur dioxide emissions, 33 per cent of the total industrial soot emissions and 22 per cent of the total soot emissions, and 70 per cent of the total amount of dust and residue in China. In 2005, soot emissions in this country amounted to 11.825 million tons, up 19.7 per cent from what they were in 2002, and sulphur dioxide emissions reached 25.49 million tons, up 27.8 per cent from 2000; both exceeded the limits mandated in the national environmental protection plan for the Tenth Five-Year Plan period. In the first half of 2006, pollutant emissions remained a major problem. Statistics show that in the first six months of that year, the nation's CO_2 emissions totalled 6.896 million tons, and its sulphur dioxide emissions totalled 12.746 million tons, 3.7 per cent and 4.2 per cent respectively more than in the same period of the previous year. Emissions of CO_2 and sulphur dioxide, which are the two principal pollutants, are worsening to various degrees throughout the nation.[2]

Ensuring safe and stable energy supply

Safe and stable energy supply requires two factors: firstly, economic security in energy supply; and secondly, energy production security. It is estimated that China's dependence upon oil imports will have reached 61 per cent in 2010 and 76.9 per cent in 2020. Any interruption in oil imports will have a major impact upon the national economy.

Although the surging international oil prices over the last few years have enabled the Chinese petroleum industry to reap handsome profits, it has also incurred high oil import costs. In 2005, the nation's crude oil imports and exports totalled 50.56 billion dollars, with a trade deficit of 45.16 billion dollars, up by 38.6 per cent from the 2004 figures; oil products imports and exports amounted to 16.8 billion dollars, with a trade deficit of 4.02 billion dollars.

With social development, energy production security is not just a cause for concern for oil producers – it is also an issue of public importance. Coal production safety has become an important issue, as the nation's coal mines that conform to safety standards have a combined coal output of 1.2 billion tons. Unsafe coal mines contributed 38.65 per cent of the nation's 2005 total coal output. As a result of consecutive years of over-capacity production, coal mines across the land have needed a total production safety investment to the tune of more than 50 billion yuan. The situation is especially bad with small private coal mines that have spent little or nothing on production safety. It is estimated that a total of 400 million tons of coal-mining capacity in China needs a safety system transformation, 150 million tons of such capacity fails to measure up to safety standards, and 200 million tons of such capacity should be closed down because it lacks conditions for safe production. Statistics show that the death toll per million ton of coal produced stands at 5.68 persons in China, three times the average level of deaths in all coal-producing nations in the world. In 2005, the number of workers who lost their lives in major coal-mining accidents (each with a death toll of more than ten people) grew by 60 per cent compared with what it was in the previous year.

Improving energy resources' utility efficiency

From 1978, the year the policy of reform and opening up to the outside world was adopted, to 2000, energy efficiency in China improved markedly, thanks to robust growth in the national economy. However, in the years that followed, the improvement has somewhat stagnated, and, in a trend that has shown no sign of a let-up, energy efficiency plummeted. In the Eleventh Five-Year Plan (2005–10), the government set the goal of reducing per-unit energy consumption by 20 per cent. In the first six months of 2006, however, GDP rose by 10.9 per cent, and consumption of coal and electricity went up by 12.8 per cent and 12 per cent respectively. Energy consumption was obviously outgrowing the national economy, and energy consumption per GDP unit rose by 0.8 per cent over the same period of the previous year. Despite a slight turn for the better in energy conservation, the entire year of 2006 saw the nation's energy consumption per GDP unit drop by a meagre 1.23 per cent, in comparison with the prescribed 4 per cent target.

It is estimated that available domestic energy resources can ensure coal supply in China for 114.5 years, oil supply for 20.1 years and natural gas supply for 49.3 years. Although coal resources are relatively abundant, given the present consumption rate, by the year 2020, China's coal reserve shortage will amount to 125 billion tons according to precision verification results, 210 billion tons according to detailed verification results, and 660 billion tons according to general survey results. To make up for such a shortage calls for a total investment of upwards of 40 billion yuan.[3] Improving the energy utility rate is therefore very important in maintaining sustained development of the Chinese economy.

Current energy policy: focal points and steps

Focal points

With a view to the problems in energy production and consumption, the weight of Chinese energy policy has been shifted from promoting production and increasing supply to such fields as optimizing the energy structure, encouraging the development of clean energy sources and attaching due importance to energy security and environment. The energy policy laid down in the Eleventh Five-Year Plan includes a number of new changes, mainly in the following fields.

Setting energy conservation and energy efficiency improvement as rigid constraining standards

Sustained quick increases have marked energy consumption in China since 2001. In 2005, national energy consumption ran as high as 2.233 billion tons of coal, nearly a 1 billion ton increase over what it was in 2000. Massive and surging energy production and consumption have brought tremendous pressure to bear on both the nation's resources and environment. For this reason, the Eleventh Five-Year Plan for National Economic and Social Development has listed energy efficiency improvement as a very important issue and raised the goal to cut 2005–10 energy consumption per 10,000 yuan GDP by 20 per cent. To achieve this goal, most provinces and municipalities have instituted a communiqué system on energy consumption indicators and include per-unit GDP energy consumption in the standards for appraising government leaders' performance. In comparison with the energy saving policy in the previous Five-Year Plans, the Eleventh Five-Year Plan has not only set energy-saving goals but also tightened up the implementation of this policy.

Stepping up the building of energy-related legislation and the energy supply system

Towards the end of the Tenth Five-Year Plan period, the government tightened up macroeconomic control of the energy industry from a strategic point of view, in an effort to cope with excessive growth in energy demand, strained energy supply and demand, and inordinate development between branches of the energy industry. A national leading panel headed by the premier was set up to provide guidance for strategic energy planning, major policy issues, and other forward-looking, comprehensive and strategic fields of work. As the top-echelon consultation and coordination team for national work on energy development, the leading panel is currently drafting the Energy Law. As a fundamental piece of legislation, this law will serve to coordinate the laws concerning different fields of the energy industry from a strategic height and overall point of view.

For the first time in China, the Eleventh Five-Year Plan issued the call to establish a 'stable, economical and clean energy supply system'. According to this author's understanding, this energy supply system will cover the following six fields of endeavour: (1) establishing a domestic energy supply system and carrying out an energy diversity strategy, that is, a supply system predicated on coal, with diversified development in coal, petroleum, natural gas, hydropower, nuclear power, solar energy and other new energy sources; (2) establishing an external energy supply system, that is, a multi-channelled energy supply system that integrates market purchases and direct development, and promoting the building of a clean, safe, economical and reliable world energy supply framework, with a view to pursuing diversity in sources of oil and gas imports and transport channels; (3) establishing a harmonious global energy diplomatic system that accords with the new concept of global energy security and matches all kinds of usable energy resources, and promoting international cooperation with the main thrust on the development of transnational oil and gas transmission pipelines and other energy shipping channels; (4) setting up a strategic energy reserve system that consists of strategic reserves, commercial reserves and resource reserves; (5) establishing legislation to coordinate energy conservation efforts; and (6) establishing an energy price system that can reflect the energy supply and demand relationship as well as the relationship between different energy values and user prices in China.

Stressing the necessity of ensuring domestic energy supply by relying on domestic resources

Looking back on the Chinese energy policy's course of development throughout the reform and opening-up years, we can see that, to tackle energy shortage, China has pushed an independent energy development policy. A number of other policies have been derived from this policy, such as those concerning energy prices and taxes, energy investment, energy technology and energy efficiency. With changes in the contradictions between energy supply and demand, the emphasis of the energy policy has been shifted to optimizing the energy structure. This energy structure policy, in turn, has given rise to the policy on new and renewable energy sources and the 'go international' policy. Energy security, which is becoming an increasingly acute issue in this nation, is also gaining prominence as a new focal point for Chinese energy policy.

With the attention of the international community focused on global warming, and the concern of all nations in the world about energy security, Chinese energy security policy is no longer merely an industrial policy. It has become something that bears on international relations and diplomacy, and on global geopolitical relations as well. Herein lies the difference between the current Chinese energy policy and its predecessors. In 2006, Hu Jingtao, General Secretary of the Central Committee of the Chinese Communist Party, emphasized China's grave concern over the energy security issue. More than a major energy-consuming country, he said, China is a major energy-producing country. Following the principles of equality, mutual benefit, and win-win situations, China is willing to step up cooperation with other energy-producing and consuming countries and join them in maintaining global energy safety. The General Secretary's new concept of global energy security involves three aspects: firstly, to strengthen mutual benefit and cooperation in energy development and utilization; secondly, to foster a framework for research, development and promotion of advanced energy technologies; thirdly, to safeguard a suitable political environment for energy security and stability.

China's energy security policy is designed to meet the following goals: to implement an energy strategy giving priority to conservation efforts; to base energy supply on domestic resources, pursue diversified development, protect the environment and step up mutually beneficial international cooperation; to foster a stable, economical and clean energy system; and to back China's sustainable socioeconomic development with sustainable energy development.

During the Ninth and Tenth Five-Year Plan periods, China formulated a 'go international' policy for the development of the energy industry with a view to energy supply and demand contradictions, but it has never relinquished the policy to base the nation on domestic energy supply. The Eleventh Five-Year Plan has gone a step further to stress the importance of relying upon domestic energy production to ensure the national energy demand and set 'basing the nation on domestic resources' as the fundamental principle for tackling the country's energy problems. Under the prerequisite of production safety, the plan called on the entire nation to strive to increase domestic energy supply and continue to maintain energy self-sufficiency at a high level.

In keeping with the policy of ensuring domestic energy supply by relying on domestic resources, the Chinese coal-mining industry has mapped out a series of plans to intensify coal prospecting, improve the recovery rate and reduce the coal-mining industry's damage of the ecosystem. The policy on active expansion of coal exports and on coal import tax breaks, as outlined in the Tenth Five-Year Plan, has been abolished. Government support for the development of oil's substitute products has been stepped up, and as a result, a number of projects, such as using grain to produce carbinol as a substitute for oil, and coal liquidification, are under way.

Major steps to be adopted in the immediate future

Setting up a sound energy price system and giving full play to the regulating role of prices and taxation

China's energy prices are in need of further readjustments, whether to improve the nation's energy efficiency or to reflect the scarcity of energy resources.

Firstly, due consideration should be given to the correlations between energy products, and the price ratio between them should be readjusted, so that energy products of the same user values can be priced at roughly the same level.

Secondly, although China has stepped up its energy price reform, the taxes and consumer prices have failed to do justice to the degrees of scarcity of energy resources. Therefore, only by properly raising the nation's energy users' tax and levying an energy consumption tax can social justice be fully embodied.

Thirdly, it is imperative to improve cost accounting for energy products, and collect fees from sales of energy products for environmental treatment purposes and from enterprises that choose to drop out of energy production. Special accounts should be established for the fees thus collected, so that they can be put to proper use.

Fourthly, it is appropriate for the government to offer income tax reductions or exemptions and consumption subsidies to promote the production and consumption of renewable and clean energy sources.

Promoting institutional building for control of environmental pollution

Trade in waste discharging rights is an effective means to control and treat environmental pollution by way of market forces. However, the government must establish a system for trade in waste discharging rights, because companies' logical choice is to turn a blind eye to pollution, which is not their targeted product. Only with a government mandated trading system can companies begin waste discharging rights trading. To establish such a trading system, the government should, firstly, set environmental quality targets for a certain region; secondly, assess the region's environmental capacity and the maximum amount of pollutant discharge allowed; thirdly, distribute the amounts of discharge among different sources of pollution by issuing licences; and fourthly, establish a discharge trade market where the waste discharge right can be sold and bought at appropriate prices. Moreover, the government has an important role to play in fields such as accurately appraising the environmental quality of a given region, establishing a market for the auctioning of waste discharge rights and determining initial waste discharging quotas, setting up second-tier markets for trade in waste discharging rights, collecting and publishing of trading information, and amending the legislation governing trade in waste discharging rights.

Establishing a collaboration framework for energy security, and warning and prevention mechanisms against energy risks

Rapid increases in oil demand have strengthened China's relations with other oil-producing and importing countries, and catalyzed the birth of the Chinese oil industry's 'go international' strategy. However, whether judging from an international trade point of view or from the stand of international investment, it is necessary for China to foster a relationship of mutual benefit and win-win situations with the world's other oil-producing and consuming countries. On no account should these countries be locked in to mutually exclusive, cut-throat competition. China's energy security need calls for the adoption of diverse steps.

Firstly, China should endeavour to solve national and international energy supply problems through friendly cooperation with other countries. Otherwise, these problems could give rise to disputes that serve only to undermine world peace and rob China of its good environment for development.

Secondly, China should have its own energy security warning and risk prevention mechanisms, and ensure energy security and reduce risks and losses by establishing strategic oil reserves.

Thirdly, China should speed up research and application of advanced technology for energy development and utilization, and reduce economic development's dependency upon non-renewable energy sources. Since China's accession to the WTO in 2001, heavy industry has been leading Chinese industrial development by the nose. This trend can be ascribed, apart from the pulling effect of domestic market needs, to the fact that developed countries are vying with each other to shift the manufacturing links of industries to China. The excessive rate of development and high density of heavily energy-consuming industries are major reasons behind the deterioration in China's energy utility rate in recent years. To carry out international cooperation in the research, development and promotion of advanced energy technologies on the basis of a sound, energy secure, cooperative framework is in the interest not only of China but also of other nations in the world.

Notes

1. Material and data used in this chapter mainly come from the Sixth to Tenth Five-Year Plans for 'National Economic and Social Development', 'Coal Industry', 'Power Industry', 'Petrol Industry' and 'The Key Specialized Programme for National Energy Development'.
2. Reference from 2005, the first half of the 2006 *Bulletin of Pollutant Emissions* jointly issued by the National Environment Protection Bureau, the National Statistic Bureau and the National Committee of Development and Reform.
3. Materials and data are taken from the Eleventh Five-Year Plan for National Economic and Social Development.

10
Energy Security Challenges to Asian Countries from Japan's Viewpoint

Shigeru Sudo

Introduction

When I talk to energy experts in Europe, I feel that there are major differences in outlooks on energy security between European and Asian experts. The basic assumption underlying European experts' arguments seems to be rather different. In the Atlantic market their major concern seems to be mainly with how to ensure economic and political stability within the EU in the aftermath of the end of the Cold War and the disappearance of geopolitical risks involving the former Soviet Union, even though the geopolitical factors seem to be increasing in recent years because of the Russian government's increasing control and involvement in the energy sector.

The EU seems to be more concerned with ensuring, as much as possible, the stable supply of energy in line with the Energy Charter Treaty. In the European market international oil companies (IOCs) dominate as major players. The European countries are basically more market-mechanism oriented in terms of their strategies and policies.

On the other hand, Asia and the Pacific remains an unstable region in geopolitical terms. This region, which may be called the 'Arc of Instability', stretching from the Middle East to Northeast Asia, is characterized by a diversity of factors of destabilization. Various efforts are being pursued to address problems arising from these factors through bilateral negotiations at a governmental level as well as in regional and sub-regional forums.

In the Asia region, national oil companies (NOCs) are still major players. Especially in the Middle East, NOCs possessing rich oil reserves are dominant players. China and India are now turning into major oil importers. In these countries NOCs, although they possess no oil reserves of their own, are major players. These factors make market conditions both in the Atlantic market and the Pacific market substantially different from each other.

Energy supply and demand in Japan

The supply of primary energy in Japan decreased for a while because of the oil crisis in 1973, but the basic trend is towards fairly steady increase. By types of energy, oil was the largest and 77 per cent of the energy supply depended on oil in 1973. After the two oil crises in 1973 and 1979, however, the dependence on oil dropped to 49 per cent in 2005 as the result of efforts made in energy saving and alternative energies such as nuclear energy and natural gas. Nonetheless, oil remains the most important energy source in Japan.

On the other hand, the total amount of CO_2 discharged was 1364 million tons in 2005, which was 8.1 per cent higher than that in the reference year 1990. It is thus necessary to take measures to reduce CO_2 by 8.7 per cent (after 3.8 per cent is ensured by taking forest-absorbing and 1.6 per cent is ensured by the Kyoto mechanism) to achieve the reduction target of reducing CO_2 by 6 per cent in comparison to 1990 in the Kyoto Protocol Target Accomplishment Plan. To definitely reduce CO_2 by 8.7 per cent, it is necessary to increase the energy supply that does not discharge CO_2 in order to save much more energy than before.

With regard to the oil supply and demand in Asia, crude oil supply is shrinking while demand is growing more and more through economic development. Asia's total oil demand is about 22 million b/d, including China, Japan and South Korea. Asia has Chinese (Daqing) and Indonesian crude oil, but this regional crude oil production can no longer cover growing regional demand. Asian countries are now procuring crude oil from the Middle East, Russia and other regions outside of Asia. As a whole, Northeast Asia now depends on imports for close to 80 per cent of its oil supply.

Looking at Japan's crude oil supply sources by region (Figure 10.1), the Middle East's share is around 90 per cent, followed by South Asia, China and African countries. Despite the effort to diversify the importing source of oil, Japan's dependence on the Middle East has been climbing again since the 1990s due to the crude oil supply decline in the East Asian nations (Figure 10.2).

The status of energy policies in Japan

Until quite recently the public's interest in the energy problem in Japan was rather low in general. In terms of their awareness of policy priorities, energy and environmental issues were ranked at lower positions compared to issues concerning the ageing population and the resultant decreasing number of children, as well as with issues of social security, etc. Such low interest in the energy problem is partly due to the fact that since the 1980s oil prices have remained at low levels and thus oil has been seen as just another commodity among many other commodities dealt with on the market. At the same

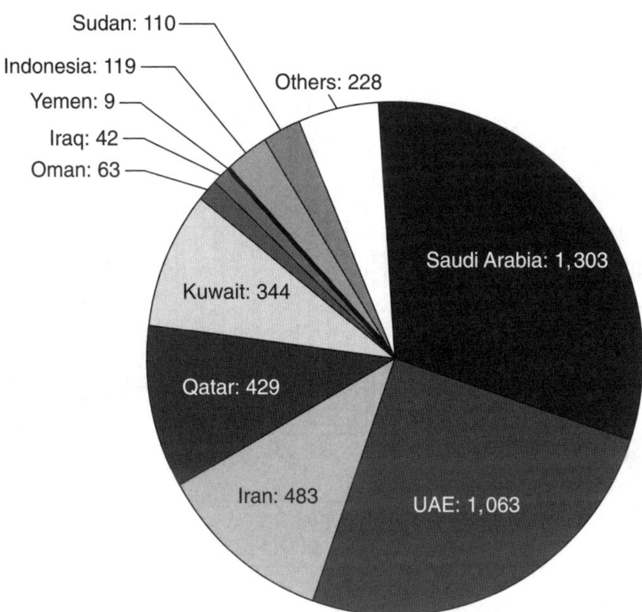

Figure 10.1   Japan's crude oil imports by country
Source: Petroleum Association of Japan, 'Oil Statistics, Crude Oil Import by Countries', http://www.
paj.gr.jp/english/statis.html, accessed 25 December 2007.

time, Japanese energy policy seemed to lack a coherent and comprehensive strategic perspective.

Now, however, in terms of the international energy environment surrounding Japan, conditions have become increasingly severe and difficult. Including oil and natural gas, 70–80 per cent of confirmed reserves of energy resources in the world are in the hands of either the governments or the NOCs of oil-producing countries. Therefore, it is becoming more apparent that though energy resources are there, private companies are not necessarily free to develop these resources. Under these circumstances, international rivalry and struggles for these energy resources, as well as diplomatic offensives for the stable supply of energy resources, are becoming increasingly intensified in Asia.

In such circumstances, the Japanese government issued a new energy strategy in June 2006. The main items of content of the strategy are the following.

With regard to a basic recognition of the current situation, the strategy describes the change in the energy supply–demand structure in the

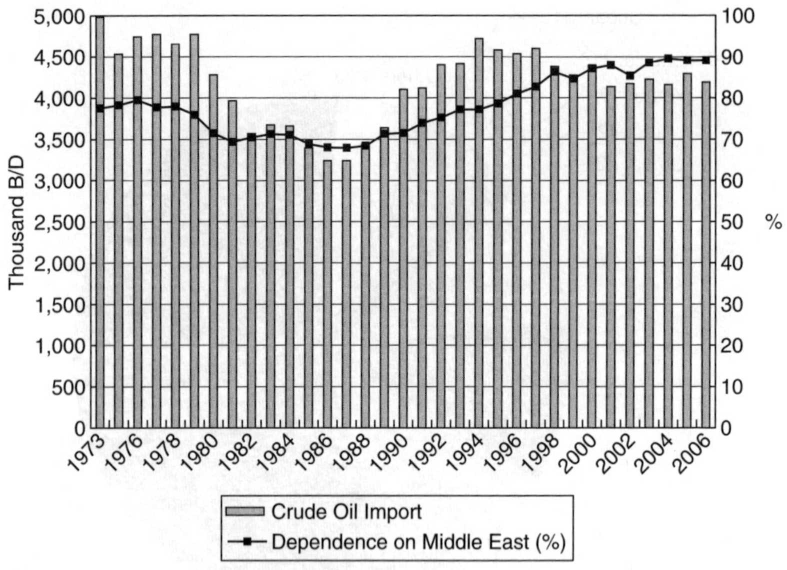

Figure 10.2   Trends in dependence on the Middle Eastern crude oil imports of Japan
Source: Petroleum Association of Japan, 'Oil Statistics, Crude Oil Import by Countries', http://www.paj.gr.jp/english/statis.html, accessed 25 December 2007.

following terms: 'in the light of the changes after the oil crises and the outlook for the next 30 years, it can be comprehended that the international energy market is facing a major structural change owing to various elements concerning both supply and demand conditions'. Furthermore, the strategy acknowledges that it is highly likely that the current high price level of crude oil will continue in the medium and long term, based on the tight supply–demand structures in the international energy market.

On the demand side, various challenges have become obvious: the rapid increase and projected growth continuation of global energy demands, especially in Asian countries; the strengthened activities of China, India and other countries' resource interests and the expanded influence of those countries on the international energy market; a possible increase of fuel demand in the transport sector; and lack of supply capacity in the consuming countries due to insufficiency of supply logistics and infrastructure.

With regard to structural change in supply, the following challenges have become obvious: the need to strengthen state control over energy resources and restrict foreign capital in oil/gas-producing countries; the lack of large-scale distribution infrastructure such as pipelines; the declining supply of power from non-OPEC nations and increasing dependence on the Middle

East; and an increased awareness of the long-term resource constraint as represented by the 'peak oil' debate.

As with the trend of debate over the international framework, there has been increasing debate over the international framework to address climate change, nuclear non-proliferation and other issues relevant to energy supply–demand structures. It becomes more and more important for Japan to be highly committed to these issues through international cooperation and to contribute to establishing new frameworks.

In these circumstances, it is essential for Japan to establish the New National Energy Strategy with focus on energy security. The New National Energy Strategy intends to achieve the following three objectives:

- The establishment of energy security measures that the Japanese people can trust and rely on.
- The establishment of the foundation for sustainable development through a comprehensive approach to energy and environmental issues.
- A commitment to assist Asian and world nations in addressing energy problems.

With regard to the first of these points, the current trend of soaring oil prices has not yet caused material damage to the overall domestic economy in Japan, and we do not see such confusion as was seen during the past oil crises. However, it is fair to say that Japan is at high risk mainly owing to the following three aspects of energy supply and demand conditions.

The energy security measures focus on the promotion of efforts to establish a state-of-the-art energy supply–demand structure, attempts to avoid various diversified or multipurpose risk elements through strengthening strategies to address foreign issues, and reinforcement of measures to minimize market confusion even in a time of emergency.

With regard to 'the establishment of the foundation for sustainable development through a comprehensive approach to energy and environmental issues', at the Gleneagles summit held in the UK in July 2005, leaders reached an agreement on the significance of a comprehensive and unified approach to address energy issues and climate change issues together. As a result, the Gleneagles Plan of Action on Climate Change, Clean Energy and Sustainable Development was adopted. As shown by this agreement, there has been a growing recognition that environmental issues are inextricably linked with energy strategy.

In the course of promoting energy security by addressing diversified or multipurpose energy supply restraints, it is necessary to pay attention to environmental concerns including climate change so that both issues can be addressed integrally. Also, such a comprehensive solution requires the implementation of medium- or long-term projects to develop advanced technologies (such as decarbonization technology) that make it possible to reduce dependence on fossil fuels.

Furthermore, as one of the world's most environmentally and technologically advanced nations, Japan should take the initiative in building various international frameworks to address global environmental issues.

Regarding the third point above, 'a commitment to assist Asian and world nations in addressing energy problems', the international energy market is interlinked with the overall trend of the world economy, including the capital markets. In addition, Japanese industries, especially frontier industries, already depend on complex, Asian-based international specialization networks.

In the light of these circumstances, Japan will have to be careful not to stir up international competition for natural resources as a result of implementing its national energy security measures, while the primary objective is to secure the stable supply of energy for the country through country-wide efforts to address both domestic and foreign issues. For this reason, Japan should introduce global viewpoints and world-level visions to its New National Energy Strategy, with the goal of maintaining a symbiotic relationship with the Asian and world economy, so that Japan's technological strengths and experience in the field of energy issues can be utilized internationally to assist Asian and world nations in addressing various problems and forming the foundation for future development.

Furthermore, the New National Energy Strategy has set five, specific, numerical targets for medium or long-term milestones in order to improve energy security. It is essential to have a long-term strategy and to clarify the direction towards which both public and private organizations should coordinate their efforts. These targets are as follows:

1. Energy conservation

Japan's economy has achieved an energy consumption efficiency of over 30 per cent since the oil shock of the 1970s. By establishing a positive cycle of technical innovation and social system reforms in the future, it aims to improve energy consumption efficiency by at least another 30 per cent by 2030.

2. Reduced dependence on oil

Japan's dependence on oil should be reduced from 50 per cent in 2005 to less than 40 per cent in 2030.

3. Transport energy for the next generation

In order to establish a highly efficient transport infrastructure that will be able to respond flexibly to the changes of the energy market, such as the demand–supply pressure in the oil market, Japan proposes to prepare the necessary

Table 10.1   Summary of the New National Energy Strategy of Japan (May 2006). Five numerical targets for the year 2030

Items	Target
Energy conservation	In the past 30 years energy efficiency was improved by about 37%, Japan aims to improve efficiency further by at least 30% by 2030
Reducing oil ratio in primary energy supply	From about 50% as oil ratio currently, Japan aims to reduce the oil dependence rate to less than 40%
Reducing oil dependence in transport sector	Currently oil dependence of the transport sector is about 100%. Japan aims to reduce the oil dependence ratio to approximately 80% by 2030
Nuclear power generation	Even after 2030, Japan aims to bring the usage rate of nuclear power generation out of total generated electricity to above 30–40%
Overseas natural resources development	While competition for acquiring resources is intensifying internationally, Japan aims to bring the rate to around 40% by 2030

Source: METI (2006), 'Energy in Japan 2006', http://www.enecho.meti.go.jp/english/index.html, accessed 25 December 2007; METI (2006) 'New National Energy Strategy (Digest)', http://www. enecho.meti.go.jp/English/index.html, accessed 25 December 2007.

environment with the aim of reducing the oil dependency of the transport sector to about 80 per cent by 2030.

4. Nuclear power

Nuclear power has excellent supply stability and is a clean energy source that does not emit CO_2 in operation. It is pivotal to establishing energy security and solving the global environment issues integrally. After 2030, Japan aims to increase its usage ratio to over 30–40 per cent of the power energy volume. As well as systematically and comprehensively tackling various issues such as the steady promotion of the nuclear fuel cycle based on the current light-water reactor and the early practical application of the fast-breeder reactor, the research and development of fusion energy technology is to be promoted.

5. Overseas natural resources development

The oil volume ratio for exploration and development by Japanese companies will be increased to around 40 per cent by 2030, through reinforcing its over-all relationship with the sources of supply and through having its businesses strengthen their support for research and development, and promoting the diversification of supply sources.

Energy-related trends in the Asian region (energy outlook by IEEJ)

The Institute of Energy Economics of Japan (IEEJ) issued the *Asia and World Energy Outlook 2007* in October 2007.[1] According to the *Outlook*, demand for energy is expected to increase in Asia on a medium and long-term basis.

The world's primary energy consumption will grow at the rate of 1.9 per cent per annum in the period up to 2030, from 10.3 billion tons (oil equivalent ton) to 16.5 billion tons (toe). Approximately 90 per cent of this growth will be due to an increase in the consumption of fossil fuels.

Geographically, approximately one half of the expected increase in primary energy consumption will be accounted for by increases in Asia, particularly in China and India. Around 90 per cent of this growth will also be satisfied with an increase in the consumption of fossil fuels.

In 2030, the primary energy consumed by China and India will represent 26 per cent of the primary energy consumed in the world. The primary energy consumed by China in 2030 will grow 3.1 billion tons (toe) from 1.5 billion tons (toe) in 2005 and India's consumption will grow 1.1 billion tons (toe) from 0.38 billion tons (toe) in 2005.

What makes these trends different from those in the 1970s which witnessed the oil crises is that the present growth trend in energy demand is not expected to be necessarily temporary. If overheated Chinese economic growth is to be redressed, there may be a temporary slowdown in energy demand. However, in terms of the overall trend for the next ten or twenty years to come, the consumption of energy will continue to grow.

In terms of energy supply sources to meet this increased demand, coal will be the largest supply source in absolute volume. Oil supplies are also expected to expand. Big increases in crude oil production cannot be expected within Asia, but the degree of dependence upon imports will rise 84 per cent by 2030. About 80 per cent of the increment of petroleum consumption is to be supplied by Middle East OPEC countries, which have the necessary resources and cost competitiveness.

Carrying out steady investment in expansion of the productive capacity corresponding to increased demand holds the key to stabilization of an international oil market. It will become the main priority for coping with the measures which Japan should take from the viewpoint of energy security (a preventive measure) so that the problems facing both the People's Republic of China and India may be avoided. Promotion of a policy dialogue, energy-saving cooperation, green engineering cooperation, the cooperation in diversification and supply capability reinforcement of energy sources, cooperation for building oil stockpiling, etc. are various options, and the they can make effective use of Japan's accumulated technology. Many of these measures will be effective also as environmental measures. Especially as energy saving environmental measures, promoting an international framework is most important in view of the importance of the greenhouse gas discharges of countries in the region. It is necessary to build a framework after the Kyoto Protocol, where all the important discharging countries participate, sharing in terms of fairness, effectiveness and efficiency.

World CO_2 emissions are expected to increase by 1.6 times, from 7500 million tons to 11,700 million tons in 2030. The increase in Asia is predicted to be by 1.9 times, from 2700 million tons in 2005 to 5 billion tons in 2030. Although Asia will be responsible for 55 per cent of the increment of the entire world, about 30 per cent of the increment in the world will be by the People's Republic of China alone. In terms of world CO_2 emissions, although Asia accounts for a big proportion, its air pollution and SO_2 contamination, which originate in coal use, are also serious as an environmental problem concentrated in Northeast Asia.

As a result, the importance of energy conservation measures is recognized in Asia. The increase of energy demand will be reduced in energy saving, CO_2 emissions will be reduced and there are three sources of reducing energy costs.

The significance of energy saving for energy security in Asia

Overview

There has been worldwide interest in the importance of measures for enhancing energy efficiency and saving energy. Energy saving is an effective measure to achieve medium- and long-term objectives in terms of promoting energy security and counter-measures against global warming.

Japan is at the forefront in the field of energy saving. In terms of the widely used index of energy consumption per GNP, if the basic figure of 1 is for Japan, it is 2 for the USA and 8 for China. Thus, Japan is regarded as one of the most energy-efficient countries in the world.

Why has energy saving been promoted in Japan? In answering this question, geographical factors such as Japan's land area and climatic conditions have played a role. However, political, economic and social factors have been more important.

Firstly, market mechanisms have played a large role in energy saving through energy prices. As was seen in the oil crisis in the 1970s, in Japan, which depends upon imports for most of its energy resources, price hikes in imported oils, and including oil products, electricity and gas, can be passed on to the final consumer relatively easily. As a result, companies endeavoured to shift to a more energy saving oriented industrial structure and to intensify the development of energy saving technology. On the other hand, consumers became more energy minded by choosing energy saving equipment and appliances.

In contrast, the USA and China are more endowed with domestic resources and have a number of energy producing companies. Energy prices in these countries are lower than in Japan. Perhaps in these countries companies have found it politically more difficult to pass oil price hikes on to the prices of other end products. In the USA and China companies are more liable to price control by the government because of the need to protect consumers' interests or regulate major energy producer companies' excessive profitability.

Furthermore, in Japan, with its scanty domestic resources, direct government regulation, including the regulation of energy saving standards for factories, automobiles and electric home appliances, seems to be politically and socially more easily accepted. There is also a general willingness in society to comply with regulatory measures as much as possible, not to mention the willingness to introduce voluntary regulation. In the USA there is a political climate that is generally hostile to government intervention. In the past, attempts have often been made to introduce taxation on gasoline and to improve companies' average fuel economy (CAFE) standards. But these attempts have been thwarted due to strong opposition from the US Congress. Recently China has embarked upon setting energy saving standards by following the example of the Japanese Energy Saving Law. However, provincial governments and companies seem to be not yet ready to comply with the central government's proposed regulations.

It should also be mentioned that Japanese success in energy saving is backed up by a culture of valuing things and avoiding any waste, traditionally nurtured by Japanese people throughout their history since the seventeenth-century Edo period. This culture is deeply rooted in the national character of the Japanese people. It is true that during the bubble economy period in the early 1970s 'use and throw away' oriented consumerism was prevalent, but it has proved to be a passing phenomenon. Supported by the public's growing awareness of environmental issues, the 3 Rs (Reduce, Reuse and Recycle) movement is widely supported. The Japanese phrase *Mottai Nai*, meaning 'too good to be wasted', is more and more heard among Japanese people. There are many Japanese people who insist that Japan should communicate this message widely to the rest of the world.

Recent international efforts to cope with energy saving

Recently a number of international frameworks for energy saving have been created. These frameworks have been conceptualized mainly with regard to the issues posed by big energy-consuming countries in Asia such as China and India. Energy saving problems used to be discussed mainly in the context of domestic problems. Now they have become an international agenda.

The enormous increase in energy demand in these countries, caused by their rapid economic growth, has strained the world energy market. Consequently, while the importance of ensuring supply sources is increasingly being emphasized in terms of energy security, the need for controlling energy demand through the efficient use of energy is also more and more called for.

Within the United Nations both developed countries and developing countries are locked in a sort of confrontational framework. A climate persists where developing countries refuse to join in action against global warming in spite of the expected increase in their greenhouse gas emissions. However, various new international frameworks prioritize energy saving measures that will result in reducing greenhouse gas emissions. These frameworks are geared to promoting efficient energy saving by starting with areas of high emissions reduction potential through technical cooperation between developed countries and developing countries. In this way they will complement the discussions within the UN in terms of bringing about consequential reduction of greenhouse gas emissions.

Essential participation of developing countries

The issue of climate change is an important long-term global issue to be coped with by humanity. The ultimate goal of the Framework Convention on Climatic Change is to stabilize the concentration of greenhouse gases in the atmosphere. Various studies have concluded that substantial reduction of greenhouse gases is needed to achieve this goal. As is shown in the fourth IPCC report released in February 2007, global warming is surely and steadily getting worse. Now consensus is being formed that very quick and substantial reduction of greenhouse gases emissions is necessary.

Even if developed countries reduced their emissions by 50 per cent by 2050, they would only contribute to approximately a 10 per cent reduction of the total world emissions. Approximately 50 per cent of the expected emissions growth is likely to originate from China and India; the latter country follows the former in terms of the size of emissions.

Therefore, it is extremely important that every single country in the world should endeavour to reduce its emissions. The participation of developing countries is essential for ensuring the effective implementation of measures against global warming.

The issue of global warming and energy security

The Kyoto Protocol provides quantitative emissions reduction targets for the First Commitment Period (2008–12). Discussions are now going on within the United Nations to provide for effective arrangements of counter-measures against global warming for beyond 2013. Developing countries argue that global warming has resulted from greenhouse gas emissions from economic activities since the Industrial Revolution and therefore it is an agenda to be tackled by developed countries. Developed countries argue that global warming is an agenda to be addressed by all humanity and therefore developing countries will also be required to reduce emissions sooner or later. Arguments on both sides do not meet. As a result, it remains difficult to reach any compromise. At the International Conference of Major Countries on

Counter-Measures against Global Warming, held on 27–28 September 2007 in Washington, parallel arguments on both sides remained unchanged.

High resources prices, resulting from the tight energy market and conditions of unstable supplies of energy resources, work as factors constraining economic development in developing countries. With respect to this, to preserve valuable domestic resources through efficient energy consumption and to save the cost of overseas resources imports is as important as securing stable energy supplies.

Moreover, developed countries' assistance to help developing countries enhance their efficiency in the use of resources will ease demand pressures on the market. It is also welcomed in terms of improving energy security. Improvement in energy use efficiency, namely energy saving, will also contribute effectively towards a solution for the global warming issue as it will reduce greenhouse gas emissions caused by energy uses.

It is against such a background that over the past few years a series of international frameworks of cooperation on energy saving have been put forward to integrate aspects of both energy security and global warming.

International frameworks for addressing issues of energy and environment

The Asia Pacific Partnership and Gleneagles Action Programme are international frameworks for cooperation in areas including energy saving, initiated in July 2005.

The Asia Pacific Partnership on Clean Development and Climate (APP) involves six countries, namely the USA and Australia, who have not ratified the Kyoto Protocol, China, India, Korea and Japan. The combined CO_2 emissions of these six countries account for approximately 50 per cent of the world total. Therefore, the potential of emissions reduction that may result from energy saving cooperation among these six countries is substantial. Both governments and industrial communities participate in the Partnership.

Eight Task Forces by sector were created under the Policy Implementation Committee composed of government representatives. The major feature is that project-based activities will be initiated and carried out on the basis of action plans formulated in each sector. Japan chairs the Steel Task Force and the Cement Task Force.

The Gleneagles summit adopted the Gleneagles Action Programme on Climate Change, Clean Energy and Sustainable Development in July 2005. The G8 process based on this action programme represents an arrangement for improving energy efficiency sector by sector through cooperation among major emissions countries. Regarding the nature of this international cooperation, the International Energy Agency (IEA) was required to carry out a number of tasks. They include the development of energy efficiency rate indexes by sector. The activities cover a wide variety of sectors. They duplicate the activities of the above-mentioned APP in many areas such as the rating of energy efficiency in industrial and thermal power sectors in countries, including developing countries, review of energy saving standards in sectors of buildings, electrical equipment and automobiles, etc., in various countries as well as evaluation of best policy practices.

International energy saving cooperation initiatives led by Japan

In the New National Energy Strategy released in May 2006, Japan set itself the goal of becoming the frontrunner in energy saving and spelled out the Asia Energy and Environment Cooperation Strategy. The Strategy recommended transferring energy saving technologies Japan has developed and stocked ever since the oil crises to neighbouring developing countries in Asia as an element of the strategic 'menu'. The Asia Energy Saving Programme spelled out, among other things, bilateral policy dialogue and action plan making as well as providing assistance to Asian countries in their efforts towards institutional framework building.

In December 2006 the first meeting of the Japan–China Comprehensive Forum for Environment and Energy Saving was held. Within this framework the project for the transfer and diffusion of energy saving equipment, plants and technologies was initiated. The second meeting of the Forum was held on 27 September 2007 in Beijing to mark the 35th anniversary of the restoration of diplomatic relations between Japan and China.

The Asia Pacific Partnership is also designed to be a framework to be used by companies possessing technological capability to promote assistance activities as well as for member governments to promote the transfer of energy saving technologies among themselves. This Partnership aims at improving energy use efficiency sector by sector through the use of excellent technologies. The development of efficiency indexes required for the benchmark approach is also regarded as one of its important activities. The collection of data on technologies, energy consumption and production as well as the definition of efficiency indexes are regarded as important end products.

Energy security in Northeast Asia (Cebu Declaration)

In January 2007 the second East Asia summit meeting was held with the participation of the heads of states and governments of sixteen countries, namely the ten ASEAN countries plus Japan, China, Korea, Australia, New Zealand and India. Discussion on energy security was the priority agenda of this meeting. The meeting adopted the Cebu Declaration on Energy Security in East Asia.

This Declaration spelled out five goals to enhance energy security in East Asia. These goals are, firstly, to improve the environmental friendliness of fossil fuel use technologies; secondly, to reduce dependence on fossil fuels; thirdly, to promote the development of the intra-regional electricity power market; fourthly, to reduce the emission of greenhouse gases; and fifthly, to promote energy-related investment and infrastructure development.

International Conference of Major Countries on Counter-Measures against Global Warming

The International Conference of Major Countries on Counter-Measures against Global Warming was held on 27–28 September 2007 in Washington. Foreign Minister Koumura represented Japan. The conference was attended by representatives from fifteen of the major greenhouse gas emissions countries such as the US, China and Japan. At this conference Japan proposed the creation of an international cooperative set-up for accelerating technological development to ensure the effective implementation of measures against global warming, in particular promoting the development of innovative technologies to reduce greenhouse gas emissions. This would be focused among other things on related technologies for high efficiency photovoltaic power generation, next generation reactors, fuel cell cars and thermal power station-generated carbon dioxide underground sequestration technologies, etc. As Prime Minister Abe had proposed on several occasions, Foreign Minister Koumura asserted that major greenhouse gas emissions countries should aim at reducing their emissions by 50 per cent by 2050, through promoting the improvement of energy consumption efficiency.

Conclusions

To maintain a good relationship with the Middle East, which has 70 per cent of world crude oil reserves, is crucially important for the energy security of Japan. Japan should also consider its energy strategy, watching the moves in the Asian region as a whole. I will give priority to the following points as concluding remarks.

Firstly, Japan should enhance its relationship with the Middle East. It should endeavour to strengthen a wide range of economic relations through a free trade agreement or an economic partnership agreement with the Gulf Cooperation Council (GCC) countries. Japan's technologies, human development capabilities and business management skills will be more important in this respect.

Secondly, the promotion of independent development of foreign oil resources is also important for Japan as a resource-poor country. The new National Energy Strategy calls for an increase in the share from 15 per cent at present to 40 per cent by 2030. It is expected to be difficult to achieve the target, but the establishment of a scheme of three-way cooperation among government, finance and business sectors will be the key to creating energy supply channels.

Thirdly, Japan should proactively provide emerging consuming countries with its energy-saving technologies and should contribute to improving the energy supply and demand structure in Asia.

Note

1. IEEJ, *Asia/World Energy Outlook 2007*, http://www.ieej.or.jp/en/index.html, accessed 25 December 2007.

11
Energy Security in Northeast Asia: Competition and Cooperation

Tai Hwan Lee

Introduction

This chapter explores the issues of energy competition and cooperation by analysing energy security in Northeast Asia with a special emphasis on its geopolitical dimension. With the rise of China and its rapidly growing oil demand, oil and gas supply has become a central concern of the consumer countries in Northeast Asia, including China, Japan and Korea. As high energy prices have persisted since mid-2000, a sense of crisis has arisen regarding Northeast Asian energy security. With the oil price hike reaching over 100 dollars per barrel, it is more imperative than ever before to address the energy security and energy cooperation issues in Northeast Asia. Even before the price hike, the rising dependence on foreign energy supply, especially the dependence on the Middle East, and increasing Chinese energy demands had led to Northeast Asian energy security problems.[1]

After the second oil crisis in the 1970s, energy security meant security of oil supply. In the 1970s the two oil shocks and the emergence of the Organization for Petroleum Exporting Countries (OPEC) led to a new round of energy security concerns, demanding their own set of appropriate policy responses. Securing access to oil has been a focus of energy security ever since. In addition to securing access to oil, energy security involves a larger question of conflicting national objectives and values. According to Daniel Yergin, the objective of energy security 'is to assure adequate, reliable supplies of energy at reasonable prices and in ways that do not jeopardize major national values and objectives'.[2] In China, for example, energy security means the acquisition of sufficient energy supplies at affordable prices to protect the Chinese leadership's core objectives.[3] It focuses on the access to sufficient energy supplies to protect the leadership's core objectives of continued economic growth, the prevention of Taiwanese independence and China's continued emergence as a global power. National security is intertwined with securing energy supply. Even though the share of oil in the world energy mix has been reduced, oil remains a strategic commodity critical to national strategies and international politics. Energy security was the driving force behind European and US foreign policy efforts to speed up the process of unlocking the huge Middle East oil reserves. Energy security concerns have been central to geopolitical interests as well as the oil supply of each country. Aggressive oil diplomacy for energy security has become part of larger foreign policy issues of the United States and China, as shown in the case of Iran and Sudan.

Energy security can be viewed from the comprehensive security perspective encompassing environmental security and economic security.[4] According to a Pentagon report issued in 1998, comprehensive security, the notion that was first advanced by Olaf Palme, the late Swedish Prime Minister, includes the security of diverse dimensions such as terrorism, environmental degradation, infectious diseases, drug trafficking, energy and humanitarian relief.[5] From the comprehensive security perspective, energy security means not only ensuring stable energy supply, but also elements related to the management of energy involving environmental aspects.[6]

The questions addressed here are to what extent Asia's high economic growth rates will widen the gap between energy demand and production of the countries in the region, and whether serious conflicts will emerge as a result of competition over energy resources with the rising resource nationalism among the countries concerned. This chapter starts with the question of why energy security matters in Northeast Asia by addressing the economic and geopolitical dimensions of energy security. On the basis of this analysis, it evaluates and explores the possibility of energy security cooperation in Northeast Asia by analysing national interests and strategies of the countries concerned based on post-Cold War geopolitics. In the final section, it addresses the prospect of energy security in Northeast Asia and proposes suggestions for energy security cooperation.

Why does energy security matter in Northeast Asia?

The economic dimension of energy security

Uneven distribution of oil and gas reserves

The energy security problems have their roots in the uneven distribution of world oil reserves (Tables 11.1 and 11.2). Three-quarters of the world's oil reserves are located in the Middle East.

In Northeast Asia, oil and gas resources are unevenly located and generally far from major centres of energy consumption. Oil and gas reserves are abundant in the Middle East and Russian Far East, while Japan and Korea have no significant domestic oil or gas fields and have to import most of their oil requirements. Although China has some oil and gas reserves, China, Japan and Korea need to import most of their oil and diversify energy supplies by reducing their heavy dependence on Middle East oil.

Table 11.1   World oil reserves by major producer country (2007)

Country/Oil reserves (billion BL)

World total	*1,317.4*		
Saudi Arabia	262.3	Canada	179.2
Iran	136.3	Iraq	115.0
Kuwait	101.5	United Arab Emirates	97.8
Venezuela	80.0	Russia	60.0
Libya	41.5	United States	21.8

Source: *Oil & Gas Journal*, Vol. 104, No. 47, 18 December 2006, pp. 24–5.

Table 11.2   World natural gas reserves by country (2007)

Country/Gas reserves (trillion cubic feet/percentage of world)

World Total	*6,183 (100.0)*		
Russia	1,680 (27.2)	Qatar	911 (14.7)
United Arab Emirates	214 (3.5)	Nigeria	182 (2.9)
Venezuela	152 (2.5)	Iran	974 (15.8)
Saudi Arabia	240 (3.9)	United States	204 (3.3)
Algeria	162 (2.6)	Iraq	112 (1.8)

Source: *Oil & Gas Journal*, Vol. 104, No. 47, 18 December 2006, pp. 24–5.

The growing gap between energy demand and supply

China is the world's second largest oil consumer after the US and Japan is the third. Korea is also included in the top ten oil consumers (Figure 11.1). China recently overtook Japan as the world's second biggest consumer of oil. China's growing energy consumption has contributed to the rise of international oil prices. In order to meet the rapidly increasing energy demand needed to sustain economic development, a stable supply of oil and gas is essential. Any supply disruption due to instability in the Middle East will have serious effects on these countries.

World energy demand will increase by 53 per cent by 2030 and 37.5 million barrels per (mbd) day need to be added in the period from 2006 through to 2015. As OPEC and non-OPEC producers have announced plans to add 25 mbd through to 2015, a further 12.5 mbd oil need to be added.[7] Energy supply problems in Northeast Asia will become even more serious by 2010 and the possibilities of energy competition and conflict between Northeast Asian countries are high.[8]

Asia has been a driver of world oil demand, accounting for about 40 per cent of world oil consumption (Figure 11.2). According to the Asia/World

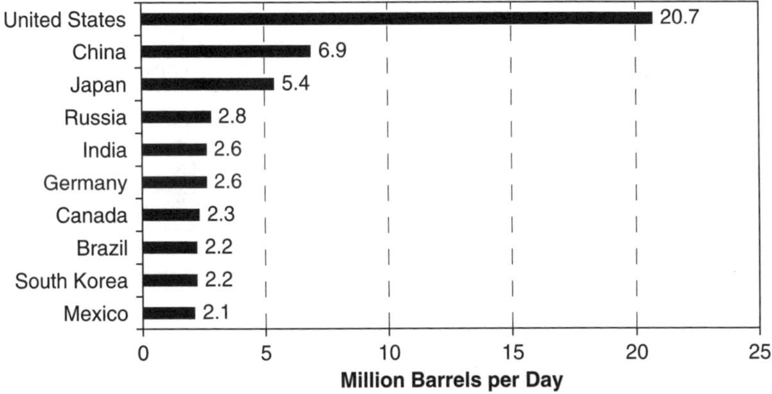

Figure 11.1   World top ten oil consumers (2005)

Source: US Department of Energy, Energy Information Administration, *Short Term Energy Outlook*, 2006, http://www.eia.doe.gov.

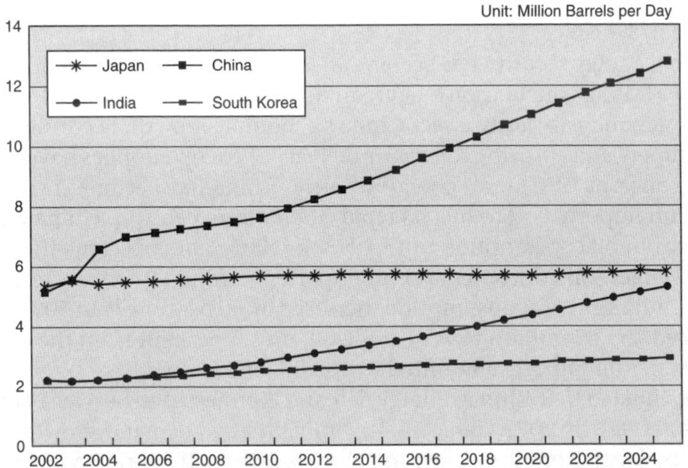

Figure 11.2   Growing oil demand in Asia (MBD)

Source: US Department of Energy, *Annual Energy Outlook 2005*, http://www.doe.gov.

Energy Outlook 2006, China and India will account for about a quarter of worldwide primary energy consumption and about 40 per cent of the increase in oil consumption by 2030.

Energy security in Northeast Asia is closely related to the Middle East factor.[9] Korea and Japan depend on Middle Eastern oil for more than two-thirds of their energy supplies.[10] China is also dependent on the Middle East to supply a large share of its oil needs: 60 per cent of China's imported oil

Table 11.3 China's oil demand and imports (MMBD)

	2000	2004	2010	2020	2020* Imports	Import Share
Actual (BP 2005)	5.0	6.7				
IEA (WEO 2004)			7.9	11.6	7.1	67%
DOE (IEO 2005)			9.2	12.3	8.8	72%
East-West Center (3/05)			8.6	12.3	8.8	72%
IEE Japan (3/04)			7.3	12.0	8.5	71%
Merrill Lynch (11/04)		10.0				

* Assuming 3.5 mbd domestic production.

comes from the Middle East while 18 per cent of US imported oil comes from the same region. According to the IEA forecast, China is likely to import 70 per cent of its total oil demand and 70 per cent of China's oil imports will come from three countries in the Middle East, likely to be Iran, Saudi Arabia and Oman, by 2015.

The China factor

In China, energy security has become an issue of the high politics of national security.[11] Price fluctuations have an immediate impact on all national economies and can easily affect China's economic growth. Securing an adequate supply and ensuring the secure delivery of energy supplies have become major concerns of China's energy security. China has become increasingly reliant on imported oil to fuel its rapid economic expansion. China was self-sufficient in oil consumption until 1993. In 2005, China became the world's second largest oil consumer and oil importer (behind Japan). From 2000 to 2005, China's energy consumption increased by 60 per cent.[12] In 2006, China produced 183.68 million tons of crude oil, up 1.7 per cent from the previous year. Its net oil imports amounted to 162.87 million tons.

It is estimated that China's energy demand is projected to be over 14 million barrels per day by 2025 (Table 11.3).[13] In China, oil demand growth will be driven by an enormous increase in vehicles. Although China had 22 million cars in 2006, it is estimated China will have from 120 to 150 million vehicles by 2020. China will probably have more cars than the United States by 2030, reaching 140 per 1000 people.

The geopolitical dimension of energy security

The geopolitical environment of Northeast Asia is basically to be competitive rather than cooperative. Rising competition in Asia over access to energy supplies could significantly affect the geopolitical landscape as regional powers struggle to secure access to energy and compete over energy prices. The Russian Far East, with vast energy reserves and relative geographical proximity to Northeast Asian markets, is already an arena for competition among the

Asian powers.[14] In addition, strategic rivalry over access to energy resources decreases trust between consuming nations and makes cooperation among them difficult.

Competition and disputes between China and Japan

The Siberian oil and gas pipeline.   The Russian Far East, with its vast energy reserves, is an arena for competition among the Asian powers. The competition between China and Japan over access to Russian oil, via a pipeline from Siberia, is a good example of this. In the dispute over the East Siberian oil pipeline route, China and Japan tried to turn the oil pipeline to their own advantage.[15] An agreement between Russia and China to construct a pipeline from Angarsk to Daqing was reached by Presidents Putin and Hu in May 2003. In 2005, however, Russia changed the route from the nearby city of Taishet to Skovorodino and then on to Daqing. Later, the pipeline would be extended to Nakhodka, as proposed by Japan. This was after the arrest of the chairman of Yukos that had brokered the deal and planned to construct the pipeline.[16] It is not easy for China and Japan to reach an agreement on this pipeline route.

The East China Sea.   The competition between China and Japan over leadership in East Asia is becoming obvious, even though economic interdependence between the two countries has increased simultaneously. China and Japan have disputes over the Chunxiao (Shirakaba) gas fields in the East China Sea. The gas exploration dispute stems from the unsettled demarcation of the exclusive economic zones claimed by the two countries. Japan argues that the median line divides the two countries' exclusive zones while China argues for Okinawa through the natural prolongation principle. China began serious exploratory operations in May 2004 and built a pipeline from the gas field to Shanghai. China has already started production in the Tianwaitian area of the Chunxiao oil and gas field, which is west of the median line that Japan says divides the two nations' exclusive economic zone (EEZ).

On the other hand, a report suggested that China would not compete with Japan or South Korea for regional energy sources in the near future.[17] This is because China will not seek to develop disputed offshore oil and natural gas in the South China Sea and East China Sea unless oil prices continue to rise dramatically in the near future.

Iran

Another important potential conflict could come from rivalry over the Middle East, including Iran. The competition between China and Japan to sign free-trade agreements with the Gulf Cooperation Council states of the Persian Gulf, during the period 2004–7, shows that the two countries could develop a rivalry over energy issues in the Middle East.[18] China made a $70 billion deal with Iran over the Yadaravan oil field while Japan cultivated Azadegan,

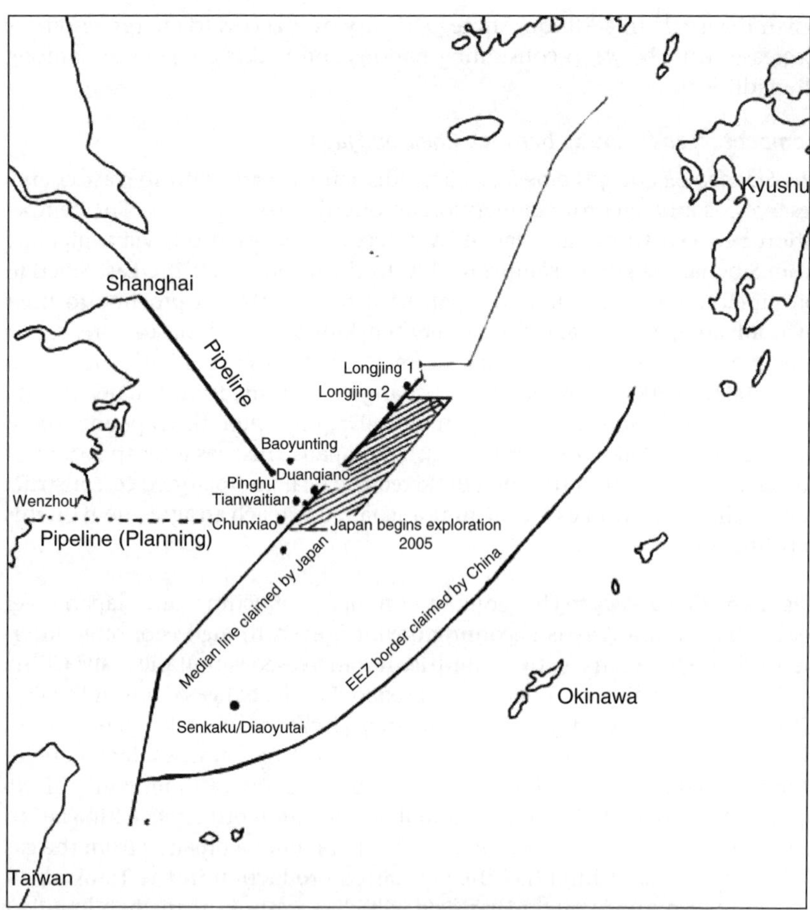

Figure 11.3 Gas fields under dispute in East China Sea

though in vain, primarily due to the US–Japan alliance. The Azadegan oil deal with Inpex Holdings of Japan was revoked because the US was concerned about the Iranian nuclear issue. The Bush administration voiced its concerns to Japanese officials about investment in Iran based on the latter's suspected nuclear weapons development programme. In December 2007, however, China finally reached an agreement with Iran in which China will invest in an oil project in the Middle East nation estimated to cost US$2 billion.[19] The original memorandum of understanding in 2004 included the export of 10 million tonnes of liquefied natural gas (LNG) annually from Iran to China for 25 years.

The North Korean nuclear issue

The North Korean factors related to energy security include the nuclear weapons programme and gas pipeline construction. The economic crisis North Korea has faced is fundamentally due to energy shortages derived from the cut off of oil supplied by China and Russia during the Cold War era. The energy shortage has led to an overall shutdown of industrial activity and, in turn, a total economic crisis. Given the energy shortages in North Korea, resolving the issue of North Korea's nuclear weapons programme through the Six-Party Talks would require careful attention to that country's energy needs.

Energy has played a central and controversial role in the ongoing Six-Party Talks between the United States, China, North Korea, South Korea, Japan and Russia to deal with North Korea's nuclear weapons programme. Under the 1994 Agreed Framework, North Korea was to be provided with two light water reactors, the construction of which was suspended after the second nuclear crisis in 2002. The North Korean nuclear crisis is to a certain extent related to the energy crisis and the peaceful resolution of the North Korean nuclear issue could have a strong influence on the future of Northeast Asian energy cooperation. If the United States, China and Russia support energy cooperation with North Korea, it could be a better model for regional energy cooperation than KEDO,[20] which has been suspended.[21] However, energy cooperation with North Korea cannot start until North Korea dismantles its nuclear weapons programme and disconnects energy issues from politics.

Energy transportation route security: sea lanes of communication

Many Northeast Asian countries depend on the route passing the South China Sea for oil and LNG transportation. The over-reliance on oil from the Middle East and Africa leads to an over-reliance on the Malacca Straits, which connect the Indian Ocean with the South China Sea and the Pacific Ocean.

Oil imports for Japan, South Korea, China and other Pacific Rim countries through the Malacca Straits reach 11.7 million barrels per day. China's oil imports will have to transit vulnerable maritime choke points and 85 per cent of China's imported oil passes through the Indian Ocean, Malacca Straits, and the South China Sea. More than 50 per cent of China's oil will have to transit the Malacca Straits. Any blockage in its transport routes will have immediate and direct effects on regional energy security. Piracy and terrorism pose another security threat in this region. The Malacca Straits are also known as an endless source of territorial disputes between seven neighbouring countries.

With its increasing dependence on foreign crude oil, China is eager to protect the Southeast Asian trade routes, which are currently protected mainly by the United States. China has distrusted energy markets which were perceived to be dominated by the United States. China believes that the United States exerts a powerful influence on global oil prices and flows because of its strategic power in the Persian Gulf and the US navy's control over sea transport lanes. This means that China has no choice but to rely on the US for its security of communication by sea lane, which is essential for the transportation of oil. China attempted to diversify the transportation routes to reduce its vulnerability. Other routes include coming by tanker from Africa, by pipeline and rail from Russia, and by pipeline from Central Asia.

National interests and energy security strategies

China's interests and energy strategies

Energy security has become a critical political and economic concern for China. China's leaders fear that domestic energy shortages and rising energy costs could undermine the country's economic growth because economic performance is one of the most important sources of legitimacy of the rule of the Chinese Communist Party (CCP).[22] It became a net importer of oil in 1993. With the rapid economic growth during the past decades, China has become the second largest oil consumer in the world and the third largest oil importer. China's economic policy, formulated during the late 1990s, was more focused on economic rather than security and geopolitical aspects. However, after 11 September 2001, China's energy policy became more strategic, focusing on securing oil supply. In order to formulate more comprehensive energy policies and coordinate all agencies involved in energy policy, the Energy Leading Group, headed by Premier Wen Jiabao, and the State Energy Office, was established in 2005. The Eleventh Five-Year Plan (2006–10) includes pursuit of comprehensive energy strategies, calling for a 20 per cent reduction of energy consumption per GDP unit by 2020. The new energy policy stresses not only assurance of energy supply but also reduction of consumption and efficiency.

A new concept of energy security was pronounced by President Hu Jintao in 2006. The new energy security concept was based on diversification, efficiency, environment and international cooperation on energy issues.[23] Hu called for cooperation with both producers and consumers because energy security could not be achieved without international cooperation. The White Paper, *China's Energy Conditions and Policies*, published by the State Council Information Office on 26 December 2007, also emphasizes the importance of cooperation in a similar vein. It says that to ensure world energy security, it is imperative to strengthen dialogue and cooperation between energy exporting countries and energy consuming countries, as well as between energy consuming countries.[24]

Securing access to the oil market and long-term contracts of crude supplies are the key to China's energy security. China has adopted the 'Go Out' (*Zhou Chuqi*) strategy in energy diplomacy which includes the following elements: to promote development of new overland oil and natural gas pipelines that will diversify future transport routes for energy imports; to diversify a long-term crude oil supply and liquefied natural gas supply contracts from a broad range of exporters; and to secure equity investments in oil and gas fields abroad to have control over oil supplies. China depends on the Middle East for roughly half of its energy imports. China has aggressively sought to buy into foreign oil fields and Chinese companies have acquired oil concessions in Central Asia, East Asia, the Middle East, Latin America, North America and Africa.[25]

China's aggressive efforts to increase energy security may lead to friction not only with the United States and Western countries but also with its neighbouring countries.[26] Chinese investment in developing Iranian oil fields is a case in point. China considers its relationship with Iran crucial to maintaining energy security. The two countries have been negotiating an estimated $100 billion agreement that would provide China with 150,000 barrels of oil a day and 250 million tons of liquefied natural gas over the next 25 years and would grant Sinopec a 50 per cent stake in the Yadavaran oil field.

China also has energy relations with both Japan and Korea. Japanese and to a lesser extent Korean firms are at the forefront of foreign participation in Chinese oil and gas development: onshore, offshore and in the refining industry.

China cooperated with Russia to develop energy supplies, mainly gas, in the Russian Far East and to ship them south through pipelines. China's growing engagement with Central Asia is motivated by a number of strategic interests. China played a leading role in the creation of the Shanghai Cooperation Organization (SCO), a regional security cooperation organization, in 1996. China has strengthened the SCO by increasing the number of member countries from five to six, which include China, Russia, Kazakhstan, Uzbekistan, Tajikistan and Kyrgyzstan. Moreover, India, Pakistan and Iran all sent high-level officials to attend the 2005 and 2006 meetings as observers, which shows the SCO's expanding influence. In October 2004, construction was started on a 988 km pipeline from Atasu in northwestern Kazakhstan to the Alataw Pass in Xinjiang which will carry ten million tons of oil a year. This pipeline, if connected to the Kazakhstan-Iran pipeline, could become an important continental oil pipeline reaching Asia's major energy consumers, including China, Japan and South Korea.[27] China has also looked into bypassing the Malacca Straits by constructing a pipeline through Myanmar.

Japan's new energy strategy

A 'New National Energy Strategy' was issued in 2006. The goals of the strategy include diversifying energy security risks, applying a 'comprehensive energy security' approach, and emphasizing a regional (Asian) energy security approach.[28] In order to achieve the goals, the strategy proposed various measures including strengthening resource diplomacy, establishing a state-of-the-art energy supply–demand structure, and energy and environmental cooperation.

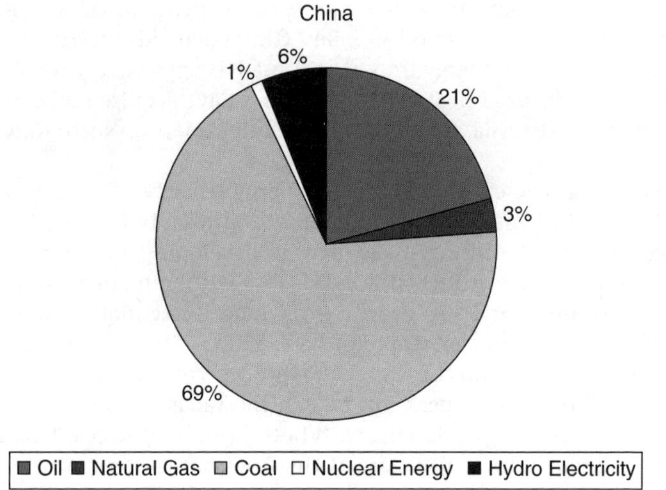

Figure 11.4 China's energy consumption mix (2006)

Table 11.4 Primary energy consumption in China, South Korea and Japan (2006) (million tons oil equivalent)

	Oil	Natural gas	Coal	Nuclear energy	Hydro electricity	Total
China	349.8	50	1191.3	12.3	94.3	1697.7
South Korea	105.3	30.8	54.8	33.7	1.2	225.8
Japan	235	76.1	119.1	68.6	21.5	520.3

Source: BP, *BP Statistical Review of World Energy 2007*,
http://www.bp.com/liveassets/bp_internet/globalbp/globalbp_uk_english/reports_and_
publications/statistical_energy_review_2007/STAGING/local_assets/downloads/pdf/statistical_
review_of_world_energy_full_report_2007.pdf

During the past decades, Japan has tried to diversify its energy sources, reducing its share of oil from over 70 per cent in 1970 to 48 per cent in 2004 and 45 per cent in 2006. While reducing oil, Japan relied on coal, natural gas and nuclear energy. Since the 1973 Arab oil embargo, Japan has increasingly relied on nuclear power to reduce its dependence on oil. Nuclear reactors provide about one-third of Japan's electricity. However, the ratio of nuclear power was 13 per cent while natural gas was about 15 per cent of energy consumption in 2006. Thus, Japan planned to add up to 12 more nuclear power plants to expand its nuclear generation by 2011.[29] Despite the attempts at diversification, Japan still imports close to 90 per cent of its oil from the Middle East.[30] Japan has actively sought supplies in the region for four decades and has maintained diplomatic relations with OPEC nations to serve its energy needs.

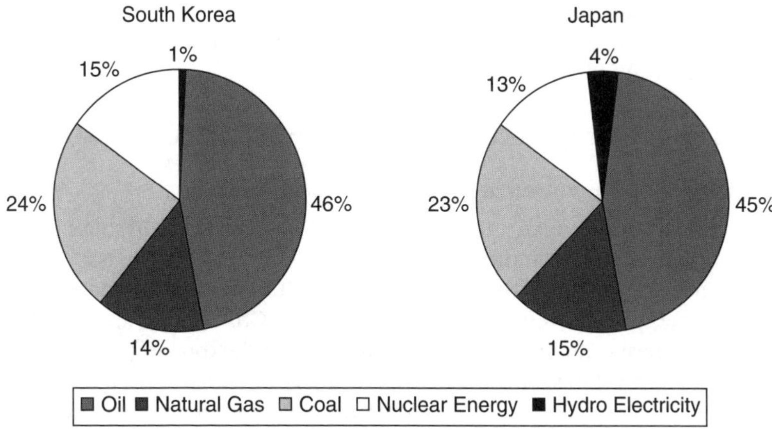

Figure 11.5   Energy consumption mix in South Korea and Japan (2006)

South Korea's energy security strategy

Like Japan, Korea lacks domestic oil and natural gas reserves and has a high level of energy consumption. Korea was tenth in primary energy consumption during 2002.[31] South Korea is the world's fifth largest oil importer and second largest LNG importer (after Japan). According to 2006 statistics, it depends on oil for 46 per cent of its energy consumption. South Korea has also adopted policies to diversify its sources of oil imports, including the Middle East, South America and Asia. Korea has succeeded in reducing heavy reliance on oil, lowering the ratio of oil to below 50 per cent of energy consumption (46 per cent in 2006).

Korea diversified the sources of energy focusing on natural gas rather than coal. The Korean National Gas Corporation (KNGC) signed a contract in July 2005 to import 1.5 million metric tons of gas a year for 20 years starting in April 2008. South Korea attempted to buy overseas oil and gas fields that would supply 18 per cent of local demand. The SK Corporation, the biggest South Korean oil refiner, for instance, started jointly developing an oil field in Kazakhstan in 2006 with LG International. SK also bought 20 per cent of a Madagascan field operated by ExxonMobil.[32] In order to help finance overseas energy projects, which was the nation's first project exclusively for oil and gas ventures abroad, Korea opened a 200 billion won ($212 million) fund in November 2006.

Nuclear power is another important source of diversification and accounts for 40 per cent of total electricity generated. Korea's reliance on nuclear power for electric power is the third highest in the world. Diversification of energy supplies and resolution of the nuclear crisis require attention to improve regional energy cooperation. One possible option is to foster nuclear energy as an export industry in cooperation with China. China plans to increase nuclear power capacity to 40GW by 2020. It means China needs to construct 4–5 units of 1GW class every year.[33]

The search for energy security cooperation in Northeast Asia

Why is energy cooperation needed in Northeast Asia?

It is not easy to establish multilateral energy cooperation because Northeast Asian countries have different interests on energy security issues. They do not share common understanding of the ultimate goal of energy cooperation. Energy importers such as South Korea, China and Japan all have different interests. Russia, as a major producer and exporting country, has totally different interests from the consuming countries.

If China, Japan and Korea link energy supply to overall security, the potential for conflict and instability is relatively high. A report suggested that China would not compete with Japan or South Korea for regional energy sources in the near future unless there are energy price hikes.[34] China will not seek to develop disputed offshore oil and natural gas in the South China Sea and East China Sea unless oil prices continue to rise dramatically in the near future. However, the price of oil at the time of release of the report was 50 dollars per barrel. Now the price is over 100 dollars. Given tight oil and gas markets and supply in the region, competition for resources among the Northeast Asian countries is likely to increase. The United States has interests in depoliticizing energy security issues all over the world. However, it is hard to disconnect national security from securing oil supply.

With respect to rivalry between China and Japan over Siberian oil pipelines, US policy opinions are divided on which of the pipeline routes better serves US national interests. The US position is to avoid getting directly involved in rivalry between China and Japan over pipeline routes from Russia.[35] Another question is arms sales. Many supply states selling oil to China, including Iraq, Iran, Sudan, Angola and Nigeria, have purchased Chinese weapons.

Evaluation of the current status of multilateral energy cooperation

Multilateral regional cooperation mechanisms in East Asia, including ASEAN plus three others, APT, APEC and the East Asia summit, have introduced programmes for enhancing energy cooperation. In APEC, for instance, the Energy Ministers' Meeting has been held on a regular basis and the security agenda has been in the spotlight within APEC. The ASEAN Energy Ministers' Meeting has been held consistently as well.

In addition to these, there are several initiatives in Northeast Asia. First, the Northeast Asian Energy Cooperation Inter-governmental Senior Official Council (SOC) was officially established in Ulaanbaatar, Mongolia on 17 November 2005 under the supervision of UN ESCAP. The main objective of the SOC is the improvement of Northeast Asian energy cooperation by sharing energy market information, cooperating on energy policy, and improving the energy business investment environment among regional countries. South Korea suggested the idea in the First International Northeast Asian Energy Symposium in June 2001. Based on that suggestion, the Khabarovsk Communiqué was adopted by UN ESCAP SOM in October 2001 and later the Energy SOM and Working Group were installed. For the SOC to be institutionalized, China and Japan need to join.

Second, the Five Country Energy Ministers' Meeting was proposed by China. China invited South Korea, the United States, Japan and India to a ministerial-level meeting to exchange information and build confidence in late October 2006. With the Chinese initiative, a ministerial level meeting of the major Asian energy importing countries, including the US, Japan, South Korea, and India, was convened in December 2006 to discuss common approaches to the importing countries' energy security concerns. The aim of the meeting was to deal with energy cooperation among the major consuming countries in terms of energy efficiency and technological cooperation in developing alternative energy, rather than to foster bargaining leverage against an energy supplier such as Russia.

Third, the Qingdao Initiative was approved to set action guidelines for regional energy cooperation in Asia at the third foreign ministerial meeting of the Asia Cooperation. It was a good start in terms of dialogues for regional cooperation mechanisms to secure regional energy security and guarantee diverse energy supplies.

Negative and positive factors for multilateral energy cooperation

Although the energy security problems have been discussed in the ASEAN+3, ARF and APEC, there are several reasons for difficulties in multilateral energy cooperation.

First, the ideological differences of regional countries and the lack of trust among the countries concerned in the region are obstacles to improving energy cooperation. For instance, historical Russo-Japan/Sino-Japan territorial issues and fishery issues are yet to be resolved to build confidence among the regional countries. Second, there is no concrete project to attract regional countries. Financing and organizing capabilities for large-scale investment are required. Finally, regional cooperative bodies are not strong enough to adjust the various interests of member countries.

On the other hand, regional countries have common interests in developing multilateral mechanisms in specific energy issues. China's interest in energy cooperation in Northeast Asia appeared to focus on energy efficiency, conservation and clean coal technology. Japan stresses international and regional cooperation because multilateral cooperation could give the consuming countries more clout and bargaining power against producers. Like other states, the Japanese government recently completed a new energy strategy which highlights the importance of regional cooperation, especially in energy efficiency. Russia stands to benefit greatly from increased regional cooperation, especially in the Russian Far East, in which resources are poorly explored.[36]

Conclusions

The geopolitical dimension in securing oil is more inclined towards competition and rivalry, while economic dimensions, such as the energy market and efficiency, need more cooperation.

Multilateral energy cooperation could be started on issues like energy conservation and alternative energy development. At the 2007 East Asia summit, for instance, leaders pushed for concerted efforts to explore nuclear, hydropower and biofuel alternatives. Energy issues and regional cooperation have been discussed within these institutions, encompassing Asia-Pacific and East Asia.[37] The scope of multilateral energy cooperation may have to be expanded to the level of the East Asia and Asia-Pacific regions. In some cases, Central Asia and Southeast Asia could also have a strategic priority.

With respect to geopolitical dimensions of energy security, bilateral dialogues are needed to build confidence among regional countries in order to avoid conflict. Particularly, dialogues between Korea and China plus Korea and Japan should be tried and institutionalized first. At the same time, bilateral dialogues between consumers and producers such as Russia are needed.

Finally, mini-multilateral mechanisms which could coordinate diverse interests of regional countries could be tried. At the seventh trilateral summit meeting in January 2007, the leaders of the three countries agreed to further promote energy security dialogue among the three countries. The necessity of strengthening regional cooperation in the energy sector was reaffirmed at the trilateral meeting of Foreign Affairs Ministers in June 2007. Based on the agreements of the two meetings, the three countries have been exploring specific ways to implement an energy security dialogue at the working level through diplomatic channels.

Notes

1. R. A. Manning, *The Asian Energy Factor: Myths and Dilemmas of Energy, Security, and the Pacific Future* (New York: Palgrave Macmillan, 2000).
2. D. Yergin, 'Energy Security in the 1990s', *Foreign Affairs*, Vol. 67, No. 1, 1988, p. 11.
3. 'Zhongguo nengyuan anquan de san zhong hanyi' ['Three implications of China's energy security'], *Zhongguo jingying bao* ['China Business'], 14 August 2006, http://www.china5e.com/news/zonghe/200608/200608140090.html; and Li Huilian, 'Zhongguo mouhua quanqiu nengyuan zhanlue xin buju' ['China formulates a new structure for its global energy strategy'], *Zhongguo jingji shibao* ['China Economic Times'], 18 July 2005, http://www.cet.com.cn/

20050718/YAOWEN/200507181.htm, cited in E. Downs, *China*, Brookings Foreign Policy Studies Energy Security Series (Washington, D.C.: Brookings Institution, 2006).
4. Currently, the main issues regarding energy security focus on overcoming the fragility of the energy supply system, minimizing risks of supply interruption, and dealing with the atomic energy safety problem and waste management.
5. US Department of Defense, *The United States Security Strategy for the East Asia-Pacific Region* (Washington, D.C.: US Department of Defense, 1998).
6. B. Buzan, O. Wæver and J. de Wilde, *Security: a New Framework for Analysis* (Boulder: Lynne Rienner, 1998).
7. International Energy Agency (IEA) Executive Director, *World Energy Outlook 2007: China and India Insights*, Washington, 16 November 2007.
8. IEA, *World Energy Outlook 2002* (Paris: IEA, 2002); Kokichi Ito, Li Zhidong and Ryoichi Komiyama, 'Asian Energy Outlook to 2020: Trends, Patterns and Imperatives of Regional Cooperation', RIS Discussion Papers, 2005.
9. M. G. Salameh, 'Quest for Middle East Oil: the US versus the Asia-Pacific Region', *Energy Policy*, Vol. 31, No. 11, September 2003.
10. Korea, China and Japan's dependence on the Middle East almost reaches 75 per cent (Korea 77 per cent, Japan 86 per cent, China 53 per cent).
11. K. Lieberthal and M. Herberg, 'China's Search for Energy Security: Implications for US Policy', *NBR Analysis*, Vol. 17, No. 1, April 2006.
12. Downs, *China*.
13. US Department of Energy, Energy Information Administration, 'China', Country Analysis Brief, 2005.
14. E. Chanlett-Avery, 'Rising Energy Competition and Energy Security in Northeast Asia: Issues for US Policy', CRS Report for Congress, 3 May 2007, p. 1.
15. D. Murphy and M. Fackler, 'Asia's Pipeline Politics', *Far Eastern Economic Review*, July 2003; K. E. Calder, 'China and Japan's Simmering Rivalry', *Foreign Affairs*, 2006.
16. Chanlett-Avery, 'Rising Energy Competition and Energy Security in Northeast Asia'.
17. US–China Energy Security Cooperation Dialogue (2006) by the Atlantic Council of the United States and the China Institute of Contemporary International Relations, Beijing, 31 October–1 November.
18. K. E. Calder, 'Sino-Japanese Energy Relations: Prospects for Deepening Strategic Competition', paper presented at the Conference on Japan's Contemporary Challenges in Honour of the Memory of Asakawa Kan'Ichi, Yale University, New Haven, Connecticut, 9–10 March 2007.
19. *South China Morning Post*, 7 January 2008.
20. For the Russian position towards the North Korean nuclear programme, see A. Fedorovskiy, 'The North Korean Nuclear Crisis and Russia', *International Journal of Korean Unification Studies*, Vol. 14, No. 1, 2005.
21. P. Kerr, 'KEDO Suspends Construction of Nuclear Reactors', *Arms Control Today*, Vol. 33, No. 10, 2003; Yoshinori Takeda, 'KEDO Adlift', *Georgetown Journal of International Affairs*, Summer 2005.
22. M. E. Herberg, 'China's Energy Consumption and Opportunities for US–China Cooperation to Address the Effects of China's Energy Use', statement before the US–China Economic and Security Review Commission.
23. http://www.fmprc.gov.cn/eng/wjdt/zyjh/t264261.htm; US–China Energy Security Cooperation Dialogue, co-sponsored by the Atlantic Council of the

United States and the China Institute of Contemporary International Relations, Beijing, 31 October–1 November 2006.

24. The State Council Information Office, White Paper: *China's Energy Conditions and Policies*, 2007 http://www.china.org.cn.

25. Chanlett-Avery, 'Rising Energy Competition and Energy Security in Northeast Asia'.

26. Keun-Wook Paik, *The Implications of China's Gas Expansion towards Natural Gas Market in Asia*, Chatham House Paper (London: Royal Institute of International Affairs, 2004); F. K. Chang, 'Chinese Energy and Asian Security', *Orbis: a Journal of World Affairs*, Vol. 45, No. 2, 2001; IEA, 'China's Worldwide Quest for Energy Security', 2000, OECD; Liu Xiaoli and Zhang You Sheng, 'China Petroleum Security and Regional Cooperation', Energy Research Institute, NDRC, 2003; V. Smil, 'China's Energy: Trends and Global Implications', POSRI International Forum on China's Development, POSRI, 2004.

27. Yuanming Alvin Yao, 'China's Oil Strategy and Its Implications for US–China Relations', *Issues & Studies*, Vol. 42, No. 3, 2006, pp. 165–201.

28. http://www.meti.go.jp/press/20060531004/20060531004.html; http://www.enecho.meti.go.jp/english/data/newnationalenergystrategy2006.pdf.

29. Chanlett-Avery, 'Rising Energy Competition and Energy Security in Northeast Asia'.

30. P. Evans, *Japan*, Brookings Foreign Policy Studies Energy Security Series (Washington, D.C.: Brookings Institution, 2006).

31. British Petroleum, *BP Statistical Review of World Energy* (London: BP, 2005); K. E. Calder, 'Korea's Energy Insecurities: Comparative and Regional Perspectives', Korea Economic Institute Special Studies Series, 2005, p. 5.

32. *International Herald Tribune*, 2 October 2006.

33. Xinmin Xue, 'Sino-Korean Cooperation on Nuclear Power Generation: Opportunity and Agenda', *Northeast Asia Energy Focus CERNA KEEI*, Vol. 4, No. 2, Summer 2007.

34. US–China Energy Security Cooperation Dialogue.

35. Chanlett-Avery, 'Rising Energy Competition and Energy Security in Northeast Asia'.

36. C. Kessler, 'Northeast Asia Energy Cooperation to Improve Regional Security', Energy and Security in Northeast Asia, KAIS-KEEI International Conference, Seoul, 16–17 November 2007.

37. S. Varadarajan, 'Energy key in the new Asian architecture', 25 January 2006, http://www.globalresearch.ca/index.php?context=viewArticle&code=VAR20060125&articleId=1802.

12
Energy Security and Investment Opportunity in ASEAN

Akhmad Nidlom and Weerawat Chantanakome

Introduction

The Association of Southeast Asian Nations (ASEAN) was established on 8 August 1967 in Bangkok by the five original member countries, namely Indonesia, Malaysia, Philippines, Singapore and Thailand. Brunei Darussalam joined on 8 January 1984, Vietnam on 28 July 1995, Lao PDR and Myanmar on 23 July 1997, and Cambodia on 30 April 1999.

The ASEAN Declaration states that the aims and purposes of the Association are: (1) to accelerate economic growth, social progress and cultural development in the region and (2) to promote regional peace and stability through abiding respect for justice and the rule of law in the relationship among countries in the region and adherence to the principles of the United Nations Charter. The ASEAN Vision 2020, adopted by the ASEAN leaders on the thirtieth anniversary of ASEAN, agreed on a shared vision of ASEAN as a group of Southeast Asian nations, as outward looking, living in peace, stability and prosperity, bonded together in partnership in dynamic development and in a community of caring societies. In 2003, the ASEAN leaders resolved that an ASEAN community should be established comprising three pillars, namely, the ASEAN Security Community, ASEAN Economic Community and ASEAN Socio-Cultural Community.

The ASEAN Centre for Energy

On 4 January 1999, the commitments, responsibilities, liabilities and assets of the ten-year long ASEAN-EC Energy Management Training and Research Centre (AEEMTRC) were handed over to the ASEAN Centre for Energy (ACE) in a simple ceremony held at the new ACE headquarters in Kuningan, Jakarta, Indonesia.

ACE is an intergovernmental organization established by Brunei, Cambodia, Indonesia, Laos, Malaysia, Myanmar, Philippines, Singapore and Vietnam. It is guided by a Governing Council composed of the senior officials on energy of the ASEAN countries and a representative from the ASEAN Secretariat. Core funding is provided by an Energy Endowment Fund established from equal contributions of the ten member countries and managed by a private fund manager.

As host country, Indonesia provides headquarter facilities and other amenities at the ACE building in the compound of the Directorate-General for Electricity and Energy Development of the Indonesia Ministry of Energy and Mineral Resources.

The Centre is envisioned to be a catalyst for the economic growth and development of the ASEAN region by initiating, coordinating and facilitating regional as well as joint and collective activities on energy. To realize this vision, the Centre will accelerate the integration of energy strategies within ASEAN by providing relevant information, state-of-the-art technology and expertise to ensure that over the long term, necessary energy development policies and programmes are in harmony with the economic growth and the environmental sustainability of the region.

Since its establishment, ACE has been instrumental in preparing the ASEAN Plan of Action for Energy Cooperation 1999–2004, a plan that is assiduously implemented by ASEAN's specialist organizations in the field of energy. ACE facilitates and coordinates the work of these specialist organizations, including the Forum of Heads of ASEAN Power Utilities/Authorities (HAPUA), the ASEAN Council on Petroleum (ASCOPE), the ASEAN Forum on Coal (AFOC), the Energy Efficiency and Conservation Sub-sector Network (EE& C-SSN) and the New and Renewable Sources of Energy Sub-sector Network (NRSE-SSN). The major programmes under this plan are:

- the ASEAN power grid;
- the trans-ASEAN gas pipeline;
- coal and clean coal technology promotion;
- energy efficiency and conservation promotion;
- new and renewable energy development;
- energy policy and environmental analysis.

The Centre acts as a catalyst for the economic growth and development of the ASEAN region by initiating, coordinating and facilitating regional as well as joint and collective activities on energy.

The ASEAN Centre for Energy will accelerate the integration of energy strategies within ASEAN through the provision of information, up-to-date technology and expertise to ensure that long-term energy development policies and programmes will be compatible with the region's economic growth and its environmental sustainability.

The goals of the Centre are the following:

- To establish the Centre as a regional institution of excellence in the initiation, coordination and facilitation of ASEAN energy programmes.

- To strengthen the region's capability in addressing global and regional energy issues by enhancing the coordination of energy strategies of the ASEAN member countries.
- To facilitate intra-regional trade in energy through the establishment of interconnecting arrangements for electricity and natural gas within ASEAN such as the proposed power grid and trans-ASEAN gas pipeline.
- To promote ASEAN cooperation in energy efficiency and conservation as effective mechanisms for demand-side management.
- To promote the development of new and renewable energy resources in ASEAN as an instrument towards sustainable energy development in ASEAN member countries over the long term.
- To serve as an energy information network and exchange centre at both regional and global levels.
- To enhance the development of ASEAN expertise in energy development and management.
- To promote private sector investment and participation in energy activities of the region.

ACE's position in the ASEAN organization

As we have already said, ACE's task is to accelerate the integration of energy strategies within ASEAN by providing relevant information, state-of-the art technology and expertise to ensure that over the long term the necessary energy development policies and programmes are in harmony with the economic growth and the environmental sustainability of the region. ACE's position in the ASEAN organization is depicted in Figure 12.1.

Energy security challenges in ASEAN

ASEAN in the global energy market

ASEAN, one of the most dynamic economic regions of the world, is a heterogeneous mix of economies, varying from developed to least developed, with greatly varying energy resource endowment and energy development situations.

- ASEAN GDP grew 5.7 per cent in 2006 (while Asia grew 6.6–7.5 per cent) due to export growth and FDI expansion, including continued growth of China and India. However, GDP for ASEAN may drop to 4.3 per cent in 2007 due to demand decline in the US, energy security risk and resource scarcity.
- ASEAN is rich in energy resources. It is a major producer of oil and gas in the Asia-Pacific region. Eight of ASEAN's members have proven oil and gas resources.

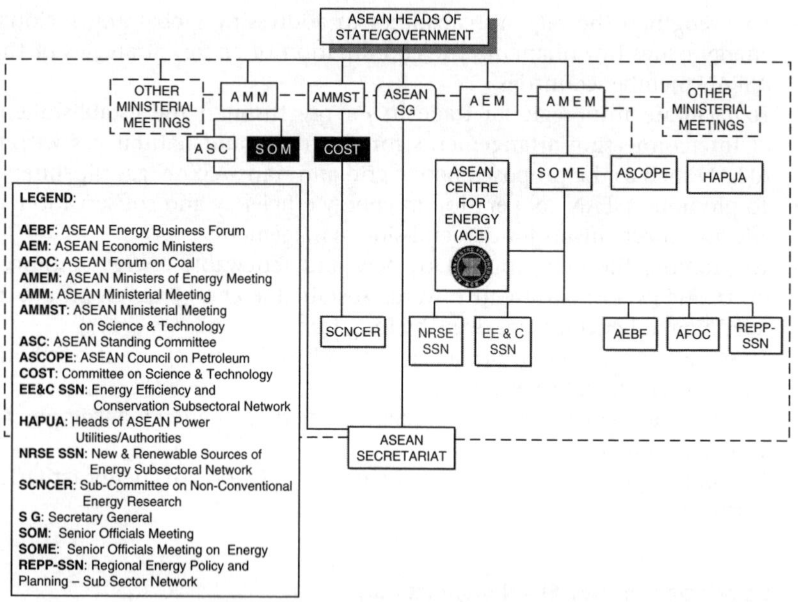

Figure 12.1 ACE in ASEAN
Source: ACE.

- Brunei Darussalam, Malaysia and Indonesia are amongst the world's top six liquefied natural gas (LNG) producers.[1]
- ASEAN controls 40 per cent of the entire oil and gas resources in the Asia-Pacific region. Oil and gas exports generate an annual value of US$48 billion for the ASEAN economies.

Approaches for future energy security

Considering the oil shock cases which occurred twice, in 1973 and 1979, ASEAN initiated some special organizations, such as the ASEAN Council on Petroleum (ASCOPE) in 1976 and the first meeting of the Heads of ASEAN Power Utilities/Authorities (HAPUA) in 1981. During the Iran–Iraq tanker war period in 1986, the ASEAN Energy Cooperation Agreement and ASEAN Petroleum Security Sharing were set up. Afterwards, in 1999, the ASEAN Centre for Energy was established and works under a directive plan of five years' activities which is known as the ASEAN Plan of Action for Energy Cooperation (APAEC).

The ASEAN Plan of Action for Energy Cooperation (APAEC)

The ACE's Plan of Action for Energy Cooperation (APAEC) is now in its second period with the same six programme areas from 1999–2004 for

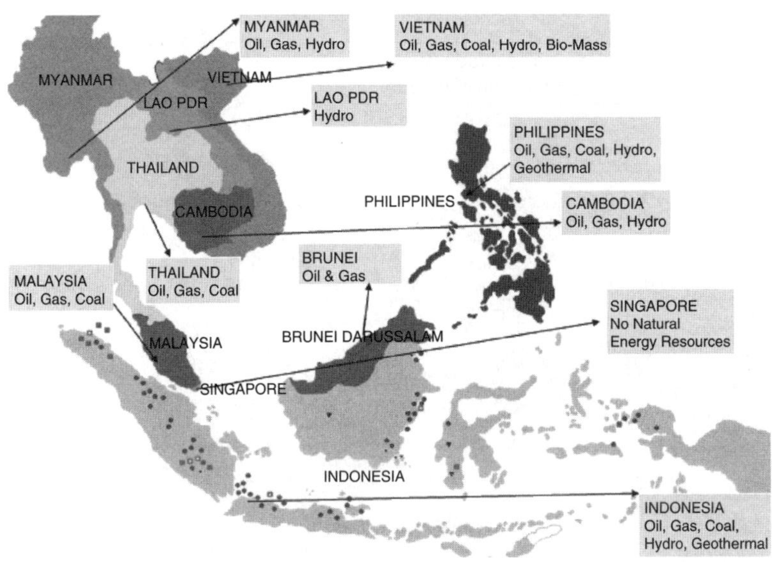

Figure 12.2   A brief of ASEAN energy resources
Source: ACE.

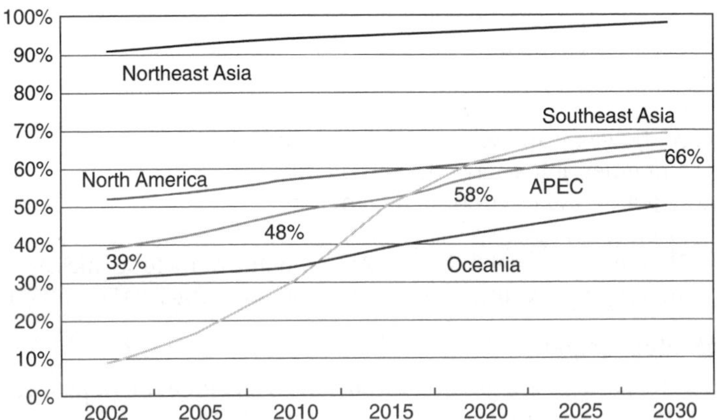

Figure 12.3   Rising oil import dependency[2]
Source: Asia Pacific Energy Research Centre (2006), 'APEC Energy Demand and Supply Outlook'.
Note: the outlook shown here includes tentative results subject to change.

2004–9. The major programmes under this plan are:

- the ASEAN power grid;
- the trans-ASEAN gas pipeline;
- coal and clean coal technology promotion;

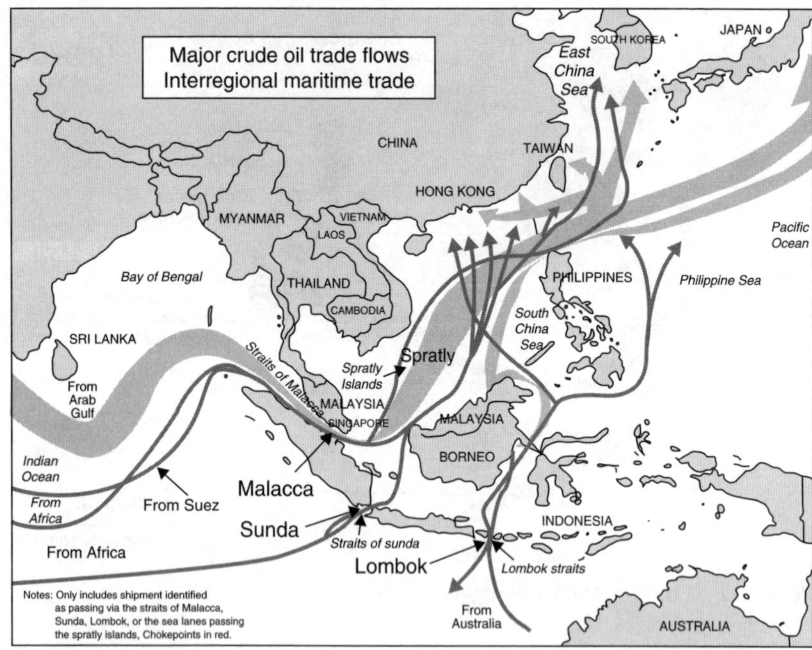

Figure 12.4   Crude oil trade flows and chokepoints[3]
Source: ACE.

- energy efficiency and conservation promotion;
- new and renewable energy development;
- energy policy and environmental analysis.

Now, ACE is developing the third APAEC which will include nuclear civilian power safety as the seventh programme area under the APAEC 2009–14.

The ASEAN power grid

The objective of the first programme area is to facilitate the implementation of the ASEAN Interconnection Master Plan and to further the establishment of the policy framework of the electricity networks comprising the APG, which consists of fourteen power grid interconnection projects.

The Heads of the ASEAN Power Utilities/Authorities (HAPUA) have the task of implementing the ASEAN power grid programme. It completed the ASEAN Interconnection Master Plan Study (AIMS) in March 2003, identifying fourteen interconnection projects. During the twenty-first AMEM in June 2003 in Langkawi, Malaysia, the ministers approved eleven of the projects

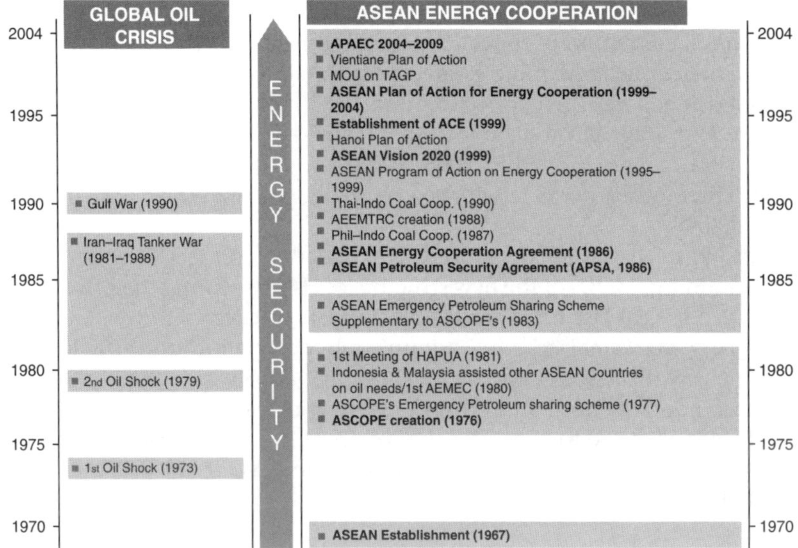

ASCOPE: ASEAN Council on Petroleum; AEEMTRC: ASEAN-EU Energy Management Training and Research Centre; TAGP: Trans-ASEAN Gas Pipeline; AMEM: ASEAN Ministers on Energy Meeting

Figure 12.5 Evolution of ASEAN energy cooperation
Source: ACE.

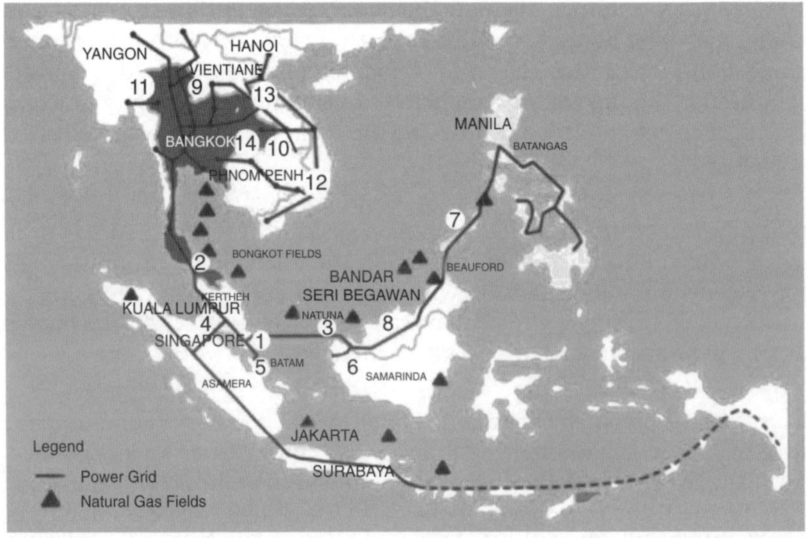

Figure 12.6 The ASEAN power grid
Source: ACE.

endorsed by HAPUA. The AIMS, as adopted, will serve as the reference guide in the implementation of the ASEAN interconnection projects.

Two interconnection projects are operational. These are the Peninsular Malaysia-Singapore interconnection and the Thailand-Peninsular Malaysia Stage 1 and Stage 2 interconnections. The Vietnam-Cambodia interconnection was commissioned in 2005–7 and the Thailand-Cambodia link in 2007. Three other projects will be commissioned by 2009, and the rest beyond 2009.

In its bid to streamline operations, HAPUA adopted the Memorandum of Understanding (MOU) of the new structure of HAPUA during their twentieth meeting. A special task force headed by Malaysia completed the review of the HAPUA organizational structure, administrative modalities and established a permanent HAPUA Secretariat on 17 December 2003 with a three-year term rotation. Indonesia hosted the HAPUA Secretariat for the period 2004–7.

HAPUA is expected to play a very important role in the development of the ASEAN power grid and it is confident that it can develop the grid and bring electricity to the people in the region.

Optimization of the generation sub-sector.   The ASEAN countries have abundant indigenous energy resources. There are large potential reserves of fossil energy sources as well as renewable energy which can be harnessed to produce electricity. However, initial results of the interconnection study indicate that it would not be economical to fully integrate the power systems of all the ten ASEAN countries. Dividing the power system into two systems – East System and West System – indicated that there are eleven potential interconnection projects that can be implemented up to the year 2020. Further optimization studies will be conducted to determine the delivery of cheap sources of energy to the load centre and the economic operation and sharing of reserves.

Invite private sector participation to develop the interconnection.   HAPUA will continue to conduct feasibility studies on the interconnection projects. As power generation and interconnection projects entail huge capital investments, which no single government can undertake on its own, the private sector will be encouraged to embark on these projects.

Address barriers to interconnections.   HAPUA will conduct studies to come up with appropriate recommendations to overcome barriers to interconnections. Studies to be undertaken will cover areas such as the policy, regulatory, legal, financial and commercial framework. The studies will be conducted in coordination with the eight Working Groups (WGs) under the new HAPUA structure. The WGs include: (a) Generation; (b) Transmission; (c) Distribution; (d) Renewable Energy and Environment; (e) Electric Supply Industry

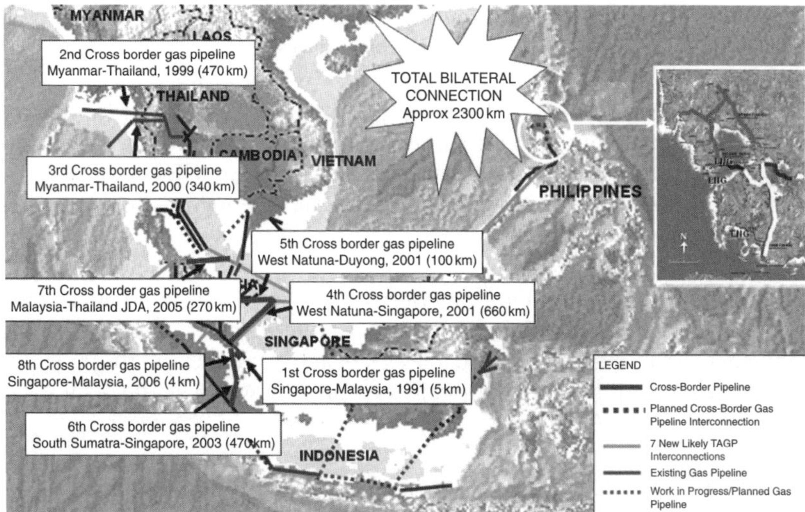

Figure 12.7   The trans-ASEAN gas pipeline
Source: ACE.

(ESI) Services; (f) Resource Development; (g) Power Reliability and Quality; and (h) Human Resources.

The trans-ASEAN gas pipeline

The objective of the second programme area is to facilitate implementation and realization of the trans-ASEAN Gas Pipeline Infrastructure Project to ensure greater economic value and security of gas supply, which consists of eight cross-border gas pipeline interconnection projects.

Under the MOU, member countries can initiate individual and/or joint studies, either on a bilateral or multilateral basis, to support and encourage the production, utilization, distribution, marketing and sales of natural gas among ASEAN member countries. Assessment and review of national and regional legal and institutional frameworks for natural gas, concerning cross-border issues relative to the commercial and economic feasibility, construction, financing, operation and maintenance of the pipeline as well as supply transportation and distribution of natural gas to member countries will be undertaken. Relevant studies on the following issues (pursuant to Article III of the TAGP MOU) will likewise be conducted.

1. Financing.   To consider available financing modes or arrangements relative to the financing of the construction, operation and maintenance of the pipelines, as well as the supply, transportation and distribution of natural gas to member countries. This considers the important role of the private sector, especially in the provision of needed capital investment.

2. Technical specifications.   To determine appropriate standardization of technical specifications of the pipeline, such as, but not limited to, design and construction standards, operation and maintenance guidelines, safety, environment and measurement standards which are internationally recognized by the oil and gas industry.

3. Access and use.   To determine effective and stable contractual arrangements for the supply, distribution and transportation of natural gas including adherence to the open access principle as well as management of the pipelines in accordance with the internationally accepted standards of the oil and gas industry.

4. Security supply and emergency supply arrangements.   To determine appropriate measures to ensure security and safety of the pipelines and the uninterrupted flow of contracted natural gas for transmission through the pipelines including a framework for cooperation in the event of serious supply disruptions, subject to mutual consultations.

5. Health, safety and environment.   To determine a framework for cooperation to mitigate risk and environmental impact which the construction, operation and maintenance of the pipelines may pose to affected communities, recognizing each member country's rights in accordance with its own national laws, safety measures and environmental requirements which are to govern the construction, operation and maintenance of the pipelines constructed within its territories, including the designation of its own safety and environmental inspectors.

6. Transit rights.   To determine acceptable measures to facilitate the issue of permits, licences, consents or other authorizations for transit pipelines and natural gas being transported through the territory of member countries.

7. Taxation and tariffs.   To determine arrangements for the mutually agreed imposition of, or exemption from, import, export or transit fees, duties, taxes or other government imposed fees and charges on the construction, operation and maintenance of the pipeline as well as the natural gas in transit.

8. Abandonment.   To explore possible cooperation and coordination measures concerning the potential further economic use of abandoned pipelines without undermining each member country's right to enforce its own national laws concerning the abandonment of pipelines within its territory.

9. Jurisdiction.   To determine jurisdiction and responsibility over the pipelines, particularly for pipeline segments located on the high seas (the Exclusive Economic Zone (EEZ). PERTAMINA and PSC partners are to undertake a detailed feasibility study for the East Natuna gas field development. Tasked to lead the implementation of the TAGP as a programme area in the APAEC, the ASCOPE formulated the Masterplan for the 'Trans-ASEAN Gas Pipeline Infrastructure Project'. The Masterplan, which was completed in October 2000, indicates that there are a total of 175 Tscf of proven and 94 Tscf probable natural gas reserves in the then seven ASCOPE member countries. Indonesia has the highest gas reserves with 90 Tscf proven and 42 Tscf probable reserves. Myanmar, which joined ASCOPE in 2003, has total reserves of 18.4 Tscf proven and 60.3 Tscf probable and possible gas reserves.

A very important finding of the Masterplan revealed that should there be no significant commercial gas discoveries in the near future, countries like Thailand, Singapore and the Philippines would see gas shortfalls. The region would increasingly be dependent on Indonesia as the future main gas supply hub for the ASEAN region, or else the region will have to import gas supplies.

The Masterplan concludes that there are enough gas supplies to meet the future growing demand for natural gas in the ASEAN region. These supply points could economically be connected to the demand centres through pipelines that would have to pass national borders and meet certain economic, technical and regulatory standards. Furthermore, the study concluded that the sustainability of the TAGP interconnection project will rely on the discovery and development of potential gas resources in the region. To this end, investment for the exploration of potential resources should be encouraged. It was also noted that the development of the East Natuna gas field in Indonesia will greatly influence the timing, occurrence and realization of the TAGP project.

10. Implement the trans-ASEAN gas pipeline infrastructure as per the approved Roadmap on the TAGP.   ASCOPE has reviewed and submitted to the ASEAN Secretariat the 'Roadmap for Integration of ASEAN: Trans-ASEAN Gas Pipeline Implementation'. Seven gas interconnection projects have been identified for implementation. Among these projects, firm commitments have been secured for the gas pipeline interconnection projects between Sumatra, Indonesia and Singapore and W. Natuna (Indonesia-Duyong, Malaysia). Ratification of the TAGP MOU by all member countries is a key factor in the implementation of this infrastructure project.

A feasibility study on a gas pipeline project covering East Kalimantan-Sabah-Philippines has been proposed with possible commissioning by 2009.

ASCOPE Gas Centre (AGC) is to implement the approved five-year Work Programme. In the near to medium term, the AGC is expected to address matters relating to harmonization and standardization of technical specification and gas quality, while the commercial aspects, as per the studies identified under the ASEAN MOU on TAGP, will be undertaken in consultation with the ASEAN Gas Consultative Council (AGCC). It will also undertake joint techno-economic studies for the implementation of the TAGP and gas-related projects. Furthermore, the AGC will develop a knowledge management system for sharing and exchange of information about the natural gas industry and will develop an exchange programme to promote research among natural gas technologists and researchers. One of the studies to be conducted will deal with using marine compressed natural gas (MCNG) as an alternative mode of transport for island demand centres.

In the long term, the AGC will enhance and promote technological capability enhancement through effective gas-related techno-economic research and development efforts, education and skills training and development. The AGC is also expected to undertake value-added activities for gas development for ASCOPE members. As agreed during the twenty-first AMEM in Langkawi, Malaysia will host the AGC.

Coal and clean coal technology promotion

The objective of the third programme area is to cooperate and promote sustainable development and utilization of coal while addressing environmental issues and facilitating intra-ASEAN coal-related issues. Accordingly, the strategies to be implemented for the next five years are: (1) strengthening the institutional and policy framework; (2) promoting clean coal technology (CCT); (3) promoting private sector investment; (4) promoting intra-ASEAN coal trade; and (5) promoting environmental assessment of coal projects. The strategies remain relatively the same as in the previous programme, with some modification on the promotion of environmental awareness. Various activities were identified to implement the five major strategies.

1. Strengthening the institutional and policy framework. The AFOC will undertake an inventory of existing policies, institutional arrangements and regulations on coal as well as the key industry players in each member country. Likewise it will conduct studies and provide assistance on policy reviews.

2. Promoting clean coal technology. Coal suffers from the negative perception that it is not a clean fuel. It is common in ASEAN countries that strong opposition is met when coal-fired generating facilities are being constructed due to the perceived pollution effects once they become operational. This is where government and private developers can work jointly for public acceptance of the project. The promotion of CCT will be highlighted in an information education campaign (IEC) plan through tri-media (print, radio and television) showing the new technologies being employed for emissions mitigation of present generation coal power stations.

Other activities that will be carried out to promote CCT are the following: (a) seminars on CCT; (b) technical visits to CCT facilities; (c) feasibility studies on CCT for rural electrification; and (d) technical training on coal usage.

3. *Promoting private sector investment.*   To promote private sector investment, the AFOC will organize Coal Business Forums wherein the private sector will be presented with business opportunities. It will conduct feasibility studies and likewise compile feasibility studies of member countries and make these available to prospective investors. When necessary, assistance in conducting feasibility studies will be provided by relevant ASEAN bodies to enhance investment opportunities. The carrying out of investment promotion road shows is also expected to boost the level of investments in the sector.

4. *Promoting intra-ASEAN coal trade.*   With the assistance of ACE, the AFOC plans to establish a directory of coal specifications, producers and consumers in ASEAN which will be uploaded to the AFOC website. It will also organize a network of coal laboratories in ASEAN to improve standards of coal analysis. AFOC will conduct studies on existing and future coal flow in the region. The studies to be conducted will focus on the coal trade flow and show how the coal commodity market can be organized and established in the future. Preliminary studies have been completed and the information gathered is compiled on the AFOC website.

5. *Promoting environmental assessment of coal projects.*   Under this strategy, the AFOC will provide assistance in carrying out environmental impact assessment (EIA) of coal projects. This will be extended to small-scale coal project entrepreneurs who will need external assistance on environmental impact assessment.

Energy efficiency and conservation promotion

The objective of the fourth programme area is to strengthen cooperation in energy efficiency and conservation through institutional capacity building and increasing private sector involvement, including enhancing public awareness as well as expanding markets for energy efficient products. The major guiding framework of the sector is to continue implementing the three strategies contained in the last plan and the inclusion of three new strategies for the next plan of action for 2004–9. The three strategies in the old programme which will be continued are the following: (1) continuation of information sharing and networking; (2) continuation of ASEAN energy labelling; and (3) expansion of private sector involvement. The three new strategies include (4) capacity building; (5) enhancing the business environment of energy services or promotion of ESCO business; and (6) promotion of energy efficiency in the transport sector.

1. Information sharing and networking.   This strategy is mainly a continuation and expansion of information sharing and networking among the members and stakeholders from the previous APAEC 1999–2004. In general terms, priorities have been set for the next five years where efforts shall be concentrated towards promoting energy efficiency. These include the following:

- Collection of policies, strategies and programmes from other member economies;
- Finalization and dissemination of a directory of EE&C products and technologies;
- Finalization and dissemination of a directory of EE&C resources in ASEAN; and
- Finalization and dissemination of papers/studies/research on EE&C best practices.

All the information gathered will be uploaded to the ACE website through regular updates by the coordinator of the EE&C-SSN for ready reference and/or dissemination to members and its stakeholders.

Overall, lack of information for consumers, manufacturers and industries hampers the inflow of investments in energy efficiency. For the 2004–9 plans, the EE&C-SSN can also strengthen public awareness of the benefits of implementing energy savings through print advertisements (e.g. newspapers, posters, brochures, handbooks, manuals, etc.) and media campaigns (e.g. radio, TV, etc.).

2. ASEAN energy standards and labelling.   The SOME of the twentieth AMEM in Indonesia endorsed a standard label to promote awareness of ASEAN energy-efficient products. The SOME requested the EE&C-SSN to identify the products to be covered by the ASEAN standard label and to formulate the required standards and procedures for certification of labelling. For this purpose, a committee for ASEAN Standards and Labelling Programme was created. The conducting of feasibility studies on the ASEAN labelling system was previously considered under the 1999–2004 APAEC plan.

3. Expansion of private sector involvement.   Private sector involvement is crucial for the successful implementation of the plans and programmes for the sector. Enhanced and closer dialogue and exchanges will be undertaken for information on energy policy, notably through the establishment of networks, forums, conferences and seminars with the private sector. These shall include EE&C industry and businesses, and other countries and organizations outside ASEAN. As an example, the sub-sector network will tap the Renewable Energy and Energy Efficiency Partnership (REEEP), which is a coalition of progressive governments, businesses and organizations committed to accelerating the development of renewable energy and energy efficiency systems.

The ASEAN Energy Business Forum (AEBF) is also a good opportunity, where EE&C can play a major part in the discussion and exhibitions with the private sector.

The extension of ASEAN Best Practices Competition Awards is expected to increase potential in energy savings through the replication and adoption of building energy management systems and other good practices towards the energy efficient operation of buildings. This will compel building owners, operators and contractors to use energy-efficient equipment, devices, and other energy conserving measures in the construction and maintenance of their buildings.

4. Capacity building.   This is a new strategy being considered for the medium term, taking into account that demand for energy and energy prices have been increasing rapidly within and outside ASEAN. To meet this challenge, EE&C-SSN has undertaken a number of initiatives for the effective utilization of energy. However, some of the ASEAN members lack experience and technology in how to facilitate development and implementation of cleaner production of energy-efficient projects. In addition, some ASEAN members lack the financial resources to carry out such projects.

For 2004–9, the sector will pursue a conservation plan to reap benefits to the greatest extent possible. Hence, capacity building will be a major focus.

5. Promotion of ESCO business.   Among the key actions to be implemented under this strategy are: (a) development of a measurement and verification protocol for ASEAN; (b) development of energy performance, contracting legal framework and standard form of contract; (c) development of project management and institutional guidelines; (d) development of energy saving potential indexes (benchmarking); and (e) E-commerce development for energy services.

The energy service companies' (ESCOs) approach has not been widely used in ASEAN due to a lack of awareness and to the financial, institutional and legal framework. As a mechanism, the EE&C-SSN will tap the assistance of an ESCO to improve energy efficiency within ASEAN. The sector will be given value-added benefits on technical assessment and recommendation with the help of a specialist. This will result in an immediate reduction of energy costs for the members who acquired the services of an ESCO.

6. Promotion of energy efficiency in the transport sector.   The new strategy was crafted in response to the clamour of the AMEM/SOME to include projects for the transport sector as the sector is a major consumer of energy. Formulation of actions to be undertaken is in its very early stage and still under discussion by the sub-sector network. Some of the actions envisaged would be the sharing of information on the energy efficiency policy and measures for the transport sector and possible research or studies. The EE&C-SSN will coordinate with the Senior Transport Officials Meeting (STOM) of ASEAN for joint studies.

New and renewable energy development

The objective of the fifth programme area is to institute and maintain sustainable development on the use of renewable energy (RE) and its technologies. The need for multilateral action to promote the commercialization of RE is apparent in the strategies and activities as elaborated below.

1. Develop a policy and institutional framework for the development of RE. Certain issues and barriers regarding RE development need to be exposed and sufficiently addressed by the ASEAN countries, which can be discussed in national workshops participated in by various agencies, including government, research institutions, and private and commercial industries. Findings from these activities are expected to be included in the formulation of a policy and institutional framework for the development of RE.

Skilled and trained personnel are essential to help realize the actual potential of RE. The necessary transfer of technology, knowledge and skills among ASEAN countries is required for capacity building. Special training sessions need to be conducted to facilitate the exchange of information on technology and successful practice among experienced ASEAN personnel.

Experience gained in the ASEAN region is valuable. Therefore, it is highly important for other countries in the region to gain access to mature technologies. Exposure through organizing bilateral dialogues and consultation workshops, training courses, study tours and exchange of visits of technical experts will be encouraged.

2. Promote the development and contribution of RE in energy supply.   The success in the development of renewable energy is gauged through its increasing importance in the national energy balance in competition with conventional sources of energy. Therefore, the target to attain at least 10 per cent of dependable capacity utilizing RE for power generation is deemed to be an acceptable and precise indicator in the ASEAN context.

3. To further strengthen information networking in RE.   Given the high acceptance of internet-based information dissemination, the existing online information networking, i.e. PRESSEA and the ASEM GRIPP Network, will be sustained to help ensure effective diffusion of RE initiatives. Selected stakeholders in the region will be invited to attend national-level RE programme workshops and seminars organized by member countries to share experience and lessons learned.

4. Promote intra-ASEAN cooperation on ASEAN-made products and services. At the moment, ACE has taken the initiative to compile existing RE specification and standards of ASEAN member countries on its infonet. This effort will be continued to ensure sufficient and updated information readily accessible to all.

Efforts will be devoted to the commercialization and marketing aspects of RE technologies. A market study will be conducted to identify and address the constraints in marketing renewable technologies in order to facilitate diffusion and to enable the renewable industry to be self-sustaining.

Lack of standards and codes of practice contribute to the perceived risk in renewable energy application among investors and consumers. To improve their confidence, RE products should comply with certain standards.

The capacity of the local industry to manufacture, assemble, service and maintain the RE products must be improved in order to assist in fostering commercialization. The capabilities of local manufacturing should be supported by strategic incentives from the government.

In spite of the merits of new RE, significant barriers to its wide-scale application involve the high cost of investment which undermines the efforts to further expand its utilization and to achieve the targeted commercialization phase. An innovative financing instrument/mechanism should be formulated to accelerate the use of RE.

Given the potential merits of RE for the ASEAN region, a compilation of prospective RE projects will be made to ascertain the accumulated potential installed capacity within the area. The activity will provide interested developers with valuable information needed for investment decision-making.

A cooperative arrangement among countries is viewed as a viable approach. Multilateral collaborations that bring in private and international agencies to invest in viable RE projects will be continued.

5. *To promote the utilization of biomass-based cogeneration technology.*

A biomass-based cogeneration system for the production of electricity and usable energy will be encouraged. In this respect, the generation of energy mainly for in-house consumption will be promoted. The supply of excess energy generated by the biomass-based generating system to the local community and to the grid will be encouraged. It is envisaged that closer cooperation with the on-going EC-ASEAN Cogen Programme will be undertaken to accelerate the acceptance of the technology in the region.

6. *To promote the utilization of biofuels.*

Some countries are trying to search for alternative fuels to reduce heavy reliance on petroleum fuels. Under the programme area, utilization of biofuels calls for focused technological cooperation in bioenergy. Links with automotive and related industries will be established in order to advance technological know-how and R&D activities. Likewise, market studies will be conducted to fully determine the commercial potential of bioenergy.

Regional energy policy and planning

The objective of the sixth programme area is to enhance national and regional energy policy analysis and planning towards sustainable development.

1. Energy policy and a supply security information sharing network.   Under the strategy of energy policy and supply security information sharing, continuous updating will be required of the ASEAN Energy Database System (AEDS). The same will be done to member countries' energy policy and plans at the REPP-SSN infonet to be developed with the assistance of ACE. A seminar/workshop on Estimation and Reporting of Energy Reserves will be conducted wherein data to be acquired will be included in the AEDS.

2. Capacity building in energy policy planning, supply security assessment and database development.   With regard to capacity building, regular training, joint studies and technical exchanges in energy policy analysis, database maintenance and supply security assessment will be conducted. These will be carried out through the technical exchange programmes such as the SOME-METI capacity building on energy database and energy supply security assessment, the EPSAP under the ASEAN-Australia Economic Development Cooperation, and the ASEAN-IEA programme. Although some ASEAN members have progressed ahead of other members in these areas, training will ensure increased technical capability and ensure uniformity in the pace of work and output expected of each country. This will greatly benefit the new members of ASEAN such as Cambodia, Laos, Myanmar and Vietnam which will be accorded priority.

3. Incorporation of environmental and sustainable development concern in regional policy formulation.   A particular area of interest that this programme area would like to focus on is the incorporation of environmental concern in regional policy formulation. The REPP-SSN will continue the information networking on environmental data related to energy development with entities such as the Climate Change Information Centre (CCIC) of the Philippines, the Centre for Energy and Environment Resources Development (CEERD) of Thailand, and the Pusat Tenaga Malaysia (PTM). These nodal networks on climate change and environment will likewise conduct cooperation studies on environmental and energy policies for sustainable development.

4. Analysis and preparation of regional energy policy and outlook.   Preparation of the regional outlook is in progress. The Institute of Energy Economics, Japan (IEEJ) will assist in developing the energy outlook models of each country using an econometric approach. The Microfit software will be used for developing the models.

5. Strengthen collaboration/cooperation among national and regional institutions in energy policy and planning.   The energy nodal network for the region will be expanded with the dissemination of reports on regional policy issue analysis and the demand–supply outlook to concerned international organizations. Cooperation/exchange programmes with regional institutions will be conducted in seminars, workshops, training courses, etc.

6. Address energy issues pertaining to ASEAN dialogue partners/other relationships.   Through the programme, dialogue will be continued with the ASEAN partners through participation in meetings/forums/training. The implications of issues arising from these dialogues will be included in policy analysis reports which could assist senior officials in decision-making.

7. Pursue studies on evolving regional energy policy reform/issues.   This strategy was formulated upon the recommendation during the Special SOME in December 2003 in Kuala Lumpur, Malaysia. This will provide special focus on ASEAN energy regulatory and market reforms as well as other areas of interest deemed sufficiently important to merit deeper studies.

8. Monitoring and evaluation on the progress of the APAEC 2004–9.   The functions of REPP-SSN under the Terms of Reference (TOR) are to assist the ACE in coordinating the implementation and monitoring of the APAEC 2004–9. This responsibility will formally rest with the sub-sector network upon approval of energy ministers at the twenty-second AMEM in May/June 2004.

Multilateral ASEAN cooperation in energy projects

ASEAN has several dialogue partners such as Australia, Canada, China, the European Union, India, Japan, New Zealand, Republic of Korea, Russia and the United States. Some multilateral ASEAN cooperation in energy projects are described briefly below.

ASEAN–European Union Cooperation

The EU is a long-standing dialogue partner of ASEAN. Cooperation between the EU and ASEAN is based on a Cooperation Agreement (1980) between the EC and member countries of ASEAN: Brunei, Indonesia, Malaysia, Philippines, Singapore, Thailand and Vietnam. In September 2001, the European Commission presented its document 'Europe and Asia: a Strategic Framework for Enhanced Partnerships', which identified ASEAN as a key economic and political partner of the EC and emphasized its importance as a locomotive for overall relations between Europe and Asia. The Commission document 'A New Partnership with South East Asia', was presented in July 2003. The EC–ASEAN Joint Cooperation Committee (JCC) promotes and keeps under review the various cooperation activities envisaged in the Cooperation Agreement. An official-level Committee usually meets every two years. Some of the energy projects between ASEAN and the European Union include the EC-ASEAN Energy Facility (EAEF) and proposed cooperation on ASEAN Energy Management Accreditation Schemes.

The EC-ASEAN Energy Facility (EAEF).   This is a programme of cooperation between the European Communities (EC) and the Association of Southeast Asian Nations to facilitate partnerships between ASEAN and European organizations in developing specific joint projects in the energy sector. The EAEF was launched in March 2002 with a duration of five years, and lasted until February 2007.

Four different categories of projects called 'facility' are available. These include: market awareness; institutional frameworks; feasibility studies; and demonstration projects. Consistent with the ASEAN Plan of Action for Energy Cooperation, the programme focuses on electricity interconnection, gas pipeline interconnection, clean coal technology, energy efficiency and renewable energy.

The total value of the programme is estimated to be 38.5 million euros including the estimated individual project partner contributions of 16.5 million euros. The commitment of the EC is fixed at 21.5 million euros as grants. ACE makes in-kind contributions to the programme at a counter-value of 0.51 million euros. Sixty-seven energy projects are covered by the facility over five years.

In previous years the EAEF worked in close cooperation with another EC-financed programme, the EC-ASEAN Cogen Programme Phase 3 (Cogen 3), which promoted the use of cogeneration from biomass, coal or gas as fuel. This was achieved through partnerships between industries in ASEAN countries and European suppliers. This programme ended in 2004, and the EAEF included activities in 2005 to monitor, follow-up and disseminate the results of eight projects which were implemented under the Cogen 3 Programme with the assistance of existing institutions and networks.

ASEAN Energy Management Accreditation Schemes (AEMAS).   Co-funded under the EAEF and coordinated by ACE, the AEMAS project is a regional scheme for the accreditation of energy managers and the certification of organizations (energy end-users). There were three projects co-funded under the EAEF related to the development and establishment of the AEMAS programme, namely:

- A feasibility study for the establishment of an ASEAN Energy Manager Accreditation Scheme for the ASEAN region.
- Development of the Theoretical Training Curricula for energy managers and training providers in ASEAN.
- Development of the Energy Management Simulation Test for the practical training of energy managers in ASEAN.

The second and third projects are a result of the outcomes/recommendations of the first project.

ASEAN and Japan cooperation

Promotion of Energy Efficiency and Conservation (PROMEEC).   This project is one of the activities under the SOME-METI Work Programme which started in 2000 and was implemented by ACE and the Energy Conservation Centre, Japan (ECCJ). It consists of three sub-projects, namely: (1) PROMEEC-Buildings, (2) PROMEEC-Major Industries, and (3) PROMEEC-Energy Management.

Currently the project is in Phase 2 of the PROMEEC project as a whole. The work plan of PROMEEC in Phase 2 was based on the recommendations and discussions made in Phase 1 covering the period of 2000–4 with accomplishments as follows:

* 100 industries and building audited;
* 600 technicians and engineers participated in on the job training;
* 40 seminar workshops;
* development of in-house database and technical directory at ACE websites;
* an award system for the best practices in 'Energy Management for Major Industries & Buildings';
* 20 company visits for promoting energy efficiency and conservation.

Energy Supply Security Planning in ASEAN (ESSPA).   The ESSPA project is one of the SOME-METI energy cooperation programmes. It supports future energy demand–supply in the ASEAN region through capacity building for the development of the energy outlook using an econometrics approach. The project is a joint undertaking of the Institute of Energy Economics of Japan (IEEJ), the Regional Energy Policy Planning Sub-Sector Network (REPP-SSN), and the ASEAN Centre for Energy (ACE).

The results of the 'Energy Demand Outlook Model in ASEAN Project' were published in 2006. The objectives of the projects are to transfer technical know-how to develop the energy outlook applying an econometrics approach, develop the energy outlook model of ten ASEAN countries, forecast future energy demand and supply in the year 2030 and extract implications based on the outlook for securing future energy supply in the ASEAN region.

Multi-Country Training Programme on Energy Conservation (MTPEC).   The Multi-Country Training Programme on Energy Conservation is funded by the Ministry of Economy, Trade and Industry (METI), Japan. The project, which started in 2005, is jointly implemented by the Energy Conservation Centre, Japan and the ASEAN Centre for Energy.

MTPEC aims to enhance the cooperation between Japan and ASEAN member countries in the field of energy efficiency and conservation. Under

MTPEC, training programmes are conducted in Japan to:

- enhance the international cooperation for EE&C between Japan and ASEAN countries through the PROMEEC projects;
- provide participants from ASEAN governments, public organizations and non-profit organizations with a clearer understanding of Japan's policies and effective activities on energy conservation;
- learn about Japanese energy conservation policy and measures, and the legal system, especially energy conservation law and the energy manager system;
- learn about excellent cases of energy conservation through site visits to be conducted at the representative building and industry/manufacturing facilities implementing energy conservation programmes. The participants are expected to collect as much 'first-hand' information as possible which they can share during the discussion;
- provide learning opportunities to enhance the ASEAN participants' understanding of the evolution and implementation of Japan's energy manager system that may find suitable application in the ASEAN member countries;
- share and discuss the energy conservation policy and measures adopted by the ASEAN member countries;
- identify the need for cooperation in energy conservation between and among ASEAN countries and Japan

ASEAN–German Mini-Hydro Power Project (AGMHP)

The ASEAN–German Mini-Hydro Project is a capacity development cooperation project jointly implemented by the ASEAN Centre for Energy (ACE) and the German Technical Cooperation (GTZ) on behalf of the German government. The AGMHP office has its headquarters in the ACE office in Jakarta.

The AGMHP is a five-year cooperation programme which aims, among other things, to improve the preconditions for sustainable utilization of mini-hydro power (MHP) sources. Proven dissemination concepts developed with GTZ's support for MHP in Indonesia will be applied in the ASEAN countries Cambodia, Lao PDR and Vietnam. AGMHP will thereby enhance the capacity for local provision of MHP equipment, sustainable MHP planning and implementation, operation, management and income generating end-use activities. Demonstration projects will showcase these efforts in an exemplary manner.

ASEAN–Australia Development Cooperation Programme (AADCP)

ACE and GSES are jointly implementing the project entitled 'Development of Regional Competency Standards for Training in Renewable Energy: Phase II – Establishing ISP Licensee in ASEAN Region; ASEAN Sustainable Energy

Training Accreditation Programme'. The project is funded by the Regional Partnerships Scheme, the ASEAN–Australia Development Cooperation Programme (RPS-AADCP) and coordinated by the ASEAN Secretariat. Phase II is a continuation of the project's first phase that developed a framework for the regional competency standards for training in renewable energy in ASEAN. Phase II of the project is aimed at strengthening this framework by establishing the ASEAN Sustainable Energy Training Accreditation Programme (ASETAP) in ACE and to train ACE staff as the ISP licensee that will manage the accreditation programme for the ASEAN region.

At the fourteenth Annual Meeting of the Renewable Energy Sub-sector Network held in Phnom Penh, Cambodia in May 2007, the Focal Points favourably recommended ACE as the most suitable organization to act as the ISP licensee.

ASEAN–United States Cooperation

The ASEAN Centre for Energy is supporting the United States Agency for International Development (USAID)'s Eco-Asia Clean Development and Climate Change Programme, a three-year programme which is implemented in China, India, Indonesia, Philippines, Thailand and Vietnam, to address major issues of economic growth, climate change and energy security. The programme focuses on the Clean Energy Financing Initiative, Energy Efficiency for Emerging End Uses, Regional Biofuels Initiative and Clean Energy Regulation Network.

ACE serves as the key channel of access to the programme for the ASEAN member countries. ACE actively participated in the country consultations on the drafting of the report which provide a useful and authoritative reference on clean energy technologies and programmes underway in the region; it also provides input into the design of the USAID's ECO-Asia regional Clean Development and Climate Programme (ECO-Asia CDCP).

ASEAN+3 cooperation (Japan, Republic of Korea, China)

This project is under the SOME+3 Energy Policy Governing Group (EPGG) and aims to ensure greater energy security in the region as a result of the rapid increase of energy demand, particularly oil and gas, working in five forums:

- energy security forum;
- natural gas forum;
- oil market forum;
- oil stockpiling forum;
- renewable energy and energy efficiency and conservation forum.

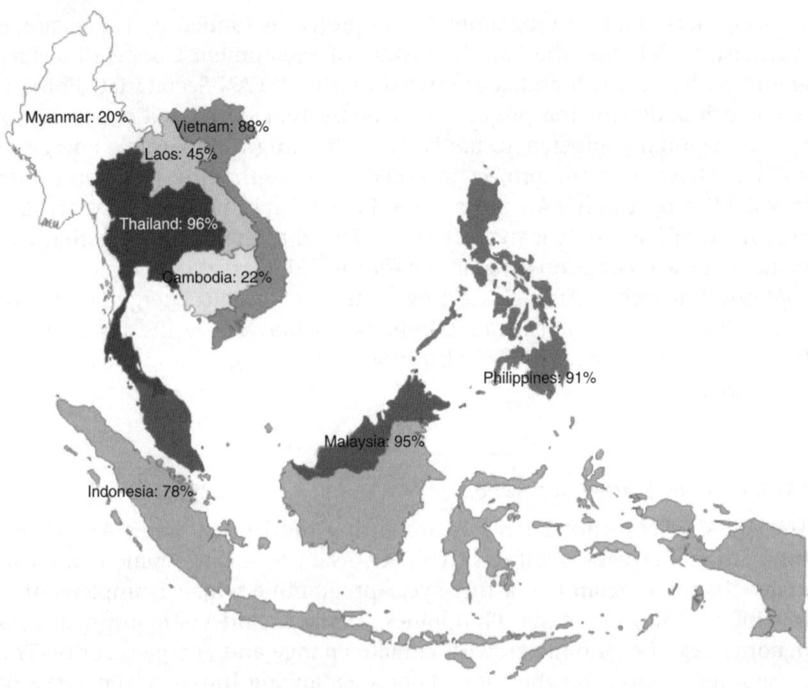

Figure 12.8 Access to electricity in ASEAN
Source: ACE.

Investment opportunity

It is estimated that ASEAN's energy requirements will grow to nearly 400 million tons of oil equivalent by 2020 from 150 million tons in 2000. The region will require at least $100 billion worth of investment in its power sector over the next 12–13 years to meet its rapidly growing energy needs.

The ASEAN power grid

Figure 12.8 and Table 12.1 show that Myanmar has the lowest access to electricity for the household and Thailand has the biggest percentage; the limitation of access should be overcome by new power plants, either using fossil fuel or renewable energy, with good support from government in the open market for the independent power industry.

Energy service access is important if the region is to achieve the Millennium Development Goals in the following areas:

- Income and increases in rural entrepreneurships: jobs, agricultural productivity and hence reduction of poverty.

Table 12.1   Access to electricity and renewable energy components

Country	Access to electricity (%)	Institution	Renewable energy component
Myanmar	15–20		Biomass, biogas
Cambodia	22	EAC, MIME, EDC	Mini-hydro, PV & biomass
Lao PDR	45	MEM, EDL	PV, mini-hydro
Indonesia	78	DGEEU, PLN	Mini-hydro, biomass
Vietnam	88	MOI, EVN	Mini-hydro, biomass, biogas
Philippines	91	NEA, DOE, NPC	Mini-hydro, wind
Malaysia	95		Biomass, PV
Thailand	96	PEA, MEA	PV, biomass

Source: ACE.

- Education and increases in school enrolment and retention rates: enabling students to study at night; reducing child labour for water and wood fuel collection.
- Health benefits of power pumps for safe water: improving health levels and powering rural clinics, particularly in maternity.
- Gender benefits in reduction of women's labour-intensive household work.
- Information and communication technology: improving access to information, television, mobile phones and computers.
- Environmental changes in patterns of fuel use.

The trans-ASEAN gas pipeline

The trans-ASEAN gas pipeline project has multiple effects on the investment opportunity in many sectors such as the following.

Exploration and production

- Intensify exploration effort to find new gas resources
- Possible strategic alliances, forming consortiums or joint ventures in E&P
- Services and support sector

Gas liquefaction and processing

- Developing more cost effective technology in gas liquefaction & processing
- Building new gas processing plants or natural gas liquefaction plants
- Building new LNG receiving terminals

Gas pipeline and shipping

- Equity participation and funding of gas pipeline infrastructure
- Gas pipeline in ASEAN member countries (Indonesia-Philippines)

- Cross border gas pipelines
- Synergizing logistic support

Transmission and distribution

- Laying new gas transmission and distribution

Gas market and end users

- Promote the use of natural gas as the fuel of choice
- Technological innovation to promote the use of natural gas, e.g. CNG, hybrid car, fuel cell, hydrogen economy
- Cogeneration
- Petrochemicals
- Industrial, NGV, GDC

Coal and clean coal technology promotion

According to the IEA's *World Energy Outlook* of 2004, East Asia is looking at expanding coal from an installed capacity of around 38,600 MW in 2003 to 311,200 MW by 2050. Coal continues to provide a large share of the world energy supply; coal-fired electricity generation provides 39 per cent of world electricity, the price is relatively low and stable, and there is abundant supply from both domestic and foreign sources.

The Southeast Asia region collectively ranks third highest in carbon dioxide emissions among developing countries, after China and India. Under a business-as-usual scenario, East Asia's carbon dioxide emissions will increase by 350 per cent by 2050 and needs mitigation technology such as zero emissions technologies (ZETs) which are state-of-the-art clean coal technologies. The most relevant technologies are:

- Supercritical pulverised coal combustion (PCC)
- Integrated gasification combined cycle (IGCC)
- Circulating fluidized bed combustion (CFBC)

The two most promising candidates for ZETs are supercritical PCC and IGCC. There is also coal-to-liquids technology which offers opportunities for:

- 'Diversification of oil supply'
- Mitigating the impact of high oil prices
- Economic value added
- A long-term and well-used option
- Oil price shocks have led to significant R&D efforts to reduce the cost and increase the yield of coal liquefaction

- Technological gains where carried out
- Process cost of converting coal-to-liquids remains above that of refining crude oil
- The main advantage of coal liquefaction is the lower cost of coal as a feedstock
- A value added opportunity for brown coal
- Provides low sulphur liquids.

Energy efficiency and conservation promotion

Various studies have noted that as economies grow, so does the lighting industry worldwide. The International CFL Market Review, *A Study of Seven Asia Pacific Economies* released in August 2006, highlighted that global compact fluorescent lamps (CFL) sales have jumped to more than 1.5 billion units from 100 million since 1990. ASEAN countries such as Indonesia, the Philippines and Vietnam were among the focus countries of this study. The Eco-Asia study also noted a report from the International Energy Agency that energy use for lighting will climb to 80 per cent by 2030. The growth of the industry – lighting in buildings, factories, industries, households – is an established fact. The IEA also noted that appropriate lighting policies, if implemented and implemented soon, could have a very positive impact on CO_2 emissions. Reducing energy for lighting use by 17.5 per cent could cut CO_2 emissions by 449 million tons annually.

CFLs compared to incandescent bulbs give better efficiency or light output, have longer life and save energy. However, there is a lack of a common or uniform set of quality standards in the manufacturing of CFLs, although well-established manufacturers do employ quality standards to maintain their positions in the market. CFL policies range from mandatory to voluntary actions. Testing procedures and specification levels exist. Some countries also have minimum energy performance standards and some still use labelling schemes either on a mandatory or voluntary basis.

Thailand is implementing a very ambitious but practical project of phasing out incandescent bulbs. The Energy Policy and Planning Office (EPPO) is distributing 800,000 CFLs for free across the country and at the same time has cut the store price of CFLs by half using the available funding from its Energy Conservation Fund. EPPO has assigned EGAT to carry out what is called 'A Project for the Nation: Stop Using Incandescent Bulbs and Use No. 5 CFL instead'. The target is to see 110 million CFLs installed and used by 2012 to reduce electricity demand and reduce CO_2 emissions.

The Philippines' Project called Philippine Efficient Lighting Market Transformation Project or PELMTP is in its third year of implementation. It is a five-year project supported by the United Nations Development Programme and Global Environment Facility with a project cost of US$15 million to increase the widespread utilization of energy efficient lighting systems such as linear fluorescent lamps, compact fluorescent lamps, high intensity discharge (HID) lamps, ballasts (low loss electromagnetic and electronic) and luminaries. The project hopes to generate energy savings of 29,000 gigawatt hours (GWH) or equivalent to 21 per cent of the electricity consumption of the lighting sector and cut GHG emissions by about 4,600 gigagrams of CO_2 equivalent. The project also aims to increase the utilization of energy-efficient lights in households, commercial and industrial sectors to 46 per cent in 2008 from 12.78 per cent and 82.5 per cent in 2012.

Vietnam, for its part, has been very successful in implementing its Demand-Side Management (DSM) Programme focusing on CFLs. The Electricity of Vietnam (EVN) followed through from the success of its Phase 1 DSM Programme in 2001–2 to undertake the Phase 2 to distribute more than 1 million CFLs to rural customers over the period 2004–7. Phase 2 is aimed at better managing its load system especially during peak hours and is intended to generate energy savings of about 64 GWh annually.

New and renewable energy development

Government leaders of ASEAN, together with the leaders of Australia, China, India, Japan, South Korea and New Zealand, have agreed to reduce their dependence on fossil fuels and promote cleaner technologies by signing the Cebu Declaration in East Asian Energy Security on January 2007. The government leaders will strengthen programmes to develop renewable energy sources such as biofuels and hydropower sources since these resources are important aspects of national energy policies. They will encourage the use of biofuels in a move towards freer trade and set a standard on biofuels used in motor vehicles. They will also aim to mitigate greenhouse gas emissions through effective policies and measures. The entire effort will be market-based. The leaders will pursue and encourage investment on energy resource and infrastructure development through greater private sector involvement, and encourage the open and competitive regional and international markets geared towards providing affordable energy at all economic levels.

According to a joint report by Greenpeace and the European Renewable Energy Council (EREC) released on the eve of the ASEAN Ministers of Energy Meeting, investing in a renewable energy future will save ten times the fuel costs of a 'business as usual' fossil-fuelled scenario, saving US$180 billion annually and cut CO_2 emissions in half by 2030.

Under the IEA's *World Energy Outlook* of 2004, by shifting to renewable energy, East Asia stands to save as much as $2 trillion in fossil fuel costs over the next 23 years and reduce carbon dioxide emissions by 22 per cent from 2003 levels. Increasing energy efficiency and shifting energy supply to renewable energy resources leads to long-term costs for electricity supply that are one-third lower than business-as-usual projections.

Brunei National Petroleum Co. is looking to partner the Philippine National Oil Co. (PNOC) to build a biodiesel plant in the Philippines.

Recently at an ASEAN Council on Petroleum meeting in Indonesia, PNOC officials revealed that they have received expressions of interest from several possible investors to pursue biofuels development.

In Indonesia, the Ministry of Energy and Mineral Resources are developing biofuels. Government policy will likely be the most important factor in determining whether the burgeoning biofuel industry in Indonesia will be a success. National banks Bank Mandiri and BNI are providing some of the financing. Plans for development will be concentrated in the eastern part of the country due to the availability of land where raw materials can be produced. There are currently only two companies that sell biodiesel from CPO to Pertamina for mixing with local diesel, while a few others are producing biodiesel on a small scale for their own use. Another two are producing ethanol. There are, however, several areas for concern, including the price of CPO. Jatropha is also being considered but it could take several years to determine the variety of Jatropha best suited to the various soil types, the right planting method, the right post-harvest handling and the right technology. Another concern is the byproduct of biodiesel production, glycerine, because the result of increased production will be oversupply of glycerine and depressed prices. Two state-owned companies, PT Rajawali Nusantra Indonesia and PT Perkebunan Nusantra III, are building ethanol plants using sugar cane and biodiesel plants using palm oil.

Malaysia will produce biofuels that are then used for running local machines, e.g. tractors, or generating electricity for local usage or for sale into the local grid. However, it is highly dependent on the price of two unrelated commodities: crude oil and agricultural crops. It is also not the whole solution but a piece of the puzzle, alongside many other options, such as biodiesel and so on.

With the passing of the Philippines Biofuels Act in December 2006, all gasoline products in that country should have an ethanol content of at least 5 per cent within two years. All diesel vehicles should use a minimum 1 per cent biodiesel blend within three months of the law coming into effect. Coconut oil is being used as the main feedstock to achieve this. The mandated blend will rise to 2 per cent for biodiesel after two years and to at least 10 per cent for bioethanol after four years.

The Singapore government has committed S$350 million (US$228 million) to develop Singapore as a global clean energy hub over the next five years, including S$170 million (US$111 million) from the National Research Foundation (NRF). While the main emphasis is on solar power, the industry development efforts will also extend to fuel cells, windpower, tidal power, energy efficiency and carbon services. It is expected that the added value of S$1.7 billion (US$1.1 billion) and 7000 new jobs will be created by 2015. Such efforts will complement clean energy investments in areas such as solar, fuel cells and wind already secured in the past two years. These include the establishment of a world-class R&D centre for wind energy by Danish wind energy company Vestas; the opening of German solar company SolarWorld's regional headquarters; the investment of S$153.9 million (US$100 million) by Rolls-Royce to conduct fuel cell R&D with local agencies like A*STAR; and the setting up of Singapore's first solar cell manufacturing plant by a local company, Solar Energy Power.

The Thailand government seeks to establish Thailand as the regional energy centre for Southeast Asia and has implemented a 'Strategic Plan for Renewable Energy Development', which aims to increase the renewable energy percentage of commercial primary energy to 8 per cent by 2011. It is currently 0.5 per cent, with hydropower accounting for most of this amount. The intended contribution from renewable energy is 2400 MW, of which 560 MW are already installed. An example of a renewable energy project already underway is a 42.5 MW solar power plant under construction in Mae Hong Son – the mountainous province (not linked to the national transmission grid) in the northwest of the country, bordering Myanmar. It will be the largest such facility in the ASEAN region and will generate 500 kilowatt hours (kWh) of power in the first phase and will ultimately be expanded to be able to produce 1750 kWh. Production costs are put at five times that of fossil-fuelled power, but construction costs will still be significantly lower than if the government had to transmit electricity to the province from outside. A large portion of the cost of the pilot project is being funded by the EPPO's Energy Conservation Promotion Fund (ECPF) with the remainder coming from EGAT.

'Twenty in Five' is part of Thailand's ambitious efforts to reduce oil imports and assist in cutting carbon emissions and global warming. The kingdom plans to replace not less than 20 per cent of its vehicle fuel consumption with renewable energy sources such as ethanol and palm oil within the next five years. After making B2 mandatory in April 2008, Thailand will thereafter compel petrol pumps and vehicle owners to accept B5, or a 5 per cent palm oil biodiesel and 95 per cent diesel mix, soon thereafter. Gasohol, a mix of 95 per cent petrol and 5 per cent ethanol, has become more popular among consumers since the government reduced its price by 10 per cent at petrol stations in March 2007.

Vietnam has huge potential in developing renewable energy sources with solar exposure being 2 to 2.5 times higher than Germany, a leading country in solar energy development. However, energy efficiency projects have faced several barriers, including a high initial investment cost, which per watt is ten times higher than that for traditional power plants. Low household incomes, poor public awareness for the need to conserve energy and inappropriate policies have also been significant hurdles. The ADB's Clean Energy Financing Partnership Facility (CEFPF) in Vietnam was established in April 2007 to provide a flexible way of responding to the needs of smaller energy efficiency projects. CEFPF Technical Assistance will be used to lower barriers to clean energy investments by supporting business and financial advisory and engineering services, linking clean energy to sustained growth and sharing costs in implementing clean energy investment programmes in combination with other government, donor and commercial funding. It will also support cooperation in transferring technology, knowledge and experience in energy efficiency to Vietnam from abroad.

Energy policy and environmental analysis

Energy security is a major concern of all ASEAN governments. It is the primary reason for regional cooperation. As the centre of energy information in ASEAN, ACE will facilitate the proposed activity in energy security and monitor the application of the ASEAN Plan of Action for Energy Cooperation programmes in future in areas such as:

- Regional gas and power interconnection
- Market liberalization of the energy industries
- Energy efficiency programmes, national and regional
- Expansion of renewable energy by:
  - Encouraging mini-hydro programmes
  - Strengthening local manufacturing of small-scale renewing energy systems
  - Promoting alternative energy such as biofuels
  - Using ethanol, gasohol, biodiesel, etc.
- Clean coal technology programme
- Civilian nuclear power plants as an alternative
- Energy supply security planning and emergency preparedness studies
- Climate change mitigation studies.

Civilian nuclear power plants

Deciding about future energy developments requires balanced and trustworthy information about issues such as the relative environmental effects of different options, the safety of installations, economics and the availability of resources. This is of particular importance now because world energy use is expected to continue to grow significantly during this century, particularly in less developed countries. In the same period, global emissions of greenhouse gases, especially carbon dioxide, will have to be severely curbed. To meet both these requirements may well involve a step away from being able to meet growing energy needs by depending on an ever-increasing supply of carboniferous fossil fuel.

Nuclear power has largely fulfilled its early promise – it now generates about one-sixth of the world's electricity, having been the fastest growing of the major energy sources in proportional terms throughout the 1970s, 1980s and 1990s. It does so safely (it is among the safest of the major energy sources, according to some studies) and without emitting significant quantities of greenhouse gases.

Perhaps the most difficult issue is over the construction of demonstration plants. If private companies are unwilling or unable to build such facilities, the financial risk being too great, then governments should be prepared to take steps to ensure that such plants are built. Governments will also have to create the circumstances in which there is a sufficient supply of suitably qualified individuals to staff the industry and the regulatory bodies – this is true whether the industry contracts or expands. Governments may also have to act to ensure that sufficient funds are put aside to deal with waste management and decommissioning in the long term. Another issue is how the industry can make itself more acceptable to the public and how to involve it in the decision-making process. Considerable thought is being given to ensuring that the public is, and feels that it is, contributing to the decision-making process.

A new understanding between the people, governments and nuclear industries in the industrialized world may be needed. Such an understanding should open the way for proper international appraisal of whether, and in what circumstances, nuclear energy might make a positive contribution to meeting the energy and environmental challenges that the world has to face in the twenty-first century.

As ASEAN member countries start plans to implement nuclear energy and the need for ensuring secure supply of energy becomes even more critical, the region's heads of states and governments look for greater cooperation. During the twelfth ASEAN summit held in the Philippines on 13 January 2007, the leaders expressed serious concern over the negative impact that prolonged high oil prices have on economic growth and development in the region. One measure looked at was to diversify energy supply by developing alternative energy sources such as biofuels and civilian nuclear power. The heads of states and governments of ASEAN member countries subsequently tasked the officials to look into a regional nuclear safety regime.

Indonesia has plans to operate nuclear power around 2016 and Malaysia will have the first nuclear monitoring facility in ASEAN in collaboration with the International Atomic Energy Agency (IAEA) to ensure that nuclear energy use is only for peaceful purposes. The Philippines will consider nuclear power for the period after 2022. Thailand is targeting 4,000 MW of generating capacity from nuclear by 2020–1 and Vietnam will operate nuclear power plants around 2020.

As ASEAN adopts and implements programmes to develop nuclear energy, the need for greater cooperation becomes more imperative. Judicious and efficient planning is necessary to look at all angles. The ASEAN Centre for Energy is in the process of reviewing and drafting the ASEAN Plan of Action for Energy Cooperation 2009–14. The creation of the Nuclear Energy Safety Sub-Sector Network (NES-SSN) will be made part of the new APAEC and the strategies, actions and activities that will be undertaken by the new NES-SSN. The new APAEC will reflect the changing times in the energy sector among countries, in the region and the world. Nuclear energy will be part of this, with its increasing role to ensure security of supply, sustain economic growth, protect the environment and safeguard public health and welfare. In order for this to happen, greater cooperation among countries is needed.

Conclusion

Energy plays a vital role in today's world, underpinning all areas of economic activity. The economic impact of supply disruptions can therefore be high and wide-ranging. This creates an incentive for governments to ensure that secure and reliable energy sources are readily available. A country's energy security policy refers to measures taken to minimize the risks of supply disruptions below a certain tolerable level. Such measures ensure that a supply of energy is readily available and affordable to meet domestic demand. This therefore involves a quantity and a price parameter. But it also involves a time parameter; a sudden price hike will have very different effects on both society and the economy than a long-term price increase. The causes of insecurity in the energy sector include the risks related to the scarcity and uneven geographical distribution of primary fuels and to the operational reliability of energy systems that ensure services are delivered to end users.

Developing countries are building up a new infrastructure for the rapidly increasing electricity demand. The next five to ten years are crucial in terms of investing in new sustainable and climate friendly power generation. Every decision about new power plants today will influence the energy mix of the next 30–40 years. Renewable energy sources do not need any fuel, which makes the operation costs independent from fluctuating world market fossil fuel prices. The future of renewable energy development in the region will strongly depend on political choices by both the individual governments and ASEAN. Renewable energy development for rural electrification is hampered by barriers, which put renewable energy at an economic, regulatory or institutional disadvantage. The barriers are numerous but fall into three broad categories: costs and pricing, legal and regulatory, and market performance.

Pipeline delivery of natural gas from country to country is growing. ASEAN estimates that bilateral gas transfers from country to country in the ASEAN region amount to around 17 per cent of regional gas consumption, emphasizing the importance of gas transfer between countries in balancing regional gas supply and demand. Over time, and provided new gas supplies can be developed economically, there is every reason to expect this trade to continue growing. In 2000 as many as seven new country-to-country pipeline linkages were being contemplated over the period until 2015 as part of the TAGP. In addition, many new pipelines have been proposed or are under development in ASEAN countries to meet projected strong growth in gas demand. All this is taking place against a very dynamic background where development plans, gas reserves, market opportunities and gas supply options are under continuous reappraisal. The TAGP Task Force, an industry group established under ASCOPE, has initiated a review of the ASEAN gas supply and demand situation, taking into account, amongst other things, recent discoveries, changes in demand patterns, infrastructure completed over recent years and the prospect of LNG as a new supply source for the region. Irrespective of the results of this review, it is clear that pipelines are becoming more interconnected in the ASEAN region. This raises a range of technical and policy issues which can only be resolved by high levels of cooperation between industry participants and between industry and governments in the region.

Some ASEAN member countries, i.e. Indonesia, Thailand and Vietnam, have shown interest in adopting nuclear power to address the domestic energy security issue and to combat climate change. Recent analysis of nuclear economics suggests that the most likely scenario for financing new nuclear building would be via some form of project finance approach probably involving a consortium of investors, reactor vendors and utility companies joining together as the reactor builder/owner/operator. From a business perspective decisions on where to site modern industrial facilities such as nuclear power stations are made in the same way as decisions on where to put any heavy industry by private sector companies seeking the best combination of such key factors as proximity to markets and materials, availability of skilled and trained labour, well-developed infrastructure, good transportation networks, electricity and water utilities, and low land and development costs. A major practical consideration in the location of new nuclear generating plants is that potential sites should be strategically placed, both for connection to the transmission grid and to supply electricity to large areas of demand. Siting plants close to areas of demand reduces the need for long-distance power transfers that in turn reduce losses from the electricity grid, improving the efficiency of the network and reducing costs. Moreover, an important factor is the ability of the grid system to accept power infeed at a particular site location without requiring costly and time-consuming reinforcement.

Planning, designing and installing energy projects are complex processes and need huge funding to accelerate the energy projects. Several financing options exist to execute the project with private sector, government and public ownership being prioritized. To enhance private investment, the government must formulate new frameworks and mechanisms that are consistent with the emerging competitive market.

Notes

1. The International Group of Liquefied Natural Gas Importers (IGLNGI).
2. As shown in the graph of the APEC Energy Demand and Supply Outlook in 2006, Southeast Asia will face oil import dependency increases, as forecasted to 2030.
3. Figure 12.4 shows oil trade flow in the Southeast Asia region; the path identifies the choked point which needs security because of piracy and traffic control to avoid tanker collisions and oil spills.

13
Energy Security: an Indonesian Perspective

Edy Prasetyono

The relationship between energy and security has been one of the most important issues shaping national, regional and international relations. Competition for energy and energy-related natural resources dominated history for many centuries, long before environmental aspects came to the fore. Many states and communities fought for energy resources for three main reasons: energy resources are limited, they are unevenly distributed, and they have strategic value in terms of development.

The need for energy is faced with the fact that the world is 70 per cent dependent upon fossil fuel energy such as oil and coal that cannot be renewed (non-renewable). It remains very doubtful whether alternative energy, such as nuclear power and other forms, will be able to sustain economic development in the twenty-first century due to security and environmental implications. In fact, this has become a political and strategic issue facing many governments. Oil pollution, environmental degradation, water pollution and climate change will force many national governments to go for cleaner and safer alternative energy.

However, the shift will not be easy as it entails political and strategic implications. The shift to alternative energy will also affect human security and individual needs as these alternative energy forms are expensive, which means access and distribution are limited to particular groups of society.

This perspective brings us to the essence of today's energy problems. First, can the availability of oil and other fossil energy resources be guaranteed with reasonable prices in the face of increasing oil consumption? In many cases, prices can fluctuate sharply due to non-economic variables. Oil supply is estimated to reach its peak in 2010, while the world's oil consumption will be at 115 mbpd (million barrels per day) and 121 mbpd in 2020 and 2025[1] respectively (the world's oil reserve is 1114 trillion barrels). Most of the oil, approximately 57 per cent, is consumed by transportation.[2] Some analysts in the US argue that it remains debatable whether new oil exploration can meet energy demands. It would also create new environmental problems. Gas consumption will increase to 125 TCFC in 2010 and 152 TCFC in 2025, while the world's gas reserve is approximately 6300 TCFC. Coal consumption will be at 5.9 billion tonnes in 2010 and 7.5 billion tonnes in 2025 (the world's coal reserve is 984.6 billion tonnes).[3] Thus, the world is facing a critical problem with the long-term availability of energy resources. Methods and approaches to address this challenge will certainly change the pattern of economic development and shape strategic interactions at individual, national and international levels.

Secondly, how far can alternative energy policy options satisfy the need to protect the environment? Today, fossil energy amounts to 26,583 billion tonnes/year.[4] Coal is certainly one important source of energy. However, it also produces high levels of pollution as is demonstrated by China's recent experience. Meanwhile, many people remain sceptical of nuclear power and perceive it as unsafe. It seems that nuclear cannot replace fossil energy in the near future. At present, nuclear energy accounts for 7.5 per cent of the world's total energy supply and generates 15.7 per cent of total electricity.[5]

Thirdly, energy needs and problems have always created a fear about dependence on external powers and geopolitical factors. This is especially true in the case of countries with limited or no energy resources, which eventually shapes their foreign and strategic policies. It can be argued that the future of world politics will be shaped by interests in energy, and world politics will be essentially a world of energy diplomacy. One extreme is perhaps the US foreign policy towards the Middle East which has been very much driven by the desire to protect energy resources and supplies for the world economy and its allies in particular. The same is true in the case of China's summit diplomacy towards African states because of energy interests.

Perhaps what is fundamentally important is the fact that there is always a conflict of interests between efficiency and population growth. There would certainly be efforts to promote efficiency to meet increasing energy demands due to population growth and economic activities. In these circumstances, the main question is which factor is more responsible for the huge consumption of energy: population growth or political-economic policies?

And lastly, investment and research into alternative energy is expensive. The IAEA estimates that the world will spend at least $200 billion on the development of nuclear energy. India has plans for 25 per cent of its energy demand to be met by nuclear energy in 2050. However, nuclear energy has always been controversial and a sensitive issue. Thus, nuclear power is likely to remain marginal in supplying energy needs. It is expected to supply 6.3 per cent and 4.7 per cent of total energy needs in 2010 and 2030 respectively.[6]

The Indonesian case

Indonesia has huge potential in energy: oil reserves amount to 9 billion barrels with production capacity of 500 million barrels/year; gas, 182 TFCS reserve, 3 TFCS production/year; and coal, 19.3 billion tonnes reserve, production 130 million tonnes/year.

In addition to this, Indonesia also has a lot of non-fossil energy: hydro-power (845 million BOE, equivalent to 75 GW of electricity); geothermal energy (219 millions BOE, equivalent to 27 GW of electricity); biomass 49.81 GW of electricity; solar energy 4.8 kWh/cubic metres per day; wind (9.29 GW); and uranium 24,112 tonnes.[7]

These resources provide legitimate grounds for those who argue for non-nuclear energy options. To this group, what is more fundamental is developing new approaches in energy policies and consumption. What is fundamental in Indonesia is that access to energy is very limited, which is only 0.5 TOE per capita. The structure of energy consumption shows a dependence on oil, accounting for 63 per cent of total energy consumption. The country now produces 1125 mbpd, with 611,000 barrels for domestic consumption and 514,000 barrels for export. Oil imports are approximately 487,000 barrels/day. Indonesia at present exports 4.88 BCF of natural gas, domestic consumption of gas is 3.47 BCF; it also produces 92.5 tonnes of coal for export, and 33 million tonnes for domestic consumption.

Dependence on oil for energy consumption and the increasing export of coal and gas have caused Indonesia to become a net oil importer. Coal, natural gas and other energy resources have not been fully used to meet energy demands.

Policy

According to the Presidential Regulation No. 5/2006, Indonesia is committed to having a primary energy mix target by 2025 with a composition of oil 20 per cent, natural gas 30 per cent, coal 33 per cent and others 17 per cent. This no doubt requires diversification and investment policies which include energy security policies to reduce CO_2 emissions, securing energy reserves, efficiency in production and use, increasing reliance on non-fossil energy resources, system incentives for investors and development of energy infrastructure.[8] Another problem with the energy mix is the nuclear option. Nuclear energy is perhaps inevitable in the future. But it is problematic due to its political sensitivity. It has been the main target of attacks from various environmental groups inside and outside Indonesia. They have been active in an intensive campaign against the development of a nuclear power plant in Gunung Muria, in the northern part of Central Java, Indonesia.

The most important issue as far as human security is concerned is how the policies provide affordability, access and energy supply to people. Indeed, the contribution of energy policy to welfare, employment generation and government income has been a political and economic issue for many years. Thus, the main purpose of the energy policy in Indonesia, as a *developing* country, is to contribute to national development by providing people with clean and cheap energy services.

However, the choice is certainly difficult. Energy security has always been dependent upon three variables: resources, supply lines and prices. In this regard, many countries are vulnerable due to overdependence: on one form; on one source; on one delivery system.[9] This problem is complicated further by environmental, climate change and global warming considerations. Even if dependence is no longer a problem, regulations on energy security will still be faced with many huge problems. Chief among these is how to protect consumers, to support investment and create economic efficiency. Equally sensitive is the strategic factor. Energy security will still shape, and be shaped by, strategic interactions of the world powers.

Notes

1. International Energy Agency (IEA), *International Energy Outlook 2003* and *2004* (Paris: IEA, 2003, 2004).
2. IEA, *Key World Energy Statistics 2006* (Paris, IEA, 2006), p. 33.
3. British Petroleum (BP), *BP Statistical Review of World Energy 2004*.
4. IEA, *Key World Energy Statistics 2006*.
5. Ibid.
6. Ibid.
7. Nenny Sri Utami, *Blueprint Pengelolaan Energi Nasional 2005–2025*, Departemen Energi dan Sumber Daya Nasional, 2005.
8. H. H. Situmeang, 'Overview of World Energy and Its Impact on Developing Countries: Energy Security – Climate Change', paper presented at Asia Cooperation Dialogue: Co-Prime Movers on Energy Security, Bali, 11–12 April 2007.
9. Ibid.

14
Philippine Energy Policy: Implications for Human Security and Regional Cooperation

Carolina G. Hernandez

Introduction

The search for energy security in the twenty-first century has become a key policy goal of states at the national, regional and global levels. Impacted upon by unprecedented economic growth, industrialization, urbanization, population increase and the technological revolution, the need for energy and its sustained supply have pushed energy security to the forefront of the national agenda of states in the domestic and external arenas.

Although a small-sized state, the Philippines shares the concern for energy security that large and medium-sized states face. Not a net producer of energy resources, it has sought energy self-sufficiency throughout most of the past half century. This is reflected in its series of energy plans, including the current one.

At the same time, energy security has implications for the comprehensive security of its people. Therefore, energy security is increasingly seen through the lens of human security, which is fundamentally about freedom from fear and freedom from want. Energy resources being unequally dispersed throughout the world, where some regions and states are blessed with great abundance and others less so, the search for energy security is necessarily a key component of the foreign and security policy of every state.

This chapter deals with the Philippines as a case study on these related issues of energy security, human security and regional cooperation. The country's energy structure and policy, its search for energy security, how energy security impacts on the Filipino people's human security, as well as opportunities and challenges for regional cooperation in achieving energy security will be discussed.

Energy security is defined as access to reliable, affordable and environmentally sustainable energy supplies. Reliability includes a condition where the sources of energy are relatively stable and the country's access to these sources is relatively assured by stable relations with the authorities governing these sources, and supply routes relatively safe from disruptions caused by both state and non-state actors. Affordability refers to a condition where energy prices are at levels the country can afford to pay in order to meet its energy needs. Environmentally sustainable refers to a condition in which the exploration, exploitation, production and use of energy resources do not create ecological damage that would deny future generations their right to meet their own needs.

Brief historical overview

Domestic and external factors have combined to shape Philippine energy policy over the years. The availability of indigenous sources of energy, the rate of economic growth and attendant implications for industrial energy requirements and changing lifestyles of the population, the stability of foreign-sourced energy imports, especially oil and gas including secure supply routes, as well as dependable domestic energy infrastructures and supply systems are key components of this energy policy context. Philippine dependence on imported energy sources in its energy mix is a persistent feature of this context. The state of political stability of foreign energy sources, particularly in the Middle East, the security of the sea lines of communication (SLOCs) through which energy supplies pass, the rise of global terrorism with implications for these external factors, as well as the phenomenal rise of China and India, both hungry for energy resources, have complicated energy security for countries like the Philippines.

Heavily dependent on foreign supplies of energy, particularly oil and coal, the country has continuously sought the goal of energy self-sufficiency through various measures including aggressive development of indigenous energy resources, energy use efficiency and energy conservation. Philippine external dependence has ranged from a low of 50 per cent in 1985 mainly due to economic decline to a high of 92 per cent during the first oil crisis in 1973. As such, it is sensitive to the dynamics of foreign-sourced energy supplies. Whenever political instability reaches crisis proportions in the Middle East, where much of the country's oil supplies come from, Philippine energy security also suffers a proportional decline. This was the case in the first oil shock of 1973 when OPEC demonstrated how effectively they could control the world's oil prices. Like most foreign oil-dependent countries, the Philippine economy suffered as oil prices skyrocketed. This experience was repeated in the second oil crisis which was triggered by the Iran–Iraq war.

Thus, Philippine energy policy has traditionally sought energy self-sufficiency to ensure energy security. This could be done by energy use efficiency and the development of indigenous energy resources. However, although rich in potential indigenous energy resources, it has not been able to meet its moving target of achieving energy self-sufficiency through the decades beginning in the Marcos era. Thus, to date, these potential indigenous resources remain largely underdeveloped and underexploited.

Among the country's available indigenous energy resources are hydrocarbons – oil, natural gas and coal reserves – as well as renewable biomass-based resources, the latter stemming from its being a largely agricultural country. According to the Department of Energy's Philippine Energy Plan (PEP) 1993–2000,[1] the Philippines had estimated recoverable reserves of roughly 400 million barrels of oil and 4.5 trillion standard cubic feet of natural gas. Between 1979 and the start of the planning period for PEP 1993–2000, the Philippines produced 40 million barrels of oil from its first oil field (El Nido in Palawan province). The country's proven coal reserves were estimated at around 370 million metric tons. However, because of its poor quality, consumer demand was low, such that annual production at that time was a little over a million metric tons. The country's geothermal steam potential was about 4000 megawatts (MW) with installed capacity at only 888 MW. Hydro potential from 293 identified sites was estimated at 14,400 MW with installed capacity at only 2257 MW. Bagasse and agriwastes consumption by large industrial users were placed at about 11.5 million barrels of fuel-oil-equivalent (MMBFOE), representing some 12 per cent of the country's primary commercial energy mix at that time.[2]

The Philippines produces oil (such as from El Nido), natural gas (Malampaya gas field offshore, Northwest Palawan), coal, and various forms of renewable energy resources including biofuels, wind and solar which are part of its energy mix. Indigenous energy development has political, economic and social implications. Politics enters into the picture in identifying sites for indigenous energy development; the tension between economic growth and environmental health has political, economic and social implications, as does the search for energy security for land use and land rights of local communities, including the indigenous peoples. Thus, all energy plans of the country have attempted to address these issues and have woven energy plans into the government's social reform agenda. Yet, the gap between rhetoric and actual implementation of these plans remains wide.

This brief energy profile suggests that both domestic and external forces shape the country's energy policy. The Philippines has responded to them in its search for energy security at various times through various ways as discussed below.

Philippine energy policy: means and ends

In spite of the fact that the Philippines had 138 million barrels of proven oil reserves as of January 2006,[3] it had no oil production until 2001. Between January and September 2006, it produced an average of just over 25,000 barrels per day (bbl/d). Production remained modest relative to its needs, although it had increased due to the development of new offshore deepwater oil deposits.

Organization of the energy sector

The Philippine National Oil Company (PNOC) has traditionally dominated the oil sector. However, deregulation of the oil industry, started in 1998, has brought several new oil companies into the country, although PNOC remains the principal player in upstream oil market activities, often in partnership with foreign companies in its large projects.

As noted above, oil production began and increased due to deepwater exploration and production activities, principally in the Malampaya oil rim lying beneath the large Malampaya natural gas field.[4] This is the country's largest oil-producing area, and began operations in October 2001 with Shell (45 per cent stake) as the operator, and Chevron (45 per cent) and PNOC (10 per cent) as partners. Natural gas production in the area is significant, but oil production in the deepwater area has been difficult to exploit, leading Shell and Chevron to give up their right to develop the oil rim project to PNOC in 2004. In 2006, PNOC awarded the contract to develop the Malampaya oil rim to Mitra Energy of Malaysia, which was terminated with the Philippine government's new regulation declaring that oil exploration and production activities in the country would be conducted through a bidding process instead of a farm-in deal such as the one awarded to Mitra Energy. Other areas are being explored, including in the Mindoro, Palawan, and Sulu Sea basins,[5] and PNOC is currently engaged in exploration of the contested Spratly area in the South China Sea with the national oil companies of China and Vietnam.[6]

The country's largest oil refining company is Petron Corporation. Formerly state-owned, it now has PNOC and Aramco each holding 40 per cent of the shares with individual stockholders controlling the remaining 20 per cent. Since deregulation of the industry in 1998, some 60 new firms have entered the retail oil sector with Petron, Shell and Chevron remaining the dominant sector players. The new entrants, however, had increased their market share from 10 per cent in 2000 to about 20 per cent by 2005.[7]

As regards natural gas, OGJ put the country's proven natural gas reserves at 3.9 trillion cubic feet (Tcf) as of January 2006, located mostly in the Malampaya natural gas field. Natural gas production started only in 2001, and while natural gas consumption has increased, in 2004, this energy source supplied less than 8 per cent of the country's total energy consumption. Domestic supply comes from the Malampaya offshore natural gas field operated by Shell, Chevron and PNOC. This field is estimated to hold 3.7 Tcf of natural gas reserves. In October 2006, another natural gas field – the Sampaguita field – was reported to potentially hold up to 20 Tcf of natural gas reserves. An interested player, Forum Energy, has plans to conduct test drills in the Sampaguita field, and will consider a liquefied natural gas (LNG) project if testing confirms substantial natural gas reserves.[8]

Philippine recoverable coal reserves are estimated at 260 million short tons (Mmst). Its coal consumption in 2004 was 10.1 Mmst, 45 per cent higher than in 1999; only 2.9 Mmst was produced domestically. It relies on Indonesia, China and Australia for its coal imports.

The electricity sector has been undergoing restructuring and privatization as a result of the server power crisis of the early 1990s. The Electric Power Industry Reform Act (EPIRA) was enacted in 2001, among other things to deregulate the power industry, break up and eventually privatize state-owned enterprises, particularly the National Power Corporation (Napocor), whose vertically integrated assets needed to be broken up into separate units for electricity generation, transmission and distribution. EPIRA also mandates the eventual sale of most of Napocor's transmission and generation assets. It appears that there is still a long way to go before the privatization goals of EPIRA can be carried out. The Power Sector Assets and Liabilities Management (PSALM) Corporation, which assumed control of Napocor's power plants in 2004, only managed to sell off 14 per cent of its power stations by April 2006, although its target was to sell off 70 per cent of these generation assets by the end of 2005.[9]

With the increased usage of natural gas-fired power plants and the rise of oil prices, conventional thermal sources of electricity generation have grown in importance. The largest projects in this category are connected to the Malampaya Deepwater Gas-to-Power Project whose natural gas pumped ashore supplies three combined cycle power plants, one of which is owned by Napocor and operated by the Korea Electric Power Corporation (KEPCO) and the other two by the First Gas Power Corporation.[10]

Second only to the United States in geothermal energy production, the Philippines has more than 1900 MW installed geothermal capacity, which the government seeks to expand to about 3100 MW during the next ten years. If carried out, the Philippines would become the world's largest producer of geothermal energy. PNOC developed most of the country's geothermal power projects, with Chevron Geothermal Philippines Holdings, Inc. and Unocal Philippines also players in this field.

Hydroelectric sources provide some 2900 MW of the country's installed electricity generation capacity (19 per cent of the total as of 2004). Due to various factors, including environmental implications and civil society opposition to the building of dams, there has not been any significant expansion in hydroelectricity capacity during the past 20 years. However, some projects are being developed to build small-scale hydropower facilities.[11]

Finally, in addition to geothermal and hydropower, the country's renewable energy consumption includes solar, wind, tide, solid biomass and animal products, biomass gas and liquids, and industrial and municipal wastes.

From the above, it can be seen that private companies play a significant role in upstream and downstream oil and gas activities, with the state-owned PNOC and Napocor continuing to play a major role. Foreign company involvement includes BP, Chevron, CNOOC, Forum Energy, Marubeni, Mitra Energy, PetroVietnam, Royal Dutch Shell and Saudi Aramco.[12]

Energy policy goals and means

Ferdinand Marcos crafted an energy policy driven by the two oil shocks cited above. He established the Ministry of Energy which responded to these externally sourced shocks by reducing oil dependence through determined and massive development and utilization of indigenous alternatives. On the foreign policy front, Marcos sought to ensure oil supply from the Middle East through forging close relations with oil-producing countries in this region, including Libya. The latter was also the leader of the Organization of Islamic Conference (OIC) and was involved in mediating the peace process between the Philippine government and the Moro National Liberation Front (MNLF), which produced the Tripoli Agreement in 1976.

Marcos' Ten-Year Energy Programme covering 1980 to 1989 was a response to the second oil crisis triggered by the Iran–Iraq war. The Programme focused on massive indigenous energy development and oil substitution especially in power generation. It aimed to reduce dependence on foreign oil imports from 72 per cent in 1979 to 48 per cent by 1984, and 31 per cent by 1989. The Programme's actual performance was 56 per cent in 1984, although it could have reached 70 per cent had the economic recession not occurred which reduced the projected energy demand significantly.[13] The recession was made worse by the effects of the Aquino assassination in 1983.

In spite of an aggressive energy policy, Marcos failed to achieve the policy's target to make the country almost self-sufficient in oil by 1984 and an oil exporter by 1979. Oil production in 1979 was at the country's highest recorded level during the Marcos years, but it still fell short of the target. During the last years of Marcos, the oil import bill took up as much as 30 per cent of total imports; the oil bill single-handedly accounted for more than 100 to nearly 400 per cent of the Philippine trade deficit.[14]

In general, the Aquino Presidency was characterized by an aversion to and reversal of policies and programmes adopted during the Marcos period. This was due to Corazon Aquino's decision to define her democratic administration as the opposite of the repressive Marcos regime. In the wake of her husband's assassination under military custody and carried to the Presidency by people power which ousted Marcos in February 1986, Aquino distanced her administration as far away as possible from that of her predecessor. One of the casualties of this approach was the country's search for energy security, signified by the abolition of the energy portfolio from the Cabinet. Persistent power outages in addition to the series of coup attempts – though unsuccessful – against her government drove foreign investment away and compromised the country's economic recovery.

During her tenure, the government adopted the five-year Medium-Term Energy Plan (MTEP) for 1988–92. Buoyed by the initial growth spurt from negative growth rates of −6 per cent and −4 per cent in 1984 and 1985 to real GDP growth rate of 4.6 per cent in 1987, there was optimism that the economy would recover from the recession of the last years of Marcos. This optimism was shattered as the actual performance of the economy was undermined by the political instability already noted above, the successive occurrence of national calamities – the country lies in the Ring of Fire and the typhoon belt where strong earthquakes and destructive typhoons followed by floods periodically occur – as well as the worsening power crisis. It did not help that the Aquino government mothballed the politically controversial, overpriced and graft-ridden Bataan Nuclear Power Plant (BNPP), which incidentally the Philippines managed to pay for in full only in 2007. It is in a way ironic that the present Arroyo administration under the recently appointed Secretary of Energy seeks to build a nuclear power plant in the country's search for energy security.

The MTEP under Aquino forecast that imported oil dependence would be reduced from 59 per cent in 1987 to 49 per cent by 1992. In fact, actual performance showed an increase in imported oil dependence to 69 per cent by 1992, or 20 percentage points higher than the target.[15] This is a telling commentary on the poor performance of the Aquino administration in energy security.

The Ramos administration not only stopped the power outages, but also established economic performance as among its signal achievements. Macroeconomic restructuring to open up the economy, accompanied by the adoption of an aggressive energy policy, with the establishment through the Republic Act 7638 in December 1992 of the Department of Energy (DOE) headed by a cabinet rank official with portfolio, made a significant difference. R.A. 7638 mandates the DOE to ensure that the country has continuous energy supply availability at affordable costs and to be cognizant of environmental concerns. Privatization of Napocor and a build-up of the country's base load capacity to meet the country's energy demands in the next century formed part of the Ramos administration's energy policy.[16]

The PEP for 1993–2000 argued the need for a national energy programme, citing the collective experience of the nation, which stressed the importance of planning for the country's energy infrastructure and supply systems as indigenous energy development and energy conservation. These were sought rigorously by the PEP so that within three years of its first Secretary of Energy taking office, the Ramos administration was able to alleviate the power outages that had plagued the preceding administration.

A successor PEP which built on the gains achieved earlier was devised for 1996–2005. Its three-pronged goal of availability of energy supply, competitive, affordable and reasonable energy prices, and socially and environmentally compatible energy infrastructures was to be achieved through the PEP with nine specific policies, including the enhancement of energy security through indigenous energy resources development, diversification of local and imported energy, and the pursuit of large-scale utilization of new and renewable energy sources.[17] It aimed for energy self-sufficiency at 40 per cent at the very least over the planning period. An increase in the percentage of imported energy is expected due to the increase in energy demand from economic growth and the resulting increased energy consumption both of industry and for private purposes. This percentage was 56.3 per cent in 1996 and is expected to be 57.2 per cent in 2010 and 58.8 per cent by 2025.[18]

President Gloria Macapagal Arroyo's energy policy was first articulated in the PEP 2002–11.[19] It forecast an increase in consumption at an annual average rate of 5.6 per cent from 2002 to 2004, and 6.5 per cent from 2005 to 2011 that was expected to be met in part through increased indigenous energy production in the amount of 1,933 MMBFOE during this planning period. This would represent a 6.9 per cent average annual increase in the production rate. The plan also sought to increase the self-sufficiency level from 45 per cent in 2000 to at least 50 per cent until the end of 2011. In particular, the Philippines sought to increase its geothermal generating capacity by developing additional geothermal fields to fuel 990 MW of power plants. As already noted, the country is second only to the United States in geothermal installed generating capacity, although Indonesia has a larger geothermal potential than the Philippines.

In addition, the PEP also planned to undertake programmes for the continuous development and utilization of new and renewable energy resources, such as mini-hydro, solar, ocean and biomass. Technologies for alternative clean fuels and energy efficiency especially in biofuels, alcogas and compressed natural gas (CNG) were also targeted for the transport sector. Privatization of power-generating plants, already begun during the Ramos administration, also remained part of a response to the goal of raising energy use efficiency. However, this view is challenged in some quarters by the claim that energy as a public utility must remain in public hands.

Ocean energy is perhaps a potentially strategic and critical resource which the country could develop. The Philippines had begun conceptualizing a project on the Assessment of Wave Power Potential to prepare wave energy maps which would then be the basis for the country's ocean energy development plan. For tidal power, Napocor undertook a preliminary resource assessment to determine the tidal current speeds and patterns in selected water passages such as the San Bernardino Straits and others in the Bohol/Talibon area[20] in central Visayas. This project, however, was reportedly shelved with the end of the Ramos administration.

The effects of the Iraq war and the continuing rise of China, and now India, have affected global energy security as never before. Skyrocketing oil prices, now at over US$108 per barrel as of mid-March 2008 have threatened the prospects for growth of the global economy, intensified the competition for energy supplies among the world's leading economies (thus raising the risks of future conflict), altered global power dynamics and structure, and posed serious social, economic and political challenges to small and medium-sized countries with continuing indigenous energy-producing capacity deficits.[21] The Philippines is no exception.

In response to these developments, President Arroyo has continued to pursue an energy plan seeking energy self-sufficiency to achieve a degree of energy security. At the same time, the energy plan also supports her administration's main thrusts of 'balanced economic growth, robust market-based industry, and poverty alleviation through social equity and good governance'. By 2006, its update on its energy plan summarized the accomplishments of PEP 2005–14 as it readjusted and refocused the plan's twin goals of attaining a sustainable 60 per cent self-sufficiency level by 2010 and beyond, and the effective implementation of reforms in the energy/power sector. The update details an Integrated Investment Portfolio of various capital investment requirements for different energy sub-sectors, incentives for prospective energy investors, as well as an indicative programme to promote long-term sustainability of the current plan's targets. In particular, the programme stresses the promotion of alternative energy resource options, emerging clean energy technologies, innovations in energy exploration and development technology among others to achieve increased energy self-sufficiency.[22]

Increased use of alternative fuels especially in the transport sector is also highlighted in the programme. These cleaner alternatives include bio-fuels (coco-diesel, fuel ethanol and jatropha curcas), CNG and autogas. In addition, solar and wind energy sources are being further developed. The Philippines could be a major producer of windpower and has showcased this potential in a number of places, including in the Ilocos region in Northern Philippines.

Implications for human security

The concept of human security has drawn the referent object of security from the state to the individual singly or collectively. Adopted by the United Nations Development Programme (UNDP) in the mid-1990s, human security is broadly seen as encompassing freedom from fear and freedom from want. In the Philippine context, it also embraces freedom from humiliation.[23] It is seen as having seven dimensions, namely economic security, food security, health security, environmental security, personal security, community security and political security.[24]

Energy security impacts on various dimensions of human security. It is presumed that when there is energy insecurity economic growth suffers as energy shortages negatively affect agricultural and industrial production, discourage existing and new investment, hamper both the building of physical infrastructure and human development, and on the whole make living as human beings more difficult. In particular, farmers, fishermen and others who live on the margins of society would be worse off than ever before.

Amidst the array of potential domestic non-renewable and renewable energy sources, the current Secretary of Energy has advocated the development of nuclear energy to attain the country's energy security goal. This option has serious traditional and non-traditional security implications, particularly in terms of human security. The issue of dual use of nuclear technology has implications for global goals of disarmament and non-proliferation, as well as risks that nuclear technology could fall into the hands of non-state actors. During the age of global terrorism, such implications cannot be treated lightly especially for countries like the Philippines that are considered major arenas where terrorists continue to operate. The United Nations has adopted conventions and resolutions to mitigate this security risk. Moreover, the disposal of nuclear waste remains a serious environmental security problem in addition to the risks of nuclear meltdown such as in Chernobyl.[25] These scenarios are ripe with human security implications.

A recent study illustrated how the search for energy security can impact on human security in the Philippines. Deregulation of the electricity generation sector is a policy option that was taken in the 1990s in order to redress energy insecurity. Such a policy has not been fully implemented to date. Yet, in a study conducted to determine the welfare impact of this reform policy, it was found that the introduction of private sector participation into the electricity generation sector, through the liberalization of the market for IPPs during the power crisis of 1990–3, promoted economic and social development. Consumers and IPPs were net gainers. Although the government was a net loser and there was an air pollution cost, the policy reform increased social welfare. The policy reform 'may have even saved lives by restoring vital social services such as water and sanitation'.[26] The study further concluded that although there were positive welfare effects from the policy reform during the energy crisis of the early 1990s, the legacy of the IPP contracts under ad hoc reform continues to weigh on the economy and society.[27] It can be deduced from the study that energy policy options have both positive and negative effects on welfare, an important element of human security.

Regional cooperation on energy security

As the Association of Southeast Asian Nations (ASEAN) moves towards the realization of an ASEAN Community of three pillars by 2015, amidst soaring oil prices since 2004, energy cooperation has become an important element in regional cooperation and integration. The region's increasing dependency on Middle East oil imports, and diminishing regional oil supplies in former oil-producing regional states, combine to push countries to increase energy flows between them as they move towards economic integration.

In this regard, the ASEAN Energy Ministers adopted in June 2004 a detailed five-year Plan of Action for Energy Cooperation (2004–9). The plan seeks (1) sustainable energy development, (2) to enhance the integration of regional energy infrastructure, (3) to promote energy security, (4) to create progressive policies for market reforms and liberalization, and (5) to address environmental concerns.

The twenty-fifth meeting of the ASEAN Energy Ministers on 23 August 2007 reaffirmed the view that 'an efficient, secure and integrated energy system is key to hastening the establishment of the ASEAN Economic Community by 2015' and in this regard agreed (1) to strengthen sustainable energy development through the expanding markets for renewable energy technologies and energy-efficient products; (2) to produce comprehensive institutional arrangements for enhanced security and stability of energy supply in ASEAN; (3) to develop regional energy infrastructure facilities; and (4) to intensify regional cooperation in enhancing energy integration.

Other important highlights at this meeting include (1) their commitment to work closely with all relevant partners, including the private sectors, the ASEAN dialogue partners and relevant international organizations, to help ensure greater regional energy security and sustainability; (2) an agreement in-principle to establish an ASEAN Nuclear Energy Safety Sub-Sector Network to explore nuclear safety issues; (3) signing of the Memorandum of Understanding on the ASEAN power grid to govern the coordination and facilitation of the programmes to implement the power interconnection projects in the ASEAN region; (4) they noted the progress made in the finalization of the new ASEAN Petroleum Security Agreement (APSA) to provide the required mechanism for a timely coordinated response in times of petroleum shortages and emergencies; (5) they noted the progress made in the implementation of the Vientiane Action Programme (VAP) Energy Agenda and the ASEAN Plan of Action for Energy Cooperation (APAEC) 2004–9; (6) and they welcomed the completion in February 2007 of the European Union (EU)–ASEAN Energy Facilities (EAEF) projects and the convening of the energy dialogue between the Senior Officials of ASEAN and the EU on 22 August 2007.[28]

ASEAN member countries have also entered into agreements to build physical infrastructures linking neighbouring countries to facilitate the flow of investments, services and goods, including energy supplies. For example, the Greater Mekong Sub-regional (GMS) Cooperation scheme includes the building of transport links between China's Yunnan province, Cambodia, Laos, Myanmar and Thailand. It is not coincidental that Myanmar is a major source of natural gas not only for its ASEAN neighbours, but for China and India as well.

The newly-launched East Asia summit,[29] consisting of the ten ASEAN member states plus three partners (China, Japan, South Korea), as well as Australia, India and New Zealand adopted the Cebu Declaration on East Asian Energy

Security at its second meeting in Mactan, Cebu, Philippines, in which they declared their commitment to seek the following goals:

(1) Improve the efficiency and environmental performance of fossil fuel use; (2) Reduce dependence on conventional fuels through intensified energy efficiency and conservation programmes, hydropower, expansion of renewable energy systems and bio-fuel production/utilization, and for interested parties, civilian nuclear power; (3) Encourage the open and competitive regional and international markets geared towards providing affordable energy at all economic levels; (4) Mitigate greenhouse gas emission through effective policies and measures, thus contributing to global climate change abatement; and (5) Pursue and encourage investment on energy resource and infrastructure development through greater private sector improvement.[30]

Twelve measures were included in the Declaration in order to achieve the goals for regional energy security, including investments in regional energy infrastructures such as the ASEAN power grid and the trans-ASEAN gas pipeline. This action was followed by the establishment of the EAS Energy Cooperation Task Force (ECTF) on 1 March 2007, whose work would be based on existing ASEAN energy sectoral mechanisms where feasible, and the convening of the EAS Energy Ministers meeting in Singapore. Held on 23 August 2007, the meeting took its cue from the Cebu Declaration and the ministers pledged to work together for the realization of the goals sought by the EAS leaders. The ministers welcomed the initiatives from Japan on (1) the Cooperation Initiative for Clean Energy and Sustainable Growth, and (2) its energy cooperation package that focuses on promoting energy efficiency, biomass and the utilization of clean coal.

In the meantime, the ECTF had already identified three energy cooperation work streams – energy efficiency and conservation, energy market integration, and biofuels for transport and other purposes – to start cooperation towards the achievement of the goals set by the Cebu Declaration. In parallel, the Economic Research Institute for ASEAN and East Asia (ERIA) had launched its work on the 'EAS Energy Outlook' as Japan launched the Asia Energy Conservation Collaboration Centre in Japan.[31]

These various regional cooperation schemes within ASEAN and the broader East Asia region of the EAS recognize the need to balance among other concerns the search for energy security, environmental security and food security. Turning to biofuels, for example, is certain to implicate CO_2 gas emissions as vast tracks of land are cleared for palm and jathropa. This would also have implications for food, economic and community security, especially among those already living on the margins of society. The search for energy security therefore creates new challenges to human security, the effective mitigation of which requires intra- and inter-regional cooperation.[32]

Conclusions

The search for energy security by the Philippines remains a work-in-progress, made even more challenging by the rise of large economies such as China and India, the increasing demand for energy by industry and households, the soaring prices of oil, the continuing instability of traditional energy sources in the Middle East, the (in)security of supply lines, the implications of renewable energy sources for the environment and human security broadly speaking, etc.

This search for energy security is not limited to specific countries or regions, but is global in character. The potential dangers that this search could lead to competition and conflict are serious. This calls for deliberate conflict preventive measures to which intra- and inter-regional cooperation can make significant contributions.

Notes

1. *Philippine Energy Plan 1993–2000* (Makati: Department of Energy), pp. 12–13.
2. Ibid.
3. As cited from *Oil and Gas Journal* by the Energy Information Administration (EIA) in its Country Analysis Brief on the Philippines, last updated in November 2006, p. 2.
4. For further information on Malampaya, see D. Young, 'Philippines Ties Energy Policy to Malampaya Gas Prices', *Oil and Gas Journal*, 22 October 2001, p. 34.
5. Ibid.
6. China, the Philippines, Vietnam, Brunei, Malaysia and Taiwan are claimants to all or parts of the islands, islets, reefs, and other geographic features in the South China Sea. To deflect tension and avoid conflict, ASEAN and China adopted an agreement called the Declaration on the Conduct of Parties in the South China Sea in 2002. The national oil companies of China, the Philippines and Vietnam entered into an agreement to conduct joint seismic studies in some of these contested areas some of which are within the Philippines Exclusive Economic Zone. This agreement is now being used as a basis by the political opposition and members of civil society in the Philippines to hold President Arroyo accountable for alleged gross violation of the Philippine Constitution.
7. Energy Information Administration, Country Analysis Brief, 2006, p. 2.
8. Ibid., pp. 3–4.
9. Ibid., pp. 4–5.
10. These facilities are the 1000 MW Santa Rita plant, the 500 MW San Lorenzo facility, and the 1200 MW Ilijan power plant. Planned projects include the Energy Park being developed by GNPower which led the construction of the country's first large-scale project by an independent power producer (IPP), a 470 MW coal-fired facility in Quezon province. The Energy Park will be built in Bataan province seeking to provide 1900 MW in new generating capacity. It includes a 600 MW coal-fired power station, a 1200 MW natural gas-fired plant and a 100 MW wind farm. From ibid., p. 5.
11. Ibid., p. 6.
12. Ibid., p. 8.
13. *Philippine Energy Plan 1993–2000*, pp. 22–3.

14. Ibid., p. 11.
15. Ibid., p. 24.
16. J. Home, 'Meeting Philippine Power Needs', *Euroweek*, No. 395, 24 March 1995, pp. 34–6.
17. *Philippine Energy Plan 1996–2002* (Makati: Department of Energy), p. 3.
18. Ibid., p. 4.
19. *Philippine Energy Plan 2002–2011* (Makati: Department of Energy), Highlights, p. 1.
20. *Philippine Energy Plan 1996–2002*, pp. 91–2.
21. Kang Wu and Fereidum Fesharaki (eds), with S. B. Westley, *Asia's Energy Future: Regional Dynamics and Global Implications* (Honolulu: East-West Center, 2007) documents the rising energy needs of countries in East and South Asia, the world's fastest energy-consuming region but with a small percentage of the world's oil resources, making it the most highly dependent region on oil imports in the world.
22. *Philippine Energy Plan 2006 Update* (Makati: Department of Energy), p. 1.
23. Human Development Network, *Philippine Human Development Report 2005: Peace, Human Security and Human Development in the Philippines* (Philippines: HDN, 2005), p. 1.
24. United Nations Development Programme (UNDP), *New Dimensions of Human Security: Human Development Report 1994* (New York: UNDP, 1994); also 'Box 1.1 Human Security: Key Concepts', in ibid., p. 5.
25. From *Food-for-Thought Papers* on 'Issues of Energy Security and the Environment in the Field of Disarmament and Non-Proliferation', prepared by Ambassador M. Karem and C. G. Hernandez, presented at the 49th Session of the UN Secretary-General's Advisory Board on Disarmament Matters, UN Headquarters, New York, 20–22 February 2008.
26. Natsuko Toba, 'Welfare Impacts of Electricity Generation Sector Reform in the Philippines', *Energy Policy*, No. 35, 2007, p. 6160.
27. Ibid., p. 6161.
28. Culled from the Joint Ministerial Statement, at the twenty-fifth ASEAN Ministers of Energy Meeting (AMEM), 'Energizing ASEAN to Power a Dynamic Asia', Singapore, 23 August 2007.
29. The East Asia summit (EAS) was convened during the eleventh Leaders summit of ASEAN in Kuala Lumpur in 2005. Countries other than the ASEAN + 3 + 3 may participate if they meet the three criteria for participation set by the ASEAN Foreign Ministers: substantive relations with ASEAN, a full Dialogue Partner of ASEAN, and accession to the Treaty of Amity and Cooperation.
30. From the Cebu Declaration on East Asian Energy Security, East Asia summit, Cebu, Mactan, Philippines, 15 January 2007.
31. Culled from the Joint Ministerial Statement.
32. Such a call for intra- and inter-regional cooperation has been aired by the Council for Asia-Europe Cooperation (CAEC) in two volumes published separately: C. G. Hernandez and G. Wilkins (eds), *Population, Food, Energy, and the Environment: Challenges to Asia–Europe Cooperation* (Quezon City: Japan Centre for International Exchange, Institute for Strategic and Development Studies and Royal Institute of International Affairs, 2000), and F. Godement, N. Grancoise and Taizo Yakushiji (eds), *Asia and Europe: Cooperating for Energy Security* (Paris: Centre Asie IFRI, 2004). See also a study by the Asia Pacific Agenda Project (APAP): P. B. Stares (ed.), *Rethinking Energy Security in East Asia* (Tokyo and New York: Japan Centre for International Exchange, 2000).

15
Nuclear Energy: World Perspectives

Eduardo González and José María Martínez-Val

The role of nuclear energy in electricity supply

Nuclear energy is the technical and economic label to identify a set of activities that transform the energy contained in the atomic nucleus into a useful type of energy, particularly electricity. The potential energy of the inner components of the atomic nucleus is very large, and it conveys nuclear radiation and nuclear reactions. The main reaction exploited so far is fission, which is usually induced by a free neutron. In one fission, about 0.1 per cent of the reacting mass disappears, and it is converted into heat. This is a much higher value than the corresponding level of chemical reactions. In fact, it is about 1 million times higher. This is why nuclear energy is so powerful, but it is also a cause for concern. To minimize the risks, nuclear reactors are designed and operated so that temperature and pressure values do not exceed the allowed levels.

Nuclear energy for electricity generation was started in the late 1950s, and evolved very fast in the first two decades. This fast early deployment was slowed down by a set of factors, particularly social and political attitudes. Accidents, such as TMI-2 (Harrisburg, USA, 1979) and Chernobyl-4 (former Soviet Union, 1986), were at the very root of social and political concern. Additionally, nuclear waste was also considered to be too complex a problem from social and political viewpoints. Last, but not least, proliferation of nuclear weapons was another fundamental issue for nuclear foes.

However, despite these social concerns, it must be stated that the actual facts are very different. First, nuclear accidents in the Western world (including TMI-2) have not had any relevant impact on people and the environment. The Chernobyl case was a collection of human and institutional safety violations such that it is difficult to believe that a similar man-induced catastrophe could happen in any country with independent surveillance of nuclear energy. Of course, this requirement of an independent nuclear regulatory body is a must for nuclear energy anywhere in the future.

Nuclear waste has some special features, namely, ionizing radiation emission and heat release, but wastes are very limited in mass and volume, and can be disposed of in deep geological repositories with an extremely low risk of interaction with the human environment any time in the future. Moreover, nuclear waste radio toxicity can be reduced by a factor of 1000 by applying advanced fuel cycles and transmutation techniques. The basic science for these activities is well known, but its deployment at a commercial level will require some technological developments which belong to the so-called 'sustainable nuclear energy' concept, which will be discussed later on.

As far as proliferation is concerned, it can be said that no country looking for nuclear weapons has used a civilian programme as an excuse or as a support. The technical requirements are totally different in each objective. Nevertheless, there is a non-negligible link between them, based on sensitive nuclear materials, namely plutonium and highly enriched uranium. The main point in this context is an international safeguard policy, improving the current level of implementation of the IAEA (International Atomic Energy Agency). Properly speaking, the proliferation issue is mainly a subject of international treaties (such as the NPT), which is not affected by the commercial programmes for electricity generation in nuclear power plants (NPPs).

It is worth underlining that NPPs generate about 2800 TWh (billions of kilowatt-hours) today, which represents more than 16 per cent of the total electricity generated in the world. Nuclear electricity is very reliable and has a high load factor, corresponding to a very large number of operating hours a year (about 8000). Hence, it contributes substantially to electricity grid stability, service quality and security of electricity supply. And last, but not least, nuclear electricity is cheaper, or much cheaper, than the average cost. It is true that an NPP conveys a higher investment-specific cost than other types of power stations, but operation and maintenance (O&M) and fuel costs are rather low, which is also an important factor contributing to security of supply.

In summary, it can be stated that nuclear energy can play the role of a fundamental contributor to electricity security of supply, without CO_2 emissions, and with a very moderate cost.

Specific features of nuclear energy

Nuclear energy has very specific features, but we can measure and monitor those special features, particularly the neutron flux and the ionizing radiation level. Of course, human beings do not have any natural sensor to identify ionizing radiation, and this fact contributes to the social fear of nuclear energy. However, radiation can be detected easily and very fast, and it is very easy to guarantee that any leak from a nuclear circuit is immediately detected, and safety countermeasures implemented. It is important to underline that all phenomena taking place in an NPP can be accurately characterized, and all conceivable accidents that could happen in an NPP are taken into account in the safety evaluation carried out by the nuclear regulatory body, on the basis of the engineering calculations and design decisions defining the NPP. This exercise is a fundamental tool in the safety culture applied to the nuclear field. In the following, brief explanations are given on the main aspects of nuclear energy, in order to help explain the physics and technology of the nuclear installations, including the sources of risk and the means we have for dealing with them at a very high level of safety, as is shown by the accumulated experience of close to 10,000 reactor-years.

Fission

Nuclear fission is a reaction in which an atomic nucleus is split into two parts, that is, two new nuclei of smaller mass. Only very heavy nuclei undergo this reaction. Some of them, particularly the largest ones, can create fission by themselves, as a natural way of achieving nuclear stability, but this is not the way this reaction is exploited in a nuclear reactor. In this case, fissions are induced by free neutrons. In our physical world, neutrons are always within atomic nuclei, although a few of them are created by the incoming cosmic radiation falling onto the earth, but the latter are not relevant for a reactor, where the free neutrons are produced in situ. This is a fact of the fission reaction, which is characterized by the following features:

- Energy production (as heat generated in the material undergoing fission, usually called nuclear fuel);
- Radioactive fragments production;
- Generation of free neutrons.

Regarding the last point, each fission generates two or three free neutrons depending on several factors (the energy of the incoming neutron and the type of nuclear fuel). This fact suggests the concept of 'chain reaction', because neutrons born from a fission can induce new fissions, and so on. In the reactors, the fission rate is kept constant in order to keep the thermal power constant. There is a risk of suffering a strong increase of power due to an expansive chain reaction, but all these mechanisms are accurately known, and every nuclear reactor is designed and operated so that a power trip cannot take place. The only case where a trip of this type happened was the Chernobyl accident, because the operators followed a flawed procedure in making a hydro-mechanical test, and they performed six severe violations of the safety rules of plant operation. In any other reactor type, the operator cannot make these violations, because the system does not allow it, and the reactor operation would be automatically stopped (in the same way as electricity is interrupted in any circuit if the current exceeds the limit of the protection units).

In relation to radioactive products generation, all nuclear fragments coming out from a fission are radioactive. In a reactor, natural radioactivity (that is, radioactivity of the natural material used as nuclear fuel) is amplified by many orders of magnitude. All natural nuclear materials, such as uranium, are radioactive and natural radioactivity is found almost everywhere on earth, which means that there is a natural background that can be used as a reference level in safety assessments. The importance of this fact is worth stressing. Radioactivity is a natural phenomenon, not a man-made one. Nevertheless, the radiation level is very important and should not surpass certain limits, and radiological protection is mainly a quantitative process to guarantee those limits are not exceeded.

The third important effect of fission reactions is energy (heat) generation, which is used in the NPP to activate a thermodynamic cycle for generating electricity in a turbo-generator. We have already said that 0.1 per cent of the reacting mass in a fission reactor is converted into heat. This is a very high energy intensity, which can be expressed in a macroscopic way: if all the atomic nucleus of 1 gram of uranium were fissioned, the energy generated would be 1 MW-day. This factor allows us to calculate the nuclear fuel consumption in an NPP. Let us take a 1000 MWe unit, which requires about 3000 MW-thermal. In operation, the reactor energy generated per day will be 3000 MW-day, which implies a fuel consumption of 3 kg/day. Of course, those 3 kg will be consumed in a rather distributed way in the reactor, not in a small part of it. During a year (let us say 330 days of full operation) 1 tonne of fuel will be consumed. In fact, most of it will be converted into other elements. Only 0.1 per cent of it will actually disappear, that is, 1 kg.

Because of the physics of nuclear chain reactors, the nuclear fuel loaded in a reactor cannot be fissioned to 100 per cent. Indeed, the consumption percentage is about 4 per cent. So, there is a discharge of spent fuel which is much higher than 1 tonne per year. It is about 25 times as large. Even so, this value is very much lower than the amount of fuel used in and discharged from a coal-fired power plant of the same power and energy, which would be about 2.5 million tonnes of hard coal (and even more if lignite is used).

Nuclear fuel

Two natural chemical elements can be used as nuclear fission fuel: uranium and thorium. A critical point has to be clarified in this context: the nuclear properties of the atomic nucleus depend on the number of neutrons in it. If it is odd, as in U-235, it is considered a truly useful fuel (fissile material).

If it is even, as in U-238 and Th-232, the fuel is of second category (fertile fuel). Unfortunately, most uranium (99.29 per cent) is U-238, and 100 per cent of thorium is Th-232. This means that we only have 0.71 per cent of

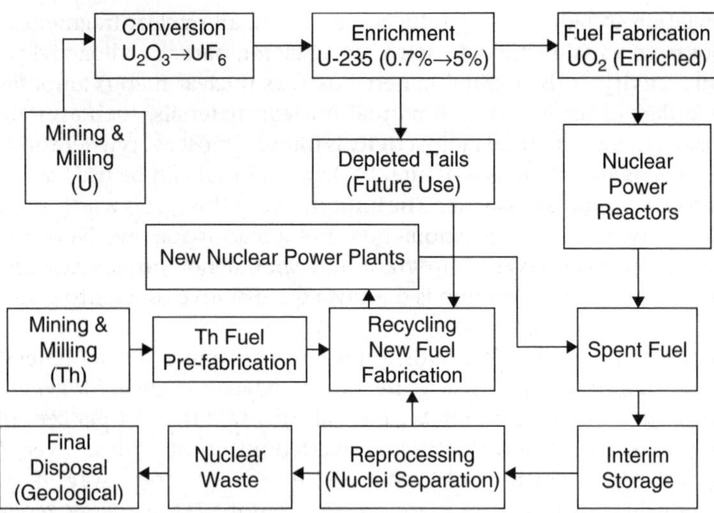

Figure 15.1   The nuclear fuel cycle

uranium which is true fuel for current reactors, being U-235. Two points must be clarified in this context.

First, standard reactors (LWR) cannot work with natural U-235 concentration. The fuel has to be enriched in U-235 up to 3 per cent or more (not above 5 per cent). This means that specific installations have to do this enrichment.

Second, U-238 and Th-232 can be used as fuels, mainly by converting them into Pu-239 and U-233 by means of a neutron capture in each case. This technique is not commercially available at the moment. Long-term use of nuclear energy in a sustainable development framework will need this type of conversion reaction, to be exploited in specific reactors called 'breeders'.

The nuclear fuel cycle

The industrial activities needed to exploit nuclear energy constitute the so-called nuclear fuel cycle, depicted in Figure 15.1. It starts with uranium mining (and thorium in the future) and the reactor is found there as the central item. Before it, the fuel only contains natural radioactivity. After it, in the spent fuel, radioactivity levels are much higher because of the new isotopes generated from the nuclear reactions.

Spent fuel is kept in suitable cooling pools in the NPP. In the medium term, spent fuel elements can be gathered in a centralized stock for many decades (or several centuries). In the longer term, a deep geological repository could be

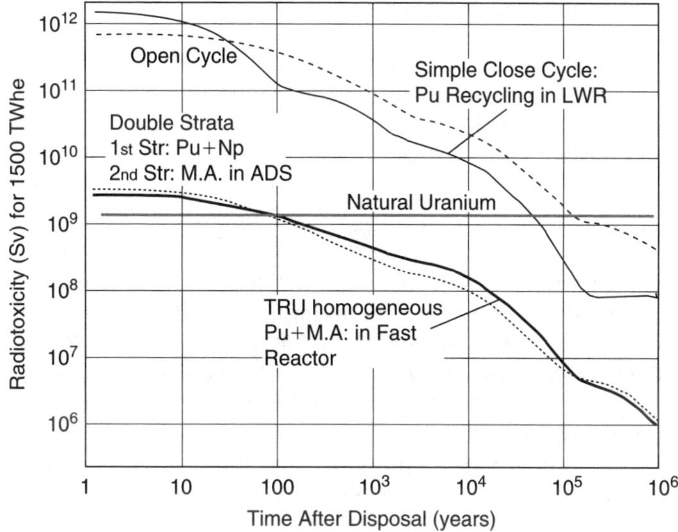

Figure 15.2   Effect of transmutation on the radio toxicity of the spent fuel

used as final destination of the spent fuel. Finland and Sweden have already identified this last stage of the nuclear fuel, but most countries are waiting for technological developments and advances before taking a decision on that point.

In fact, transmutation of selected isotopes from the spent fuel could reduce quite a lot of the radio toxicity of the spent fuel and its heat load (which are the main burdens for the interim and final storage). In Figure 15.2, radio toxicity (measured in sieverts per TWhe generated) of the spent fuel is shown as it is, and the value after transmutation of the actinides (or trans-uranium elements, such as Pu, Np, Am and Cm) is also shown. The open cycle is the current activity, where the spent fuel is not recycled. Plutonium (Pu) can be recycled in current reactors (LWR) but the transmutation effect is not very relevant. It becomes relevant if actinides are recycled either in double strata cycles or in homogeneous burn-up in advanced reactors (in a later section, those reactors will be discussed).

It goes without saying that transmutation is accompanied by additional energy generation, which can be maximized by appropriate reactors, already identified on paper, but not built so far. In this context, it is important to underline that the potential for nuclear energy is much larger than the industrial level commercialized so far. Mastering the activities and installations to take advantage of the full potential of nuclear energy is a fundamental challenge that will briefly be addressed in the next section.

Security of supply for nuclear energy

It has already been said that electricity generation in NPP is very reliable and is based on a continuous operation of the plant (around 8000 hours a year) suffering from a very small number of non-programmed stops. This fact is in turn based on two facts:

- Technology maturity and availability;
- Nuclear material and nuclear services availability.

As regards the former, technology has always been an asset of nuclear energy, and it has always been under continuous improvement. In fact, reactors being built nowadays are a development of the former families, with better performance. Any country interested in nuclear energy (such as Japan, France, Korea, Finland, China and others) can make their choice between a set of new reactor types, labelled Generation 3.

With respect to the latter, uranium ore availability is based on an international market with very stable features, although prices have gone up (and down) in recent years. Uranium inventories at a given price are currently evaluated by the IAEA[1] and they are currently estimated as 4.5 million tonnes at a price lower than 130 US$/kg. Reserves are distributed across the world: 24 per cent in Australia, 17 per cent in Kazakhstan, 9 per cent in Canada and 7 per cent in the United States.

U-235 enrichment services and fuel fabrication are also international commercial activities that do not show any bottleneck for nuclear programmes as defined at the present time, and there is a sound capability to increase those services if the programmes expand much more than current forecasts. The nuclear services industry reaction can be faster than the deployment of expanded programmes. Commercial plants for U-235 enrichment have a capability bigger than 50 million SWU (unit of separate work) which is in excess of the demand. New facilities are being built, based on ultra-centrifugation, to replace older diffusion plants.

In summary, it can be said that analysis of all the activities and material availability in nuclear energy clearly shows that there is no roadblock jeopardizing the role of nuclear energy as a main contributor to security of supply in electricity generation.

In some cases, the so-called 'regulatory risk' is cited as a problem for this role. According to the actual experience of many countries over many years, this risk is actually non-existent, that is, there has been no nuclear regulatory decision to close a certain family of reactors for safety reasons. A totally different subject is the 'political risk', that is, the political decision to phase out nuclear reactors, as was the case of Sweden and Germany. In both cases, the decision was not taken overnight, and it was discussed in terms of utilities, not only for economic reasons, in order to adopt a suitable schedule for replacement by other types of power station.

Technology perspective: sustainable nuclear energy

As has been already said, the potential of nuclear fission energy exceeds the current level of commercial application considerably. This potential was known from the very beginning of the nuclear era, as a scientific reality that could be converted into practical applications through the corresponding R&D programmes, which need the corresponding budget. Those budgets and efforts were not fully justified because the available technology in the early days was good enough for the first stage of this history.

The concern over climate change and the need to contain and reduce CO_2 emissions have pushed several governments and energy agencies to reconsider the long-term role of nuclear energy and to revisit and re-analyse its potential. From these analyses, the concept of sustainable nuclear energy has emerged. This concept considers not only the potential, but also the drawbacks and risks of nuclear energy, and it is established on four principles: non-proliferation, enhanced nuclear safety, nuclear fuel exploitation and waste minimization.

The first principle can be addressed by technology innovations, but it is mainly an international, diplomatic issue. In fact, the US Department of Energy invented and proposed the GNEP initiative (Global Nuclear Energy Partnership) in order to guarantee that new deployments in nuclear energy do not serve as a platform for spreading proliferation.

Nuclear safety records in the Western world are very positive, but it is obvious that there is room for improvement. Moreover, the experience acquired in more than 400 reactors over many years has driven continuous improvement, both in safety features and economic performance, including repowering (a 10 per cent increase in LWRs).

From this experience, a new brand of reactors was developed late in the twentieth century, and they are currently available for commercial applications. They are labelled Generation 3 reactors, and they include enhanced safety features, many of them based on natural mechanisms (such as free convection) for performing the safety functions. They are much better designed and equipped to deal with accidental situations inside the plant, so that an accident with external effects outside the plant is extremely unlikely. Like previous reactors they have self-stabilizing mechanisms in the neutron chain reaction, but they also have better capabilities to guarantee reactor cooling with the emergency system. Indeed it would be very difficult to design other reactors with still higher safety standards.

For the long term (around 2030 and beyond) Generation 4 reactors are under consideration. They will be mainly oriented to achieve a better exploitation of natural nuclear materials, particularly U-238, by means of the so-called nuclear breeding mechanism. When a U-238 nucleus captures a neutron, it undergoes two consecutive beta-decays and becomes Pu-239, which is a very good fission fuel. This breeding mechanism needs fast neutrons (which are very scarce in current and Generation 3 reactors) and this is why they are called fast breeders.

With current reactors, the energy obtained from their fuel is less than 1 per cent of the total potential energy of the uranium ore. With fast breeders, this percentage could be higher than 60 or 70. However, a strong effort in R&D is still needed for those reactors to become commercial. (Similarly, some reactors can be developed to 'burn' thorium, although they need to be fed initially with U-235.)

Sustainability of nuclear energy in terms of reserves can be explained as follows: current nuclear energy production implies a consumption of 2.8×10^{19} J per year, in terms of energy contained in the natural uranium. Total U reserves (at any price, that is, not actually in the market) are about 15 million tonnes, which represents an energy content of 1.2×10^{24} J. We must add 8 million tonnes of thorium reserves, with a content of 7×10^{23} J. In total, it means close to 2×10^{24} J, that is, 60,000 times the annual consumption. However, current reactors only exploit about 0.6 per cent of the potential energy of the ore. Hence, those reserves only represent about 360 years at the current consumption level. This is why it is so important to develop fast breeders (Generation 4 reactors) because they will be able to exploit 60 or 70 per cent of that energy, which will completely change the long-term scenario.

Besides being good machines to get the energy from U-238, fast breeders will also be useful to reduce the long-term radio toxicity of the waste per unit of energy generated in the total fuel cycle. To achieve this objective, some dedicated reactors could be built, called accelerator driven systems (ADS), because they will be sub-critical reactors needing an intense neutron source activated by a beam of accelerated protons. They will be able to eliminate neptunium and americium, and eventually curium isotopes, so leaving much cleaner waste. In fact, this transmutation policy will produce waste reaching the natural reference value of radio toxicity in less than 1000 years, instead of the non-transmuted waste, that will need about 100,000 years (see again Figure 15.2). This reduction is very important, because the time span of the waste-associated risk will be of human historical perspective, not a geological dimension.

In summary, nuclear technology is a mature engineering field producing around 17 per cent of the world's electricity today. It now offers new (Generation 3) reactors, which can give better performance with higher safety standards, using the same fuel cycle. And it can offer new fuel cycles for Generation 4 reactors, with a substantial reduction of the radiological waste burden, and a much higher capability to exploit the natural ores, with non-proliferation technologies and international safeguarding agreements. So, besides being a sound commercial activity in the present, it can evolve towards a truly sustainable development scenario to contribute to fulfilling the energy requirements of mankind.

Table 15.1 Development of nuclear power in different regions/continents (GWe)

	1980	*1985*	*1990*	*1995*	*2000*	*2005*
North America	56	84	110	114	106	111
Latin America	0	2	2	3	4	4
Western Europe	46	95	117	122	126	124
Eastern Europe	14	32	43	45	45	48
Africa	–	2	2	2	2	2
Middle East and South Asia	1	1	1	2	3	3
South East Asia and Pacific	–	–	–	–	–	–
Far East	17	32	43	56	63	76
Total	134	247	319	343	350	368

The renaissance of nuclear energy

It must be underlined again that, today, nuclear energy represents 17 per cent of worldwide electricity production at a very competitive cost. It is a proven technology for base-load electricity generation. Installed capacity at the end of 2007 was 368 GW. Its development has undergone very different time evolution in past decades, as can be seen in Table 15.1. There was a first business cycle in the US from the mid-1960s until the mid-1980s, and a second construction cycle in Europe some years later. Nowadays, the cycle is mainly taking place in the Far East, with a timid renaissance in OECD countries.

Nuclear power faces many challenges in many parts of the world, but policies encouraging the construction of nuclear reactors are becoming less rare than a few years ago. Public opinion is often presented as the cause for this lack of positive attitude, and there is no doubt that this is a strong factor. Nevertheless it has to be said that a change of public attitude seems to be taking place.

As already said, concerns are based on nuclear safety, long-term waste disposal risks and proliferation of nuclear materials. On the other hand, financing of nuclear programmes is often considered a key aspect for the deployment of this technology. While the costs are competitive in the overall lifetime of the plants, the high initial investment requires a stable legal framework so as not to jeopardize the investment recovery thanks to the proper operation of the plant.

Nuclear power and CO_2 emissions

Nuclear power is a very low carbon emitting technology, in these terms similar to most renewable ones. In fact, electricity produced by nuclear power plants today saves 2800 million tons of CO_2, which amounts to 10 per cent of total worldwide CO_2 emissions (because coal-fired power plants emit 1 kg of CO_2 per kWh, on average, and it is the type of plant that could substitute for nuclear power with similar features of cost and reliability). This is the reason why countries with a high per capita nuclear energy production yield a lower per capita CO_2 emission.[2]

The cost of nuclear power

The installation cost structure of electricity generated by nuclear power is characterized by high investment costs, typically in the order of 2000–2500 euros per installed electric kW. This means that a 1000 MWe installation will have a cost of 2000–2500 million euros and it takes between 60 and 70 months to be built.

Nuclear plants may operate from 40 to 60 years at an average of 8000 hours per year. As a consequence, interest rates play an important role in the final amortization costs whatever other questions are taken into consideration. The operational costs are in the order of 10 euros per MWh for operation and maintenance, 3–6 euros per MWh for fuel, and 3 euros per MWh for fuel treatment, waste disposal and final dismantling.

This results in a cost of 35–40 euros per MWh, but it may differ from one NPP to another because of the conditions for recovering the initial investment. OECD studies have compared costs from different electricity sources, including nuclear, at different interest rates, and taking into account the possible costs of CO_2 emissions. The conclusions of these studies show that nuclear power is competitive with fossil fuels for electricity production and that the CO_2 price may have an even more positive impact if it goes to levels above 20 euros per ton.

One of the most critical studies on nuclear energy was produced by Greenpeace in 2007 (*The Economics of Nuclear Power*, by S. Thomas et al.). Although it puts a lot of emphasis on the fact that NPP construction was halted in many Western countries two decades ago, it cannot contradict the fact that nuclear electricity is currently in the lowest level of cost in every country with nuclear energy. The study is also extremely weak when it tries to demonstrate that Finland's decision to build its fifth NPP was not based on economic arguments. In fact, the main argument of the NPP owner, TVO, was purely economic. The main shareholder of TVO is PVD, a consortium formed by Finnish electricity-intensive industrial companies. These companies are extremely interested in guaranteeing low electricity cost in the long run, besides having reliable supply. They studied different options and concluded that nuclear power was the right choice. The outcome of that study was clear: without political interference, nuclear power is a front-runner for securing electricity supply.

Table 15.2 presents some projections on nuclear power development. They are closely related to economic growth projections and the needs for additional energy in different countries and continents. Indeed the Far East and South Asia will be a macro-region absorbing a high share of the new nuclear business cycle. Richer countries with much lower economic growth seem to

Table 15.2 Projections of nuclear power capacity in the lowest and highest estimates (GWe)

	2005	2010		2020		2030	
		Low	*High*	*Low*	*High*	*Low*	*High*
North America	111	114	116	120	131	126	158
Latin America	4	4	4	6	7	6	18
Western Europe	124	122	124	91	129	48	149
Eastern Europe	48	48	50	68	76	78	107
Africa	2	2	2	2	4	2	10
Middle East and South Asia	3	10	11	17	27	23	46
South East Asia and Pacific	–	–	–	–	1	1	5
Far East	76	81	83	119	145	130	187
World total	368	381	390	423	520	414	679

Source: IEA, *World Energy Outlook 2006* (Paris: IEA, 2006).

rely on natural gas, although some of them, including the US and France, have also started a new cycle that is still to be seriously launched. However, it is well known that natural gas is facing increasing problems in price, transport and storage, and it is also useful for other applications (including the organic chemistry industry), which poses some problems as an electricity source.

On the other hand, renewables are being promoted and subsidized in many countries, but they do not offer the features of nuclear power in terms of reliability and availability. Moreover, the cheap long-term price of nuclear kWh is the best help for the development of renewables.

Without doubt, the energy sector has to change towards a sustainable development scenario, with much lower CO_2 emissions, because of the threats of global warming. At the same time, energy supply will remain a major social and economic objective. In order to solve such a difficult equation, nuclear power must be part of the answer.

Notes

1. OECD Nuclear Energy Agency and International Atomic Energy (2006), *Uranium 2005: Resources, Production and Demand*.
2. IEA, *World Energy Outlook 2006* (Paris: IEA, 2006).

16
Human Security: European and Asian Approaches

Antonio Marquina and Mely Caballero-Anthony

Introduction

The concept of human security has its roots in the debates on security carried out before and after the Cold War. The Independent Commission on International Development (1980), the World Commission on Environment and Development (1987), the Commission on Global Governance (1995) and the United Nations Conference on the Environment and Sustainable Development (1992) were influential in broadening the concept of security and the subjects of security, not only states but also the planet as a whole and its citizens and individuals, its actors, threats, risks and security mechanisms. The internal conflicts and the civilians that were at the epicentre of conflicts in many parts of the world after the Cold War contributed to the reformulation of the concept of security. Many threats to human survival and well-being were internal threats. To this has to be added the awareness of global risks induced largely by the actions of people living in different states.

If Lincoln Chen coined the term 'human security', Mahbub ul Haq, a respected Pakistani development economist and consultant to the UNDP, who played a key role in the construction of the Human Development Index, initially developed its content. Given the inspiration provided by ul Haq, the UNDP *Human Development Report* of 1994 conceptualized human security in three distinct ways. First, it shifted the referent objects of security from the state to individuals or the people. Second, it identified four essential characteristics of what are considered to be 'human security issues'. These are: that the issue is of universal concern; the components are interdependent; it is best ensured through early prevention rather than later intervention; and finally, it is people centred.[1] Third, the concept was further focused on two main aspects. The first one is 'safety from such chronic threats as hunger, disease and repression', and second, 'protection from sudden and hurtful disruptions in the patterns of daily life – whether in homes, in jobs or in communities'.[2] Following these features, the UNDP report identified seven core human security values. These are: economic security, food security, health security, environmental security, personal security, community security and political security.[3] Despite these expanded definitions, the UNDP's human security concept was essentially narrowed down to mean 'freedom from fear and freedom from want'. This definition subsequently became the point of reference of the many writings on human security.

The problem of conceptual clarity

The 'comprehensiveness' of the UNDP schema of human security was criticized by many security analysts for its lack of conceptual clarity. The contention was that without a clear focus human security as a concept loses its utility.[4] In arguing for a narrower definition of human security, Sverre Lodgaard stressed that it should focus only on the 'vulnerability to physical violence during conflict'.[5] Another writer, Astrid Suhrke, advocated concentration only on 'vulnerabilities' as its defining feature, specifically pertaining to the vulnerabilities faced by those victims of war and internal conflict, those living at or below subsistence levels and those who are victims of natural disaster.[6] To both these writers, the concept of human security would be best served if it were confined to 'freedom from fear of man-made physical violence', which is referred to as direct, personal violence.

Apart from scholars who argued for more clarity in the definition of human security, there were also critics who were dismissive of the concept.[7] Roland Paris, for instance, argued that human security is too broad to be analytically meaningful or useful as a tool of policy-making, and thus provides 'policy-makers with little guidance in the prioritization of competing policy goals and academics little sense of what, exactly, is to be studied'.[8] Others also found the concept too normative, thus making the realization of the goals of human security unrealistic.[9]

The problem of conceptual ambiguities was also reflected in the different formulations of human security as found in the foreign policies of certain states. As a matter of fact, Canada, the first state to adopt the concept of human security in its foreign policy agenda, and many other Western countries have defined the concept rather narrowly through focusing on 'freedom from fear'. As a result, Western countries represent a more pro-active approach that includes the possibility of collective use of force, as well as sanctions in the interest of protecting civilians from violent conflicts.[10] In contrast to that, Japan, as the second state after Canada to promote the concept quite prominently in its foreign policy, follows the UNDP's comprehensive and broad view of human security through adding the aspect of 'freedom from want'. This is why the Japanese government's approach to human security has been noted by many observers as presenting the 'other school of thought' on the question of how policy establishments should conceptualize and articulate human security in foreign policy statements. In Europe, the European Commission and in particular formerly neutral, European countries tend to favour the broad view of human security.

In this chapter we will provide two contrasting approaches to human security based on the European and Asian experiences. The European experience will focus largely on the role of the European Union (EU) as an international actor and a global player, and the implications of its European Security Strategy (2003) and the Lisbon Treaty (2007) on the present debates about the concept of human security. While the EU's Common Foreign Security and Defence Policy puts more emphasis on the *freedom from fear*, the traditional approach of the European Commission was and still is in line with *freedom from want*. The EU approach therefore needs a more coherent and operational re-elaboration. The discussion on Asia will focus on the different Asian perspectives on human security.

The European Union as an international actor and its implications for human security

The EU has been depicted in many ways: as an international actor, a global power in the world economy, a political and diplomatic actor, and a military actor. This is reflected in several recent key EU documents:

> The EU has a history and cultural ties that gives it links with every part of the world. Now, with 27 states and over 490 million people producing a quarter of the world's Gross National Product (GNP), it has no choice but to be a global player.[11]

> As a union of 25 states with over 450 million people producing a quarter of the world's Gross National Product (GNP), and with a wide range of instruments at its disposal, the European Union is inevitably a global player...Europe should be ready to share in the responsibility for global security and in building a better world.[12]

But the EU has not become a great power and there is no clear picture of the kind of power it will be. This lack of clarity is reflected in the wide academic and political debates in Europe about what kind of international actor the EU is and is going to be.[13] It is clear that the European Community during the Cold War and later the EU at the beginning of the 1990s has been an unusual and distinct actor, given its ability and intention of extending its own model of ensuring stability and security through economic and political means. It was characterized as a civilian power.[14] It tried to give a distinct flavour to international relations. But this novel type of power in the international system implies some assumptions and has some characteristics:

- its international role was distinct from the role of states and great powers;
- its emphasis is on non-military instruments in foreign policy;
- territorial sovereignty is not crucial.[15]

This liberal-idealist approach[16] also presupposed that military power was less important, and that a strategic environment and international order could be maintained without the necessary use of military power.

The European approach is largely influenced by its historical experience, especially after the end of the Cold War. The absence of military threats to Europe after the Cold War as well as the security guarantees provided by the US have essentially shaped the EU's approach to a new international order, where the promotion of its soft power outweighs military instruments as a means to conduct international relations. Western norms and Western world views could be expanded and the world would become more peaceful as a result. As war was considered very unlikely, the EU focused on promoting multilateral cooperation, institution building and supranational integration rather than national interest, unilateral policies and defence of national sovereignty. Instead of military coercion, the EU preferred the modalities of persuasion, rewards, deference, attraction, negotiation, even condition-alities and to some extent sanctions. With this approach, the EU tried to promote international cooperation, solidarity and domesticate international relations, expanding democracy, market economies and Western values. Later, after 1995, it tried to promote international conflict prevention in order to maintain and sustain peace in the world.

For different analysts the EU's weakness in military capabilities supported this notion of the EU as a civilian power. This weakness was highlighted in its ineffectiveness to manage the conflict in the former Yugoslavia. The EU had failed in being a neutral and effective actor in controlling and preventing the spread of the conflict, showing the limits of civilian means.

Despite this perceived failure, some authors still maintained that the EU could be considered as an effective civilian actor through the promotion of norms and values rather the use of military force. Arguing that the EU can be a normative power, Ian Manners stated in 2002 that 'the discussion about the conceptions of the EU as either a civilian or a military power, both located in discussions of capabilities, need to be augmented with a focus on normative power of an ideational nature characterized by common principles and a willingness to disregard Westphalian conventions'.[17] For this pioneer of EU normative power there is a clear differentiation between civilian power and normative power: 'the emphasis on EU cosmopolitics within normative power representations clearly indicates a huge change of political culture away from the Westphalian frames of reference in which many discussions of civilian power take place'; 'normative power can be differentiated from civilian power by the extent to which Westphalian culturation is changing'.[18] Thus the EU does not rely on military or other capabilities to achieve its objectives and its power rests on norm leadership and persuasion.[19]

However, what kind of values and norms? Depending on the author, the list can be extensive. Ian Manners, for instance, identified the following core values: peace, liberty, democracy, the rule of law and respect for human rights and four subsidiary values: social solidarity, anti-discrimination, sustainable development and good governance. Nathalie Tocci included the promotion of peace, democracy, human rights, the rule of law and sustainable development.[20] Finally the Lisbon Treaty, signed by the European Council in December 2007, establishes the values and norms of the EU. Thus the debate is closed at least for a while.

Article 1-a and Article 2,5 of the Lisbon Treaty state:

> The Union is founded on the values of respect for human dignity, freedom, democracy, equality, the rule of law and respect for human rights, including the rights of persons belonging to minorities.

> These values are common to the Member States in a society in which pluralism, non-discrimination, tolerance, justice, solidarity and equality between women and men prevail.

And in Article I-3, 4 the Treaty states that:

> In its relations with the wider world, the Union shall uphold and promote its *values and interests*. It shall contribute to peace, security, the sustainable development of the Earth, solidarity and mutual respect among peoples, free and fair trade, eradication of poverty and the protection of human rights, in particular the rights of the child, as well as to the strict observance and the development of international law, including respect for the principles of the United Nations Charter.

Thus, values and interests are connected. In addition to this, the Treaty presents the missions and capabilities of the EU. Articles 28A and 28B establish that:

> the common security and defence policy shall be an integral part of the common foreign and security policy. It shall provide the Union with an operational capacity drawing on civilian and military assets. The Union may use them on missions outside the Union for peace-keeping, conflict prevention and strengthening international security in accordance with the principles of the United Nations Charter. The performance of these tasks shall be undertaken using capabilities provided by the Member States.

> States shall make *civilian and military capabilities* available to the Union for the implementation of the common security and defence policy, to contribute to the objectives defined by the Council.

> The tasks referred to in Article 28 A(1), in the course of which the Union may use civilian and military means, shall include joint disarmament operations, humanitarian and rescue tasks, military advice and assistance

tasks, conflict prevention and peace-keeping tasks, tasks of combat forces in crisis management, including peace-making and post-conflict stabilisation. All these tasks may contribute to the fight against terrorism, including by supporting third countries in combating terrorism in their territories.

And Article 10a establishes the values and interests to be preserved in the international arena.[21]

Tensions in translating the EU's normative stance and other means to peace

Conceptual discourses have to take into account this complexity of civilian and military means and different tasks that imply the possible use of force,[22] such as conflict prevention, crisis management, peace-making and the fight against terrorism, and in particular the distinction between interests and values. There are means and methods that can be used by the EU that can be considered more normative than other means at its disposal. It is more useful to define the appropriate means at the disposal of the EU in a quite normative foreign policy as 'means and instruments regardless of their nature that are deployed within the confines of the law'.[23]

The EU, in order to be an actor capable of challenging the established norms of the international order, needs to reach a consensus and a clear picture of the new international order to be created, and to become a capable agent that can successfully challenge the actual international system. That is not obvious. A broader vision like a cosmopolitan order induced by EU international action is a dream.

Another point to be made is that other states also put emphasis on the diffusion of norms and values. Normative power is not new; all states are based on normative values. But the main difference is that the EU tries to promote democracy, the market economy and human rights, considering them as the principal tools for promoting sustainable peace in international relations and as contributing to shape the preferences and behaviour of other international actors. This stance has some limits:

- Experience shows that the EU has not been successful in projecting its normative power when it could not offer full membership to other countries.
- There is a difficult problem in interacting with other states and international actors that do not follow the same norms, standards and rules, in particular if these countries can diversify their relationships connecting themselves with powers or great powers that do not play by the same rules and norms and can provide a substitution.

- There is a crisis in international institutions, international law and human rights that affects the EU proposals and objectives.
- The ability to be a normative power and to carry out norm diffusion will become non-viable given the development of the Common Foreign, Security and Defence Policy (CFSDP) of the EU.

To this we can add that its normative power depends on the interaction between its policy goals, means and policy justifications and varies between different issue areas.

Several recent critics have been particularly sound on these issues. Some point at the lack of sufficient analysis of EU behaviour and the stress on the construction of the EU's identity. This emphasis may contribute to blinding the actors from their failings and deficiencies both in internal affairs as well as in their engagement with others.[24]

In December 2007 and January 2008 CEPS presented two working papers on the EU as a normative foreign policy actor. Some of the conclusions are strongly critical:

- The EU is more likely to pursue normative means when power relations between the EU and a third state are relatively balanced and relations develop within the confines of mutually negotiated agreements. On the other hand, power and particularly relational power seems to be of critical importance in engendering a normative impact given that even the best of intentions may be an insufficient condition of success.
- The EU is driven by possession goals just like any other international actor. While it can certainly influence the external context, particularly in its neighbourhood where it has real foreign policy presence, it is bound to also rely on fortuitous external circumstances to effectively assert its normative power.

It is also suggested that the Union could strengthen its web of contractual relations with third states in a manner that would 'tie its own hands', thus reducing its ability to act non-normatively.

Other authors emphasize that the growing discourse on insecurity, projecting the EU as protector of its citizens from different threats, is incompatible with the presentation of the EU as a normative power.[25]

These critics show the difficulties in maintaining a continuum in the approach to a political entity in deep transformation. The CFSDP and the development of the military component imply an alteration in the EU's essence and its traditional conceptualization, making it difficult if not impossible to maintain the conceptualization of the EU as a civilian power and a normative power. Power based only on the first pillar capability was something from the past. Petersberg tasks,[26] the lessons learned and the new, more multi-polar international environment, where the interests of states are more salient and the promotion of European interests and values more difficult or impossible to realize, forced a reconsideration of the international role of the EU.

Human rights in trade agreements, emphasis on regional cooperation, strengthening of international institutions, lack of military instruments and the turn to sustainable peace as characteristics of normative power have to be complemented with other approaches. The normative practices based on the Commission are now complemented with a full spectrum of instruments for defence and intervention based on the Council.

In this context we can stress that human security addresses the same objectives as sustainable peace. But in some aspects the application of this concept to the EU CFSDP is becoming problematic.

The EU and human security

The concept of human security is now accepted by the Commission and more ambiguously by the Council. We quote several recent official documents of these EU institutions:

> Central to the EU's approach is the concept of human security – an idea of security which places people at the heart of our policies. It means looking at the comprehensive security of people, not the security of states, encompassing both freedom from fear and freedom from want.
>
> A world in which people can live in freedom, security and dignity, free from poverty and despair, is still a dream for many. Yet only in a world based on the rule of law and the freedom from fear and want can people develop their individual and collective potential. Respect for human rights is one of the most fundamental and universal values of our world. All of us have a responsibility to promote and protect the rights of our fellow members of the human family, be that at home or elsewhere in the world.
>
> The EU takes this obligation seriously. We have been pursuing an active human rights policy with our partners for many years, through political dialogue, human rights clauses in our agreements with partner countries, in the international fora as well as through our development aid programs, in particular the European Initiative for Human Rights and Democracy (EIHRD).[27]

The EU High Representative for the Common Foreign and Security Policy that has convened the Human Security Study Group apparently has been reluctant to use the concept. We can quote this recent statement dealing with the concept of security and not with EU security: 'Security in the modern sense is a very broad concept. It is about people, about Human security.'[28]

There are important approximations to the concept in the document *The European Security Strategy: a Secure Europe in a Better World*. In the introduction it is clearly stated that 'Europe should be ready to share in the responsibility for global security and in building a better world.' The normative approach is clear in the document. Some books[29] that have analysed the document did not mention the concept of human security. Other authors consider that the document means a compromise with the concept of human security. We share this view.

Basic components included in the *European Security Strategy*

In the presentation, the document remarks that the EU has been central in the achievement of a period of peace and stability unprecedented in European history. It stresses the route the EU has taken and the progressive spread of the rule of law and democracy, as the path other countries have to follow.

The EU considers as global challenges questions centrally included in the conceptualization of human security such as:

- *Protection of civilians in conflict*: 'Since 1990, almost 4 million people have died in wars, 90% of them civilians. Over 18 million people world-wide have left their homes as a result of conflict.'
- *Poverty*: 'In much of the developing world, poverty and disease cause untold suffering and give rise to pressing security concerns. Almost 3 billion people, half the world's population, live on less than 2 Euros a day. 45 million die every year of hunger and malnutrition.'
- *Health*: 'AIDS is now one of the most devastating pandemics in human history and contributes to the breakdown of societies. New diseases can spread rapidly and become global threats.'
- *Environment and natural resources*: 'Competition for natural resources – notably water – which will be aggravated by global warming over the next decades, is likely to create further turbulence and migratory movements in various regions.'
- *Economic failure*: 'Sub-Saharan Africa is poorer now than it was 10 years ago. In many cases, economic failure is linked to political problems and violent conflict.'
- *Conflicts*: 'Conflict not only destroys infrastructure, including social infrastructure; it also encourages criminality, deters investment and makes normal economic activity impossible. A number of countries and regions are caught in a cycle of conflict, insecurity and poverty.'... 'Violent or frozen conflicts, which also persist on our borders, threaten regional stability. They destroy human lives and social and physical infrastructures; they threaten minorities, fundamental freedoms and human rights. Conflict can lead to extremism, terrorism and state failure; it provides opportunities for organised crime.'
- *State failure*: 'Bad governance – corruption, abuse of power, weak institutions and lack of accountability – and civil conflict corrode States from

within. In some cases, this has brought about the collapse of State institutions. Somalia, Liberia and Afghanistan under the Taliban are the best known recent examples. Collapse of the State can be associated with obvious threats, such as organised crime or terrorism. State failure is an alarming phenomenon that undermines global governance, and adds to regional instability.'

- *Good governance and the rule of law*: 'The best protection for our security is a world of well-governed democratic states. Spreading good governance, supporting social and political reform, dealing with corruption and abuse of power, establishing the rule of law and protecting human rights are the best means of strengthening the international order.'

- *International law:* 'We are committed to upholding and developing International Law. The fundamental framework for international relations is the United Nations Charter.'

- *Development of international institutions and regimes*: 'We want international organisations, regimes and treaties to be effective in confronting threats to international peace and security, and must therefore be ready to act when their rules are broken.' . . . 'We have an interest in further developing existing institutions such as the World Trade Organisation and in supporting new ones such as the International Criminal Court. Our own experience in Europe demonstrates that security can be increased through confidence building and arms control regimes.' . . . 'Strengthening the United Nations, equipping it to fulfil its responsibilities and to act effectively, is a European priority. We want international organisations, regimes and treaties to be effective in confronting threats to international peace and security, and must therefore be ready to act when their rules are broken.' . . . 'The development of a stronger international society, well functioning international institutions and a rule-based international order is our objective; establishing the rule of law and protecting human rights are the best means of strengthening the international order.'

- *Multilateralism*: 'In a world of global threats, global markets and global media, our security and prosperity increasingly depend on an effective multilateral system.'

- *The attraction of the EU*: 'It is in the European interest that countries on our borders are well-governed. Neighbours who are engaged in violent conflict, weak states where organised crime flourishes, dysfunctional societies or exploding population growth on its borders all pose problems for Europe. The European perspective offers both a strategic objective and an incentive for reform.'

- *On the instruments and means to use*: 'Trade and development policies can be powerful tools for promoting reform.' . . . 'Contributing to better governance through assistance programmes, conditionality and targeted trade measures remains an important feature in our policy that we should further reinforce.' . . . 'None of the new threats is purely military; nor can any be tackled by purely military means. Each requires a mixture of instruments.'...'In failed states, military instruments may be needed to restore order, humanitarian means to tackle the immediate crisis. Regional conflicts need political solutions but military assets and effective policing may be needed in the post conflict phase. Economic instruments serve reconstruction, and civilian crisis management helps restore civil government. The European Union is particularly well equipped to respond to such multi-faceted situations.'

In the third part of the document concerning policy implications the document insists on the missions and means:

> (There is a) full spectrum of instruments for crisis management and conflict prevention at our disposal, including political, diplomatic, military and civilian, trade and development activities. Active policies are needed to counter the new dynamic threats. We need to develop a strategic culture that fosters early, rapid, and when necessary, robust intervention... Preventive engagement can avoid more serious problems in the future.

Thus, in the *European Security Strategy* crucial elements for the development of the concept of human security as *freedom from fear* and *freedom from want* are included. But the most significant elaborations on this document from the human security angle have followed the line of human security as *freedom from fear* not as *freedom from want*. The task to develop all these elements in a coherent framework as *freedom from want* is a very complicated task but it needs to be carried out in the coming years.

A European security doctrine for Europe

In 2004 a report entitled 'Human Security Doctrine for Europe: The Barcelona Report of the Study Group on Europe's Security Capabilities'[30] was made public. The Study Group, convened by Mary Kaldor at the request of Javier Solana, the secretary of the Council, presented several proposals on the application of principles of human security understood as the freedom for individuals and communities from basic insecurities caused by gross human rights violations. The centre of attention was insecurity as the consequence of conflicts in which individuals and communities are deliberately targeted with impunity. *Freedom from fear* was the approach.

They concurred that Europe needed military forces but maintained that these forces had to be configured and used in new ways different from classic defence and war fighting. Europe also needed to be able to deploy more police, human rights monitors, aid specialists, and many other kinds of civilian experts.

The Study Group considered that in the new global context, the European Union's security policy should be built on human security and not only on state security. The justification is based on morality, legal obligations from the UN Charter and enlightened self-interest. They believed that this concept could give new direction and coherence to the European security strategy.

Focusing on situations of severe insecurity and the Petersberg tasks elaborated in the draft of the EU Constitution, they try to fill a vacuum: the lack of a comprehensive doctrine for implementing these military operations, supporting law and order and defending human rights (the overall aim of these operations). This point is not evident. They present the EU as a promoter of values, in a normative role. Later they move in another direction, presenting the need for European citizens to support the process because of feeling that the EU contributes to their security. But, in their opinion, this could only be achieved through a European contribution to the security of human beings in general.

Later the document proposed a set of principles intended to guide the actions of high-level EU officials, politicians, diplomats, soldiers and civilians:

- The primacy of human rights, avoiding killing, injury and material destruction. In human security operations protection of the individuals, not defeating the enemy, is an end in itself.
- Legitimate political authority. Interventions must provide the conditions for restoring or establishing a legitimate political authority. With this, the internal situation can be stabilized. Command and control of the human security missions has to be exerted by a political authority. And the missions have to be led by a civilian.
- Effective multilateralism. Working with international institutions and through their procedures, ways of working, coordination and common rules and norms. Multilateral authorization is needed for human security missions.
- The bottom-up approach. Success depends on the local population for advice, information and implementation. It is necessary to use the local capabilities if they are available.
- Regional focus. The reason is that the new wars do not have clear boundaries and insecurity spills over borders.
- Use of legal instruments. The primary task in any deployment is to assist law enforcement. For the military it means a shift from the traditional use of military force, fighting wars, to that of law enforcement.
- Appropriate use of force. Minimal force, not overwhelming force, is key. The defence of people living in a territory has priority over the protection of military forces. It means that the lives of the forces deployed cannot be privileged. Like the police, they have to risk their lives to save others at more immediate risk.

For the implementation of these principles the Study Group proposes other capabilities for the EU: an integrated set of civil-military capabilities, a multinational 'Human Security Response Force' of 15,000 personnel, where substantial contingents of civilians are included, and a legal framework that can legitimize the decisions to intervene. The question of intervention is clearly accepted but the ways in which the civil-military forces are used in crisis and conflicts are different from the past.

Three years later, in 2007, the Study Group presented a new report entitled 'A European Way of Security' where they added the principle of clear and transparent strategic direction. The new report, answering the critics, emphasizes the EU's tasks of crisis management, conflict prevention and civil-military cooperation capabilities,[31] and defends the thesis that a human security approach is more realistic and effective for tackling crises. They also try to define the type of military power the EU is and find lessons from the recent EU missions and interventions. They propose an EU public declaration of human security principles in order to affirm the core beliefs and values in relation to international operations, something that will appear as quite redundant once the Lisbon Treaty is signed by the members of the European Council, where EU values are clearly stated. They also put forward a new strategic framework for ESDP missions, including military missions, headed by a civilian commander, with the aim of placing even short-term, rapid responses within a long-term time frame providing time and space to the local communities to build the conditions for peace; and several practical measures to translate the commitment to human security into ESDP operations.[32]

This approach, as was stated by the convenor of the Study Group, is based on Kantian principles.[33] It is clear that conflicts after the Cold War are different: they are very complex, asymmetric, internal, they propel regional instability and the distinctions between civilians and regular forces are difficult to maintain. All this has to be managed in a different way. There are different situations in which the necessity of intervention is a must. The problem is that the experience of the last fifteen years shows that normative approaches are not cost free and the European Union not only did not react on time, but also did not agree on possible interventions and the maximum obtained was a coalition of the willing. Human security approaches have to be linked with the interests of the states, including the costs – often colossal costs – of intervention. It is sobering to see how many times the EU only provided money and delegated moral responsibilities to third countries.

Another question is the possible scenarios that the Study Group has in mind for the deployment of the 'Human Security Response Force'. That is a mystery. Without knowing this, the proposal lacks credibility. What will the relationship be between the Human Security Response Force and the EU battle groups? How can one manage the possible conflicts on the European periphery, achieving a ring of well-governed countries with which it can enjoy close and cooperative relations, when possible US intervention is not clear? For example, in the Mediterranean and Middle East, the Balkans, Ukraine, Belarus and the Caucasus, are the ways and means proposed sufficient?

In security and defence matters, the EU has a solid connection with NATO in a process of transformation. The question is how to link these principles and recommendations with new NATO approaches such as EBAO[34] and achieve a 'comprehensive approach' in a possible crisis situation. How can the EU improve its collaboration with NATO when this organization is looking for non-military instruments and resources from other actors and organizations? What kind of crisis does the Study Group consider possible? What is the concept of crisis they are using? In a crisis escalation, if the EU is unable to manage it with its civilian-military means, can NATO enter into the crisis, accepting a previous EU soft mandate or a law enforcement mandate? How is a law enforcement mandate associated with an increasing UN strong mission slide towards peace enforcement?

European human security approaches depend as a precondition on the global security – including military security – order established by the US.[35] On the other hand, EU approaches and conditionalities on human rights (primacy), democracy and values are fragile when confronted with state security approaches (Russia and China) whose agenda does not include these matters in their strategies and policies concerning the different regions and conflicts. To be effective, the EU as normative power would need a unipolar Western world or no competition with other effective competing states that use different principles and rules. The topic of this book, energy security, shows clearly these EU shortcomings.

Thus, the human security doctrine for Europe as *freedom from fear* needs new reflections and discussions, while the human security doctrine for Europe as *freedom from want* needs substantial theoretical development and articulation.

An Asian perspective on human security

In Asia, ever since the concept of human security gained resonance in the mid-1990s, and particularly after the Asian financial crisis in 1997, human security appears to have taken on a momentum of its own. This can be seen in the way the concept has become part of the security lexicon in regions and in the way some regional organizations like the Association of Southeast Asian Nations (ASEAN) have started to adopt this concept in their official statements. More importantly, human security has also been used to frame many of the emerging security issues confronting the region, particularly non-traditional security issues like climate change, resource scarcity, migration and pandemics.

These developments are very significant especially if one looks back to the kind of climate that prevailed during the period when the concept was first introduced in the region. We note for instance how concerned some countries in Asia were about the veiled motivations behind the promotion of the concept; and how they objected to the way this concept had become part of the foreign policy agendas of certain Western governments. Hence, compared with the kind of attitudes displayed then, it seems that much has changed. But whether these changes are temporally or indeed qualitatively different, will depend largely on which vantage point one is coming from.

Against this background, this part of the chapter will focus on two things: first, to provide a review of the evolution of the concept of human security in Asia and the different perspectives and issues that emerged in the region with regard to the promotion of this concept. The second is to examine how human security has remained salient in the security agenda of states and provide an assessment of its outlook in the years to come. In doing so, the argument will be that while human security was once marginalized, the concept is now being mainstreamed in the security agenda in the region since human security provides the platform that embodies the other security concerns of states and societies in the region.

Revisiting the concept of human security: what, why and how?[36]

The evolution of the human security concept in the region can be linked closely to the academic debates that emerged after the end of the Cold War, which were essentially about reconceptualizing the concept of security. Disenchanted with the limited focus on military security, several scholars have offered various ways of defining security beyond the conventional notions of military threats to the state. We can group these scholars broadly into two schools. The first refers to studies that seek to widen the scope of security beyond military security, to include among others, political, economic and ecological security concerns. The main thrust of this first school is to challenge the dominant thought within the field of neo-realism that highlights the anarchic international system in which states had to compete for survival to achieve their security.[37] The second group includes those that not only widen the scope of security concerns beyond the state and military threats, but also seek in the process to achieve a goal of human emancipation. Human emancipation, in this context, is defined as 'the freeing of people (as individuals and groups) from the physical and human constraints which stop them from carrying out what they would freely choose to do. To this group therefore, emancipation is the other side of security.'[38]

Beyond the academic contestations there have also been efforts at the policy level to broaden the traditional notions of security. Although the contestations about drawing the boundaries of security continue even today, it is noteworthy that it was not until 1994 that the concept of human security actually gained international attention. Also important was the fact that the person who was responsible for [re]introducing this concept was an Asian, Mahbub ul Haq. Haq was a Pakistani developmental economist whose work on human development became the basis of the United National Development Programme's (UNDP) *Human Development Report* where this concept was first used.[39] Kanti Bajpai, in tracing this concept, had noted that the UNDP report was in fact inspired by and based largely on Haq's original paper entitled 'New Imperatives of Human Security', wherein he passionately argued that for any formulation of development thinking and policies, the primary focus is the welfare of individuals rather than simply the state's macroeconomy.[40] It was in this seminal work that Haq raised the question, 'security for whom?' He argued that what matters in security is not just the security of nations but more so the security of individuals. Haq's main contention therefore was '*to fashion a new concept of human security that is reflected in the lives of our people, not in the weapons of our country*'.[41]

Asian debates on human security

The debates on the conceptualization of human security and the controversy about which area to focus on were not uncommon in states in Asia. However, much of the earlier discussion on the so-called Asian focus of human security came from Japan.

Although the official Japanese articulation of this policy started in 1998 when former Prime Minister Keizo Obuchi introduced human security as one of the pillars of Japan's foreign policy, Japan had in fact already articulated this concept much earlier at a speech by former Prime Minister Tomiichi Murayama. In his address to the fiftieth anniversary special session of the UN General Assembly in October 1995, Murayama advocated for human security to be the UN's new strategy. But it took the Asian financial crisis of 1997–8 for Japan to clearly articulate and promote human security in the international arena. In his speech at the First Intellectual Dialogue on Building Asia's Tomorrow in December 1998,[42] Mr Obuchi said that human security (as a concept) 'is the key which comprehensively covers all the menaces that threaten the survival, daily life, and dignity of human beings and strengthens all efforts to confront those threats'.[43] Among the menaces or threats were 'environmental degradation, violation of human rights, transnational organised crime, illicit drugs, refugees, poverty, anti-personnel landmines and infectious diseases such as AIDS'.[44]

The stark difference in the Japanese approach, when compared with the Canadian approach, is its comprehensive way of listing human security threats which correspond to the UNDP's view of human security. Thus, by having an inclusive agenda of human needs 'human security can only be ensured when the individual is confident of a life free of fear and free of want'.[45] And, while not necessarily in sequential order, the thinking is that the realization of human security covers the three phases of 'human survival, human well-being and human freedom'. The nature of 'human security thinking' in Japan was clearly articulated by a Japanese official, who stated that:

> We believe that freedom from want is no less critical than freedom from fear. So long as its objectives are to ensure the survival and dignity of individuals as human beings, it is necessary to go beyond the thinking of human security in terms of protecting human life in conflict situations.[46]

This foreign policy orientation has been translated into the various official development assistance (ODA) schemes that Japan has introduced within the framework of human security. These schemes are wide-ranging, from the IMF-led assistance packages and assistance in economic structural reforms to assistance for human resources development and assistance to the socially vulnerable. The most important development assistance programme under the human security scheme has been the establishment of the Human Security Trust Fund under the United Nations in 1998. The fund, approximately US$190 million in total, was slated for projects that address specific human security concerns like poverty eradication, health care and refugee assistance. Japan, like Canada, has also been in the forefront in the campaign against anti-personnel landmines, having advocated the 'Zero Victims Programme'. This programme calls for a comprehensive approach not only to effectively ban anti-personnel landmines but also the strengthening of de-mining and victim assistance.[47] Moreover, Japan has also played a leading role in the adoption of the Convention against Transnational Organized Crime and its Protocol on Trafficking in Persons, especially Women and Children, by the UN General Assembly.[48]

Moreover, Japan has been largely instrumental in the establishment of the International Commission for Human Security. Formally launched in January 2001, the Commission has Sadako Ogata and Amartya Sen serving as co-chairs. The Japanese government has also initiated the UN Trust Fund for Human Security to assist in poverty alleviation projects and refugee assistance.[49]

From the above, it is clear that while Japan's human security policy may be more inclined towards the UNDP's developmental approach, it has gone beyond addressing the 'freedom from want' issues to also include the issues that fall under 'freedom from fear'. However, Japan has ruled out the possible use of collective force in advancing human security. While it supports and cooperates in international efforts in such issues as anti-personnel landmines, international criminal tribunals and controlling small arms, it has so far dissociated itself from international efforts of humanitarian intervention. As argued by an official from the Japanese Foreign Ministry, 'the use of force for humanitarian intervention ... is an ill-conceived concept of human security.

So long as its objectives are to ensure the survival and dignity of individuals as human beings, it is necessary to go beyond the thinking of human security solely in terms of protecting human life in conflict situations.'[50]

Perspectives from other Asian countries: the case of ASEAN

Although this concept has generated a lot of interest in Southeast Asia, it took a while for the concept to achieve a major breakthrough. Among the reasons for this lack of impact is the concern about the implications of human security approaches for state sovereignty. Some countries in the region have had reservations regarding the emphasis placed on certain elements belonging to the 'freedom from fear' category – for example, political security (freedom to exercise one's basic political rights) – that would allow certain states to interfere in their internal affairs and to adopt a more confrontational attitude in promoting regional security. Such practices have been considered as going against the regional norm of non-interference.

But while this concern about possible intrusion into domestic affairs is a shared concern among states not limited to Southeast Asia alone, the other more interesting aspect about human security is the way this has been perceived as challenging the dominant security paradigm in the region, which is that of comprehensive security. Comprehensive security is conceptualized as going beyond (but does not exclude) the military to embrace political, economic and socio-cultural dimensions.[51] There are two essential points that have to be underscored in the way comprehensive security has been promoted in the region. One is the paramount importance placed on regime stability and the other is the emphasis given to economic development as a major means/instrument to bring about domestic stability. As a consequence of this formulation, the position of the state was reified as the primary unit of analysis. It has become the main actor in defining and providing security, which in the process has legitimized further its pre-eminent role in not only bringing about economic development, but more importantly in shaping the security doctrines of states. Hence, while ASEAN states may have had an expanded notion of security beyond military concerns, their idea of comprehensive security was no different from the dominant state-centric approach to conceptualizing security.

It took the experience of the Asian financial crisis for the concept of human security to make some headway in the region. In the aftermath of the crisis, many observers and policy-makers in the region were dissatisfied with the way regional institutions, especially ASEAN, had responded to the problems that followed. It should also be noted that the enthusiasm for human security also coincided with calls for ASEAN's norm of non-interference to be reviewed. Among the most significant developments in this regard was the Thai proposal for 'flexible engagement' which called on ASEAN member states to be open and frank about discussing certain issues, albeit domestic ones, but of regional concern and that had serious repercussions for the security of member states as well.

Although some ASEAN members considered the proposal as ill-timed, given that the region was still reeling from the devastating effects of the 1997 Asian financial crisis, the proposal nevertheless exposed the differing opinions within ASEAN on how regional problems were to be addressed. These dynamics were succinctly summarized by Withaya Sucharithanarugse, who observed that:

> [when] Thailand, supported by the Philippines, proposed moving from a policy of 'constructive engagement' with Myanmar to one of 'constructive intervention' or 'flexible engagement', Indonesia came out strongly against the idea, arguing that it ran counter to ASEAN's basic principle of respecting sovereignty of the state. Malaysia then weighed into the argument by reportedly suggesting that Thailand would not like it if Malaysia started commenting on the treatment of Muslims in southern Thailand.[52]

Despite the lack of consensus in the region on promoting human security, the concept did not lose its appeal, especially among NGOs and Track II bodies who continued to challenge the dominant idea of state-centric security and raised issues of human rights protection, social justice and equitable development. In effect, these calls indirectly sustained the calls for adopting human security as a common framework for promoting security and development in the region.

Tipping points in advancing human security in the region

The 1997 Asian financial crisis triggered a series of 'human security' crises which, in effect, added to the impetus to reconceptualize the notion and approaches to security. Among these was the emergence of three major security threats: economic dislocation as an offshoot of Asian financial crisis; the threats posed by transnational crime; and the outbreak of infectious diseases. These are discussed briefly below.

Poverty and economic dislocation

The onslaught of the Asian financial crisis (AFC) and its economic impact on many affected states in the region proved to be a watershed in the way security was thought of. As the story of the crisis has shown, the economic effects were not only devastating but came in rapid succession. The economic crisis also brought about a host of problems in a short period of time. These included massive private sector debt, a credit crunch, decline in economic production, decline in consumption, falling investment, high unemployment, inflation, labour migration, rising social problems and political unrest.

As these countries geared up for economic recession, it soon became clear that they were up against not merely a financial crisis, but – particularly for badly hit countries like Indonesia[53] and Thailand – also a social and political crisis which reverberated across the region, and was indeed a wake-up call to the states in the region. At the very least, it brought out two salient points about security in Asia. First, that while emergence of human security threats reaffirmed the close nexus between economics and security, it also reinforced the region's notion that security was more than just a military concern. Secondly, no matter how convincing the arguments were for regime security and its emphasis on economic development, these approaches had become dismally inadequate against the new types of security threats that transcended borders. Among these new types of security threats were illegal migration, environmental pollution, drug trafficking and other types of transnational crimes. To be sure, the relationship between territory and security had drastically changed. But more to the point was the fact that the domain of state authority had contracted and its capacity to handle an increasing number of security threats was already being stretched to the limits.

The problem of transnational crime

In Southeast Asia and the wider Asian region, the problem of transnational crime is severe and consists primarily of the illicit trafficking of drugs, money laundering, piracy, arms smuggling, cyber crimes, credit card fraud and others. Some of the most dangerous criminal organizations operate in the region. Transnational crime constitutes a threat to states by violating national borders, compromising national administrations and eroding the rule of law, and is also a threat to national economies and civil societies. The problem of transnational crime therefore requires a transnational response. Yet inter-state cooperation in the region is often complicated by the fact that it touches on sensitive questions such as domestic jurisdictions, the sharing of information, extradition laws and problems of corruption.[54]

Despite these constraints, regional efforts in fighting transnational crime can now be seen on several fronts. At the ASEAN level, the regional mechanism addressing this issue is the ASEAN Ministerial Meeting on Transnational Crime (AMMTC). ASEAN has also worked with its regional partners to enhance international cooperation in fighting transnational crime. One of the more significant regional arrangements in this area is the ASEAN–China Joint Declaration on Cooperation in the field of non-traditional security (NTS) which was signed at the ASEAN-China summit in 2002.[55] The agreement seeks to complement national and international efforts in addressing issues like drug trafficking, people and arms smuggling, sea piracy, money-laundering, cyber crime and terrorism. The ASEAN–China Joint Declaration on NTS also dovetails with ASEAN and China Cooperative Operations in Response to Dangerous Drugs (ACCORD) to respond to this rising problem.

Infectious diseases

Since the Asia-wide outbreak of the SARS virus in 2003, the threats from infectious diseases appear to have become more severe. As the SARS experience has shown, in this era of globalization and regionalization, some infectious diseases have the capacity to detrimentally affect the security and well-being of all members of society and all aspects of the economy.[56]

The region's recent experience with SARS and the looming threat of a new pandemic, possibly from the mutation of the H5N1 virus (Bird flu), have highlighted the need for the region to address an emerging human security threat that is potentially of immense proportions. Given the complex problems faced by states at the national level, such as the lack of contingency planning and coordination among state agencies, people now realize that health issues are also security issues. Initiatives are, therefore, emerging at the regional level to institutionalize cooperation in averting the possibility of pandemic outbreaks, through measures such as building regional capacity for surveillance and disease control.

In summary, the different security challenges that have confronted Southeast Asia and the wider region since 1997 have brought home the salience of human security to the well-being of states and societies in the region. More importantly, this has made the states, as well as a number of international organizations and many civil society organizations, increasingly aware of the breadth and the complexity of human security threats and of the urgency to address these kinds of challenges on many fronts. As a result, human security issues are increasingly gaining an important place in both national and regional forums.

China and human security

The proliferation of various regional initiatives that attempt to address a number of human security issues – whether it is fighting infectious diseases or combating transnational crimes – have also seen the active participation from what was once Asia's most vocal opponent of the concept of human security. As a country that has and continues to be faced with a number of human security threats, China has indeed been very active in many regional mechanisms that have been established in Asia to respond to these challenges. As one Chinese scholar observed recently, the urgency to respond to a host of global security challenges has led to a slow shift in Chinese thinking and approaches towards security, where security 'not only refers to security at the state level, but also to the international, the global and individual levels'.[57] It is important to note, however, that the term 'non-traditional security' is used to refer to human security issues rather than human security itself. The reason behind such preference, according to scholars, is the fact that while human security issues are important issues, national security still remains the core of security and 'without national security, there is no human security'.[58]

Nevertheless, it can be observed that 'non-traditional security' is now a term used widely by Chinese leaders, academics and the mass media.

Moreover, notwithstanding the reticence to adopt human security in the national security lexicon, there is nevertheless a perceptible trend particularly among scholars in China to promote the notion of human security. Albeit advanced in a more nuanced form, there are now several Chinese works that study issues of human security. Among these are the important works that have been generated by the Chinese Academy of Social Sciences (CASS) in Beijing. This trend is best captured by Wang Yizhou, Director of World Economics and Politics, CASS who noted that: 'human security and social security are the foundations for national security ... To seek national security at the expense of human safety and social stability is to treat the symptom rather than the root of the problem.'[59]

Discourses from below: civil society organizations and Track II networks on human security

In tandem with these developments at the official level are also significant movements at the non-official levels, with a number of civil society organizations (CSOs) in the region actively advocating human security in various regional forums. In Southeast Asia, for instance, the ASEAN People's Assembly (APA) has been at the forefront in promoting human security on the ASEAN agenda. In fact, the genesis of the APA provides some salient insights on how social movements or NGOs in ASEAN have developed links with Track II networks in pushing for their agendas on development and security.[60]

For the last six years since its formation, the APA has focused its engagement with ASEAN on outlining and pursuing an ambitious people's agenda that highlights the human security issues of the people in this region. This can be found in APA's Action Plan which it has been developing since its inception. The Action Plan has identified specific areas where urgent attention needs to be given to address issues of security and development. These include issues such as the protection of human rights, the promotion of democracy and attention to critical areas of human development – poverty, illiteracy and health.[61]

At another level, discussions about human security also indicate significant attempts by different groups of actors to address the more difficult issues of human security that pertain to prospects of humanitarian intervention. One of these is the attempt by a Track II organization, the Council for Security Cooperation in the Asia Pacific (CSCAP), to define the principles of humanitarian intervention.[62] This was initiated in the light of the bitter debates that ensued following the NATO intervention in Kosovo in 1999 and the peacekeeping operations in East Timor. Against these developments, a workshop was organized by the CSCAP Working Group on Comprehensive and Cooperative Security to reflect on the challenges posed to the principle of non-intervention. The findings of that workshop, which were outlined in the Summary of Discussions, were instructive in that it was perhaps one of the pioneering attempts to reflect on some of the emerging ideas on the controversies found in the region, and on the calls to review the principle of non-interference in the domestic affairs of states. Among these were the criteria that must be considered before any humanitarian intervention can be allowed, which include consent from the local people, support from the international community and a high probability of success.[63] Given that one of the difficult hurdles in humanitarian intervention lies in the lack of consensus on principles and procedural safeguards to ensure that it is properly carried out, the CSCAP efforts in this regards are notable. It belies the assumption that states in the region are unwilling to discuss intervention in multilateral forums.[64]

Discussions on related topics on humanitarian intervention are also found in Track III circles. For example, at the 2002 ASEAN People's Assembly, there was a special session devoted to debating the ideas propounded by the Report on the Responsibility to Protect (RTP).[65] The main objective of these sessions was to get the reaction of the civil societies in the region on the various proposals related to the responsibilities to protect, react and rebuild. It is significant to note that at the discussions on intervention in the APA meetings, the cases cited where intervention was needed centred largely on Myanmar. Many NGOs represented at APA issued calls to governments in the region to 'intervene' in Myanmar to stop alleged cases of human rights abuses. But, interestingly, while the language of humanitarian intervention was often used, the types of interventions suggested did not include deployment of military force against the regime in Yangoon.[66] Instead they called for the promotion of human rights mechanisms, and also promoting the role of civil society in conflict prevention.[67] Moreover, among the interesting points raised in the RTP was how women's NGOs could make use of the RTP proposals to create new norms for the protection of women and children in conflict areas, and also how to refocus the RTP doctrine away from its emphasis on reaction and instead think more about the responsibilities to prevent and to rebuild.[68]

In summary, the evolution of these types of regional discourses when put together, albeit mostly found at a non-official level, are indeed indicative of the willingness by several actors in the region to address the difficult issues related to humanitarian intervention. More importantly, it also reflects the growing constituency of actors in the region who are seriously examining intervention issues and how multi-sectoral actors can play a role. These activities therefore dovetail well with the on-going efforts by other actors to promote the adoption of proposals within the broader framework of the UN reforms, specifically those that are outlined in the UN Report on *A More Secure World*, which include the RTP's ideas on sovereignty-as-responsibility.[69]

Conclusion

The preceding discussions have shown how human security is evolving to be part of the security lexicon in Europe and in Asia.

In Europe the recent studies and approaches have focused on the European Union as an international actor for good. It is accepted at the official and academic level that the conceptualization of security inherited from the Cold War is not viable. The task is to forcefully link EU human security approaches with a new, more multi-polar and more complex, international environment. Interventions, even for good, are not for free. The use of force is problematic. The way that civil-military forces are used in crisis and conflicts is different from the past and its articulation is complicated. But the utility of military forces, even for conflict prevention and internal conflicts, which are often very complex and violent, cannot be so generally devalued. And the myriad of instruments at the EU's disposal have to be more effectively articulated for an EU human security approach such as *freedom from want.*

In Asia, by highlighting the different narratives on discourses on security at both official and non-official levels, and by identifying some of the concrete policies that have been introduced to address human security issues by different governments in the region, one can see that human security is now gaining a place on the regional security agenda.

Moreover, it can be observed that there is indeed an effervescent constituency out there that has begun to define security beyond the conventional, comprehensive notions to a multilevel perspective of what security should be. These include the proposals made by civil society groups which adopt an 'emancipatory' vision of human security that argues against the division and exclusion that the idea of comprehensive security has engendered. This has, in effect, challenged the dominant notion of comprehensive security in the region which had been been shown to be inadequate in addressing the emerging security challenges faced by states and societies in Asia. While many of these developments still need time to yield more definite results, these emerging trends and attempts to mainstream human security on the security agenda in the region point to a sea change, in both the attitudes and approaches to security from different actors in the region. To be sure, the new rhetoric about human security has paved the way for more policies and actions in addressing a host of security threats in the region.

Notes

1. United Nations Development Programme (UNDP), *Human Development Report 1994* (New York: Oxford University Press, 1994), pp. 22–3.
2. Ibid.
3. Ibid.

4. Harvard University Conflict Resolution Project, 'The Human Security Report', unpublished manuscript, 2000.

5. S. Lodgaard, *Human Security: Concept and Operationalization* (Oslo: Norwegian Institute of International Affairs, 2001), http://www.cpdsindia.org/globalhuman security/operationalisation.htm.

6. A. Suhrke, 'Human Security and the Interests of States', *Security Dialogue*, Vol. 30, No. 3, September 1999.

7. See the plural definitions in A. Marquina, 'Environmental Security and Human Security', in A. Marquina (ed.), *Environmental Challenges in the Mediterranean 2000–2050* (Dordrecht, Boston and London: Kluwer Academic Publishers, 2004), pp. 14–17.

8. See R. Paris, 'Human Security: Paradigm Shift or Hot Air', *International Security*, Vol. 26, No. 2, Fall 2001, pp. 88, 87–102.

9. See W. T. Tow and R. Trood, 'Linkages between Traditional Security and Human Security', in W. T. Tow, R. Thakur and In-Taek Hyun (eds), *Asia's Emerging Regional Order* (New York: United Nations University Press, 2000) p. 14.

10. See 'Freedom from Fear: Canada's Foreign Policy for Human Security', http://www.dfait-maeci.gc.ca/foreignp/humansecurity/HumanSecurityBooklet- e. asp.

11. Council of the European Union and European Commission, 'Europe in the World: Working for Peace, Security and Stability', 2007.

12. J. Solana, 'A Secure Europe in a Better World: European Security Strategy', Brussels, 12 December 2003.

13. See for instance H. W. Maull (2007) 'Europe as a Global Power', p. 3, http://www.gwu.edu/~sigur/pubs/9-14- 07%20Major%20Powers%20Conference/ Maull%20on%20Europe.pdf; I. Manners, 'Normative Power Europe: a Contradiction in Terms?', *Journal of Common Market Studies*, Vol. 40, No. 2, 2002, pp. 235–58.

14. See F. Duchêne, 'Europe's Role in World Peace', in R. Mayne (ed.), *Europe Tomorrow: Sixteen Europeans Look Ahead* (London: Fontana, 1972), pp. 32–47.

15. H. Sjursen, 'What Kind of Power?' in H. Sjursen (ed.), *Civilian or Military Power? European Foreign Policy in Perspective* (London and New York: Routledge, 2007), p. 4. For Hans W. Maull, a civilian power implies: the acceptance of the necessity of cooperation with others in the pursuit of international objectives; concentration on non-military means; military power as a residual instrument serving essentially to safeguard other means of international interaction; and willingness to develop supranational structures to address critical issues of international management.

16. A. Hyde-Price, ' "Normative" Power Europe: a Realist Critique', in Sjursen (ed.), *Civilian or Military Power?*, p. 50.

17. Manners, ' "Normative" Power Europe', p. 239.

18. I. Manners, 'Normative Power Europe Reconsidered', CIDEL Workshop, Oslo, 22–23 October 2004, p. 3, http://www.arena.uio.no/cidel/WorkshopOsloSecurity/ Manners.pdf.

19. T. Diez and M. Pace, 'Normative Power Europe and Conflict Transformation', paper presented at EUSA Conference, Montreal, 17–19 May 2007, p. 1, http://www.unc.edu/euce/eusa2007/papers/diez-t-01a.pdf.

20. N. Tocci, 'Profiling Normative Foreign Policy: the European Union and its Global Partners', CEPS Working Document No. 279, 2007.

21. The values and interest mentioned are: safeguarding EU values, democracy, rule of law, human rights, principles of international law, peace, economic, social

and environmental development of developing countries, integration of all countries in the world economy, sustainable development, assistance in confronting natural and man-made disasters, and multilateral cooperation and good global governance.

22. Ian Manners was of different opinion: 'Paramount amongst these norm diffusion factors is the absence of physical force in the imposition of norms. This absence of physical force and the importance of cultural diffusion has led me to argue that "the most important factor shaping the international role of the EU is not what it does or what it says, but what it is".' Manners, 'Normative Power Europe Reconsidered', p. 5. Later this pioneering author has shown his dissatisfaction: 'given the prioritization of military intervention over non-military conciliation, I have little doubt that normative conceptions of the EU are being undermined'. I. Manners (2007) 'Normative Power Europe Reconsidered: Beyond the Crossroads', in Sjursen (ed.), *Civilian or Military Power?*, p. 26.
23. Tocci, 'Profiling Normative Foreign Policy', p. 6.
24. Diez and Pace, 'Normative Power Europe and Conflict Transformation'.
25. C. Bretherton and J. Vogler, 'The European Union as a Normative Actor: Contradictions in the Union's Collective Identity', paper presented to 47th Annual ISA Convention, San Diego, 22–25 March 2006, http://www.allacademic.com/meta/p99571_index.html.
26. Petersberg tasks included humanitarian and rescue tasks, peacekeeping tasks including peace-making, and tasks of combat forces in crisis management.
27. Foreword by Commissioner Ferrero-Waldner, 'The European Union: Furthering Human Rights and Democracy across the Globe', European Commission, External Relations, 2007, p. 3.
28. Opening greeting by J. Solana, EU High Representative for the Common Foreign and Security Policy at the annual New Ukraine in New Europe Conference, Brussels, 4 February 2008, http://www.consilium.europa.eu/ueDocs/cms_Data/docs/pressData/en/discours/98569.pdf.
29. For example, S. Biscop, *The European Security Strategy* (Aldershot: Ashgate, 2007); S. Biscop and J. Joel Andersson, *The EU and the European Security Strategy* (Oxford and New York: Abingdon, 2008).
30. 'A Human Security Doctrine for Europe: The Barcelona Report of the Study Group on Europe's Security Capabilities', presented to EU High Representative for Common Foreign and Security Policy J. Solana, Barcelona, 15 September 2004, http://www.lse.ac.uk/Depts/global/Publications/HumanSecurityDoctrine.pdf.
31. These ideas were presented previously by M. Kaldor, M. Martin and S. Selcho, 'Human Security: a New Strategic Narrative for Europe', *International Affairs*, Vol. 83, No. 2, 2007, pp. 273–88.
32. 'A European Way of Security: The Madrid Report of the Human Security Study Group, comprising a Proposal and Background Report'. Madrid, 8 November 2007, http://www.lse.ac.uk/Depts/global/PDFs/Madrid%20Report%20Final%20for%20distribution.pdf.
33. M. Glasius and M. Kaldor, 'A Human Security Vision for Europe and Beyond', in M. Glasius and M. Kaldor, *A Human Security for Europe: Project, Principles and Practicalities* (Oxford and New York: Routledge, 2006), p. 3. They also say that 'the European Union itself can be viewed as a "perpetual peace" project'.
34. See for instance: E. A. Smith, 'Effects Based Operations: Applying Network Centric Warfare in Peace, Crisis, and War' (Washington: DOD-CCRP, 2003); J. D. Celeski, *Operationalizing COIN* (Hurlburt Field: JSOU Press, 2005).

35. We agree with the arguments of Professors Hedley Bull and Adrian Hyde-Price. See A. Hyde-Price, ' "Normative" Power Europe: a Realist Critique', in Sjursen (ed.), *Civilian or Military Power?*, p. 50.
36. This section draws largely from the earlier works of the author on examining the various approaches to human security. See for example, M. Caballero-Anthony, 'Human Security and Comprehensive Security in ASEAN', *Indonesian Quarterly*, Vol. 27, No. 4, 2000, pp. 413–22; and M. Caballero-Anthony, 'Human Security in the Asia Pacific: Current Trends and Prospects', in D. Dickens (ed.), *The Human Face of Security: Asia Pacific Perspectives*, Canberra Papers on Strategy and Defence, No. 144 (Canberra: Strategic and Defence Studies Centre, Australian National University, 2002), pp. 18–29.
37. See, for example, R. Ullman, 'Redefining Security', *International Security*, Vol. 8, No. 1, 1983, pp. 129–53; J. T. Matthews, 'Redefining Security', *Foreign Affairs*, Vol. 68, No. 2, 1989, pp. 162–77; K. Krause and M. C. Williams, 'Broadening the Agenda of Security Studies: Politics and Methods', *Mershon International Studies Review*, Vol. 40, Supplement 1, 1996, pp. 229–30; B. Buzan, O. Wæver and J. de Wilde, *Security: a New Framework for Analysis* (Boulder: Lynne Rienner, 1998).
38. K. Booth, 'Security and Emancipation', cited in K. Booth, 'International Relations Theory vs. the Future', in K. Booth and S. Smith (eds), *International Relations Theory Today* (University Park: Pennsylvania State University Press, 1995), pp. 328–49.
39. In most writings about human security, scholars have traced this concept specifically to the 1994 UNDP *Human Development Report*. See, for example, A. Acharya, 'Human Security: East Versus West', *International Journal*, Vol. 61, No. 3, 2001, pp. 442–60; K. Bajpai, *Human Security: Concept and Measurement*, J. B. Kroc Institute Working Paper No. 19 (Notre Dame: University of Notre Dame Press, 2000); and M. Caballero-Anthony, 'Human Security in the Asia-Pacific: Current Trends and Prospects', in Dickens (ed.), *The Human Face of Security*, pp. 18–29.
40. M. ul Haq, 'New Imperatives of Human Security', RGICS Paper No. 7 (New Delhi: Rajiv Gandhi Institute for Contemporary Studies, Rajiv Gandhi Foundation, 1994), cited in Bajpai, *Human Security*.
41. Ibid., p.10 (emphasis added).
42. The project 'Intellectual Dialogue on Building Asia's Tomorrow' was initiated by the Japan Centre for International Exchange (JCIE) with the advice and support of Prime Minister Obuchi. This has been an on-going project with subsequent Intellectual Dialogues held in Singapore and Thailand. The fourth Dialogue is currently being planned (personal communication with Mr Tadashi Yamamoto, President of JCIE).
43. Opening remarks by Prime Minister Obuchi at the Intellectual Dialogue on Building Asia's Tomorrow, 2 December 1998.
44. *Japan Diplomatic Bluebook 1999*.
45. Statement by Yukio Takasu, Director-General of Multilateral Cooperation Department, at the Third Intellectual Dialogue on Building Asia's Tomorrow, Bangkok, 19 June 2000.
46. Statement by the Director-General (Ministry of Foreign Affairs, Japan), at the International Conference on Human Security in a Globalized World, Ulan-Bator, 8 May 2000.
47. Ibid.
48. Ibid.
49. See *Japan Diplomatic Bluebook 1999*.

50. Statement by Yukio Takasu.

51. Muthiah Alagappa, *Asian Security Practices: Material and Ideational Influences* (Stanford: Stanford University Press, 1998), and 'Comprehensive Security: Interpretations in ASEAN Countries', in R. Scalapino et al. (eds), *Asian Security Issues: Regional and Global* (Berkeley: Institute of East Asian Studies, University of California, Berkeley).

52. See Withaya Sucharithanarugse, 'Regionalising Human Security in the Asia-Pacific: Asianising the Paradigm', in W. Tow, Ramesh Thakur and In-Taek Hyun (eds), *Asia's Emerging Regional Order* (Tokyo: United Nations University, 2000), p. 59.

53. See, for example, M. Caballero-Anthony, 'Challenges to Southeast Asian Security Cooperation' and R. Sukma, 'Security Implications of the Economic Crisis in Southeast Asia', in G. Wilson-Roberts (ed.), *An Asia-Pacific Security Crisis? New Challenges to Regional Stability* (New Zealand: Centre for Strategic Studies, 1999), pp. 51–65 and pp. 39–51, respectively; and Japan Centre for International Exchange, *The Asian Crisis and Human Security* (Tokyo: Japan Centre for International Exchange, 1999).

54. See, for example, A. Dupont, *East Asia Imperilled: Transnational Challenges to Security*, Cambridge Asia Pacific Studies (Cambridge: Cambridge University Press, 2001).

55. 'Joint Declaration of ASEAN and China on Cooperation in the Field of Non-Traditional Security Issues', http://www.aseansec.org/13185.htm.

56. For more on SARS and its security impact, see for example, M. Caballero-Anthony, 'SARS in Asia: Crisis, Vulnerabilities, and Regional Responses', *Asian Survey*, Vol. 45, No. 3, 2005, pp. 475–95; M. Curley and N. Thomas, 'Human Security and Public Health in Southeast Asia: the SARS Outbreak', *Australian Journal of International Affairs*, Vol. 58, No. 1, 2004, pp. 17–32; E. Prescott, 'SARS: a Warning', *Survival*, Vol. 45, No. 3, 2003, pp. 162–77.

57. See Li Dongyan, 'China's Approach to Non-Traditional Security', paper prepared for Non-Traditional Security Workshop, CSIS, Washington, 5 March 2007.

58. Ibid.

59. Yizhou Wang, 'China Facing Non-Traditional Security: a Report on Capacity Building', in R. Emmers, M. Caballero-Anthony and A. Acharya (eds), *Studying Non-Traditional Security in Asia: Trends and Issues* (Singapore: Marshal Cavendish Academic, 2006), p. 66.

60. For more on the genesis of APA, see M. Caballero-Anthony, 'Non-State Regional Governance Mechanism for Economic Security: the Case of the ASEAN Peoples' Assembly', *The Pacific Review*, Vol. 17, No. 4, 2004, pp. 567–85.

61. See *Second APA Report: Challenges Facing the ASEAN People* (Jakarta: Centre for Strategic and International Studies, 2003), pp. 5–7.

62. The use of the term Track I usually refers to official diplomacy between government officials, while Track II refers to non-official activities that usually includes epistemic communities and government officials participating in their personal capacity. For more discussion on the role of Track II institutions in East Asia, see M. Caballero-Anthony, *Regional Security in Southeast Asia: Beyond the ASEAN Way* (Singapore: Institute of Southeast Asian Studies), pp. 157–93.

63. See 'Summary of Discussions of the Seventh Meeting of the CSCAP Working Group on Comprehensive and Cooperative Security', in D. Dickens and G. Wilson-Roberts (eds), *Non-Intervention and State Sovereignty in the Asia-Pacific* (Wellington: Centre for Strategic Studies, 2000).

64. While CSCAP is widely regarded as a non-official, Track II organization, its member-state representatives in the 17-member body are also drawn from official circles, albeit participating in CSCAP meetings in their private capacities.

65. The RTP is the more popular term to refer to the International Commission on Intervention and Sovereignty, *Responsibility to Protect: Report of the International Commission on Intervention and State Sovereignty* (Ottawa: International Development Research Centre, 2001).

66. See APA Report: *Challenges Facing the ASEAN People* (Jakarta: Centre for Strategic and International Studies, 2002).

67. Ibid. See also the first APA Report: *An ASEAN of the People, by the People, for the People*, Report of the First ASEAN People's Assembly, Batam, Indonesia (Jakarta: Centre for Strategic and International Studies, 2001).

68. Third APA Report: *Towards an ASEAN Community of Caring Societies* (Manila: Institute for Strategic and Development Studies, 2003), pp. 104–11. See also N. Morada, 'R2P Roadmap in Southeast Asia: Challenges, Prospects and Proposals', manuscript, 2005.

69. See High Level Panel on Threats, Challenges and Change, *A More Secure World: Our Shared Responsibility*. Report of the Secretary-General's High Level Panel on Threats, Challenges and Change (New York: United Nations Foundation, 2004).

Index

NB: Page numbers in **bold** refer to figures and tables